WORKERS' CONTROL

IN LATIN AMERICA, 1930–1979

D1558654

EDITED BY JONATHAN C. BROWN

WORKERS' CONTROL

IN LATIN AMERICA, 1930–1979

The University of North Carolina Press
Chapel Hill and London

© 1997 The University of North Carolina Press
Manufactured in the United States of America

The paper in this book meets the guidelines for permanence
and durability of the Committee on Production Guidelines
for Book Longevity of the Council on Library Resources.

Library of Congress Cataloging-in-Publication Data
Workers' control in Latin America /
edited by Jonathan C. Brown.
p.   cm.
Includes bibliographical references (p.) and index.
ISBN 0-8078-2362-7 (cloth: alk. paper).—ISBN 0-8078-4666-X (pbk.: alk. paper)
1. Working class—Latin America—Political activity.
2. Railroads— Employees—Latin America—Political activity.
3. Miners—Latin America— Political activity.
4. Strikes and lockouts—Latin America—History—20th century.
5. Industrial relations—Latin America—History—20th century.
I. Brown, Jonathan C., 1942–   .
HD8110.5.W67   1997
322'.2'098—dc21   97-1880
                                                                                    CIP

01   00   99   98   97   5   4   3   2   1

In everything there should be dignity,
and that's what we were fighting for.
—*Maria Pavone, Brazilian textile worker*

CONTENTS

ILLUSTRATIONS

MAPS AND FIGURES

PREFACE

The original essays in this book attempt to make Latin American labor history accessible to the widest possible readership. In covering some of the most important events to take place in Latin America between 1930 and 1979, we authors have taken special care to describe how workers influenced the outcomes. For this alone, the book would contribute new knowledge to Latin American history. But we seek to add not only to factual information but to conceptual understanding as well, and to do this, we employ many analytical concepts including, most prominently, that of "workers' control." The objective is to explain *why* the working class of each country participated in public affairs at critical junctures in history. Readers will learn from these essays that the reasons motivating workers' actions are as important as how they behaved. After all, understanding causality is more useful for analyzing the patterns of Latin American labor history than the mere memorization of specific worker-inspired events. Causality of one set of events may be compared with the causality of another in a different time and place in order to test extant hypotheses and ultimately to build new, more universal paradigms.

The writers of this volume have aspired to present their arguments in the clearest fashion, to make these vignettes intrinsically interesting, and to write well. Each chapter is formatted identically and can be read in one sitting. Each contains a brief introduction on the prior role of workers in their nation's history in order to provide the proper context for the intelligent but perhaps not knowledgeable reader. At the end of each chapter appears a brief postscript placing the story into the subsequent history of the country. A bibliography is appended at the end of the volume so that the readers may follow up with their own investigations into the history of Latin American workers.

As much as possible, the authors aspire to have this collection read like a single-author volume. Each chapter strives to make a rigorous argument, the summaries of which are located in both the introduction and the conclusion. These arguments comment on the causality that connects workers' actions to the great historical events. Quotations are minimized; abstract concepts are clearly defined in the text. The authors keep the arcane jargon of social science to a minimum and avoid the endless and confusing acronyms that frequently pepper the writing of labor history. This volume also underwent a rigorous, collective editing and rewriting. The contributors have commented on each other's chapters, so that the whole volume benefits from the insights of many authors. Moreover, we sent out each essay to the leading scholars in the field. Therefore, this volume has also benefited from the suggestions of Jack Womack, Alan Knight, Tom Skidmore, Barry Carr, Lou Perez, Rodney Anderson, Florencia Mallon, Jeff Gould, Paul Goodwin, Torcuato Di Tella, Julian Laite, Joel Horowitz, Steve Stern, Erick Langer, Paul Drake, Ginny Burnett, Mike Conniff, Mike Jimenez, Adrian Bantjes, Steve Stern, and Carl Van Ness. Susan Long drew the maps. María Fernanda Tuozzo in Argentina and Marcos Tonatiuh Aguila M. in Mexico assisted us in acquiring some of the photos. In essence, we have produced this book collectively, the same way in which our subjects have so often contributed to their own history.

WORKERS' CONTROL

IN LATIN AMERICA, 1930–1979

WHAT IS WORKERS' CONTROL?

JONATHAN C. BROWN

U ntil recently, Latin American history had been written principally from the top down. That is to say, history books often reflected the viewpoints and lives of the elites: the rulers, politicians, intellectuals, newspaper editors, and professionals. Even studies of the "popular classes," the peasants and workers, have reflected the attitudes and views of their leaders, even though they might have assumed perspectives and goals different from those of their followers. That this top-down approach to history was dominant should not cause surprise. After all, those who could read and write left records, and historically in Latin America, the literate formed only a small minority. To reconstruct the past, the historian used these elite records in the form of newspapers, proclamations, letters, and account books.

But what of the voiceless in history? What of the laborers and peasants who, even if literate, had been so busy making a precarious living that they had little time to edit newspapers or leave written records of their lives? Can we assume that their lives had little meaning? Little influence? Most of all, students of history must inquire whether workers and peasants actually counted for little in history just because few of their documents have been preserved or just because the extant documentation inflates the role of the elites.

The authors of this volume protest. We believe that the full parameters of history cannot be known until scholars sharpen their focus to reveal patterns of behavior of the common people. By focusing our research as much as possible on their lives, we are both following and seeking to influence an increasingly important trend in the study of Latin America's popular classes. This line of inquiry concentrates on how historical events affected the workers and how— and why—the workers acted to shape their own environments.[1] Therefore, this volume brings together several studies of the urban and industrial workers. Such a focus does not automatically eliminate rural workers. In twentieth-century Latin America, peasants and farm workers have moved into industrial work, bringing their values and strategies of resistance. Rural-urban migration also has contributed to the growth of cities in the region. Therefore, the study of the formative history of urban and industrial workers certainly treats an important precedent for Latin America.

However, we make no pretense that our treatment of even this industrial sector of the popular classes will be comprehensive, because our essays deal principally with organized workers, that is, those laborers who belonged to unions. Depending on time and location, organized laborers may have counted for only a quarter or a third of a country's working class. These essays do not represent the lives of the mass of unorganized workers such as bootblacks, housemaids, laundresses, petty sellers, peddlers, and construction laborers, among others. Obviously, some workers were more privileged and active than others. In Latin America, the artisans of the colonial period and the nineteenth century were noted for clannishness, restricting competition, and dunning the government for concessions. In the twentieth century, workers in the more dynamic industries—many owned by foreign companies—received high wages and acquired considerable skills. Most of the chapters in this volume, in fact, deal with just such workers, be they the oil men of Mexico, the railroaders of Guatemala, the textile employees of Brazil, or the copper miners of Chile. Our workers tended to be highly skilled, well paid, and politically active. Many of our subjects may be said to be "labor aristocrats," the privileged few who could be quite militant in preserving their privileges vis-à-vis other members of the working class. By the same token, the highest-paid laborers provided the leadership in forming unions and in advancing the interests of the working class as a whole. This collection, therefore, does not claim to be comprehensive. But it does offer a wide variety of cases, suggestive of comparative analysis and supportive of a new line of historical inquiry.

All of these episodes in labor control share a common time frame: they all occurred during the trend period from the Great Depression through the fall of the Allende government. It comprises the half century spanning from 1930 to the late 1970s. Let us call this era the middle years of the twentieth century. The middle years were critical economically, politically, and socially.

The Great Depression shocked Latin America's previous economic reliance on exporting raw materials and importing manufactured goods from the United States and northern Europe. Thereafter, most Latin American countries followed similar developmental paths. They tended to reject certain free-market economic doctrines (though not necessarily capitalism itself), to increase state regulation of the economy, to stimulate domestic industrialization as a substitute for the import of industrial products, to display economic nationalism, and to nationalize the basic industries. Politically, this fifty-year period was one of populism, revolution, and growing state centralization. Socially, this trend period was also a time of urbanization. Previously massive European immigration tapered off in southern Brazil, Argentina, Chile, and Cuba. Interregional migration now took over to swell the urban population of Latin America and to exacerbate the urban maladies of slums, congestion, pollution, and underemployment. Nonetheless, most migrants did not return to the countryside. In the city, they felt they had greater access to health care, cultural improvement, industrial employment, schools, and perhaps individual choice.

The economic and social changes that occurred between 1930 and the late 1970s made possible significant political transformations as well. Leaders such as Cárdenas of Mexico, Perón of Argentina, Vargas of Brazil, and Siles of Bolivia forged multiclass political movements, introducing urban labor to the political life of the nation. Their regimes nationalized urban utilities, oil and steel industries, and transportation facilities—often removing them from the control of the foreign interests. This was also a time of revolution. Guatemala, Bolivia, Cuba, Peru, and Chile experienced political movements that attempted to institute fundamental economic and social change. Although varied, all these movements declared themselves revolutionary. Once again, labor and land reforms accompanied the strengthening of the state apparatus. Foreign-owned industries were nationalized in order to achieve economic independence for Latin America, but the foreign debt of many countries grew alarmingly too. Inflation was high in many cases. Although the national militaries, with United States support, aborted the revolutions of Guatemala and Chile, the army actually led the so-called revolution in Peru. The period between 1930 and 1979 in Latin America certainly was not bereft of idiosyncrasies.

The middle years of the twentieth century, begun by a depression, also ended in one. The shock of the debt crisis of the 1980s has tempered Latin America's rejection of free-market capitalism. Currently, politicians claiming to be "market reformers" are going out of their way to slash government spending, deregulate the economies, and invite foreign capital back on favorable terms. By the same token, Latin American officials are now denouncing the populist and revolutionary policies of the previous age. Encouraged by the International Monetary Fund to control inflation, they have created economic policies that seek to increase labor's productivity while freezing wages at the same time. Since 1980, Latin American workers have faced new hardships. The focus of this volume, nevertheless, remains on the previous period of economic regulation, urbanization, and populism—that is, the middle years of the twentieth century, lasting from 1930 to the late 1970s.

The question remains: What was the role of the urban and industrial workers in the changes that took place during that trend period? Despite the centrality of workers to the period, the existing literature tends to treat them as having been led rather than as having acted on their own. These essays seek to demonstrate that the workers were capable of influencing national events. They assumed a large role in undermining the foreign interests in industries that eventually were nationalized. By strikes and factory takeovers, they forced the elites to acknowledge their struggles. They rallied and voted and pushed politicians to adopt more popular policies. In most cases, the urban and industrial workers were better positioned to influence national events than were peasants and rural workers. Urban workers did not live isolated and dispersed, like their country cousins, and their labor organizations aided industrial workers in resisting the dictates of employers and political authorities. The following essays demonstrate that the role of urban and industrial workers looms large. That being the case, several additional questions follow.

For what did the workers struggle during the middle years? We believe that the answer to this question lies at the level of the shop floor. It is here that workers defined their lives, their individual worth, their cherished independence, and their regard for their peers. Above all, the worker on the shop floor wished to assure his or her livelihood and the material well-being of his or her family. In most of our cases, the laborers had already been proletarianized. That is to say, they had given up most alternate forms of subsistence and lived almost exclusively on their industrial wages. Employment in industry had motivated many migrants from the country to give up their ties to the land, while former artisans may have long since moved from their own shops to the employer's factory. This new dependence may not have rankled, so long as the paychecks came regularly. But a number of conditions rendered proletarians vulnerable in their wage-earning lives. A downturn in the economic cycle caused the employer to slash wages, reduce hours, or lay off workers. An upswing in the cycle forced up the cost of living. The employers also desired, at times, to increase productivity at the workers' expense. Owners speeded up the production line or reorganized work on the shop floor in order to save on labor. Finally, factory supervisors might be arbitrary. They often prevented a worker's just promotion, favored undeserving subordinates, and disrupted camaraderie among employees. The proletarian's life in Latin America could be rewarding in terms of skill acquisition, higher pay, and greater social status; but, by the same token, industrial work was fraught with dependence, vulnerability, and indignity. Consequently, two items formed the agenda of the workers' struggle: to enhance the dignity of their work and diminish their vulnerability.

How did Latin American workers struggle to achieve their goals? The following essays demonstrate that laborers struggled on several different levels. At base, individuals might resort to single acts of resistance. They might absent themselves from work without permission in order to attend to urgent family matters. Tools and raw materials might disappear. A machine could break down unexpectedly. An unpopular supervisor might become subject to practical jokes or insults. On other occasions, workers might resort to collective solidarity, to labor organization and union action, in order to intensify the struggle. Most often, the internal debate preceding action will take the form of factionalism and leadership struggles. Eventually, revitalized labor organizations demanded wage increases, job security, work regulations, and labor contracts. When negotiations failed, the workers went on strike. Unions representing workers in one sector of the economy will cooperate and support labor organizations in others, forming federations and confederations. But foreign and domestic employers in Latin America have been notoriously reluctant to give in to labor agitation. They blamed unions for promoting a pampered, lazy proletariat and accused labor leaders of being radicals and communists. Troublemakers were fired. Employers also had a history of calling on local and national officials to use force in repressing strikers. Therefore, workers and their organizations also sought finally to raise their struggle to the political level.

These essays deal explicitly with the conundrum of rank-and-file politics. Certainly, none of us wishes to oversimplify ideological issues by giving the same weight to worker absenteeism as to factory seizures. Therefore, each author clarifies when workers engaged in individual acts of resistance and for what objectives. Recognizing different levels of workers' actions to control their working and community environments, we take pains to contrast the individual acts of resistance with the less frequent moments of union militancy and with the even rarer attempts to alter national history directly. The answer as to why workers choose different tactics in order to gain a measure of control over their lives has to do with their workplace experiences. Each chapter shows that workers on the shop floors were sensitive to the ebb and flow of capital accumulation, to the vagaries of the world economic system, and to political openings. They were capable of pursuing those great and small tactics according to a considered estimation of their likelihood of success. Workers knew how to read the economic and political situation in order to decide on propitious moments for action. This is why strikes were so infrequent.

Since the Great Depression, laborers in Latin America had increasingly resorted to politics. They goaded politicians to pass labor legislation and pressured judicial authorities to carry out the laws. This political activity was nothing new, for the state's role in employer-employee relations extends back into the colonial period, and artisans and workers since independence had not forsaken their traditions of appealing to political authorities. However, the trend period from 1930 through the 1970s introduced new forms of political participation for the urban masses—much of it of their own doing. Governments established labor ministries, recognized unions, intervened in labor strikes, and negotiated with employers. National leaders instituted labor reforms.

The reason why particular politicians accomplished these prolabor actions was partially pragmatic. Urban and industrial workers had grown in number, universal and woman suffrage had enlarged the voters' lists, and labor rallies manifested popular demands in a powerful manner. In an environment in which the landed elites had been discredited and the middle class remained underdeveloped, the politician ignored the groundswell of popular demands at his peril—unless he had solid support of the military. Not all of them did. As these essays demonstrate, leaders such as Cárdenas, Perón, Vargas, Siles, and Allende became potent political forces even in the face of significant patrician and military opposition. In other cases, workers mounted defensive actions so as not to lose all previous gains. They collaborated with governments not of their own choosing and cooperated with conservative leaders or institutions (such as the military government in Peru) so as to preserve labor's gains rather than to demand new concessions. Confronted with military repression in Guatemala and Chile as elsewhere, the working classes strategically retrenched to await more appropriate moments for pressing their demands.

When did workers struggle? Factory laborers did not always agitate or struggle at the level of union organization and even less at the level of national politics. Indeed, these cases are relatively discreet. We can assume that, during most of the trend period, workers carried on their daily struggles on an individual basis. For one thing, the composition of the new industrial working class and competition among its various sectors often operated to divide rather than to unite. In Latin America, the popular classes were racially and ethnically heterogeneous. European immigrants often worked in the same industries as did the native-born, although the immigrants held the skilled and well-paying positions. Moreover, the native-born of Argentina were darker-skinned *criollos* from the interior provinces, and many native-born migrants in Brazil were blacks. In Peru and Bolivia, the Spanish-speaking *cholos* who worked regularly in the copper and tin mines may have looked down upon the Quechua- and Aymara-speaking peasants and itinerant laborers. Racially, there may have been little difference between them. Likewise, native-born, Spanish-speaking Cuban mill workers might have been predominantly black, but the blacks whom the companies employed as cane cutters were English- and patois-speakers from the British West Indies and Haiti. Mexican workers might have been uniformly mestizo and Spanish-speaking, but skill and position in the oil and rail industries prompted them to observe a social hierarchy that reflected the racial hierarchy of the colonial past. There were also sex and age differences. Employers hired women and children to suppress wages, and male workers retaliated by harassing not the employers but the women and children. The working class of Latin America was divided among itself, sometimes by employer design, sometimes by its own composition.

What, pray tell, prompted the urban masses to rise above these differences on specific occasions and influence the course of national events? Cause and opportunity. Employers gave them the cause, and the economic structure and political conditions afforded them the opportunity. Employers took advantage of the proletarians' vulnerabilities by cutting wages, reducing employee privileges, firing workers, abusing authority, speeding up production, violating accepted work rules, and hiring outsiders. Often, increased competition, political backing, or economic hard times motivated the employers to undertake these measures. During periodic business recessions, the working class responded to the layoffs mutely. But workers did not accept employer attacks complacently. Most of the time, they responded with individual actions to survive and retain some measure of income and dignity. At other times, the economy assisted workers to redress past grudges. In moments of economic revival, when employers began rehiring, workers organized new and stronger unions. They selected tough labor bosses and supported—even urged—their leaders in calling for strikes. When thousands of urban workers took actions simultaneously, the politicians could not ignore them. All across Latin America in this fifty-year period, there was a strong coincidence of strike activity and populist and revolutionary movements. Indeed, the timing of the business cycle of the international economy provided workers of many countries with some of the same moments of opportunity. (See figs. 1, 2, and 3.)

Once having contributed to political movements, however, the workers did not entirely control them. The entourages of populists and revolutionaries represented other constituencies. Thus, a popular government's nationalization of an industry—such as the railways of Mexico or the copper mines of Chile—provided no guarantee that workers would achieve their goals. Even

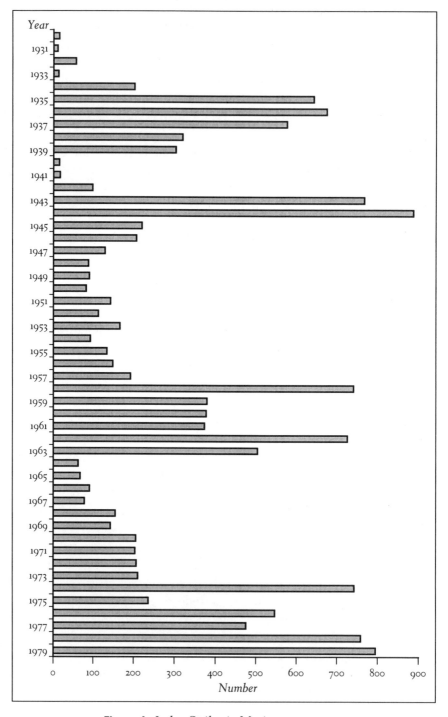

Figure 1. *Labor Strikes in Mexico, 1930–1979*

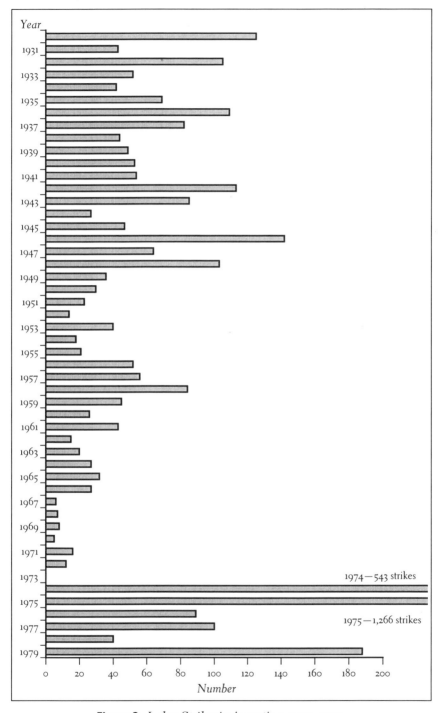

Figure 2. *Labor Strikes in Argentina, 1930–1979*

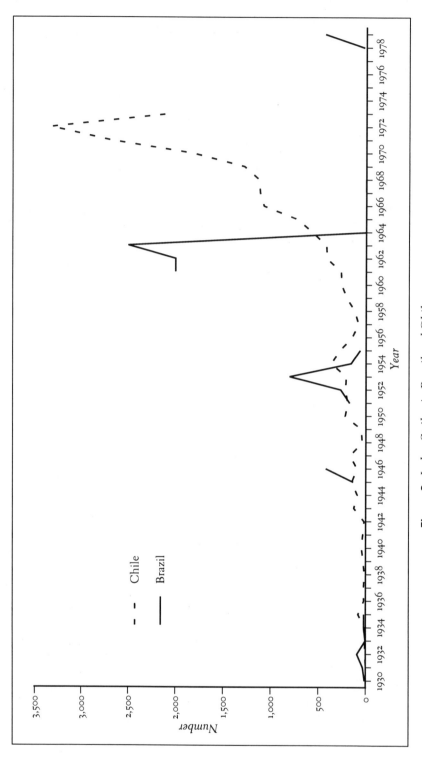

Figure 3. *Labor Strikes in Brazil and Chile, 1930–1979*

the popular governments had their own agenda, separate from that of the workers who supported it, and government administrators often behaved suspiciously like the old employers. So the struggle never completely ended.

The following chapters, therefore, show the variety of the urban and industrial workers' contributions to their own history and to their nations' histories. These vignettes depict remarkable successes and tragic failures but seldom total defeat and never crushing blows that permanently subordinated the working class to the whims of the elite. Our survey takes us to the important struggles in Latin America. We journey from the sugar mill seizures of Cuba, to the oil nationalization and railway strikes of Mexico, to the attempted revolution in Guatemala, to the railway nationalization and Peronism of Argentina, to Brazil's textile strikes, to the miners-cum-revolutionaries in Bolivia, to Peru's copper strikes, and finally to the revolutionary miners of Chile. There the saga ends with a military counterrevolution. Perhaps the latter forms too tragic and forlorn a conclusion to this volume. We really wish to emphasize that the struggle for workers' control never ends. It is constantly being negotiated everywhere, at all times, and at some level. What, finally, does this term really mean?[2] Here is our definition.

Workers' control refers to the struggle of workers on the shop floor to gain sufficient command of the work process to bring dignity to their proletarian lives.[3] Most often, workers struggle against wage cuts, layoffs, arbitrary supervisors, declining real wages, and reorganization of work that makes them bear the cost. Workers' control, of course, is never achieved but always under renegotiation between workers and their employer—whether that employer is a foreign company, a domestic entrepreneur, or the nation-state itself. Most often, the struggle continues sub rosa with workers undertaking individual acts of resistance. But workers overcome their internal class divisions during propitious economic times such as a resurgence of the economy and relative full employment or during favorable political events, some of which they may help to bring about. They attempt to take their shop struggles into the community and also into national life. Workers form labor unions and engage in strikes during these moments. Frequently, they seize the opportunity to replace complacent labor leaders with aggressive ones. If political leaders respond to such popular demands occurring simultaneously in many places of work, the result leads to a populist or revolutionary movement that brings about significant changes at the national level. These changes have included labor legislation, social reforms, labor participation in government, and the nationalization of industries. All too frequently, these worker-inspired actions produced a political backlash and repression, of which this volume contains numerous examples.

In subsuming the concept of workers' control of the work process to the broader idea of workers' control over their working lives, we desire to to draw a clear distinction between them. The former refers to "workers' power over the means of production"—or the productive processes—in the more traditional sense.[4] We use the idea of workers' control over their working lives to refer to the multifaceted struggle including, but not limited to, the battle for wage increases, job security, better working and housing conditions, and control over the productive processes. The locus of this broader struggle is usually the shop floor or the work site.

For this reason, each chapter is focused on the work process in various industries, in different countries, and in distinct historical contexts. Moreover, we propose one particular theoretical contribution for the particular utility of the workers' control paradigm as it applies to Latin America: that is, the workers' demonstrated ability—at certain conjunctional moments—to bring their workplace struggles to national attention and thereby to influence national events. We are not the first scholars of Latin American labor to make the connection between workplace struggles and labor's participation in national events. Such connections already have received abundant notice in the works of James, Bergquist, French, Brennan, Winn, and Gould, among others.[5] But we believe we are the first to reformulate the concept of workers' control in order to include the idea that ongoing workplace struggles motivate the larger political commitments of Latin American workers.

Of course, the concept of workers' control, like gender and culture, is a theoretical abstraction. One way we see workers' control as a useful concept is that it refers to the struggles of working people to gain power for a variety of ends. Workers seek leverage in order to limit the power that their employers wield over their lives. The struggle for control, as Montgomery and others have pointed out, is long term and unrelenting. At rare instances, workers use dramatic tactics such as voting, strikes, or violence to resist being exploited by their employers. They attempt to achieve particular objectives (wage increases, health care, removal of abusive supervisors, and appointment of sympathetic public officials). By thinking of discreet episodes of resistance as moments in this long-term struggle for power—regardless of their immediate objectives and tactics—we get away from reducing labor history either to a melee for money or to a great, predestined march to socialism.

Ours is a history from the bottom up, and our treatment of politics reflects this vigorous orientation. We concentrate on the experience of the working people in the mines and factories as well as in their communities. Labor historians often claim to present the view from below but usually settle on quoting the views of the labor leadership. In contrast, when we deal with politics, we do so from the level of the rank and file.[6] Thus, we subordinate formal ideology in an effort to re-create the culture of the working class, which has been shaped by what the workers brought with them to their places of work as well as by their concrete experiences with the labor processes and relations of production they found there. The bottom-up approach is fruitful and revealing, because the rank and file did not always follow the ideological trends set by their anarchist, syndicalist, communist, and nationalist spokespersons. But the bottom-up approach is also difficult. It requires the historian to go beyond the union halls to the workplaces themselves.

Given the constraints imposed upon us by available resources about the workplace, the workers' own ideology (or "politics") is not easily discerned. We have clearly unearthed previously undocumented forms of behavioral resistance from which we may posit some broader conclusions, even what the workers "really thought." However, we have to admit that few of us really know "what the workers were thinking." Only three of us were able to interview them. Others of us attempt to deduce their thinking based on an interpretation of their actions and the demands voiced by their leaders. Nevertheless, we cannot decide definitively whether they intended their actions to have the political consequences they did have. Indeed, historical actors may rarely consider the long-range effects of their actions. The following chapters explain how the struggle for workers' control in Latin America during the middle years contributed to the making of history.

Notes

1. Some of the most influential of these works include Rodney D. Anderson, *Outcasts in Their Own Land: Mexican Industrial Workers, 1906–1911* (DeKalb, Ill., 1976); Samuel Baily, "The Italians and the Development of Organized Labor in Argentina, Brazil, and the United States, 1880–1916," *Journal of Social History* 3 (1969): 123–34; Charles W. Bergquist, *Labor in Latin America: Comparative Essays on Chile, Argentina, Venezuela, and Colombia* (Stanford, 1986); Peter Blanchard, *The Origins of the Peruvian Labor Movement, 1883–1919* (Albuquerque, 1976); Philippe I. Bourgois, *Ethnicity at Work: Divided Labor on a Central American Banana Plantation* (Baltimore, 1989); James P. Brennan, *The Labor Wars in Córdoba, 1955–1976: Ideology, Work, and Labor Politics in an Argentine Industrial City* (Cambridge, Mass., 1994); Barry Carr, *El movimiento obrero y la política en México, 1910–1929* (Mexico City, 1981); Ruth Berins Collier and David Collier, *Shaping the Political Area: Critical Junctures, the Labor Movement, and Regime Dynamics in Latin America* (Princeton, 1991); Michael L. Conniff, *Black Labor on a White Canal: Panama, 1904–1981* (Pittsburgh, 1985); Peter DeShazo, *Urban Workers and Labor Unions in Chile* (Madison, Wis., 1978); John D. French, *The Brazilian Workers' ABC: Class Conflict and Alliances in Modern São*

Paulo (Chapel Hill, 1991); Jeffrey Gould, *To Lead as Equals: Rural Protest and Politi-cal Consciousness in Chinandega, Nicaragua, 1912–1979* (Chapel Hill, 1990); John Mason Hart, *Anarchism and the Mexican Working Class, 1860–1931* (Austin, 1978); Joel Horowitz, *Argentine Unions, the State, and the Rise of Perón, 1930–1945* (Berkeley, 1990); Daniel James, *Resistance and Integration: Peronism and the Argentine Working Class, 1946–1976* (Cambridge, England, 1988); Alan Knight, "The Working Class and the Mexican Revolution, c. 1900–1920," *Journal of Latin American Studies* 16 (1984): 51–79; Roberto P. Korzeniewicz, "Labor Unrest in Argentina, 1887–1907," *Latin American Research Review* 24, no. 3 (1989): 71–98; Deborah Levenson-Estrada, *Trade Unionists against Terror: Guatemala City, 1954–1985* (Chapel Hill, 1994); June Nash, *We Eat the Mines and the Mines Eat Us: Dependency and Exploitation in Bolivian Tin Mines* (New York, 1979); Hobart A. Spalding, *Organized Labor in Latin America: Historical Case Studies of Workers in Dependent Societies* (New York, 1977); and Peter Winn, *Weavers of Revolution: The Yarur Workers and Chile's Road to Socialism* (New York, 1986). For discussions of the central issues in this growing historiography, see Emilia Viotti Da Costa, "Experience versus Structures: New Tendencies in the His-tory of Labor and the Working Class in Latin America," *International Labor and Working-Class History*, no. 36 (Fall 1989): 3–24; Ian Roxborough, "Issues in Labor Historiography," *Latin American Research Review* 21, no. 2 (1986): 178–88; Eugene F. Sofer, "Recent Trends in Latin American Labor Historiography," *Latin American Research Review* 15, no. 1 (1980): 167–76; John Womack Jr. "The Historiography of Mexican Labor," in *El trabajo y los trabajadores en la historia de México*, ed. Elsa Cecilia Frost, Michael C. Meyer, and Josefina Zoraida Vásquez (Mexico City, 1979), 739–56.

2. The concept of workers' control has been developed in Carter L. Goodrich, *The Frontier of Control* (New York, 1921); Goodrich, "Problems of Workers' Control," *Locomotive Engineers Journal* 57 (May 1923): 365–66; Antonio Gramsci, *Selections from Political Writings (1921–1926)*, trans. and ed. Quintin Hoare (Minneapolis, 1978), 10–11; David Montgomery, "Workers' Control of Machine Production in the Nine-teenth Century," *Labor History* 17 (1976): 485–509; and Montgomery, *Workers' Con-trol in America: Studies in the History of Work, Technology, and Labor Struggles* (Cam-bridge, Mass., 1979). Like James Scott, we assume that the "subaltern" classes are capable of effective resistance and that the elite's cultural hegemony confronts certain limitations in controlling the workers. See James Scott, *The Moral Economy of the Peasant: Rebellion and Subsistence in Southeast Asia* (New Haven, 1976); Scott, *Weap-ons of the Weak: Everyday Forms of Peasant Resistance* (New Haven, 1985). But we also find inspiration in the works of Antonio Gramsci, Eric Hobsbawm, E. P. Thompson, the Colliers, Charles Bergquist, and Emilia Viotti Da Costa. Most of all, our research and writing has been guided by David Montgomery's usage of the older concept of "workers' control." Our research indicates that workers' behavior, in large measure, is determined by their experiences in the workplace. Montgomery hypothesizes that workers act to resist those arbitrary managerial reforms that make labor pay the price of increased efficiency. They fight against extended hours, reduced pay, Taylorism, and

altered work rules. We further suggest that, in Latin America, these shop floor battles sometimes motivated workers to take their struggles into the community and, less frequently but more dramatically, into national politics.

3. As one historian has defined the basic objective, "The struggle for job control was at the heart of the Córdoba autoworker factory rebellions in the 1970s." Brennan, *Labor Wars in Córdoba*, 316.

4. See Antonio Gramsci, "Workers' Control," in *Selections from Political Writings*, 10–11; Goodrich, "Problems of Workers' Control," 365–66, 415; Montgomery, "Workers' Control of Machine Production," 485–509. Although the authors of this volume make no claim to be Marxist historians, we do acknowledge that the influence of Marxists such as Gramsci, Montgomery, Da Costa, Scott, Hobsbawm, Thompson, and Gutman have led us to privilege the struggles of laborers in the workplace. These Marxist historians have defined the critical issues as few others have—especially the conflictive interplay between workers' culture and the labor process.

5. For citations of these authors, see note 1 above.

6. For an excellent example of this perspective, see Joel Wolfe, " 'Father of the Poor' or 'Mother of the Rich'?: Getúlio Vargas, Industrial Workers, and Constructions of Class, Gender, and Populism in São Paulo, 1930–1954," *Radical History Review* 58 (1994): 80–111.

CHAPTER ONE

TO RELIEVE THE MISERY

Sugar Mill Workers and the

1933 Cuban Revolution

MICHAEL MARCONI BRAGA

The standard of living of Cuban sugar mill and cane field workers declined steadily during the 1920s as the sugar industry attempted to reduce costs of production and to battle the effects caused by worldwide overproduction. With the onset of the Great Depression in the 1930s, the living standards of sugar workers declined even further. Mill owners slashed wages and reduced employment, leaving both cane and mill workers in a state of abject misery. At first, sugar workers were prohibited from protesting against their deteriorating position by the strong-arm tactics of President Gerardo Machado. But when the Machado government fell in August 1933, sugar workers reacted explosively. They demanded higher wages, shorter workdays, improvements in living conditions, job security, and the recognition of labor unions by employers. Management refused to meet these demands, and workers seized the majority of sugar mills on the island. They threatened the lives of managers. They helped themselves to food and supplies from company storehouses. The workers remained in control of the mills for most of September, forcing changes in legislation governing practically every aspect of sugarcane production. As a result, workers obligated owners to pay a minimum wage to both mill and field workers. They also compelled management to obey work rules on the shop floor and prohibited the firing of employees without just cause. These were certainly among the most significant reforms that occurred as a result of the revolution of 1933.

Thus far, the historical literature has overlooked the role of sugar workers in this revolution. Historians of the events of 1933 prefer to deal with the student uprisings, increasingly violent defiance in urban areas, and the rebellion within the military. Cuban and Soviet authors have recently given more than passing attention to sugar mill takeovers, but many questions still remain unanswered.[1] For instance, why did sugar workers take over the sugar mills? To what extent was the power vacuum created by the fall of Machado and the rebellion in the military responsible for the success of their movement? What did the workers do when they were in charge of the mills? Why did they eventually return the mills to the owners? What were the major points of contention between management and labor during contract negotiations? And what were the long-term consequences of the workers' actions?

In order to answer these questions, this chapter draws on documents contained in the Braga Brothers Collection at the University of Florida at Gainesville. The collection houses the complete records of the Czarnikow Rionda Company, its affiliates, and subsidiaries, which at the time of the uprisings owned five sugar mills and had an interest in a number of others.[2] Based on the information gleaned from these and other sources, it is possible to conclude that workers rebelled because they were hungry, because they were frustrated at a decade-long decline in their living standards, and because they were angry at management's intransigent neglect of their conditions. The collapse of the Machado administration in August 1933 and the Sergeants Rebellion led by Fulgencio Batista in September of the same year provided workers with a window of opportunity. Cane cutters and railway and factory employees, led by a vanguard of skilled mechanics and technicians, consequently established control over sugar mills across the country. The uprising was largely spontaneous and led by local union leaders, many of whom were labor agitators who had taken jobs at the mills in the years immediately preceding the revolution. Communists and other labor organizers acknowledged that the movement took them by surprise. They had to scramble to send delegates to the distant mills to help direct worker activities. Although managers called for assistance to put down the insurgency, the government and the military were in a complete state of disarray at the time and could not respond. Managers found themselves with few alternatives other than to concede to most of the labor demands. When workers finally opted to return the mills to owners, they had completely restructured relations of production in the weakened sugar industry. In the process, they restored lost dignity to themselves and gained greater control over their lives.

Working-Class Tensions

The sugar industry dominated Cuba's economy and society since the late eighteenth century. The single-minded focus on this one product brought occasional prosperity to the island. At the same time, Cuba depended on overseas markets and was vulnerable to dramatic swings in international commodity prices. Periodic recessions, triggered by changes in market conditions, accentuated already simmering tensions between members of the sugar industry's multiethnic workforce and also between labor and capital. Rebellions, racial conflicts, insurgency, and all-out guerrilla warfare were often the consequences.[3] By the time of the sugar mill takeovers in 1933, the sugar industry was directly or indirectly responsible for the livelihood of two-thirds of the Cuban population. Sugar sales represented four-fifths of the country's export earnings.[4] In Cuba, the cyclical nature of the sugar economy and tensions within the working class set the pace for political and social life.

The Cuban sugar industry consisted of an agricultural sector devoted to the cultivation and harvesting of cane and an industrial sector concerned with the processing of raw sugar. In 1933, foreign capital dominated both the agricultural and industrial sectors of the sugar industry. United States and Canadian corporations and banks owned or controlled approximately 100 of the 135 operating sugar mills as well as 20 percent of the arable land, producing some three-quarters of Cuba's total sugar output.[5] These North American–owned mills tended to place English-speaking foreigners in the top-level management and technical positions. This meant that Cubans did not control the profits from their principal industry and were relegated to the role of servants to foreign capital. The relationship between Cuban workers and North American managers was consequently tainted by feelings of resentment. These feelings were easily exploited by nationalists, which contributed to the unrest of 1933.

Similar antagonism existed among sugar workers themselves. The labor force consisted of hundreds of thousands of workers with varying skill levels, racial and ethnic backgrounds, and standards of living. Such heterogeneity made it difficult for workers to form a united front against capital and fight for their needs. But over the years, workers learned to broaden their movement as much as possible, incorporating workers with widely disparate skills and backgrounds. Although the diverse groups of sugar workers never truly bonded, they were all equally frustrated by their declining living standards and lack of control over their lives. Their simultaneous explosion in 1933 helped many workers to achieve what they wanted.

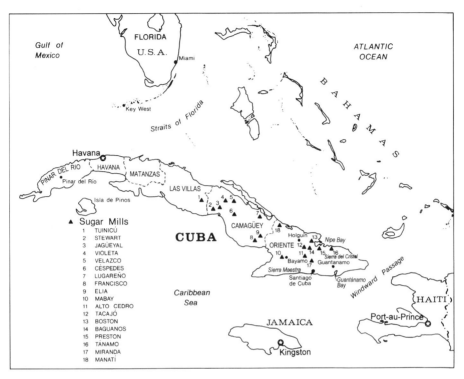

Map I. *The Rionda Company sugar mills in Cuba, 1933*

Field workers employed at plantations were the most divided of all. They came from different countries, did not speak the same languages, and had dissimilar standards of living. Cane farmers and sugar companies hired field workers on a temporary basis during the harvest season. They cut cane by hand and loaded the stalks onto oxcarts and railway cars to be taken to the mills. At first, field work was done primarily by former slaves, poor white peasants, and seasonal European immigrants from the Canary Islands. But when these workers declined to work for low pay and began agitating for wage increases from 1912 onward, the larger and more modern plantations at the eastern end of the island increasingly began to import black workers from other Caribbean islands.[6] Haitians and Jamaicans were willing to work for less money than native Cubans and endured the miserable living and working conditions. In turn, these immigrants spoke Creole French or English, making them less easily influenced by Spanish-speaking labor organizers. By 1933, approximately half of the five hundred thousand cane cutters working the harvest were Haitians or Jamaicans. Although they were originally supposed to return to their countries of origin after the harvest season, most of them resided in Cuba year-round. In the dead season, when harvest activity ceased, they would simply drift off into the countryside or head to the cities to find work.[7]

Native Cubans strongly objected to the presence of Haitian and Jamaican workers, because these immigrants represented a threat to their livelihood. In response, native Cubans took their struggle to the political level, attempting to convince the government to impose bans on the hiring of immigrant labor. Although workers finally succeeded in getting laws passed in the 1920s, sugar companies paid no attention to the bans and continued to import workers.[8] As a result, native Cubans retained a deep animosity for the immigrant cane cutters and never joined with them to fight against the capitalist class. Field workers also bore similar feelings of antipathy toward Spanish-born supervisors, as well other foreign administrators, for hiring immigrants in the first place. Tensions and animosity, therefore, divided the class of workers that labored in the cane fields and also set one class against another.

Some heterogeneity also divided the mill workers. Yet they had proved more willing than field workers to join together in labor unions. The milling process required both skilled and unskilled labor. The unskilled tasks, such as cleaning the mill floor and keeping the channels under it from getting clogged, were handled by African Cubans, whereas the jobs requiring mechanical, electrical, chemical, or woodworking skills were monopolized by Spaniards and white Cubans. Following independence in 1902, Spanish immigrants flooded into Cuba to take advantage of expanding job opportunities. They were initially preferred by mill owners because they tended to work hard to establish themselves in Cuba and also because they often remained aloof from Cuban labor struggles during the years preceding World War I. Consequently, Spaniards displaced Cubans from technical and middle-level management positions in the mills, thereby creating sources of animosity.[9] In addition to ethnic conflict between Spaniards and Cubans, considerable racial tension existed between white and black workers within the mills. But these considerations tended to be played down as the effects of the Great Depression and industry recession wore on and the need to develop a united front became apparent.

Ultimately, Spaniards and Cubans, blacks and whites, fought together during the takeover movement, presenting unified lists of demands in many places that called for an end to racial discrimination.[10] By 1933, mill workers realized the power of an uprising of the masses of field workers and the fear it generated in the capitalist class. So mill workers began to associate themselves with that power in order to obtain their demands. In return, petitions began to include the requirements of both industrial and agricultural labor. Throughout, however, the approximately fifty thousand mill workers on the island clearly represented the vanguard of the takeover movement.

By the time of the 1933 revolution, workers were loosely organized into unions affiliated with the Cuban National Confederation of Workers and the National Sugar Industry Workers Union.[11] However, management had not recognized these unions. With the help of the government troops, known as the Rural Guard, mill owners had made every effort to repress union activity. Perhaps an even harder task than unifying their own members, therefore, was the workers' struggle against management to be allowed to organize and form unions. Most sugar mills in Cuba operated like independent fiefdoms. The owners had almost complete control over who could live and work within the mill compound and the adjoining fields. Utilizing the Rural Guard, management usually found it easy to rout out union agitators from the general population of workers and exile these troublemakers and their families from the plantations.[12] Consequently, mill workers had to overcome two significant obstacles prior to the takeover movement of 1933. They had to unify the working class, and they had to organize in the face of intense opposition from mill owners and the Rural Guard. Communists, anarcho-syndicalists and other prolabor organizations helped workers overcome these barriers. Organizers were clandestinely sent to the mills to help disseminate ideas at the beginning of the decade, and many of these organizers played a crucial role in the pending uprisings even though they were often cut off from their central labor organizations.

Preceding the 1933 revolution, many factors conspired against efforts of Cuban sugar workers to obtain improvements in living conditions and to gain control over their lives. The mills were usually located far from population centers, which made management less beholden to the laws of the state and more likely to police workers on its own terms. The mills also had mostly seasonal workforces and large influxes of foreigners, making union organization extremely difficult. Moreover, during the depression, the living conditions of workers deteriorated rapidly, their pay diminished, and tens of thousands of jobs were eliminated. Agricultural, industrial, skilled, and unskilled workers of diverse racial and ethnic backgrounds still succeeded in coordinating a widespread revolt in an effort to take control of their lives.

Dance of the Millions

In order to explain why living conditions declined and workers eventually rebelled in 1933, it is necessary to go back to the beginning of World War I to show how the sugar industry evolved and how sugar workers were affected by and reacted to political and economic changes. The period from 1914 to 1918 was characterized by the expansion of the Cuban sugar industry. World War I was fought on the beet fields of Europe, causing European sugar production to decline from 8.6 million tons in 1913 to 3.1 million tons in 1918.[13] The Cuban sugar industry expanded rapidly to fill the void. (See fig. 4.) Foreign capital poured into the country in order to finance the construction of new sugar mills, modernize port facilities, and extend railway lines. As a result, Cuba's sugar production rose dramatically, and its share of the world sugar market grew from 16 to 34 percent. Annual profits increased from $120 million to more than $400 million by 1918.[14] The owners were not particularly inclined to share these earnings with workers.

Along with growth and profits, the war years were also a time of high inflation and increasing conflict between labor and capital. The war caused shortages of goods, forcing prices of basic necessities to rise by more than 100 percent. At the same time, real wages fell.[15] The drop in purchasing power caused sugar workers to begin agitating for pay hikes, for lower consumer prices, and for the right to form labor unions. In October 1917, strikes broke out at forty-eight sugar mills. They were led by the skilled workers—machinists, mechanics, electricians, iron workers, and carpenters, who were mostly of Spanish origin. Agricultural workers, most of whom were transient Haitians and Jamaicans, the most populous part of the sugar industry workforce, did not participate. Unwilling to concede to mill workers' demands, the owners asked the government to send in the Cuban army. They also called on assistance from the United States Marines, who had established a presence in the sugar districts since the outbreak of violence following the 1916 presidential elections. The combined U.S. and Cuban forces quickly succeeded in repressing the workers' movement. Sugar companies then sent strikebreakers to replace striking workers, while the government arrested national leaders and deported foreign ones.[16]

The mill owners gave the workers a 10 percent wage increase in the hope that this would satisfy them, but labor's efforts to achieve greater control over the workplace were stifled. Despite their failure to achieve many of their demands, sugar workers learned a great deal from their participation in the strikes. One of the reasons that they were so easily defeated was that the field workers had not joined with the mill laborers. Moreover, workers from related sectors of the economy, such as railways and ports, had not allied with the strike movement in order to form a united front against capital. Another factor that contributed to their defeat was the willingness of the U.S. government to deploy troops. In succeeding struggles, sugar workers were careful to form

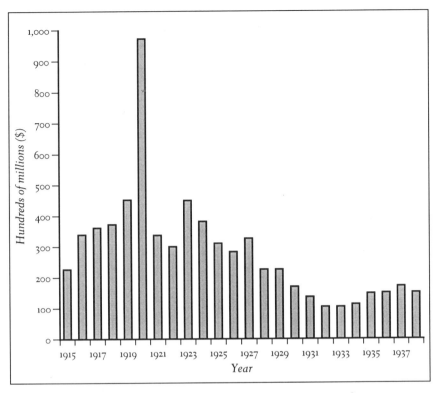

Figure 4. *Value of Cuban Sugar Harvest, 1915–1938*

alliances with workers in other branches of the economy and also to step up propaganda campaigns against the threat of U.S. intervention.

In 1919 and 1920, sugar companies experienced an astronomical increase in profits owing to rising sugar prices and an equally precipitous drop in profits when prices suddenly plunged. Following World War I, rumors circulated that the United States was benefiting from wartime price controls by reselling Cuban sugar at a profit. Cuban producers responded by withholding their supply, forcing the United States to abandon its pricing policy. Between June 1919 and May 1920, prices rose from 6.5¢ to 22.5¢ a pound, and Cuba was awash in money.[17] The total value of Cuban sugar reached nearly a billion dollars. Thinking that the boom would last at least until the following harvest, mill owners, cane farmers, and speculators raced to expand production. They borrowed heavily from local and international banks on terms relating to the eventual sale of sugar at prices ranging from 15¢ to 20¢ per pound.

However, by the end of the summer, sugar prices sank as fast as they had risen. In December 1920, they hit a low of 3.75¢ a pound. The sugar and banking industries were devastated. Seventy-nine percent of all sugar mills went into receivership, and nineteen Cuban banks with outstanding loans of more than $130 million went bankrupt. The only survivors were industries and banks that held significant assets abroad. National City Bank and the Royal Bank of Canada emerged the strongest of all. The former took over approximately sixty sugar mills after the crash, representing one-third of Cuba's productive capacity.[18] The dominance of international banks following the market collapse ushered in a new era. From 1920 on, banks only tended to loan money to properties in which they held financial interest. Smaller independent mills either had to form an alliance with one of the huge foreign-owned conglomerates or go out of business, which caused the sugar industry to become more consolidated.[19] At the same time, banks pressured sugar mills to continue expanding production and to reduce costs in every conceivable way. This strategy ultimately proved to be a burden for both the workers and the Cuban industry as a whole, contributing greatly to the coming rebellion.

After the crash, from 1920 to 1924, sugar workers intensified their protests because capital was forcing them to assume an overwhelming share of the sacrifices. Sugar mills dismissed workers and reduced wages in order to bring costs in line with revenues and to begin paying off debts. The international banks favored these initiatives. Banks also provided additional funds to encourage industries to increase mill efficiency through the incorporation of economies of scale.[20] As a result of protests from local workers about their declining real wages, sugar mills and cane farmers increasingly turned to imported labor. Sugar mills encouraged more than ninety-five thousand Haitians and Jamaicans to come to Cuba to work the harvests between 1920 and 1925. Besides their willingness to receive less pay, these immigrants also proved reluctant to join labor unions.[21] Sugar companies, therefore, benefited from transient labor. They saved on their wage bills and also avoided some of the bottlenecks in production caused by periodic protests. Native Cubans who had previously worked the sugar harvests had to pay the price.

Cost cutting, the incorporation of economies of scale, and the importation of cheaper labor from Haiti and Jamaica cost many native Cubans their jobs. For instance, management at the Tuinucu sugar mill laid off 150 workers in 1921 and reduced wages by 20 percent. Similar cuts were made at mills throughout the island. In response, there was an increase in protest activity, culminating in the strikes of 1924. In that year, workers protested at approximately thirty mills.[22] The strikes started at Central Morón, a Cuba Cane Corporation factory. Spurred on by the Morón faction of the Railway Brotherhood, an anarcho-syndicalist union made up primarily of Spaniards and Spanish Cubans, mill workers boycotted work after management decided to reduce the payroll by two hundred dollars a day. Workers suggested that if the company was going to reduce pay, then the workday should be reduced accordingly. They also objected to the fact that North American employees did not suffer equal pay cuts. The Morón factory workers demanded that the company stop paying employees in tokens or script, that workers be permitted to purchase goods at other locales besides the company store, and that Cuba Cane refrain from hiring foreign workers. In addition, they petitioned for the right to unionize and for the cessation of terror and repressive tactics. The company responded by immediately firing the striking workers and evicting them from company houses. Cuba Cane management also informed the mill restaurant and grocery stores that striking workers were no longer in its employ, stopping these enterprises from supplying workers with food and supplies. Incensed by these actions, the Railway Brotherhood encouraged mill workers at four other Cuba Cane factories (Jagüeyal, Stewart, Violeta, and Velasco) to walk out in solidarity with the Morón workers. Management responded once again by firing the striking workers. Railway workers and stevedores at area ports, both affiliated with Railway Brotherhood, then struck in solidarity with the Cuba Cane mill workers, refusing to unload machinery and supplies from cargo ships and transport these items to Cuba Cane mills. Cut off from the ports, the company was forced to negotiate. Management agreed to reinstate the men who had gone on strike and to pay them fortnightly and in cash. The company also granted workers the right to unionize and to appoint shop stewards to each department.[23]

The success of the strikers at Cuba Cane mills stimulated approximately fourteen thousand workers at other sugar mills in Cuba to adopt similar tactics. Management was forced to make concessions to labor in many of these places as well.[24] Compared with the strikes of 1917, the 1924 protest movement was a huge success. Mill workers still did not unite with Haitians and Jamaican field workers, which is evident from the fact that they called for management to stop importing foreign labor. However, mill workers did receive assistance from workers in other vital sectors of the economy. Another factor that assisted the sugar workers in 1924 was that the incumbent political administration was involved in an electoral campaign and proved reluctant to call troops into the mills for fear of losing votes.[25] The delay on the part of government gave sugar workers their first opportunity to obtain some of their demands.

Labor's triumph did not last long. Between 1925 and 1929, the Cuban government clamped down hard on organized labor and repealed most of the gains that workers had achieved during the 1924 strikes. Although President Gerardo Machado played lip service to the needs of workers and at first appeared to be a populist, he soon supported capital at labor's expense. He once promised U.S. businessmen in New York not to let any strike last longer than twenty-four hours. Machado made good on his word. During his seven-year regime, he ordered the arrest, deportation, and assassination of labor leaders. He also prohibited union meetings and strikes.[26] Despite Machado's reign of terror, unions continued to operate underground. The Communist Party, founded in 1925, gradually gained control of the Cuban National Labor Confederation from the anarcho-syndicalists. Communist labor leaders organized several urban strikes in 1927 and 1930. However, the communists did not succeed in organizing sugar workers until the onset of the Great Depression.[27]

For the first five years of the Machado administration, labor disturbances at sugar mills were effectively stifled. Machado did attempt to relieve unemployment and social tensions caused by a slump in the world sugar market, by borrowing and investing in public works projects such as the construction of a central highway and a presidential palace in Havana.[28] Some workers displaced from sugar mills after 1926 found jobs on these projects. Because of the worldwide oversupply of sugar at the time, sugar mills had sought to stimulate prices by cutting back production. Prices rose briefly in 1927, but they headed downward again soon afterward, dipping below 2¢ a pound in 1929.[29] Instead of improving the economy, therefore, crop restrictions actually forced mill owners to reduce their labor force, while declining prices prompted them to slash wages. The onset of the Great Depression only made matters worse. Sugar industry profits continued to decline, and bank financing for public works projects rapidly dried up. Suddenly, Machado had to confront increasing unemployment, falling standards of living, and the ramifications of years of political repression—all at the same time.

During the first years of the Great Depression, from 1930 to 1933, Cuba suffered from an absolute deterioration in social, economic, and political conditions. The United States in 1930 implemented the Hawley-Smoot Tariff, raising import duties on Cuban sugar. This law, designed to protect domestic cane and beet producers, actually benefited sugar producers in the U.S. possessions of Hawaii, Puerto Rico, and the Philippines. Increasing exports to the United States from these territories caused Cuba's share of the North American market to fall from 51.9 percent in 1929 to 24.6 percent in 1934. Total Cuban exports to the United States dropped from 3.7 million to 1.4 million tons.[30] Falling production, prices, and profits crippled the Cuban sugar industry's ability to pay the interest on its massive debts. Banks reacted by tightening their supply of credit. Sugar mills became involved in a running battle with banks to obtain the funds necessary to remain in production. Producers cut wages and employment even further and reduced expenditures on repairs and planting.[31]

In the meantime, economic conditions failed to improve. Sugar prices dropped below 1¢ per pound, forcing many mills to close down. By 1933, only 135 mills were operating, as compared with 183 in 1925. It is difficult to ascertain exactly how many jobs in the sugar industry were lost. According to several sources, more than 250,000 heads of families, representing approximately 1 million persons, were permanently unemployed at the time.[32] With regard to wages of those who managed to retain their jobs, cane cutters found their pay reduced from 80¢ to 25¢ per 100 *arrobas* from 1925 to 1933. (An *arroba* equals roughly twenty-five pounds of cut cane.) Average wages of mill workers fell from $2.40 per day in 1925 to less than $1.00 a day in 1933. To make matters worse, these wages were often paid in tokens or script, which had to be exchanged for marked-up goods at the company store. The harvest season was reduced by two months, and dead-season budgets were slashed by half.[33] Now, the majority of workers were unemployed for eight months instead of six, and the prospects of earning income in the dead season were practically eliminated.

Hunger became an acute problem. In lieu of money, the workers were ultimately given seeds and parcels of land on which they could grow vegetables in order to survive.[34] "Many people come to the [mill compound] who are going hungry and we have offered them meat and milk," reported the general manager of the Manatí Sugar Company. "Every day we have 110 to 112 men to eat and everyone here is giving. . . . In 20 years that I have been in Cuba I have never seen the neediness of people like this year."[35] Another Rionda official issued a similar report shortly before the dramatic events of September 1933. In this case, the manager asked for "money or food to relieve some of the misery." He added that something should be done quickly, "because with all this hunger no one can control the state of anarchy that is spreading throughout the island."[36] Since the onset of the Great Depression, social unrest increased in both the cities and countryside. Declining economic conditions and frustration with the Machado government caused opponents of the regime to rise up. Violence escalated, as did labor agitation. The Cuban National Labor Confederation, led by members of the Communist Party, intensified efforts to organize sugar workers. In 1932, the National Sugar Industry Workers Union was established, and delegates from thirty-two sugar mills attended a labor conference in February of that year.[37] Plans were drawn up for a widespread response to deteriorating economic conditions.

The collapse of the Machado regime and a rebellion within the army created a power vacuum that workers both helped to create and quickly took advantage of. At the beginning of 1933, sugarcane workers had stepped up their protests. Cane fields were set afire, while some twenty thousand mill workers struck for higher wages at twenty-five sugar factories. The government retained enough power at that time to repress the workers and force them to complete the harvest.[38] Then in August, a general strike, initiated by Havana bus drivers and other urban workers, was called by the Cuban National Confederation of Workers. The entire economy came to a halt. The strike forced President Machado to step down, and an interim government under Carlos Manuel Céspedes was formed. But the Céspedes government barely survived three weeks before it was toppled by a military rebellion.[39]

On 4 September a group of noncommissioned officers led by Sergeant Fulgencio Batista rebelled and took over Camp Columbia in the center of Havana. They were reacting to rumors that many enlisted men were going to be discharged and their wages reduced. But there were other reasons as well. Enlisted men objected to their deteriorating living standards and the contrasting corrupt and opulent lifestyles of the officers. Believing that U.S. armed intervention was imminent and would result in their reinstatement, officers barricaded themselves in the National Hotel in downtown Havana, where they conspired for the rest of the month. U.S. troops never arrived. After much anticipation, fighting finally broke out on 2 October between the officers inside the hotel and the enlisted men surrounding it. Two days later, the officers surrendered, allowing Sergeant Batista to assume undisputed control of the army.[40] During the period in which officers occupied the National Hotel, plantation workers rebelled and seized sugar mills across the island. This brief span of time was the opportunity sugar workers had been waiting for. Because of the breakdown in the military, there was no one to stop them.

The Old Feeling Has Disappeared

Sugar workers joined the strike movement somewhat later than workers in urban areas. It was the middle of the dead season, and because of the depression, many mills were completely closed down. Nevertheless, sugar workers presented lists of demands to management at the end of August. When these demands were not met, tensions escalated. At the Preston mill, owned by the United Fruit Company, workers revolted. The situation must have been serious, for the company authorized its manager to sign whatever agreement he thought necessary to avoid loss of life and property.[41] Similar events occurred at other mills, but it was really the Sergeants Revolt in September that released the pent-up frustrations and anger of sugar workers. Throughout the country, an estimated two hundred thousand mill and field workers, led by a vanguard of skilled laborers, seized nearly 120 sugar mills.[42] The workers remained in control of the mills for most of September.

What did the workers want? They requested higher wages, improvements in living conditions, job security, and greater control of the workplace. With respect to wages and work time, both field and mill workers asked for an eight-hour day and a corresponding minimum daily wage for unskilled workers of $1.00. They requested proportional wage increases for skilled labor. Sugar workers also demanded to be paid on time and in cash instead of with tokens or script. They asked that prices be reduced at the company store. With regard to improvements in living standards, both field and mill workers required sugar companies to provide them with free housing, water, and electricity all year round. They petitioned for improvements in mill compounds such as repairs to houses and buildings and the installation of better drainage and sanitation systems. The workers also asked for improved educational and health facilities, for a doctor to be stationed permanently at the mills, and for the provision of accident insurance. Concerning workplace control, workers demanded that unions be recognized by employers and that the Rural Guard cease from repressing legitimate protests. Workers solicited promises from sugar companies, stating that labor would not be punished after strikes ended. No worker was to be fired without just cause. Management was also required to stop evicting families from plantations after their jobs had been terminated.[43] Of these demands, wages and control of the workplace led to fundamental disagreements between capital and labor.

When managers refused to meet worker demands, arguing that because of market conditions they could not possibly comply, the workers rebelled. They seized sugar mills across the country, becoming completely responsible for law and order at the plantations for two to three weeks. How were the takeovers organized? What exactly did workers do while they were in charge of the mills? Although conditions varied somewhat from place to place, sugar workers followed similar strategies. After taking the mills by force, the workers usually set up strike committees, made up of three to nine members, under the auspices of local unions. The workers elected members of the strike committee by majority vote, usually selecting skilled personnel pertaining to the mill but occasionally appointing outside organizers linked to the National Confederation of Workers and the National Sugar Industry Workers Union.[44] The two labor organizations were dominated by members of the Communist Party at the time. But the communists were not completely in charge of the takeover movement. In fact, Communist Party officials in Havana admitted that the mill seizures took them by surprise and that they had to scramble to keep up with worker initiatives. Communist Party representatives rushed from mill to mill throughout September in an effort to consolidate the takeover movement. At the same time, representatives of other ideological and political persuasions, such as anarcho-syndicalists and representatives of the new Grau San Martín government, were doing exactly the same thing.[45] Therefore, it is difficult to claim that the communists were in control of the movement. There is no question that the Communist Party helped to disseminate information and ideas to strike committees during the uprisings, but local union representatives were in charge at most mills.

Strike committees took on the task of running the plantations. They issued orders and delegated responsibilities subject to a vote by their members. They disarmed the mill's guards, who generally did not attempt to obstruct worker activities. As the soldiers stationed at the mills were not receiving commands from their officers because of the Sergeants Revolt, they also tended to side with the workers. In their place, strike committees appointed militias, made up of workers, to patrol the properties and to restrict exit and entry. They ordered that storehouses and cafeterias be opened, distributing food and supplies to workers and to the unemployed. Strike committees also confiscated and butchered company livestock to feed the hungry. Occasionally, as at the Mabay sugar mill, the strike committees parceled out land to peasants. At several mills, strike committees even sold sugar from company warehouses to local towns in order to raise money to pay for supplies and munitions.[46] While in charge of the mills, workers used the company railroads to transport goods and to communicate with other mills and field workers in the interior. Out of revenge, they often discharged office personnel, warning them not to appear at work and providing them with only minimal food rations.

Throughout the ordeal, managers feared for their lives. If the managers were present at the mills at the time of the takeovers, the workers usually confined them to their residences or offices; anyone who wanted to see them had to obtain a pass from the strike committees. This occurred at the Manatí, Francisco, Tuinucu, Alto Cedro, Tacajo, Baguanos, Miranda, and Tanamo mills.[47] At these and other places, workers prohibited domestic servants from carrying out their tasks, leaving managers and upper-level staff to prepare their own meals and wash their own clothes. Strike committees also regulated the use of water and electricity, which caused managers to complain that they were deprived of the use of these necessities. The workers often vented their frustrations on the managers by threatening to kill them or burn down plantation houses if they failed to sign their demands. In some cases, workers also expressed their anger by destroying office furniture. Some withheld food or banged constantly on the walls and water pipes of the managers' residences so that they were unable to sleep at night, such as occurred at the Baguanos and Tacajo sugar mills. Managers repeatedly sneaked telegraph or handwritten messages to their base offices in Havana, asking for military assistance. Direct

Plowing a field for sugarcane in Cuba, 1928. (Courtesy of the Braga Brothers Collection, University of Florida Library)

contact with the outside world was often impossible, because the strike committees ordered telephone lines to be cut. Where telephone service remained in operation, workers monitored the conversations, making managers feel they could not talk freely.[48] Despite the physical discomfort and threats of violence, however, no manager was injured during the takeovers.

Similar events, all tightly controlled by local strike committees, occurred across the countryside. "More than 500 workers and peasants, armed with revolvers, machetes and sticks, have taken over the mill," wrote the manager of Central Lugareño. "In essence, they represent the law at this time, because the attitude of the army could not be more complacent. The strike committee guards the mill, storehouses of sugar, the offices, and the entrances and exits to the [mill compound] with thirty or forty men, who are relieved every four hours day and night."[49] The mills were highly organized under workers' control, but from management's perspective, the events appeared completely chaotic. Many managers conveyed a general feeling of anarchy augmented by the shortage of food and by economic paralysis. "At all the mills, [the workers] are running off with pigs, chickens, and livestock," said one Rionda company official. "It is impossible to realize the disorder that reigns in all parts."[50] Hunger was ever present. In the western part of the island, this need for food was especially severe; a hurricane swept the island at the beginning of September, destroying crops. "The inactivity of the mills cut off [the farmer's] only money crop," a U.S. consular agent explained, "and heavy rains this fall either wholly washed away or greatly crippled his rude plantings of vegetables." The official concluded that these disasters prompted the farmers to "assault the provision stores of the Hormiguero mill."[51] The Céspedes sugar mill, pertaining to the Rionda family, was also raided by workers and local farmers during the period. The mill was the least profitable of all the Rionda mills, and the family decided to close it down as soon as the harvest ended in June 1933. Therefore, workers at Céspedes "did not receive a penny" during the entire dead season.[52] The workers responded by seizing the mill in September. The manager was not present at the time, leaving the workers with no one with whom to negotiate. Failing to receive any assurances that the mill would grind, workers began to strip the factory. "I have just received advice to the effect that the robbing and plundering of the mill has commenced: tools, bronzes, spare parts, pieces of machinery, etc. etc. are being taken away and sold in the towns near Céspedes," said the manager in December 1933. "The cattle is feeding on the cane, and the workers and dwellers of the neighborhood have practically taken possession of the mill."[53] From management's perspective, this activity appeared criminal. It was, however, a matter of survival to the workers.

Faced with the urgency of worker demands and the depth of the sugar market crisis, management tried to procrastinate as much as possible. Companies even attempted to withdraw their managers to Havana so that workers would not have anyone with whom to negotiate. Managers of the Rionda mills were urged to return to Havana if they could. "The most important thing is to gain time by putting things off," the official said. "The mills that are faring best in this storm are those where workers have no one to deal with. Therefore, I suggest that we remove the managers from the mills and shut down all work so that workers see that it is their fault that the mills are not completing the harvest."[54] By holding managers hostage, the workers prevented them from abandoning the mills. By threatening their lives, the workers forced them to sign new contracts.

But why did the workers try to make the lives of managers miserable? The workers took these actions mainly because they wanted to show that they were in charge. Perhaps they also wanted to let managers know what it felt like to be unable to control their own lives, to be denied basic necessities, and to be threatened with starvation. The shutting off of public utilities, however, was not always done to be vindictive. Workers shut off the power at sugar mills to conserve energy. The economy was at a complete standstill, and there was no way of knowing when additional fuel supplies could be obtained. The workers also cut telephone lines so that managers would be unable to call for assistance. They prohibited managers from receiving unauthorized visitors because the workers feared that the managers would try to create conflict within their ranks. By promising favors to certain individuals, workers believed that managers could weaken the movement. That is why the manager of the Francisco mill wrote that a worker who came to visit him without a pass would be "in danger."[55]

The workers formed militias and patrolled the properties to protect themselves. They were not particularly worried about the Cuban military in its contemporary state of disarray, but they definitely feared U.S. intervention. After all, the marines had landed in Cuba in 1917, and during the height of the takeover movement, U.S. destroyers entered most Cuban harbors.[56] To warn sugar mills across the country of the impending danger from these vessels, the strike committee at the Mabay sugar mill issued a circular: "The Imperialists and their national lackeys, the Wall Street bankers, threaten with an imperialistic military intervention, already started by dispatching thirty ships of war to Cuban waters. . . . [The] warships, the military array, the technicians of the Department of the Navy and other big military men who are now in Cuba, have come to our country chiefly and principally to intimidate the laboring class, the peasants, the soldiers, and the students, and to drown the movement in blood."[57]

The warships made workers extremely nervous. Strikers at the Manatí sugar mill nearly panicked when a U.S. destroyer entered the harbor. Its commander came ashore to confer with the general manager of the Manatí sugar company, who remained at the mill during the uprising. The manager reported that, during conversations with the commander, "three (workers) broke into the dining room violently. . . . The men stated that they wanted the chief of the company police to hand over the company's arms. . . . The result of all this was that the strikers took over the rifles, revolvers and machetes of [the company] police, the army corporal here not doing anything to prevent them."[58] The commander of the U.S. destroyer returned to his ship shortly after his visit to the plantation and sailed it just over the horizon. Nevertheless, workers at the Manatí sugar mill remained vigilant in their preparations for defense, as they did at other sugar mills. With the help of the Communist Party and university students in Havana, workers from sugar mills such as Mabay disseminated propaganda throughout Latin America to stir up public opinion opposing the use of force. The noninterventionist sentiments of Latin American countries at the time greatly influenced U.S. foreign policy, helping to restrain

U.S. aggression.[59] In sum, the actions of workers were usually both calculated and rational during the takeover movement, but workers were often confronted with events that caused them to react out of panic or necessity.

If they were able to establish control over the mills and form militias in order to protect them, why did workers begin to return the mills to their owners at the beginning of October? The principal reason was that workers lacked the financial resources to run the plants. Financing a sugar harvest cost nearly one-half million dollars in the 1930s. Sugar companies usually borrowed necessary funds against future sugar sales or by mortgaging property and buildings. Because of depressed market conditions, bankers were already reluctant to lend to sugar mill owners, let alone to a group of insurgent workers. Besides the intricacies involved in financing a crop, selling sugar also required marketing connections. Sugar mills owned by refineries sold their supplies directly. Other mills used brokerage firms.[60] It is impossible to imagine that refineries and brokerage firms would sever their ties with capital in order to market sugar for insurgent workers. Realizing this, the workers knew that they had to turn the mills back to the owners while they still retained an advantage.

At the beginning of October, Batista consolidated control over the military and was in a position to order troops into the mills. Shortly after the battle at the National Hotel, Batista informed mill owners that he was ready to "dislodge from any sugar central all individuals other than the employees whom the manager desired to retain." Batista also said that "the army would seize all foreign agitators and arrange for their immediate expulsion from Cuba and imprison communist leaders, and would also guarantee the right of the legitimate managers of such properties."[61] Sensing the increasing power of Batista and the Cuban military, and realizing that there were still factions in the revolutionary government of Ramón Grau San Martín that opposed the takeovers, the workers entered negotiations at an advantage. They controlled most of the mills and held the lives of managers and the condition of sugar properties in the balance.

What did the two sides struggle over during contract negotiations? Wages and control of the workplace. Management representatives at most mills freely acknowledged that wages were extremely low but argued that there was little they could do about it. A senior Rionda official remarked that "if prices were two and a half cents a pound and mills were allowed to grind two million tons then [the Riondas] would be the first to raise wages," but with prices at current levels such an increase was impossible.[62] Nevertheless, every mill in the country eventually agreed to minimum wage increases for both field and mill hands. A manager for the Manatí Sugar Company stated that if he had not accepted wage demands, "there would have been considerable loss of property and lives." He added that the company would just have to postpone repairs on the mills and run fewer trains in order to meet the wage increases.[63] Management understood the need to raise the wages of skilled technicians and department supervisors. One manager admitted that the plantations' current labor problems derived from the fact that crop supervisors were being paid so little. He explained that the added responsibilities of these men, which included riding around the fields on horseback and ensuring that other work-ers were doing their jobs, had to be compensated accordingly. "How is it possible to convince this man that he must earn less than a worker? This is the person we must help to resolve the problem," the manager said.[64] At least with regard to skilled workers, the issue of wages did not always produce a stum-bling block to negotiations between labor and capital. After all, these skilled workers had provided the leadership for the mill seizures, and they needed to be assuaged.

What really embittered the negotiations was labor's insistence on greater control over the workplace. Workers at many mills demanded that co-workers be rehired and that certain managers and strikebreakers be fired. They also stipulated that sugar companies were to adhere to contract terms and allow unions to appoint shop stewards to protect against contract violations. In addition, workers fought to make management promise not to fire workers for their participation in the strike movement and to refrain from evicting families from plantations. Labor won most of the battles over these issues. Manatí sugar mill workers demanded that the assistant manager be fired because he treated them in a "gruff manner" and repeatedly refused to meet their de-mands. At first, the general manager of the mill strongly objected. In the end, he conceded. The general manager stated that he had feared "the workers (would) carry out their threats of personal injury." Therefore, for "the assistant manager's own good," he was requested to resign.[65] Not every struggle ended as favorably for labor.

On the whole, however, when workers did not win outright, they were usually able to neutralize management's position. During contract negotia-tions at the Francisco sugar mill, for instance, employees demanded that seven of their co-workers be fired for attempting to block the strike movement. The president of the company refused. Desiring to divide the workers at the mill, he stated, "We will not fire certain workers others want us to fire even if there are demonstrations or a mutiny to remove workers not in agreement with the strike."[66] In this case, the striking workers were forced to give in, but not before making the company agree to let the union appoint all the shop stewards at the Francisco mill and to promise that no worker be punished for his participation in the strike.[67] This agreement forced workers to allow potential strikebreakers in their midst. But the inclusion of the clause regarding shop stewards gave local unions greater power to police the shop floor, making certain that contractual agreements were not violated. The clause preventing punishment after the strike gave workers a sense of security that their jobs would not be eliminated in favor of their more servile comrades. Therefore, the compromise weakened management's position regarding control of the workplace and strengthened that of the workers.

A similar compromise was reached during negotiations between labor and management at the Tuinucu sugar mill. In this case, the company fought to retain the right to expel any family from the plantation for disorderly conduct. The workers ultimately agreed, but they forced the company to include a clause that no worker was to be fired for his participation in the strike. The two clauses tended to conflict with each other. Different interpretations of the two clauses provided the source for future conflicts.[68] Nevertheless, agreements between labor and management were eventually reached, and workers promptly ceded control of the sugar mills.

As a result of their struggle, workers could claim victory. They had gained much and lost nothing, because they compelled managers at least to compromise on every issue of importance. After the completion of Tuinucu negotiations, the president of the company expressed the feeling of loss. He lamented that the union delegates "behaved so badly." He was especially chagrined by the fact that they were children of men who had worked for the family for a long time and "had received a great many favors." "They were much tougher than I imagined them to be," the president of the company said, "and one could see that the old feeling that existed between management and workers at Tuinucu has disappeared."[69] Although workers had reached agreements with management at most mills by the beginning of October, this did not signify the end of the takeover movement.

In November, troubles started again when management broke some of its agreements. At the Elía sugar mill, workers claimed that the company breached its contract by failing to investigate the behavior of the mill's manager as it said it would. The company argued that it had investigated the manager and concluded that he had not treated the employees in a "despotic and unjust way," as workers had claimed.[70] The Elía sugar mill employees walked off the job. Similarly, Francisco sugar mill workers requested the reinstatement of two of their comrades who had recently been fired. Management refused, explaining it did not have the funds to pay the two fired men. The manager said that because the two workers were some of the last people hired, they had to be the first to go. However, the workers told the manager that they would be willing to work less each week to allow their co-workers to stay on. They suggested that three men could work ten days each instead of one working for the entire month. But again the manager declined, causing the workers to strike. Workers said the company had agreed to not fire anyone for his participation in the takeover, but that is exactly what happened. Both of the fired workers had been leaders of the mill seizure.[71] Despite the conflict, workers remained calm. An attorney representing Rionda interests maintained that the workers did not want to be obstructionist but just wanted their demands to be met. However, there was no quick resolution to the strike at the Francisco mill. The company held fast to its desire to retain the freedom "to determine who [would] be in its employ." The strike dragged on well into February, and finally the Rural Guard was called in.[72] Therefore, the strike movement did not end with the return of the mills to the owners. It ended when a new government was strong enough to start a campaign of repression.

By February 1934, the Mendieta-Batista government was in a position to send in troops to the mills, pressured to do so by the U.S. legation in Havana and plantation owners who were eager to begin the harvest. Labor leaders urged workers to stand firm against the coming "brutal terror" and to form armed militias. They claimed that their "goal was not to provoke struggles but to put an end to the slaying of defenseless workers."[73] In early 1934, the Mendieta-Batista government prepared for repression by first safeguarding most of the gains that workers had achieved during the past four months. Legislation passed guaranteeing the minimum wage, an eight-hour day, and the provision of accident insurance. At the same time, the Mendieta-Batista government changed the rules regulating the right to strike. From then on, workers had to seek the permission of the recently formed Department of Labor in order to mount a strike. The government then could declare strikes legal or illegal; troops could be sent in against illegal strikes.[74] During February, Batista sent two hundred troops to the Preston mill, owned by the United Fruit Company, and several workers died as a result. Thirty families were also expelled from the plantation. Blood was shed at several other mills as well, eventually compelling employees "to work or vacate company property."[75] Many labor leaders were deported, and several individuals sympathetic to the labor movement were assassinated. Workers abandoned the strike movement to begin working the harvest.

However, from time to time, when opportunities presented themselves, workers struck to obtain what they had been denied. At the Tuinucu sugar mill, for instance, protests broke out again in September 1934. This time the workers demanded that the company agree to a "closed shop" clause under which it had to refrain from hiring anyone not affiliated with the sugar workers' union. They also required that the company promote employees on the

basis of seniority, telling management to maintain existing wage scales rigorously. Any worker who left his position was to be replaced by someone at the
exact same wage. Besides these clauses, the workers also demanded that any
extra work around the mill be given to the unemployed and that delegates be
appointed to every department to help management uphold work rules. Management ultimately conceded to all these demands.[76] Clearly, the workers had
obtained greater control of the workplace. By the end of 1934, they had a say in
practically every issue affecting their lives at the plantations, from how much
they would be paid to who was to be hired and fired.

Conclusion

In many ways, sugar mill owners had brought the takeover movement on
themselves. Their callous treatment of workers since independence in 1902
and especially their importation of foreign workers in order to depress wages
and stymie union activity after 1912 created animosity on the part of Cuban
sugar workers. But the primary cause of the sugar mill takeovers in September
1933 was the collapse of the world sugar market after "the dance of the millions" in 1920. Sugar mills struggled to remain solvent and pay off their debts,
resorting to the incorporation of economies of scale and cutting costs to the
bone. These efforts dramatically reduced the standard of living of sugar workers. Had they been permitted to protest, workers might have effected some sort
of change that would have altered their fate, such as the establishment of a
minimum wage, but the Machado government severely restricted the workers'
right of free speech. When Machado ultimately fell in August 1933, the reaction of workers was explosive. They seized control of mills and threatened the
lives of managers. Through their united and spontaneous action, workers rose
above the ethnic and racial conflicts that divided them, forcing capitalists to
change the way they had done business. At the same time, workers forced
government to legislate these changes. By 1940, most of the demands workers
had fought for during the 1933 revolution were incorporated in the new Constitution of 1940, a document containing some of the most advanced labor
legislation in Latin America. Workers received a minimum wage linked to the
price of sugar, an eight-hour day, and better living and working conditions.

  Most important, they gained more control over the workplace. Sugar companies agreed to recognize unions and to deal with them directly. The unions
were permitted to appoint shop stewards to prevent management and nonunion workers from breaking work rules. In turn, most mills eventually adopted
clauses regarding hiring and firing. No employee could be hired unless the
union indicated his acceptance as a member, and no employee could be

dismissed without union approval. Furthermore, management agreed to promote workers according to seniority and to uphold existing wage scales.[77] These developments meant that management no longer absolutely dictated policy on employment, promotions, or pay at the sugar mills or in the fields. Henceforth, workers took over a share of these responsibilities through their local unions. Greater authority at the factory level also translated to greater power at the political level. After the revolution of 1933, no government that came to power could ignore organized labor.[78] As a result, workers emerged from the revolutionary period with greater control over their lives and the realization that collective action translated into political power.

However, the revolution of 1933 did not solve all of the workers' problems. Although sugar prices, profits, and wages initially rose from their 1933 levels, the economy stagnated. Increased regulation on the sugar business, continued political instability, and the lingering effects of the Great Depression discouraged foreign investment.[79] Without investment, there was little economic growth. Without growth, no new jobs were created, and unemployment and underemployment remained high. In addition, new trade agreements made the island nation more economically dependent.[80] The United States was in a position in which it could withdraw its favors at any moment and wreak havoc on the Cuban economy, and it did this several times in the late 1930s to block liberal reforms that might have additionally benefited rural workers. Economic stagnation, high unemployment, and dependence on the United States plagued Cuba for the next twenty-five years. The malaise eventually contributed to the revolution of 1959, which brought Fidel Castro to power. Sugar workers played an important role in this revolution as well. By setting fires in cane fields and destroying company property, the workers let management and the government know that they were not satisfied with the status quo. Although their wages increased and they obtained greater control of the workplace following the 1959 revolution, their struggle was not over. By embracing some of Castro's labor strategies and rejecting others, Cuban workers continue to struggle for greater control over their own lives.

Notes

The author thanks Louis A. Pérez and Carl Van Ness for their helpful comments and suggestions.

1. Three recent books include Lionel Soto, *La revolución del 33* (Havana, 1977); Angel García and Piotr Mironchuk, *Los soviets obreros y campesinos en Cuba* (Ha-

vana, 1987); Instituto de Historia del Movimiento Comunista y de la Revolución Socialista de Cuba, Anexo al Comité Central del Partido Comunista de Cuba [hereafter referred to as Instituto de Historia], *Historia del movimiento obrero cubano: 1865–1958*, vol. 1 (Havana, 1985). For an anticommunist view, see Justo Carrillo, *Cuba 1933: Students, Yankees, and Soldiers* (New Brunswick, N.J., 1994).

2. For information regarding the Rionda family holdings, see Farr & Co., *Manual of Sugar Companies: 1951–1952* (New York, 1952), 35–269.

3. Ramón Eduardo Ruíz, *Cuba: The Making of a Revolution* (New York, 1968), 40–47; Robert L. Paquette, *Sugar Is Made with Blood* (Middletown, Conn., 1988), 71–72.

4. F. T. F. Dumont, "Cuban Economic and Financial Problems," 25 February 1931, National Archives and Record Service, Washington, D.C., Record Group 59, General Records of the Department of State, Confidential U.S. Diplomatic Post Records: Central America, Cuba, 1930–45 (hereafter cited as Diplomatic Post Records), 2116956596.

5. Louis A. Pérez, *Cuba under the Platt Amendment, 1902–1934* (Pittsburgh, 1986), 72–74, 188. See also Francis White to Harry F. Guggenheim, Havana, 8 February 1930, Diplomatic Post Records, 2116956483; Commission on Foreign Affairs, *Problems of the New Cuba* (New York, 1935), 268; Lowry Nelson, *Rural Cuba* (Minneapolis, 1950), 95.

6. Louis A. Pérez, *Intervention, Revolution, and Politics in Cuba, 1913–1921* (Pittsburgh, 1978), 72; Pérez, *Cuba under the Platt Amendment*, 81. Commission on Foreign Affairs, *Problems of the New Cuba*, 286; W. H. Harris to secretary of state, Havana, 31 May 1919; Harold L. Williamson to secretary of state, Havana, 29 August 1919, National Archives and Record Service, Washington, D.C., Record Group 59, General Records of the Department of State, State Department Correspondence for Cuba, 1910–1929, Decimal Files (hereafter cited as State Dept. Decimal Files), 837-504/0-315.

7. Commission on Foreign Affairs, *Problems of the New Cuba*, 285; Instituto de Historia, *Historia del movimiento obrero cubano*, 179; Franklin W. Knight, "Jamaican Migrants in the Cuban Sugar Industry, 1900–1934," in *Between Slavery and Free Labor: The Spanish Speaking Caribbean in the Nineteenth Century*, ed. Manuel Moreno Fraginals, Frank Moya Pons, and Stanley L. Engerman (Baltimore, 1985), 100.

8. Pérez, *Cuba under the Platt Amendment*, 77, 84, 162; Arthur C. Frost to secretary of state, Havana, 20 June 1924, State Dept. Decimal Files, 837-504/316-837.5073/8; *Havana Post*, 26 December 1929, State Dept. Decimal Files, 837-504/0-315. Manuel Rionda y Polledo to Salvador Rionda, New York, 8 November 1928, Braga Brothers Collection at the University of Florida at Gainesville (hereafter referred to as Braga Brothers Collection), ser. 10, Manatí Files; Knight, "Jamaican Migrants in the Cuban Sugar Industry," 105, 109.

9. Commission on Foreign Affairs, *Problems of the New Cuba*, 285; Edwin Schoenrich to Samuel S. Dickson, Camaguëy, 2 January 1934, Diplomatic Post Records, 2116956632; Pérez, *Cuba under the Platt Amendment*, 78–79, 149.

10. Havana Embassy to secretary of state, enclosure 2 to dispatch 143, 29 September 1933, Diplomatic Post Records, 2116956552. For antidiscrimination clauses in labor contracts, see note 46.

11. Commission on Foreign Affairs, *Problems of the New Cuba*, 280; Instituto de Historia, *Historia del movimiento obrero cubano*, 271–73.

12. Instituto de Historia, *Historia del movimiento obrero cubano*, 271.

13. United States Cane Sugar Refiners Association, *Sugar Economics* (New York, 1938), 70.

14. Oscar Pino Santos, *El asalto a Cuba por la oligarquía financiera yanqui* (Havana, 1973), 79.

15. Instituto de Historia, *Historia del movimiento obrero cubano*, 178.

16. Pérez, *Intervention, Revolution, and Politics in Cuba*, 41–45, 87–97, 101; J. L. Mayer to M. R. Polk, Havana, 12 December 1918, State Dept. Decimal Files, 837-504/0-315; Instituto de Historia, *Historia del movimiento obrero cubano*, 181–85; Telegram 981 from U.S. Embassy in Havana to U.S. State Department, 14 April 1919, State Dept. Decimal Files, 837-504/0-315.

17. Leland Hamilton Jenks, *Our Cuban Colony* (New York, 1928), 214–19.

18. Ibid., 245, 282; Grosvenor M. Jones to the U.S. Department of Commerce, Havana, 7 August 1923, State Dept. Decimal Files, 837-00B-837-00/6.

19. Jenks, *Our Cuban Colony*, 282.

20. Ibid.

21. Instituto de Historia, *Historia del movimiento obrero cubano*, 179; Knight, "Jamaican Migrants in the Cuban Sugar Industry," 103.

22. Oliver Doty to Rionda y Polledo, Tuinucu, 13 May 1921, Braga Brothers Collection, ser. 10, Tuinucu Files; Francis R. Stewart, Santiago, 4 November 1924; E. H. Crowder to secretary of state, Havana, 17 October 1924, State Dept. Decimal Files, 837-504/0-315.

23. Crowder to secretary of state, 17 October 1924, State Dept. Decimal Files, 837-504/0-315.

24. Interview with Railway Brotherhood leader Enrique Varona, *El Heraldo*, Havana, November 1924. For information about strikes at other mills, see Francis R. Stewart to E. H. Crowder, Santiago, 4 November 1924 and 6 December 1924; Mr. White to Mr. Manny, Havana, 22 November 1924; Crowder to U.S. State Department, Havana, 24 November 1924, State Dept. Decimal Files, 837-504/0-315.

25. Crowder, Havana, 17 October 1924, State Dept. Decimal Files, 837-504/0-315.

26. Instituto de Historia, *Historia del movimiento obrero cubano*, 240–41.

27. Pérez, *Cuba under the Platt Amendment*, 239–40, 263, 282–83; Instituto de Historia, *Historia del movimiento obrero cubano*, 271; Ruíz, *Cuba*, 123.

28. F.L.W. to Guggenheim, 9 July 1926, State Dept. Decimal Files, 837-504/316-837-5073/8; Guggenheim to secretary of state, Havana, 11 April 1930, Diplomatic Post Records, 2116956450.

29. Nelson, *Rural Cuba*, 98; Luis E. Aguilar, *Cuba: 1933* (Ithaca, N.Y., 1972), 56.

30. Soto, *Revolución del 33*, 263; Pino Santos, *Asalto a Cuba*, 183–86.

31. Guggenheim to secretary of state, Havana, 10 April 1931, Diplomatic Post Records, 2116956483; George E. Crawley to Manuel Rionda y Polledo, Francisco, 3 De-

cember 1929; Salvador Rionda to Rionda y Polledo, Manatí, 26 April 1929; Rionda y Polledo to Salvador Rionda, New York, 24 July 1931, Braga Brothers Collection, ser. 10, Francisco and Manatí files.

32. Soto, *Revolución del 33*, 261; Commission on Foreign Affairs, *Problems of the New Cuba*, 87; Hugh Thomas, *Cuba: The Pursuit of Freedom* (New York, 1971), 688.

33. Commission on Foreign Affairs, *Problems of the New Cuba*, 287; Instituto de Historia, *Historia del movimiento obrero cubano*, 264. George E. Crawley to Rionda y Polledo, Francisco, 12 March 1928, Braga Brothers Collection, ser. 10, Francisco files; Guggenheim to secretary of state, Havana, 10 April 1931, Diplomatic Post Records, 2116956483.

34. Rionda y Polledo to Salvador Rionda, New York, 11 April 1928; Salvador Rionda to Rionda y Polledo, Havana, 6 January 1930, Braga Brothers Collection, ser. 10, Manatí files.

35. Salvador Rionda to Rionda y Polledo, 24 July, 25 November 1931, Braga Brothers Collection, ser. 10, Manatí files.

36. José B. Rionda to Aurelio Portuondo, Francisco, 2, 14 September 1933, Braga Brothers Collection, ser. 11.

37. Pérez, *Cuba under the Platt Amendment*, 282; Thomas, *Cuba*, 598; Ruíz, *Cuba*, 125.

38. Salvador Rionda to Irving Trust Company, Manatí, 2 March 1933, Braga Brothers Collection, ser. 10, Manatí files; enclosure 1 to dispatch 1541, Havana, 3 March 1933, Diplomatic Post Records, 2116956552.

39. "Chronology of Events Leading to Machado's Resignation," Havana, 16 August 1933, Diplomatic Post Records, 2116956552.

40. Edmund A. Chester, *A Sergeant Named Batista* (New York, 1954), 33–141; Louis A. Pérez, *Army Politics in Cuba, 1898–1958* (Pittsburgh, 1976), 72–75.

41. L. H. Woolsey to Mr. Wilson, 30 August 1933, Diplomatic Post Records, 2116956574.

42. It is difficult to get an exact figure of how many sugar mills were seized, but the number is probably close to 120. See A. F. Nufer to the U.S. ambassador, Havana, 1 November 1933, Diplomatic Post Records, 2116956574.

43. Confederación Nacional de Obreros de Cuba (hereafter cited as CNOC), Sindicato Nacional de Obreros de la Industria Azucarera, Sección de Tuinucu, Tuinucu, 3 September 1933; CNOC y Pro Organización, Francisco, 9 September 1933; Strike Committee of Central Gómez Mena to José Gómez Mena, Havana, 11 September 1933, Braga Brothers Collection, ser. 10, Labor Troubles file.

44. Instituto de Historia, *Historia del movimiento obrero cubano*, 290–94. See also Salvador Rionda to Rionda y Polledo, Manatí, 22 September 1933, Braga Brothers Collection, ser. 10, Labor Troubles file.

45. Ruíz, *Cuba*, 126; Thomas, *Cuba*, 185–86.

46. Salvador Rionda to the government secretary, Manatí, 17 September 1933, Braga Brothers Collection, ser. 10, Labor Troubles file. Sumner Welles to U.S. State Department, Havana, 14 September 1933, Diplomatic Post Records, 2116956574. With regard

to Central Mabay and other mills, see García and Mironchuk, *Los soviets obreros*, 102–13; Instituto de Historia, *Historia del movimiento obrero cubano*, 258; Soto, *Revolución del 33*, 157; Commission on Foreign Affairs, *Problems of the New Cuba*, 183; José A. Tabares del Real, *La revolución del 30: Sus dos últimos años* (Havana, 1973), 158.

47. A. M. Douglass to Frederick G. Herbst, Céspedes, 11 September 1933; Manolo Rionda to Rionda y Polledo, Havana, 12 September 1933; S. Clark, Manatí, 22 September 1933; Vicente Estrada to José B. Rionda, Elía, 25 September 1933, Braga Brothers Collection, ser. 10, Labor Troubles file. Sumner Welles to secretary of state, Havana, 6, 13 September 1933; José M. López Oña, enclosure 1 to dispatch 197, Havana, 31 October 1933; Horace Dickson to Freeman Matthews, Antilla, 17 December 1933, Diplomatic Post Records, 2116956574.

48. Vicente Estrada to Higinio Fanjul, Francisco, 15 September 1933; Salvador Rionda to Irving Trust Company, Manatí, 25 September 1933, Braga Brothers Collection, ser. 10, Labor Troubles file.

49. Oscar Baéz to Bartolo Estrada, Central Lugareño, 10 September 1933, Braga Brothers Collection, ser. 10, Labor Troubles file.

50. Fanjul to Portuondo, Havana, 25 September 1933, Braga Brothers Collection, ser. 11.

51. Schoenrich to Dickson, Santa Clara, 29 December 1933, Diplomatic Post Records, 2116956574.

52. Douglass to Herbst, Céspedes, 15 December 1933, Braga Brothers Collection, ser. 10, Labor Troubles file.

53. Douglass to Herbst, 9 December 1933, Braga Brothers Collection, ser. 10, Labor Troubles file.

54. Fanjul to Portuondo, Havana, 25, 29 September 1933, Braga Brothers Collection, ser. 11.

55. José B. Rionda to Vicente Estrada, Francisco, 12 September 1933, Braga Brothers Collection, ser. 10, Labor Troubles file.

56. Hudson Strode, *The Pageant of Cuba* (New York, 1934), 317–23.

57. Confederación Nacional Obrera de Cuba, enclosure 4 to dispatch 143, 29 September 1933, Diplomatic Post Records, 2116956552.

58. Welles to secretary of state, Havana, 3 September 1933, Diplomatic Post Records, 2116956552; The American Assembly, Columbia University, *The United States and Latin America* (New York, 1959), 147–57.

59. Salvador Rionda to Irving Trust Company, Manatí, 25 September 1933, Braga Brothers Collection, ser. 10, Labor Troubles file.

60. Commission on Foreign Affairs, *Problems of the New Cuba*, 231–33.

61. Welles to secretary of state, Havana, 1, 4 October 1933, Diplomatic Post Records, 2116956552.

62. Fanjul to Vicente Estrada, Havana, 12 September 1933, Braga Brothers Collection, ser. 11.

63. Salvador Rionda to Irving Trust Company, Manatí, 29 September 1933, Braga Brothers Collection, ser. 10, Labor Troubles file.

64. Salvador Rionda to Manuel E. Rionda, Manatí, 30 September 1933; Vicente Estrada to Fanjul, Francisco, 15 September 1933, Braga Brothers Collection, ser. 10, Labor Troubles file.

65. Salvador Rionda to Irving Trust Company, Manatí, 29 September 1933, Braga Brothers Collection, ser. 10. See also "Piden los obreros la destitución de Mr. Wood y Mr. Hicks," *Ahora*, 27 January 1934, Diplomatic Post Records, 2116956621.

66. José B. Rionda to Armando Loret de Mola, Francisco, 14 October 1933, Braga Brothers Collection, ser. 10, Labor Troubles file.

67. Telephone message from Francisco workers' union to José B. Rionda, Francisco, 7 October 1933, Braga Brothers Collection, ser. 10, Labor Troubles file.

68. José B. Rionda to Rionda y Polledo, Havana, 28 September 1933, Braga Brothers Collection, ser. 10, Labor Troubles file.

69. José B. Rionda to Rionda y Polledo, Havana, 30 September 1933, Braga Brothers Collection, ser. 10, Labor Troubles file.

70. Ramón de la Cruz to Leandro Rionda, Havana, 1 December 1933, Braga Brothers Collection, ser. 11.

71. "Exposición que hacer los delegados de los obreros del Central Francisco sobre las causas de la huelga," Francisco, 26 November 1933, Braga Brothers Collection, ser. 10, Labor Troubles file.

72. De la Cruz to Leandro Rionda, Havana, 1 December 1933, Braga Brothers Collection, ser. 11; Instituto de Historia, *Historia del movimiento obrero cubano*, 318.

73. "H. F. Matthew's Translation of a Communist Organization Paper," Havana, 26 February 1934, Diplomatic Post Records, 2116956621.

74. Memorandum 6624, Havana, 27 June 1936, Diplomatic Post Records, 2116957034.

75. Instituto de Historia, *Historia del movimiento obrero cubano*, 317–18. The quote is from Jefferson Caffery to secretary of state, Havana, 16 February 1934, Diplomatic Post Records, 2116956632.

76. M. Reyes, César Pruna, and Walfredo Legón to José B. Rionda, Tuinucu, 19, 20 October 1934, Braga Brothers Collection, ser. 10, Labor Troubles file.

77. Commission on Foreign Affairs, *Problems of the New Cuba*, 290–91; Jorge I. Domínguez, *Cuba: Order and Revolution* (Cambridge, Mass., 1978), 89.

78. Letter 1769 to Welles, Havana, 15 December 1937, Diplomatic Post Records, 2116957034; letter to Welles, 15 March 1939, Diplomatic Post Records, 2116957089.

79. Domínguez, *Cuba*, 90.

80. Thomas, *Cuba*, 692–94.

CHAPTER TWO

ACTING FOR THEMSELVES

Workers and the Mexican

Oil Nationalization

JONATHAN C. BROWN

T he nationalization of the foreign oil companies seemed to define Mexican national character so sharply in 1938 that the chief protagonists attempted to appropriate its meaning for their own ends. National labor leader Vicente Lombardo Toledano depicted the crisis as one in which rapacious, money-grubbing foreign capitalists had been ravaging the national patrimony. Intellectually anti-imperialistic, he suggested that the nationalization represented nothing less than economic emancipation of Mexico.[1] President Lázaro Cárdenas also desired to explain the event in nationalistic terms. In his nationwide radio speech of 18 March 1938, Cárdenas projected the crisis as one of national sovereignty. The oil companies had brought the nationalization upon themselves, he said, when they defied Mexican courts, sought diplomatic protection, intervened in domestic politics, and provoked capital flight.[2] Politicians, writers, and scholars—not all of them Mexican—subsequently have interpreted this event basically within its international dimensions.[3] Few inquire as to what the oil nationalization meant in terms of the relationship between labor and the state, essentially an internal matter. After all, it had been an oil workers' strike that precipitated the crisis leading to nationalization.

This chapter casts aside the standard perspectives to examine why Mexican labor had played a prominent role in the Mexican oil nationalization, for the oil workers had pressured the Cárdenas government to expropriate the Mexican oil industry. They had begun seizing oil industry assets prior to the actual nationalization and immediately thereafter took the leading role in replacing refinery and oil-field supervisors, both foreign and Mexican, with loyal union members. The oil workers had seemed quite resolved to shut down the oil industry, threatening ruin to the oil-dependent national economy, if the need had arisen. In the process, they joined the political process rather than shunning it. If the workers did indeed force the nationalization of the oil industry, why did they? What motivations did their behavior—as opposed to the rhetoric of their leaders—obey? How did the struggle engender strong, sometimes tyrannical, leadership?

Among the nation's better-paid proletarians, the Mexican petroleum workers were reacting to economic deterioration within the industry. Oil production and prices dropped precipitously in the 1920s and early 1930s. Oil workers organized to demand job security. Seniority rights were as important as wages. Workers wished to control who was hired and who was fired. Their reactions to job insecurity gave rise to internecine struggles, intense turf battles, and militant political action. Workers negotiated with employers and politicians and among themselves to achieve greater control of their workplaces. Of necessity, the struggle strengthened those labor leaders who could deliver results, by whatever means. Nationalization of a weakened and much reduced industry may not necessarily have been the only solution guaranteeing the security of the workers. It was, nonetheless, the logical outcome, given the oil companies' inability or refusal to allay the insecurities of their own employees. Therefore, the oil workers took their struggle from the refineries and oil fields into the arena of national and international politics. The result was the most spectacular takeover of a foreign-owned industry in Latin American history.

Memories of Desperation

The oil industry affected Mexico and, in turn, was affected by the host country. Developed initially in the first decade of the twentieth century, the foreign-owned industry experienced a boom in the First World War, by the end of which Mexico was the world's second leading producer of petroleum after the United States. Located along Mexico's gulf coast, these oil fields escaped the worst depredations of the Mexican Revolution. The violent period of that national watershed lasted between 1910 and 1920, but subsequent governments effected land and labor reforms in partial fulfillment of revolutionary aspirations. The revolution changed the relationship between the foreign oil companies and both labor and the state. The state sought increasingly to raise taxes on the companies and, bolstered by the new Constitution of 1917, to make crude petroleum a public property rather than a private asset owned by foreign interests. Labor, too, gained new status from the Mexi-

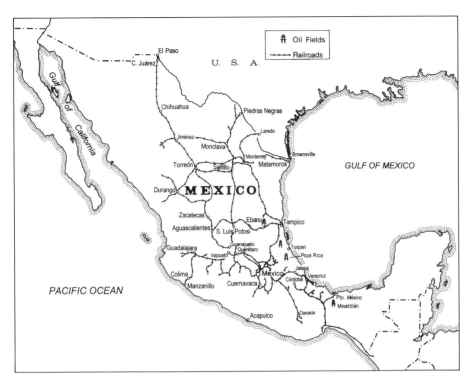

Map 2. *The oil fields and railways of Mexico, 1940*

can Revolution. The oil companies employed approximately fifty thousand Mexicans at the height of the industry in 1920. Many thousands more migrated to the refining towns of Tampico and Minatitlán to find work in the construction and service industries. They developed industrial skills, earned three times the wage of agricultural peons, and severed their ties with peasant villages. In a word, they became proletarianized.

Even so, the consequences of their increasing dependence on selling their labor power did not become immediately apparent to the oil laborers. High wages and burgeoning production helped the Mexicans tolerate the even higher wages and greater privileges accorded to American workers. The honeymoon ended in 1915. The economic dislocation of revolution at home and the industrial scarcities produced by world war abroad raised the workers' cost of living. When the foreign companies refused to adjust wages upward, laborers began organizing. Even before the 1917 constitution recognized their rights, mechanics, boilermakers, firemen, pipefitters, carpenters, and boatmen formed craft unions and struck for higher wages and parity with foreign workers. They often succeeded in raising wages, at least. Nonetheless, the oil workers had never desired to smash foreign capital. Nor did they organize worker militias to participate in the military events of the revolution.[4] By 1919, their militancy abated considerably, as wartime shortages eased worldwide.

Then, the boom ended abruptly in 1920, once again disrupting the livelihoods of the oil proletarians. Salt water invaded the Mexican oil wells, and prices slumped as a result of overproduction in other parts of the world. In 1921, the companies streamlined their operations and laid off several thousand laborers. Even as the industry declined, its ownership became more consolidated. In 1919, Royal Dutch Shell purchased the largest of the Mexico-based companies, El Aguila. This British firm handled approximately 60 percent of the nation's oil business. The Standard Oil Company of New Jersey (today Exxon) in 1932 bought Mexico's second largest company, the Huasteca. In the process, Jersey Standard also acquired more valuable oil properties in Venezuela. Other foreign concerns shared but a small portion of Mexican production and markets.

Labor militancy came in fits and starts. The workers were motivated by, but did not unionize during, times of economic stress. They quietly suffered the postwar depression, but the slight recovery motivated those still retaining their jobs to organize anew. The old craft unions formed the nuclei of the refinery and terminal unions of the mid-1920s. Workers at the El Aguila refinery at Tampico, assisted by local politicians, engineered a remarkable triumph in 1923. Their organizational strike forced the company to sign the first collective contract in the industry. Pay raises, the eight-hour workday, and indemnities for layoffs were among their important gains.[5] Laborers at other refineries soon followed suit. Great rivalry existed between the labor leaders. They competed with the companies—and each other—to control the workplace. Foreign, mostly American, supervisors and workers were resented for their superior pay and privileges and for their racism.

Labor militancy now gained national significance. The Mexican Regional Labor Confederation (Confederación Regional Obrera Mexicana, or CROM) sought to bring the oil unions into its national organization, but with limited success. The Minatitlán refinery union came under CROM affiliation, only to have the national leaders in Mexico City negotiate an end to their 1925 strike directly with El Aguila in return for a hefty fee.[6] Tampico, however, remained beyond the clutches of national labor leaders, and rivalries between labor organizations often undermined the gains. Such was the case with the 1925 strike against Huasteca. Refinery workers had just succeeded in unifying most of Huasteca's oil-field laborers into the first companywide union. But the new union's officials rashly called a strike to force the company to dismiss rival labor leaders. The government disapproved, the workers broke ranks, the strike failed, and Huasteca's companywide union disintegrated. Most of its members were never rehired.[7] Softening prices and additional production decline in the late 1920s intimidated workers, permitting companies to curtail and economize their operations in Mexico.

The depression contributed to the grudges that oil workers—or at least those who remained—were storing up. Crude production declined even further as international prices once again took a nosedive. Newly acquired by Jersey Standard, Huasteca took advantage of the soft markets to rebuild its refinery at Mata Redonda, across the river from Tampico. Coming back onstream in 1932, the new refinery somewhat relieved the unemployment in the city, but its operations now were more efficient.[8] For those still retaining their jobs, wages were reduced by 10 to 15 percent. Smaller companies shut down installations and merged with larger ones.[9] At the Penn Mex Fuel Company, which would soon merge with Huasteca, the readjustments for labor in 1931 included the following: 15 percent of the workers were temporarily reduced; 10 percent were to work five days instead of six; and 25 percent of the workers (the highest paid) had their wages reduced by one-tenth.[10]

Oil workers in all the companies, great and small, had to accept the cuts. It was no time to strike while companies economized in order to stay competitive in the international oil industry. Oil proletarians had suffered mightily in the great layoffs of 1921 and the early 1930s. The decline in Mexican production and price fluctuations in the world market reduced the number of oil laborers from fifty thousand in 1920 to fifteen thousand in 1935.[11] Still, along with the railway and mining laborers, oil workers constituted the cream of the Mexican working class. When militancy returned to the refineries and oil fields, these "labor aristocrats" would seek control of their workplaces with the same measure of intensity with which they had suffered conditions of insecurity during the depression.

Two events provided the opportunity for oil workers to redress past grievances. First, Mexico pulled out of the depression. In 1934, exports returned to their 1929 levels, and oil prices recovered. The efficiencies and mergers accomplished by the foreign companies had permitted Mexico to remain competitive in export markets with the new petroleum entrant, Venezuela. El Aguila had brought in the first new oil discovery in a decade at Poza Rica, which would eventually produce 40 percent of Mexico's total crude oil. The domestic economy also rebounded, and domestic demand for petroleum rose significantly. Encouraged by the government, El Aguila constructed a new refinery outside Mexico City at Azcapotzalco and connected it to Poza Rica with a pipeline.

The second event, not unrelated, was political. National leadership had been in flux since the assassination of President-elect Alvaro Obregón in 1928. Opportunities existed for the mass organizations to be heard and to make alliances with politicians seeking to consolidate national power. The breakup of the CROM, a victim of the inchoate political climate, permitted Lombardo Toledano to form the nucleus of an alternate national labor group. The political opening encouraged peasants and workers throughout the country, taking advantage of the economic resurgence, to reorganize. Strike activity rose along with demands for land reform. Seeking to canalize these popular demands, the politicians lurched to the left. Lázaro Cárdenas was elected president.[12] No matter what the state's intentions were to control popular demands, Cardenismo was to be no top-down reform movement.

The pressure from below in the petroleum industry began in Minatitlán and soon spread to Mexico City, Tampico, and Poza Rica. The oil workers, motivated by keen memories of depression-era desperation, were about to rebuild their labor organizations from the ground up. Why? Because the companies refused to reinstate some of the benefits and wages taken away from workers at the depth of the depression. Oil workers had to struggle to restore a modicum of workers' control. The necessary by-product would be a tough, demanding intermediate leadership, the powerful labor bosses.

A State of Racial Superiority

Labor militancy had to resolve questions of power sharing between rival oil unions before the workers could take their struggles into national politics. This was particularly so in the southern Veracruz oil zone. El Aguila reigned supreme on the Isthmus of Tehuantepec. Its assets—several small oil fields of indifferent production, the oil terminal at Puerto México, and the refinery at Minatitlán—provided the scene of much competition among rival unions to retain the declining number of jobs. The drive for labor's control of the workplace contributed to factional disputes between groups representing the different facilities. Their internecine rivalries spilled over into national politics and propelled local contestants to solicit outside alliances in order to dominate each other. The refinery leaders won out over the oil-field and terminal groups. They did so, ultimately, by cooperating with unions representing other refineries in fashioning a national union.

Following the depression, when El Aguila began rehiring, the competition among workers and their representatives became more intense. Two rival unions represented the workers in the isthmian oil fields. The minority union became annoyed when the company stopped deducting union dues from paychecks of its members, thus depriving the group virtually of its existence.

Union officials accused the company of favoring the rival "white union," a buzz word for company union. Moreover, those of its members who had suffered demotion during the depression now discovered that their old jobs were going to men with less skill and seniority. Few of the smaller union's men were being reinstated to their old jobs.[13] But the majority union, whether a "white" group or not, did not permit El Aguila complete freedom in its personnel matters. Two Mexican drillers, having learned a skill that American workers had for so long monopolized, had been laid off elsewhere. El Aguila had wanted to transfer the trained men to the isthmian oil field, but the majority union blocked the transfer.[14]

Union leaders on the isthmus believed—and government officials agreed with them—that a closed shop would reduce much of the intense competition and divisiveness between workers. The unions would decide which applicants would be sent to company openings. Free workers could remain at their jobs, but when they left, they would be replaced by union members. The so-called exclusionary clause also had its disciplinary features. If the union expelled a worker from membership, the company was obliged to fire the man. The exclusionary clause was the major demand of the isthmian oil workers in the spring of 1934. All the companies opposed it. El Aguila called it unjust. While the nation's enlightened labor laws limited the exploitation of workers by bad employers, El Aguila claimed, they did nothing to curb the abuses of immoral labor bosses. The exclusionary clause also promoted mediocrity in the workplace. It meant that that skilled workers would be replaced by union members, El Aguila claimed, who were "the most ignorant and least skilled."[15] And how did some Mexican workers feel about the foreign management? "It treats the Mexican workers with a racial superiority," wrote one worker of El Aguila. The foreign supervisors got the best jobs and company housing, while the Mexicans lived "in the worst and least hygienic habitations."[16] Not seeing eye to eye with the managers, the workers at the terminal went on strike in May. They demanded both the exclusionary clause and the mandatory unionization of all foreigners. The managers surmised that this was one way that the Mexicans could rid themselves of foreign competition for the better oil jobs.[17] Get all foreigners into the unions, then expel them, forcing the companies to let them go.

In the big isthmian strike of May 1934, thirty-five hundred oil workers walked off the job. The Minatitlán refinery union became the dominant group and formed a loosely organized federation of unions representing the oil fields and the terminal.[18] The chief demand was the exclusionary clause, which labor leaders wanted in order to combat their rival "white" unions. Local union leaders showed themselves to be less than united in this strike.

They could not agree on the selection of a committee to represent them and missed the scheduled negotiating meeting in Mexico City.[19] Nonetheless, the unions forced the company to agree to binding presidential arbitration. The American companies were to be furious at the British company for giving in to the workers, for the Presidential Settlement of 1934 would soon encourage other oil workers to request the Minatitlán contract. The Presidential Settlement consisted of the exclusionary clause; establishment of seniority rights for promotion; reduction of the workweek to 46½ hours; a basic three-month severance pay in case of layoffs; half salaries for sick workers; medical benefits for families of workers; equal pay for equal work; retirement benefits; obligatory pay for days of rest; and salary increases for workers making less than 5 pesos per day.[20]

Very soon, El Aguila was to see how the exclusionary clause was going to work. Unions activated the clause when they were sensitive to any loss of advantage in their struggle with other unions over *radio de acción*, radius of action or jurisdiction. The exclusionary clause gave labor leaders additional ability to interrupt the transfer of persons within the industry. For example, the refinery union at Minatitlán claimed jurisdiction over the new exploratory oil field, reserving the jobs for fifty-one part-time workers from the refinery. Then, when some of the workers were transferred to the Puerto México terminal, the latter's union asked that they be fired for being hostile.[21] One hundred nineteen men involved in drilling still could not get jobs on the isthmus, and the closed shop meant that the company was forced to let them go, paying them all severance pay.[22] These out-of-work oil-field men were also not exactly welcomed by their fellow workers elsewhere either.

Having consolidated majority unions within their own installations, labor leaders now began to fight among themselves. They disputed questions of transfers and pay equalization between the refineries and the oil fields. Most of all, they disagreed about which union in the federation would represent the isthmian oil workers at the regional and national levels. It was a tug-of-war between the Minatitlán refinery and the Puerto México terminal. When the terminal union seemed to gain the upper hand in the federation, the refinery workers denounced its leaders as "outside persons who only [sought] their personal betterment" and withdrew.[23] The terminal union attempted to outflank its isthmian rivals by forming a national oil workers' union. This time, the refinery men at Minatitlán called on aid from refinery unions at Tampico to deflect this threat. Ultimately, as we shall see, the refinery workers—not the smaller terminal and oil-field groups—would successfully create the national oil union.

Internal strife and the fact that oil unions elsewhere began winning better contracts than the 1934 settlement kept the isthmus in a constant state of agitation right up to the nationalization. The federal labor inspector at Mina-titlán expressed the opinion that most workers did not favor constant strikes and threats of strikes but were under the influence of "leaders lacking in scruples."[24] One thing the presidential arbitration of Abelardo Rodríguez may have accomplished was the conversion of isthmian oil workers to the popular coalition supporting Lázaro Cárdenas. In the first Cárdenas-Calles showdown in 1935, the union leaders led their workers in a victory march. "¡Viva el General Cárdenas!" they shouted, and "Down with Calles!"[25]

El Aguila, Mexico's largest petroleum company, fulfilled a long-term commitment to the government when it began construction, in 1930, of the refinery at Azcapotzalco, outside Mexico City. El Aguila provided employment for several hundred Mexican construction workers. Most were unskilled peons, engaging in transitory work under individual contracts guaranteeing them no rights to longevity. Skilled workers received a three-day trial period before they could sign on more permanently. "The Company will be the only authority," El Aguila officials announced, "to determine the number of workers it needs in each construction place and the dates on which their services are no longer necessary."[26] Long accustomed to the Mexican proletarians' demands, El Aguila obviously sought to avoid labor agitation at its new facility.

A nucleus of workers, nevertheless, organized a union in August 1931, long before the refinery came on-line. Responding to that year's new labor law, they presented the company with a collective contract that featured the exclusionary clause. They demanded that the company recognize the union, abolish individual contracts, and accept members for new jobs.[27] The new group claimed that the company intended to replace its present employees with workers from Minatitlán. El Aguila's managers replied that the construction work was transitory and that refining operations necessitated workers with specialized skills. But a government-sponsored vote of workers indicated that only one out of five favored a strike.[28] No sooner had this fledgling union's initiative ended than a rival group of workers presented their demands, much less demanding, to the company. A second government-monitored vote, by a 4–1 margin, awarded this second group as representative of the refinery's constructors.[29] It did not have the exclusionary clause.

The high turnover among construction workers may have weakened this second union, for a leadership struggle split it into two factions. Another government-monitored election in July 1934 gave one faction of the union a 2–1 majority over the other.[30] But the defeated leaders were not giving up and started a third union in alliance with the rising national labor leader, Lombardo Toledano. Each rival group at Azcapotzalco accused the other of being the "white union" and blamed the company for discharging its own partisans. Fights broke out at the construction site, and shortly after Cárdenas took office, the latest union's leaders recruited the clerical workers at El Aguila's downtown office and reconstituted itself as the Azcapotzalco Refinery Workers Syndicate. Eventually, this new majority union gained a labor contract, complete with the exclusionary clause.[31] The one refinery where El Aguila officials had hoped to avoid labor problems now had an aggressive union on very good terms with Lombardo Toledano and with sympathetic friends in Cárdenas's labor department. Although the struggle had been between rival unions, the company was the final loser. The new collective contract made it quite difficult for the company to dismiss anyone who did not wish to leave. Much the same was occurring in Tampico.

A State of Injustice

As elsewhere, the proletarians at Tampico suffered the unemployment of the depression silently. When the oil companies began rehiring in 1933, however, they too began to take matters into their own hands, struggling as much among themselves as against their dependence in the industrial workplace. They demanded the assistance of the political authorities, and they got it.

At Mexico's largest refinery of El Aguila, located in Tampico's industrial suburb of Ciudad Madero, worked one of the nation's largest concentrations—perhaps five thousand—of skilled and semiskilled Mexican laborers. They had also formed the most important and powerful unions in the country. It contracted for an eight-hour day, a week's paid vacation, and severance pay for laid-off workers. From 1928 to 1932, when oil prices were low, many of its workers had collected severance pay at one time or another.[32] In 1933, however, new labor leadership was spoiling to regain some of the old hegemony of earlier days. The refinery union broke up into two factions. Three hundred workers met in March to form a splinter refinery union. It presented El Aguila with a labor contract, which the company ignored. A turf battle also broke out between oil workers and boatmen who labored on the Pánuco River for El Aguila. At one point, gunmen ambushed and killed one faction's leader, for which five labor organizers were convicted. State and local officials were also implicated in the confused affair.[33] The interunion struggle intensified when the company began rehiring beginning in May 1933. At the reopening of the canning factory at the Tampico refinery, the breakaway group accused company officials of excluding its members—in conspiracy with the older union. Armed guards at the gate of the canning factory even threatened members of the new group.[34]

In the election year of 1934, the factionalism among the workers of Tampico became clearer. El Aguila's resurgent refinery union gained sufficient political backing to survive the factional infighting. It joined the Tampico Chamber of Labor, a citywide labor federation, and got other Tampico unions from the Huasteca and Pierce/Sinclair refineries also to join the Chamber of Labor. Cooperation between the powerful local unions enabled each to maintain control of its own members, especially during the restive years in post-depression Tampico.[35] The labor struggle was emerging from the shop floors to local, state, and eventually national levels.

The workers of the Huasteca Petroleum Company (from 1932 owned by the Standard Oil Company, New Jersey) may have been more typical of the workers from many smaller companies. Their whole labor struggle centered on resisting the layoffs brought about by loss of production, by improvements in efficiencies, and by business decline. The company had laid off hundreds of workers during the 1921 depression, following the broken strike of 1925, and again when it rebuilt its Tampico refinery in 1930. Unlike El Aguila, Huasteca had discovered no new oil field since 1920. Owing to attrition, the company had been able to keep the union relatively weak at its refining plant at Mata Redonda, across the Pánuco River from Tampico. Workers' representatives, for that reason, relied on assistance from the government and from fellow unionists.[36] In 1934, the refinery union presented the company with a new collective contract, based on the Minatitlán settlement. The union demanded the exclusionary clause for itself and for a nearby Huasteca oil-field union as well, and severance benefits for ninety-three part-time workers laid off by Huasteca.[37]

The Huasteca union made its big push in 1935, taking on both the company and the free workers. The strike began on 23 January and idled six hundred men in the refinery and terminal for several months. Union leaders offered to return to work if the company would agree to arbitration by President Cárdenas. Huasteca would have none of it. The strike dragged on through April, exhausting the strike funds of the Huasteca refinery union and those of its affiliate unions in Tampico.[38] Huasteca managers took a very hard line against organized labor. (The managers were under orders from the New York headquarters of Standard Oil New Jersey to prevent Mexican labor militancy from spilling over into the more productive Venezuelan oil fields.) They preferred to keep the Tampico refinery permanently closed, said an American diplomat, "rather than compromise with the workers, who [had] struck eight times in the past twelve months."[39] A confrontation at the refinery between union and nonunion workers resulted in one death. Ultimately, the nonunion workers requested military protection from the government, which federal officials

were unwilling to provide because the union might consider it a provoca-
tion.[40] The strike failed at the end of November 1935. The union's ultimate
lack of success in gaining a collective contract similar to that of El Aguila's
refinery union rankled its leaders. They would cooperate with their brethren
at the larger El Aguila refinery in forming a national oil union, but they were
in no position to provide leadership.

The struggle to form the national oil workers' union further enhanced the
strength of the Tampico refinery unions. Apparently, the idea had begun in
Puerto México and enticed a number of small oil-field unions to attempt to
form a national syndicate. But the Tampico workers as well as the refinery laborers at Minatitlán viewed this national petroleum union as a threat. Based
on their larger membership and importance to the industry, these refinery
unions wanted to be the organizers of a national union—or have none at all.[41]
When the smaller groups of petroleum workers met in Mexico City in July
1935, the refinery unions and their supporting labor organizations from around
the country denounced them as "white unions" (company unions) and requested government officials to deny them support.[42] The oil-field and terminal workers, therefore, failed to effect a viable national union.

Plainly, 1935 was a critical year for cooperation between the large refinery
unions within the oil industry. Newly dominant local unions now began to cooperate with each other. They communicated between Minatitlán, Azcapotzalco, Tampico, and Mata Redonda, frequently launching sympathy strikes
for each other and for the smaller oil-field groups that cooperated with them.
Allied unions at Tampico could also be counted on to strike on their behalf,
especially the aggressive taxi drivers' union, an influential member of the
Chamber of Labor. Tampico's El Aguila refinery union expanded its membership to several of El Aguila's oil fields in northern Veracruz. They had members at several oil fields, the loading terminal at Tuxpan, and the new oil field
at Poza Rica. In 1935, numerous strikes broke out within the industry in efforts
to equalize pay and benefits between the refineries and the oil fields. Said
President Cárdenas of the rash of strikes in the oil and other industries: They
were "a simple manifestation of the state of injustice in which certain companies [kept] the workers."[43] Later, when the national oil union was formed,
however, the president did not view these strikes so tolerantly.

In the meantime, the mounting political tension between President Cár-
denas and former president Plutarco Elías Calles on the national level had
repercussions in Mexican industrial cities such as Tampico. The Chamber of
Labor became allied with the left wing of the Mexican Senate and with
Cárdenas. The group sponsored "direct action" against the local supporters of
Calles. The chamber's supporters visited city council chambers and the press

rooms of local newspapers. Rumor had it that the Chamber of Labor also wanted to purge the leadership of the dockworkers' union, Tampico's oldest, dating from 1911, by inciting a mob takeover of the dockworkers' headquarters. The February 1936 parade in support of the Tampico mayor, who had just been dismissed by the governor, provided the occasion. Shots rang out at the end of the parade, and an angry crowd set upon the building. The local police and military authorities were either unprepared to intervene or actually favored the Chamber of Labor. They did nothing to stop the riot. At the end of the day, three members of the dockworkers' group had been killed and thirteen injured, compared with one killed and four wounded among the attackers.[44]

Once Calles was forced into exile in 1936, the plans for the formation of a national petroleum union solidified. The refinery unions were in the vanguard. The El Aguila refinery group christened itself as Section 1 of the Mexican Oil Workers Syndicate. The Huasteca refinery union became Section 2. Several small petroleum unions still opposed a national oil union over which they would have insufficient influence. Some small companies had no unions at all. However, Lombardo Toledano, who had just organized the Confederation of Workers of Mexico (Confederación de Trabajadores de México, or CTM), came to court the Tampico labor leaders behind closed doors. Local refinery unions refused to declare their intentions of joining the CTM just yet.[45] By virtue of the fact that it gathered together the largest conglomeration of workers, El Aguila's refinery union served as vanguard in the formation of the national petroleum union. Oil union leaders next sought confirmation of their power with an industrywide labor contract.

Lack of Control and Discipline

The formation of the Mexican Oil Workers Syndicate, as we have seen, was not the beginning of labor's attempt to control the workplace. This struggle against layoffs and for stability in the lives of the proletarians had been occurring since 1915. The destitution that oil workers suffered during the depression intensified that process in the early 1930s. Formation of the national union, therefore, was but another stage in this struggle. Yet the formation of one union within the oil industry raised the level of combat from the refineries and oil fields to national and international politics. It did not mean that shop floor militancy was now over. On the contrary, local struggles for leadership and for the loyalty of workers continued, keeping relentless pressure on national labor leaders and politicians. Leaders of the oil union and the CTM knew that if they did not satisfy the demands from below, their claim to the power and perquisites at the union helm was worthless. Doubtless, President Cárdenas felt these same pressures.

Mindful that they had to gain a victory to keep the loyalty of their members, the union leaders conferred tirelessly to propose an industrywide collective contract. They demanded a 30 million peso (approximately $8.3 million U.S.) wage increase and the equalization of salaries among the eighteen petroleum, terminal, and ship companies whose workers the Mexican Oil Workers Syndicate represented.[46] For the workers, there were to be eighteen holidays (including Day of the Petroleum Worker), ample death and sick benefits, twenty to sixty days of paid vacation, vacation travel, and complete medical insurance. Many of these benefits were to embrace the families as well as the worker. Laid-off workers would lose no seniority rights and would receive preference in rehiring.

The contract assaulted the remaining employer privileges in the workplace: the supervisory positions and the right to hire and fire. Supervisory positions traditionally lay outside union control altogether. Now the oil union demanded that they be reduced to 110 throughout the entire Mexican oil industry. At its Azcapotzalco refinery, El Aguila would retain only one of thirteen managerial positions, that of the general manager.[47] All other supervisory positions would be filled by union men according to seniority. Above all, much of the power to hire and fire workers was removed from the company to the union, the ultimate implication of the exclusionary clause. "The Companies are obliged to suspend workers whom the Syndicate decides to discipline," the proposed contract stipulated, "and without the Companies having any authority to question the basis for such discipline."[48] Assuming that the abilities to punish and to reward were the twin pillars of power, then oil union leaders fully expected to wrest that power from the companies. The workers were in agreement.

The Mexican Oil Workers Syndicate delivered the contract to the companies on 3 November 1936 and demanded approval before a 17 November strike deadline. The companies' response was predictable. "The Union draft contains over 250 clauses, covers 165 pages of legal size script of which almost 40 embrace the wage schedule, and took several months to formulate," said the companies. "And yet, the companies were to 'discuss' and 'approve' the document in the peremptory period of ten (10) days."[49] The smaller firms protested that they could not agree to equalization because they were unable to pay the high salaries that El Aguila and Huasteca were paying their workers. The latter two big companies, on principle, also resisted raising the wages of the highest-paid workers in the country. Although executives and labor leaders alike couched their public utterances in terms of salaries, the pay issue actually was subservient to the issue of worker control.

The proposed contract of 1936 would have eroded capital's flexibility to compete in the marketplace, said the companies. Labor's efforts to unionize even the occasional and part-time workers meant that companies would no longer be able to hire short-term labor for special projects. If they did, they would never be able to let workers go when the job was completed. The 1936 contract also would have signaled the end of contracting work within the industry. Companies depended upon construction and drilling contractors to perform ad hoc jobs, for which the contracting agency provided its own workers. Moreover, the companies objected to the difficulties they would encounter in firing incompetent or poor workers. A worker was to be discharged only for "grave and infamous" causes, which would be reviewed by a union-management panel. The companies said that, under the 1936 contract, they would have lost all rights to transfer or promote their employees.

Since the companies could not agree to the new contract, an industrywide strike appeared inevitable. Such a strike would have disrupted urban transit, power generation, industrial production, and agricultural harvests throughout the country. It threatened additional labor unrest in other sectors. Therefore, President Cárdenas intervened to convince the workers and employers to discuss the contract while oil workers continued at their posts. The state acted as host and moderator of the talks. The companies, too, wanted labor stability over a long period of time, but not at the expense of worker control. Moreover, each company needed to approve the final accord. For its part, the Oil Workers Syndicate had to deliver a contract that was better than any existing contract or face a dissatisfied rank and file.[50] The hiatus between the positions of the workers and employers seemed insurmountable. Indeed, it was. These state-sponsored labor talks broke down at the end of May 1937.

President Cárdenas intervened a second time, after a brief national oil strike, by getting the unions to accept an investigation of the oil companies' financial accounts. As stipulated in the 1931 labor law, the economic study would determine whether the companies could afford the proposed labor contract. Professor Jesús Silva Herzog of the National University led a team of three experts who made up the investigative commission. During the months of June and July 1937, Silva Herzog collected statistics, testimony, and evidence on taxes, profits, expenses, and wages. The companies told the commission that the labor bill was much higher than the wage hikes indicated. El Aguila calculated the contract would increase its labor costs by 142.6 million pesos per year.[51] Working under pressure, the commission's study was presented to the public on 14 August. It came in the form of recommendations to the Federal Board of Conciliation and Arbitration, which was to settle the labor dispute that the companies and labor leaders had been unable to negotiate. The arbitration board's deliberations continued throughout the remainder of 1937. It finally confirmed the commission's findings, giving the workers a $26.4 million peso pay raise and granting the labor leaders many of their managerial demands. The companies filed an injunction (*amparo*) against the board's ruling, but Mexico's supreme court, having been reconstituted thoroughly during the Cárdenas years, upheld the ruling on 2 March 1938. In effect, the state was attempting to resolve a conflict that employers and labor leaders could not.

However, the companies still refused to abide by the decision. The foreign oilmen had been saying that the union's demand for pay increases and participation in management would bankrupt the already unprofitable Mexico-based companies. "Owing to the present restricted number of supervisory positions," they claimed in December 1937, "the industry is already suffering the consequences of lack of control and discipline."[52] If labor agitation made Mexican oil any more expensive, they warned, it would be undersold in foreign markets by cheaper Venezuelan crudes. Moreover, the companies did not believe that the Mexicans could run an oil industry themselves. Thus, they laid the challenge before President Cárdenas. He would have to discipline the workers for them. The companies simply refused to operate in Mexico under the labor conditions arranged by the Mexican political system.

One thing should be made clear: Cárdenas did not need to expropriate the industry to uphold the Mexican constitution. In December 1937, Cárdenas and El Aguila signed an agreement in which the oil company seemed to renounce its private property rights to the new Poza Rica oil field. The British company agreed to "concessionary" status at Poza Rica, paying government royalties amounting to 25 to 35 percent of production. Therefore, one foreign company had tacitly conceded government ownership of its oil property, as stipulated in Article 27 of the Mexican constitution.[53] Cárdenas expected that the other oil companies, in time, would come round to accept the provisions of the Mexican constitution. Article 27, after all, did not mandate the establishment of a state petroleum monopoly—only national ownership of the petroleum deposits. However, workers' control would soon give another meaning to Article 27.

Mexican workers and their leaders had always appealed to the state to attend to their grievances. Oil laborers carried these traditions forward into the twentieth century. They corresponded directly with the president, with the appropriate national agencies, and with state and local political factions. They also calculated their strike activity to gain the intervention of the state into their affairs—preferably on their behalf. Especially critical to the oil workers, political activity aided them in their struggle to preserve for themselves positions of security in an industry notorious for the prerogatives of ownership. Shell and Standard Oil New Jersey, which controlled El Aguila and Huasteca, respectively, were among the largest industrial enterprises in the world. Part of their economic power was due to their ability to adjust production and employment on an international scale. The companies' power did not deter the workers. But it made state intervention so much more critical to the achievement of their goals. If the workers were to gain any security in the industry, they needed strong leaders who could negotiate successfully with politicians. When the government faltered, the workers were capable of prodding them. When their own union leaders faltered, the workers knew how to prod them as well.

From the moment that the national contract was delivered to the companies, the oil workers applied direct, unrelenting pressure on all the parties. The strike was their weapon. As the Mexican Oil Workers Syndicate finished its draft of the proposed contract in November 1936, Tampico's El Aguila workers returned after a twenty-three-day walkout. Their colleagues at the nearby Pierce-Sinclair refinery ended a fifty-six-day strike.[54] Certainly, labor factionalism did not end just because the national oil union had entered into negotiations. Labor talks had to be suspended in January 1937 so that Section 1 could deal with the stevedores' unions over which group controlled the loading of oil cargos at Tampico. Then, when employers were reluctant to resume national talks, Section 1 ordered a one-day work stoppage.[55]

The major oil strike in the industry began at the end of June 1937, following the breakdown in the labor-management talks. All major companies had to suspend operations. Oil tankers left Tampico without their usual cargoes of exported petroleum, and cargo vessels could not get fuel oil in any of the ports of the Mexican gulf coast. Port cities suffered a loss in port fees; the federal government, a loss in customs duties.[56] Within a week, the strike produced confrontations in Mexico City. Oil workers placed red-and-black strike flags at oil depots selling to tourists and private companies. The *taxistas* and truckers were annoyed that the government favored the bus drivers with rationed gasoline. They blocked several major thoroughfares in the city. Finally, Cárdenas intervened directly with labor, getting them to suspend the oil strike after thirteen days, in exchange for an economic investigation of the companies.[57]

The rank-and-file oil workers were miffed about the compromise. They began a series of their own "wildcat strikes," local uncoordinated shutdowns of short duration. Several members of the oil union delegation, which had

Mexican workers drilling an oil well, 1938. (Courtesy of the Fototeca del Instituto Nacional de Antropología e Historia, Pachuca, Hidalgo)

ended the strike at the insistence of President Cárdenas, were voted out of office when they returned to their union locals. Part-time workers at the Cerro Azul oil field of Huasteca accosted four Huasteca officials, two of whom were Mexican. "The workers seem to feel that the union leaders in Mexico did not properly back up their demands," a U.S. diplomat at Tampico reported, "and that accordingly they have to act for themselves."[58] These wildcat strikes were intended to force the investigative commission to make a favorable report. From Yucatán, where he was turning over land to campesinos, President Cárdenas wired a request for no more wildcat oil strikes.[59] Few petroleum workers paid much attention.

Animosity still existed at the Huasteca refinery and terminal at Mata Redonda. Section 2 struck on a number of occasions in September and October 1937 to obtain its own local contract, in lieu of a national contract. The labor agitation there continued intermittently in November and December. Several of the renegade work stoppages of December indicated the locals' frustration at the length of the federal arbitration board's deliberations. At least, that was the reason why Section 1 threatened a twenty-four-hour stoppage at the Tampico refinery of El Aguila. Cárdenas expressed his displeasure in the nation's newspapers.[60] The Huasteca company's hostile response to the board's decision, which, it thought, was favorable to the workers, provoked additional worker resentment. The Standard Oil affiliate closed twenty-three wells and ordered all the oil stored in the field to be moved to its terminal at Tampico. In his last pay envelope of December 1937, each Huasteca worker got a message saying the company would not be able to comply with the board's decision. Subsequently, Section 2 leaders became angered at the Mexican managers of Huasteca who were determined to close down portions of the Mata Redonda refinery. The foreign oilmen concluded that more than ninety unauthorized strikes had plagued the petroleum industry during the last six months of 1937.[61] The positions of the workers and their employers did not seem to leave much room for negotiation.

The oil proletarians of Poza Rica gained the reputation as the biggest troublemakers in the entire petroleum industry. Much of the grassroots militancy at Poza Rica stemmed from problems connected to jurisdiction. El Aguila's new, expanding oil field during the 1930s did not suffer, like most other oil workplaces, a deterioration in the number of workers. But even in expansion, workers competed against each other for rights to work, and their organizations, for rights to represent. In expanding its workforce here in the early 1930s, the British company had sent out experienced workers from Tampico. Therefore, the Sindicato de Trabajadores, later Section 1, from El Aguila's Tampico refinery claimed first jurisdiction over Poza Rica. Prior residents of the area felt slighted, thinking that they ought to have gotten the jobs.[62] Section 1 had gained enormous power in controlling Poza Rica workers. A strike here was felt in Mexico City, supplied via pipeline from Poza Rica, and the capital had only ten days' worth of fuel in storage at any one time.[63] The nation—and government officials—could withstand prolonged oil strikes anywhere else but Poza Rica.

These oil-field unionists found their opportunity to break away from Section 1 following the June 1937 strike, when the rank-and-file anger at the economic investigation undermined some oil union leaders. By July, Poza Rica had its own union representation, Section 30, which defied the government as well as the national oil union. It shut down the flow of oil to Mexico City with wildcat strikes throughout the summer and fall. Other companies and other facilities attempted to make up the shortfall in supplies at the capital, but transportation and industrial slowdowns occurred, as did speculation in fuel supplies.[64] So great was the grassroots concern for job stability that the contract ending the dispute in early September took pains to name workers to specific posts and at specified wages. Nevertheless, not everyone was satisfied. When additional walkouts at Poza Rica exasperated him, Cárdenas once again felt compelled to criticize the "lack of discipline" of the oil unions. He suggested that they may be working for "capitalist interests," inasmuch as their tactics were turning the country against the labor movement.[65] The Poza Rica workers came in off the picket lines, not because their president had requested it in the national interest, but because the company agreed to pay 75 percent of the workers' salary during the strike and to give 25,000 pesos ($7,000 U.S.) to the union.[66]

A brief review of the minutes of the Section 30's assemblies for the months leading up to the oil nationalization reveals what did and what did not motivate the rank and file at Poza Rica. There was no discussion at all of the companies' defiance of the arbitration board and supreme court rulings. There were no denouncements of foreign imperialism or demands for the nationalization of the industry. Workers at the oil fields concerned themselves with jurisdiction. They discussed agreements with affiliate unions over who obtained the rights to work in the outlying fields. They argued over to whom a contract should be let for road building. Questions of union membership for individuals were also discussed, sometimes heatedly if there was a hint that the new worker had once collaborated with management. They sometimes defied the union's national leadership on these issues. And they also discussed what happened to three months' worth of union dues that had disappeared from the treasury. At one point the secretary recorded: "Compañero Domingo spoke up saying that the money is in the same mess as always, that no one ever knows in reality how much there is in the union treasury nor how much is owed."[67] But the Poza Rica rank and file did not express any opinions whatsoever about the nationalization of the industry in which they worked. And yet their relentless pressure on their own union leaders led to just that outcome.

The direct demands that the men in the refineries and fields placed on the labor leadership explain why the oil union, in February and March 1938, refused to meet the companies halfway. The Mexican Oil Workers Syndicate ignored an offer by the oil companies to raise salaries by a total of 23.5 million pesos rather than 26.4 million pesos as stipulated by the arbitration board's decision. It represented a 100 percent raise in the company's offer of the year before. They also prevented the government from compromising on the labor contract. At the CTM's second national congress in February 1938, the oil workers' delegation suggested that all five thousand labor delegates call on the president of the supreme court to request that the justices hasten their final decision.[68]

Given their activism right up to the last moment, the oil unions were not mere bystanders at the nationalization itself. They participated actively. When the companies disclosed that they could not obey the supreme court decision, the Mexican Oil Workers Syndicate called for a strike to begin at midnight on 18 March 1938. It announced a day of protest against the foreign oil companies for 23 March, the CTM promising to sponsor a giant demonstration in the Zócalo. The workers themselves anticipated their leaders. They seized control of the El Aguila loading terminal at Tampico and shut down the Huasteca pipelines days before the strike was supposed to have begun.[69] One might wonder what labor unrest might have occurred if Cárdenas had not nationalized the oil industry on 18 March, hours before the strike deadline. Workers thereupon seized the rest of the oil facilities throughout the nation: gas stations, distribution depots, tugboats, barges, trucks, refineries, wells, pipelines, company offices, and payrolls. Foreigners and Mexicans who had held *puestos de confianza* were dismissed, and union locals appointed their own officials to supervisory positions. The transition was particularly vindictive at the Huasteca facilities. Managers fled the oil fields. For several days, Section 2 leaders detained two unpopular Mexican officials of the company until national labor leaders arrived to negotiate their release. These had been the Huasteca officials in charge of dismissing workers in the depression. They were eventually released unharmed.[70] In the meantime, the CTM turned its 23 March protest into organized labor's celebration of itself.

Conclusion

The enthusiasm with which most oil workers welcomed the nationalization cannot be diminished by the fact that they never did obtain their wage increases. The activities of workers at the refineries and oil fields following the depression of 1930 show that the level of wages, although important, may have been secondary to most oil workers. First and foremost, the individual who lent his services to the oil industry wanted a steady job. He wanted to leave at his own choosing—not the company's. Deterioration of the foreign-owned Mexican oil industry had produced the very antithesis of security for the proletarians. Nearly seven out of ten jobs were lost between 1921 and 1935.

Their struggle, however, most often pitted members of the working class against each other. Why? Workers wanted to control the competitive labor market as much as possible, at the same time that they strove to effect guarantees that the disastrous layoffs would not occur again. To accomplish these two objectives, they reconstituted their unions, making them stronger and more able to confront the companies. Those unions emerging from the internecine strife of 1934 and 1935 proved exceptionally combative. Their leaders were tough minded and bold. The struggle for the closed shop met part of the agenda of the rank-and-file workers. But it did not fulfill all of the workers' criteria for security. As long as the companies retained control of personnel matters, the workers could not be certain that their gains might not be reversed. The same uncertainty held true if a few pockets of employer privilege remained in the form of nonunionized companies and of some unions having no exclusionary clause. The remedy was a collective contract severely limiting employer prerogatives. For security, therefore, the worker was counting on the union and its tough leaders. It was certainly more tangible and familiar to him than the distant and unpredictable world economy. Neither the state, nor the Constitution of 1917, nor the 1931 labor law, nor Cárdenas himself would deliver that security like an industrywide union could. Therefore, the workers made the Mexican Oil Workers Syndicate, from the ground up.

For its part, the state under Cárdenas promoted labor unity, consistent with its policy of balancing the "antagonistic interests" of capital and labor. The state conceived of all workers being organized into large industrial unions partly as a means to providing social peace in the industrial world. Cárdenas himself tolerated strikes when workers were organizing their unions. But once unions were formed, Cárdenas also expected that labor strife would end, as evidenced in his condemnation of the wildcat oil strikes. The state obviously viewed the labor union as a form of social discipline. The laborer viewed it as a form of workers' control.

Given these perspectives, was the Mexican oil nationalization inevitable? Perhaps it was in the long run, but the state did not necessarily need to create a national oil company in 1938 to achieve social discipline. Likewise, the workers did not demand it. Both parties seemed to act on the belief that the proposed collective contract of 1936 sufficed to provide security and discipline. Aside from what analysts have said about sovereignty and economic emancipation, the Mexican oil nationalization came about as a historical quirk. The international oil interests had already passed on to Venezuela and were soon to enter the Middle East. Under these circumstances, the petroleum companies did not think the Mexican petroleum industry was worth the compromise of its traditional employer prerogatives. Mexican oil workers thought otherwise and got the state to agree with them.

In retrospect, the workers were mistaken. They did not take control of the administration of the nationalized petroleum industry. Cárdenas soon established a new state oil company, Pemex, with headquarters in Mexico City, and appointed seasoned bureaucrats and technicians to command it. The oil workers' union gained minority membership on the board of directors, but the workers definitely lost control of the oil fields and refineries throughout the country. At this point, the union leaders began to consolidate their control over the rank and file. Strikes became a thing of the past, although worker resistance continued sufficiently to disrupt government plans to completely restructure production. However, the successors of President Cárdenas turned toward industrialization in the 1940s, and cheap petroleum fuel subsidized the energy needs of Mexican factories. To get the workers to accept their no-strike pledge and the state's cap on oil prices, governments in the 1950s grew to accept the often corrupt and violent suzerainty of labor leaders over the oil union. The labor bosses rewarded loyalists with absolute job security. Dissidents were greeted with loss of jobs or, if necessary, violence. Bosses "sold" part-time jobs in the industry and enjoyed favored positions as contract suppliers to the Pemex; corruption tied the government and labor bureaucracies closer together. The oil boom of the 1970s solidified this alliance.[71] But the fall in oil prices beginning in 1982 shocked both the economy and the political system.

The state found itself inhibited when, in 1988, it sought to reform the Mexican economy according to the standards of free-market capitalism. The oil union unsuccessfully backed the leftist challenger against the official government candidate for president. Powerful oil union leaders subsequently were jailed, although the president has said that the oil industry will not be sold to foreign interests along with other state companies. Nonetheless, a new effort to assault workers' control appears to be under way.

Notes

Research for this chapter was made possible by the Mellon Fellowship of the Institute of Latin American Studies and by a grant from the Policy Research Institute, both of the University of Texas. The author thanks John Womack Jr., Alan Knight, Rodney Anderson, and Paul Goodwin for their comments and Adrian Bantjes for his research assistance.

1. See Worker's University of Mexico, *The Oil Conflict in Mexico, 1937–1938* (Mexico City, 1938); *El Universal,* 21 March 1938.

2. *El Universal,* 19 March 1938.

3. The classic study is that of Lorenzo Meyer, *Mexico and the United States in the Oil Controversy, 1916–1942* (Austin, 1977). See also George Philip, *Oil and Politics in Latin America: Nationalist Movements and State Oil Companies* (Cambridge, England, 1982).

4. S. Leif Adelson G., "Historia social de los obreros industriales de Tampico, 1906–1919" (doctoral thesis, College of Mexico, 1982); Jonathan C. Brown, *Oil and Revolution in Mexico* (Berkeley, 1993), chap. 5.

5. S. Leif Adelson G., "Coyuntura y conciencia: Factores convergentes en la fundación de los sindicatos petroleros de Tampico durante la década de 1920," in *El trabajo y los trabajadores en la historia de México,* ed. Elsa Cecilia Frost et al. (Mexico City, 1979), 632–60.

6. Marjorie R. Clark, *Organized Labor in Mexico* (Chapel Hill, 1934), 118–19; Barry Carr, *El movimiento obrero y la política en México, 1910–1929* (Mexico City, 1976), 161, 187–88.

7. J. C. Brown, "Foreign Oil Companies, Oil Workers, and the Mexican Revolutionary State in the 1920s," in *Multinational Enterprise in Historical Perspective,* ed. Alice Teichova et al. (Cambridge, England, 1986), 265–66; Leopoldo Alafita Méndez, "Trabajo y condición obrera en los campamentos petroleros de la Huasteca, 1900–1935," in *Anuario IV, Universidad Veracruzana* (Jalapa, Ver., 1986), 169–207.

8. C. E. Macy to secretary of state, 1 April 1931, 6 June, 31 December 1932, 29 March 1933, National Archives and Record Service, Washington, D.C., Record Group 59, General Records of the Department of State, State Department Correspondence, 1910–29, Decimal Files (hereafter cited as State Dept. Decimal Files), 812.00-Tamaulipas/23, /53, /92, /101.

9. L. Ralph Higgs, "Prevailing Wage Scale, Tampico Oil Industry," 6 October 1932, U.S. Consular Records, Tampico, General Correspondence, Decimal File 850.4, Record Group 84, National Archives; "Penn Mex Fuel Co. contra trabajadores de la terminal Alvarez," 8 June 1932, Archivo General de la Nación, Mexico City (hereafter cited as AGN), Junta Federal de Conciliación y Arbitración (hereafter cited as JFCA), C69, E9.

10. Pedro Noyola to Junta Regional Permanente de Conciliación, no. cuatro, 7 September 1931, JFCA, C53, E20.

11. AGN, Archivo Histórico de Hacienda, Papeles de la Comisión Pericial (hereafter cited as AHH), C1866-157, f44.

12. See especially Alan Knight, "Mexico, c. 1930–1946," in *The Cambridge History of Latin America*, ed. Leslie Bethell, 9 vols. (Cambridge, England, 1982–89), 7:3–82.

13. José Pera et al. to president, 15 June 1933, AGN, Papeles Presidenciales, Fondo Abelardo Rodríguez (hereafter cited as FAR), 561.8/130.

14. Hermanegildo Vásquez et al. to president, FAR, 561.8/130.

15. P. J. Jonker to president, 2 May 1934, FAR, 671.4/51.

16. Gabriel Morán to president, 22 February 1933, FAR, 561.8/97.

17. Macy to secretary of state, 31 May 1934, State Dept. Decimal Files, 812.00-Tamaulipas/150.

18. Torres to J. H. Dyball, 6 April 1934, AGN, Departamento Autónomo de Trabajo (hereafter cited as DAT), C46, E1; doc. dtd. 6 May 1934, DAT, C28, E1, f48.

19. Thomas D. Bowman, "El Aguila and Other Strike Movements in Mexico," 11 June 1934, State Dept. Decimal Files, 812.5045/168.

20. J. Rennow to Luis J. Rodríguez, 15 December 1934, AGN, Papeles Presidenciales, Fondo Lázaro Cárdenas (hereafter cited as FLC), 432.2/8, E1. For the 1934 Laudo, see FLC, 432.2/2.

21. Docs. dtd. 27 June, 26 December 1934, DAT, C28, E1 fs. 332, 591–95.

22. P. J. Jonker to president, 3 September 1934, FAR, 561.4/51-7; doc. dtd. 5 October 1934, DAT, C28, E1 f449; extracts, 4, 13 February, 6 March 1935, FLC, 432/69.

23. Luis R. Torres et al. to president, 10 July 1934, FAR, 06/22; docs. dtd. 10, 23 January 1935, DAT, C28, E1, fs. 383, 797.

24. Doc. dtd. 24 January 1935, DAT, C28, E1 fs. 816–18.

25. Doc. dtd. 28 June 1935, FLC, 432/87.

26. J. M. Torres to JFCA, 21 May 1931, JFCA, C51, E2.

27. Sindicato de Obreros to JFCA, 4 August 1931, JFCA, C51, E5, fs. 3–6.

28. Sindicato to JFCA, 7 August, Pieter Jan Jonker to JFCA, 12 August 1931, JFCA, C51, E5; "Sindicato de Obreros y Empleados de la Cía Mexicana de Petroleo El Aguila: Huelga," 17 September 1931, JFCA, C66, E1.

29. Luis E. Galindo, [Report,] 23 October 1931, JFCA, C51, E5. The refinery's construction employed 536 workers.

30. Bernardo G. Gortera et al., [Report,] 3 July 1934, FAR, 561.8/272.

31. John S. Little, "Strike Movements," 10 December 1934, 7 January 1935, State Dept. Decimal Files, 812.5045/184, /188; J. Rennow to Luis I. Rodríguez, 15 December, Armando T. Vázquez to president, 20 December 1934, FLC, 432.2/8, E1.

32. "Sindicato de Obreros contra El Aguila," 23 May 1932, JFCA, C69, E8.

33. G. Polanco G. to president, 14 April, Sindicato de Empleados y Obreros to president, 25 April 1933, FAR, 561.5/40, 501.3/40.

34. R. Castillo to Juan de Díos Bojórquez, 3, 10 May 1933, DAT, C9, E13.

35. "JFC en Tampico: Convocatorio para elección de representates obreros y patronales," 1934, DAT, C20, E3.

36. Francisco Dávila to president, 9 July 1934, FAR, 561.6/196.

37. Littel, "Strike Movements," 10 December 1934, State Dept. Decimal Files, 812.5045/184.

38. Macy to secretary of state, 30 April 1935, State Dept. Decimal Files, 812.00-Tamaulipas/187; docs. dtd. 1 March, 11 April, 18 October 1935, FLC, 432.2/2.

39. R. Henry Norweb to secretary of state, 26 April 1935, State Dept. Decimal Files, 812.45/212.

40. Docs. dtd. 20 July, 5, 8 October 1935, FLC, 432.2/2.

41. Macy to secretary of state, 29 June 1934, State Dept. Decimal Files, 812.00-Tamaulipas/152; Agustín Haro to Sindicato de Obreros, 9 November 1934, DAT, C28, E1, f398.

42. Extracts, 14, 16 August, 3 September 1935, FLC, 437.1/37.

43. Docs. dtd. 11, 15, 27 January 1935, FLC, 433.2/8; John S. Littel, "Strike Movements," 4 February 1935, State Dept. Decimal Files, 812.45/191.

44. Macy to secretary of state, 13 February 1936, State Dept. Decimal Files, 812.00-Tamaulipas/253.

45. Doc. dtd. 30 April 1936, FLC, 432.3/191; Macy to secretary of state, 30 September 1936, State Dept. Decimal Files, 812.00-Tamaulipas/282.

46. See "Proyecto aprobado en la primera Gran Convención Extraordinaria del Sindicato de Trabajadores Petroleros de la República Mexicana," no date, AHH, C1857-117.

47. Doc. dtd. 1 July 1937, AHH, C1844-3, f25.

48. "Proyecto aprobado en la primera Gran Convención Extraordinaria," AHH, C1857-117, f422.

49. *The Mexican Oil Strike of 1937*, 2 vols. (Mexico City, n.d.), 1:3. Additional company objections are found in Macy, "Proposed Collective Labor Agreement," 21 May 1936, State Dept. Decimal Files, 812.00-Tamaulipas/421.

50. See transcripts of sessions dtd. 26 November, 12 December 1936, AHH, C1858-119, fs. 36, 79, 102.

51. Doc. dtd. 24 June 1937, AHH, C1844-3-bis, legajo 1, f19.

52. *The Mexican Oil Strike*, 2:25.

53. "Convenio que celebran . . .," 11 November, Josephus Daniels to secretary of state, 17 November 1937, State Dept. Decimal Files, 812.6363/3064, /3042. On Cárdenas's expectations of the El Aguila contract, see Daniels to secretary of state, 22 March 1938, State Dept. Decimal Files, 812.6363/3101.

54. Macy to secretary of state, 30 November 1936, State Dept. Decimal Files, 812.00-Tamaulipas/287.

55. S. Roger Tyler Jr., "Developments in Petroleum Labor Code in Mexico," 15 January 1937, State Dept. Decimal Files, 812.504/1635.

56. Jack D. Neal to secretary of state, 1 June 1937, State Dept. Decimal Files, 812.000-Tamaulipas/310.

57. Pierre de L. Boal to secretary of state, 5, 7, 9 June 1937, State Dept. Decimal Files, 812.45/397, /409, /402; El Aguila to Anglo-Mex, 2 June 1937, Public Record

Office, London, Foreign Office General Correspondence, 1906–38 (hereafter cited as FO), 371-20639/A4049/132/26.

58. S. Roger Tyler Jr., "End of Petroleum Strike in Mexico," 11 June, L. S. Armstrong, "Resume of Events in the Oil Industry," 16 June 1937, State Dept. Decimal Files, 812.45/419, 424; Joseph Pyke to Foreign Office, 18 June 1937, FO, 371-20639/A4795/527/26.

59. Gallop to Foreign Office, FO, 371/20639/A6194/527/26; Boal to secretary of state, 10 August 1937, State Dept. Decimal Files, 812.45/495.

60. Armstrong to secretary of state, 1 December 1937, State Dept. Decimal Files, 812.00-Tamaulipas/328; extract, 9 December 1937, FLC, 432/87; *El Universal*, 10 December 1937.

61. Armstrong to secretary of state, 4 January 1938, State Dept. Decimal Files, 812.00-Tamaulipas/331; Rafael Mazatán R., 9 March 1938, DAT, C180, E1; Daniels to secretary of state, 20 October 1937, State Dept. Decimal Files, 812.45/576.

62. Extract, 21 September 1936, FLC, 432.3/226; Alberto J. Olvera, "Origen social, condiciones de vida y organización sindical de los trabajadores petroleros de Poza Rica, 1932–1935," *Anuario IV*, 11–55.

63. H. W. Foote, "Dificultades con los Sindicatos," 26 September 1936, FLC, 432.2/8; James Espy, "Strike Situation in the Petroleum Industry in Mexico," 30 October 1936, State Dept. Decimal Files, 812.45/336.

64. Boal to secretary of state, 25, 26 July, James B. Stewart to secretary of state, 17 August 1937, State Dept. Decimal Files, 812.45/463, /479, /501.

65. Daniels to secretary of state, 8 September 1937, State Dept. Decimal Files, 812.34/548; *El Universal*, 13 September 1937.

66. Jack D. Neal to secretary of state, 30 September 37, State Dept. Decimal Files, 812.00-Tamaulipas/320. See also Alberto J. Olvera, "Working Class Culture, Union Organization, and Petroleum Nationalization in Poza Rica, 1932–1940," in *The Mexican Petroleum Industry in the Twentieth Century*, ed. Jonathan C. Brown and Alan Knight (Austin, 1992), 63–89.

67. "Acta de sesión de la Sección 30 del STPRM," 27 January 1938, typescript, 37. The author thanks Fabio Barbosa Cano for providing him with copies of these documents.

68. O'Malley to Holman, 13 January 1938, FO, 371-21462/A887/10/26; Daniels to secretary of state, 25 February 1938, State Dept. Decimal Files, 812.504/1720.

69. *Excélsior*, 18 March 1938; *El Universal*, 19 March 1938; Daniels to secretary of state, 17, 18 March 1938, State Dept. Decimal Files, 812.5045/697, /726.

70. Mazatán Rodríguez to chief, 21, 22 March 1938, DAT, C180, E1; Daniels to secretary of state, 24 March 1938, State Dept. Decimal Files, 812.6363/3120.

71. See Brown and Knight, *Mexican Petroleum Industry in the Twentieth Century*; Angelina Alonso and Carlos Roberto López, *El sindicato de trabajadores petroleros y sus relaciones con Pemex y el estado, 1970–1982* (Mexico City, 1986).

CHAPTER THREE

REHABILITATING
THE WORKERS

The U.S. Railway
Mission to Mexico

ANDREA SPEARS

etween 1942 and 1946, the U.S. Railway Mission to Mexico, in cooperation with the Mexican government, worked to rehabilitate the Mexican railway system.[1] The Railway Mission represented a token of conciliation between the two countries. During the Cárdenas administration (1934–40), relations between the two nations were often strained, especially after the nationalization of the petroleum industry in 1938. War on the European front, however, brought the United States and Mexico into close alliance. Although Mexico sent relatively few troops to the war, raw materials and minerals from Mexico fueled U.S. wartime industrial production. Mexican migrant workers called *braceros*, which literally means "arms," toiled in U.S. fields, factories, and railway yards. The rapid movement of goods and personnel depended on the Mexican railways. But many tracks still bore the destructive marks of the Mexican Revolution (1910–20), and half of the locomotives were twenty-five to fifty years old. A U.S. survey concluded that "if a wartime load were thrown on the Mexican National Railways the system would undoubtedly break down within a short period of time."[2] In the meantime, the administration of President Manuel Avila Camacho was pursuing the nation's project of industrialization and was placing renewed emphasis on modernizing and upgrading the transport system. The two nations, therefore, cooperated to rehabilitate the Mexican railways.

Yet the human element could not be overlooked: the industry employed sixty-five thousand workers. Mission planners and Mexican railway administrators considered the workforce and the existing workers' collective contract as infrastructural deficiencies. During the Cárdenas administration the Union of Mexican Railway Workers, which represented all workers, won important labor gains. For a brief period of time, between 1938 and 1940, the railway workers themselves even administered the National Railways after the Cárdenas administration had nationalized the company. The line between management and labor blurred. In 1940, the government secured labor's support in concluding this experiment: the Mexican National Railways became a state-run enterprise. But the workers' collective contract, which protected them from the arbitrary actions of the managers, remained in force. The U.S. Railway Mission tended to ignore the serious administrative problems. It overlooked managerial incompetence and concentrated instead on modifying the collective contract. The conflict over the collective contract that culminated in 1944 represents just one example of the ongoing struggle between workers and managers for control in the workplace. Workers of the Mexican National Railways resisted even though, unlike the oil laborers during the expropriation crisis, they rarely carried their struggle into the national arena. Instead, railroaders struggled daily to define and control their work experience. Although they shaped and influenced national political developments, the railway workers were most concerned with the daily struggles within the factory walls and train yards. In this case, the Mexican railway workers refused to make all the sacrifices for modernization when management itself bore much of the blame for the continuing problems in the Mexican railway industry.

Impossible to Work in Filth and Misery

U.S. interests figured prominently in the railroad system's development beginning in the late nineteenth century. By 1900, North American investors controlled 80 percent of the railway lines, and gringos dominated the skilled labor force. North Americans who worked in the best jobs on those early Mexican lines commonly referred to the less skilled native workers as "'greasers'" and "'our peons.'"[3] Mexican railway workers, however, refused to accept discrimination in their own country and fought to eliminate "'that terrible foreign element that [was] trying to take over everything and occupy all jobs.'"[4] The Mexican government actually set in motion the "Mexicanization" of the labor force when it bought up railway stock to control the two largest railway companies in Mexico. In 1908, the Mexican government created the Mexican National Railways to administer the new system and established hiring practices favorable to native workers. Spanish rather than English became the official operating language on the railways. Together, these new "nationalistic" work rules and the violence of the revolution (1910–20) prompted nearly all the foreign workers to abandon their jobs on the Mexican railways. Mexican workers soon proved that skill and expertise were not the sole prerogative of foreign workers. Still, U.S. influence did not end. U.S. investors figured prominently as stockholders, and the enterprise's international debt continued to grow. During the 1920s, several studies conducted by international experts had recommended cuts in personnel and wages and encouraged administrative reforms. Railway administrators followed up on some of these recommendations in 1931 and 1932 and fired ten thousand workers; it was a "painless adjustment," according to the general manager of the National Railways.[5]

Although major infrastructural deficiencies remained, many U.S. observers and Mexican railway administrators in the 1940s considered the Mexican labor force to be the greatest obstacle to transporting goods efficiently to the United States. The planners of the U.S. Railway Mission, therefore, determined to remold the Mexican worker to create a "modern," productive worker. Modern, productive workers were to toil in safe, hygienic surroundings. They were to follow operating regulations. Because these conditions did not exist on the Mexican railway system, Mission designers considered the "rehabilitation of the personnel and their habits, methods and practices" the most critical component of their railway reforms.[6]

It was undeniable at the time that dangerous and precarious working conditions existed in the shops, in the work camps, and on the tracks. Workers rarely used goggles or gloves, because management often neglected to provide even the most basic safety equipment. Dangerous machinery lacked the proper protective covers, and scattered parts and equipment posed serious safety hazards. The unpaved shop floors, littered with trash and covered in spilled oil, proved especially hazardous.[7] Conditions worsened during the rainy season, when many shop roofs leaked. Inadequate ventilation and poor lighting created hazardous conditions. Basic conveniences such as bathrooms, showers, and potable drinking water did not exist in many shops and work camps. When workers went on location, the managers provided only leaky tents to sleep in.[8]

Such work conditions contributed to low morale and poor health among the workers. Cold, wet shop conditions and the often dramatic temperature changes experienced by operating crews contributed to the high rates of respiratory illnesses, rheumatism, and "nervous conditions" among them.[9] Railway workers benefited from hospitals and clinics funded, albeit inadequately, by the railway administration. But those workers stationed in rural or desolate areas enjoyed far fewer benefits. Traveling medical teams, for example, periodically visited the work camps, but, as one laborer reported, they stayed only long enough to pass out medicines indiscriminately.[10] The overall conditions on the Mexican railways violated the federal labor laws as well as the workers' collective contract. What were the workers to do, especially considering that the employer was the government itself? They still sought to pressure management to comply with its obligations as if it were a private employer.

Poor work conditions and management's inadequate attention to the workers' needs also contributed to low labor productivity. Shop workers found it "humanly impossible" to work in "filth and misery." Even the U.S. experts admitted that such work conditions could "nullify" the effects of introducing new equipment.[11] To clear up traffic jams, for example, the Mission introduced diesel locomotives that pulled heavier loads and operated around the clock. Two such diesel locomotives were to operate in the overburdened Monterrey rail yards. In February 1943, more than three thousand cars were jammed into the Monterrey yards, which had been constructed to handle only eighteen hundred cars. The city consequently experienced periodic shortages of gas and other essential items that arrived by rail. Vegetables and fruit spoiled in waiting cars, and the local smelters could not ship their metal products to the United States. More than fifty locomotives were awaiting repairs. Responding to local and national criticism, the workers blamed the poor repair record on a scarcity of needed tools and parts. Carpenters, for example, used their own tools. However, U.S. technicians blamed the situation on low productivity of the workers.[12] Improving work conditions, therefore, constituted an important goal for the Mission as well as for the railway workers. In 1944, the railway administration announced plans to construct or reconstruct bathrooms, dining rooms, and showers in the larger shops and stations.[13] Many of these new facilities opened in 1946.

Improving work conditions served two purposes: to increase labor productivity and to garner workers' support for the Mission. The railway union itself had advocated a number of measures to modernize the railway system and place it on a profitable footing, including an increase in transport rates. The Mexican railway workers eagerly pledged to cooperate in the Allied war effort, and the union supported the goals of the U.S. Mission. "We are not chauvisists [*sic*]," a union spokesman stated; "we know that [the U.S. technicians] are competent [and] that their counsels will be useful to the Mexican technicians."[14] But some workers did oppose the presence of U.S. technicians in Mexico. Then the Mission sought to improve work conditions as a way to secure the cooperation of all workers. Two public health officers were employed especially to address the medical needs of maintenance-of-way workers. Hoping to stamp out malaria in the work camps, the Mission also distributed twenty-four thousand atabrine and quinine pills. The Mission's director stated that the "railway workers . . . [would] come to realize that only through the efforts of the Mission [had] help in their malarial troubles been brought to them."[15]

Besides health, the workers and the Mission were also concerned about safety on the Mexican railways. Precarious work conditions, compounded by greater traffic on the railway lines, had resulted in a rise in accidents. Between 1940 and 1945, cargo transportation and passenger travel increased 29 percent and 32 percent, respectively. In 1944, the railway administration ordered the workers to redouble their efforts.[16] Workers were to repair and load the rail cars as rapidly as possible in order to sustain the increased traffic. The average workweek for shop workers and train crews, for example, increased by 18 percent overall during the Second World War.[17] Retired railway workers even today remember the war as a period of intense activity in the shops and on the tracks. "For about three years, we worked twelve and fourteen hours a day," says one retiree, Manuel Sotelo Pallares. "Saturdays and Sundays did not exist. We entered at seven in the morning and left at seven at night to increase production . . . to ship out the metals, to prepare the cargo cars, because we were at war."[18]

The new transportation demands, however, affected some workers more than others. Yard engineers, for example, were working an average of fifty-five hours a week in 1944, compared with thirty-four hours in 1942. Train crews worked up to sixty hours without a day off. As a consequence, the number of operating accidents rose from 306 in 1941 to 652 in 1944. One-fifth of all workers were being injured on the job every year.[19] Félix Celestino, a champion boxer and brakeman, lost both of his arms when his hands slipped while trying to connect two cars. In 1944, sixty-seven railway workers died in work-related accidents on the National Railways. Engineer Jorge Olvera, for example, lost his life in a train accident in March 1944; he had been working nonstop for seventy hours.[20] Poor track conditions caused the deaths of four track workers in Durango. A fellow worker recorded their tragedy in a *corrido*:

A cargo train coming from Durango was to blame,
it sent out a message that the tracks were damaged.
They climbed onto the locomotive to try to help,
but a break in the tracks marked their destiny.
The accident occurred; my heart hurts,
four men have died, the locomotive killed them.
They were railroaders that worked on the tracks,
poor *compañeros*, it was their fate.[21]

Faulty equipment, poor track conditions, and incompetent management caused most accidents. In one of the worst recorded railway accidents, sixty-eight passengers died when two trains crashed in February 1945. Most of the victims, who were en route to a religious pilgrimage in Guanajuato, were riding in wooden box cars. Although the press blamed the railway workers, antiquated operating rules caused the accident.[22] Thirty-five passengers were injured and one died when a train derailed in August 1944. A damaged rail, laid in 1906, caused the accident. Faulty equipment, bad track conditions, and "other causes" were responsible for 55 percent and 63 percent of all accidents on the National Railways in 1944 and 1947, respectively.[23] As the number of accidents rose, the railway workers became the easiest scapegoat for the complex problems affecting the railway system. Critics cried sabotage whenever an accident occurred. Train crews, however, defended themselves as professional, skilled workers who followed operating procedures and used sound judgment.

Mission personnel did acknowledge unsafe track conditions and faulty equipment yet blamed most accidents on train crews that violated operating rules. According to U.S. technicians, safe operating procedures did not exist among the workers. Few trains carried the mandatory red flags or red and white lanterns for night signaling. Red handkerchiefs served for all signaling purposes. But could the workers be blamed for such discrepancies? According to the Mission's director, the managerial personnel also lacked training in basic safety standards.[24] Extensive training and safety awareness programs did not exist. Improving shop and equipment safety also required greater monetary investment in the railway system than the Mexican government could afford. New parts and equipment, generally U.S.-made, represented costly expenses.

To redress the situation, the Mission engaged in an extensive campaign to reinvigorate safety committees, which had been designed ostensibly to increase safety awareness in the workplace as well as report unsafe conditions to management. The railway union fully supported these efforts. The collective contract, in fact, stipulated that workers failing to observe safety committee recommendations could face disciplinary actions. Yet safety committees operated sporadically. In 1941, for example, Labor Department inspectors began reestablishing a number of local safety committees.[25] The combined interests of the Mission, the railway union, and the railway administration also provided greater impetus to safety awareness. Safety committees were to meet ideally every week. They distributed posters that exhorted workers to employ safe work habits and clean up their work areas. The Mission distributed thousands of safety manuals covering every facet of railway operations. As in the United

States, ideas of wartime "patriotism" permeated these safety campaigns. Each manual had a large, red "V" for victory on the cover and the word "PATRIOTISM" graced the opening page. "Be PATRIOTIC in your daily work," one such manual exhorted the worker, "and make materials last longer—Bring victory closer."[26] After five crewmen died in a train derailment, an editorial in the railway administration's magazine stated: "The death of a railway worker is just as important as that of any soldier who dies from a Nazi bullet."[27] Safety campaigns invigorated local efforts to improve work conditions and reflected efforts to "modernize" the worker.

Unsafe conditions, however, did not change overnight. By early 1945, seventeen local committees functioned erratically with varied effectiveness. Some workers embraced new safety standards, but others continued to ignore safety precautions. Children still rode on switch engines in the yards.[28] Local safety committees often struggled to be heard; shop supervisors frequently ignored safety recommendations. In Aguascalientes, for example, foundry workers engaged in a sit-down strike because managers refused to distribute work gloves—even though more than five hundred pairs were in stock. The gloves were finally distributed.[29] Poorly trained supervisors as well as individual workers undermined the safety campaigns and impaired the workers' safety. Perhaps to deflect attention from their own problems, railway administrators persisted in blaming the workers for their perceived deficiencies.

Arrogant in Bearing and Insulting

"Rehabilitating" the workers included more than just improving work conditions and encouraging the observance of work rules. Mission personnel also sought to "modernize" work practices. The plan required shifting workers according to local exigencies, transferring workers from traditional daytime jobs in order to create second and third shifts, and "serially" repairing equipment. The workers and their union certainly were not adverse to increasing productivity. In 1943, for example, the union proposed the creation of Wartime Cooperation Committees. The railway administration then adopted the idea. Local and national committees sought to stimulate labor productivity as well as enthusiasm and discipline among the workforce.[30] But the changes envisioned by the Mission and by the railway administration violated the workers' collective contract, provoking much resistance among the workers.

The various rehabilitation projects necessitated the elimination or transferal of workers depending upon changing labor requirements. Arbitrary transfers violated the collective contract and annoyed workers. One case in point: the reclamation plant established in San Luis Potosí. Reclaimable materials and equipment generally rotted alongside the tracks or were sold by workers to supplement their pay. In the new reclamations facility, used materials were to be reconditioned for reuse or sold to private companies to recoup the company's losses. The list of recyclable materials also included old machinery. According to the collective contract, only employees of the Motive Power Department could retool old machinery. If retooling was to take place in the new reclamation plant, as management desired, then workers in the Motive Power Department could lose their jobs. Labor and management negotiated a solution. Employees transferred from the Motive Power Department would retool machinery in the reclamation plant. All other positions would likewise be filled by workers with the appropriate specialties.[31] Despite the delays caused by the negotiations, the railway administration saw an almost immediate profit. Between 1943 and 1944, the reclamation program resulted in a net savings of $450,000 and continued to produce savings for the National Railways' administration. The U.S. reclamations expert considered the new plant one of the Mission's crowning achievements. "I don't believe that the Mexican people will soon forget how much they owe to the Mission for having started something . . . of such permanent value," he crowed.[32]

These rehabilitation projects also necessitated the geographical relocation of workers. Managers refused to respect the stipulations of the collective contracts that prevented forced transfers. Shop workers at Aguascalientes even engaged in a four-hour work stoppage when management arbitrarily transferred twenty-four workers. Similar stoppages occurred in Cárdenas and San Luis Potosí.[33] Nevertheless, in December 1943, management transferred workers from Torreón to a new railway station. The workers fought the move. They argued that the transfer "forced [them] to seek living accommodations in private homes—often at exorbitant rates—and that their children—violently uprooted from their homes—would no longer receive an adequate education."[34] Arbitrary transfers became a constant source of labor-management conflict.

The U.S. technicians and the Mexican railway administrators also established second and third shifts to increase labor productivity. In February 1943, for example, the Mission and the railway management embarked on a sixty-day emergency plan to clear up the traffic jam in the Monterrey yards. Mission employees assumed the direct management of the yards and shops, and Mexican supervisors were to follow their orders. Extra shifts were also to be established in the yards and shops to clear out the traffic. The plan, however, required labor's cooperation, because the collective contract prohibited extra shifts. The Monterrey-based workers agreed to support the sixty-day plan and to suspend the prohibitive contract stipulations. From the onset, however,

Mexican workers cleaning up following a train wreck, 1946.
(Courtesy of the Fototeca del Instituto Nacional de Antropología e Historia,
Pachuca, Hidalgo)

local union representatives made it clear that they would not accept other unwarranted contract violations. Union representatives also reminded the U.S. technicians that the workers would not accept direct orders from them; all suggestions were to come from local supervisors.[35] Many workers remembered when U.S. interests and gringo workers controlled the railroads. Moreover, taking orders from too many supervisors complicated the workers' tasks. The sixty-day plan successfully accomplished its immediate goal at the Monterrey yards because the Mission and the railway administration did not ride roughshod over the workers and their collective contract but worked out an agreement with the workers that all parties could respect. The railway workers cooperated.

In Monterrey and throughout Mexico close contact with Mission personnel provoked questions and unrest, but the workers' responses were diverse. The last Mission director, characterized as "pompous and officious," provoked considerable ire among the workers. He traveled in his own private rail car, which doubled as a traveling office, and his wife prohibited the Mexicans from entering.[36] The director of the U.S. Mission further insulted Mexican sensibilities when he publicly declared that the "U.S. government couldn't produce locomotives fast enough to replace those destroyed in Mexico."[37] Prior to the sixty-day experiment, Monterrey workers threatened to strike if U.S. technicians did not stop directly interfering and violating the collective contract. Since workers received orders from both their local supervisors and the Mission technicians, confusion reigned. The railway workers often could not be sure who was in command. Local newspapers contended that U.S. technicians routinely criticized the workers. In Mexico City, workers complained that U.S. technicians "had been arrogant in their bearing and even insulting" toward them.[38] However, the Mission personnel were well received in Aguascalientes, where few negative incidents occurred between the workers and the U.S. technicians. Workers who had no contact with the Mission personnel, on the other hand, actively solicited the Mission's intervention in an effort to improve their working conditions. Chihuahua workers complained that the railway administration ignored their problems, "no doubt" because they were so far from Mexico City. "We beg of you [U.S. technicians], with all respect, that you intervene," they pleaded.[39] Conflict and animosity, although occasional, did not by any means characterize the relations between the gringos and railway workers.

Mission personnel rigorously sought to defuse any hostility. After receiving several reports of imprudence, the Mission director threatened to fire all his technicians involved in future misconduct.[40] He advised his technicians to maintain a friendly attitude, avoid direct criticism, and refrain from making easily misunderstood comments, especially in front of their personal interpreters. "Young" and "inexperienced," the interpreters could easily misconstrue what they heard and engage in detrimental gossip. "Remember," the director told his men, the United States "was colonized and civilized by strong, far-seeing people; people who had come to seek freedom and to make a new home." Mexico, on the other hand, "had always been the object of conquest, enslavement and exploitation. . . . Mexicans had the perfect right to look with suspicion."[41] Interpreters received similar warnings. The Mission expected them to exercise patience and to choose their words wisely.[42] These cautions, however, did not prevent the workers from hardening their resistance to elements of the rehabilitation program that placed the burdens on them.

In mid-1943, the Mission embarked on an ambitious plan in Aguascalientes: to modernize shop production. More than three thousand workers toiled in the Aguascalientes shops—the workers referred to the shops as the "Railway

Workers' University"—and the installations compared favorably to similar U.S. shops. "Good" mechanics worked in the shop, according to one technician, but they were "very largely idle" and unproductive. Although workers completed the repair of fourteen engines at the shop each month, the U.S. technicians believed that they could repair twenty.[43] The organization of work was primarily to blame for the low figure. Workers repaired cars and locomotives one at a time. Boilermakers, mechanics, carpenters, painters, and welders all worked on the same car at the same time, resembling a "wholelistic" method of reparation. The Mission advocated a form of serial production known more commonly as Fordism. Cars repaired serially would move along an assembly line much as Henry Ford's employees had used to make automobiles. Each worker was to perform a specific task before the rail car moved on to the next point, where another specialist completed a separate task. Beginning on a small scale, in March 1944, the Mission set up the serial reparation of seventy-eight cabooses. Workers were assigned to twelve work stations. One hundred eighty men repaired the cabooses at a total cost of 8,909 pesos per unit—an apparent success.[44] Fordism represented a radical departure from traditional shop practices.

Despite the initial optimism, U.S. technicians soon revised their enthusiasm for serial production. Neither the workmen nor their supervisors, they said, would "take advantage of the new methods."[45] Supervisors routinely reassigned workers without regard for the overall production goals. On one occasion, for instance, Mexican administrators reassigned all of the men engaged in serial production to the rapid construction of five cabooses. The administration wanted to show off the work at Aguascalientes and needed a few shiny, new cabooses for the event. The result was "chaos."[46] Work assignments changed from one day to the next, and workers did not know what was expected of them or who was in charge. Material shortages further delayed progress. "[Workers] become indifferent and loaf about, leaving their positions, for which they cannot be held responsible," reported one U.S. technician.[47] The shop workers also resisted the new production system, because it increased managerial supervision. Traditionally, these repairmen exercised a great deal of freedom and personal initiative in the shops. Supervisors (or the U.S. technicians, for that matter) did not lean over their shoulders; no one timed their work. The Mission director even proposed paying bonuses to workers as an incentive to increase their unsupervised productivity, but the railway administration did not follow his advice.[48] Instead, the administration established an annual production prize: the Copa de Producción. The most productive shop would receive the cup, and the workers would receive diplomas—but no extra money. Their aversion to incentive pay for the workers did not, however, prevent the railway administrators from awarding themselves a bonus of an extra month's pay in December 1944.[49] Reportedly "very, very discouraged," one U.S. technician advised his superiors to forget about the idea: serial production would never succeed. Production did increase 30 percent by 1945 but primarily because the workers had doubled their efforts.[50]

Arguing that an unskilled workforce doomed much of their own work, Mission planners also sought to expand technical training. The Mexican railway worker, according to the Mission director, possessed "absolutely no knowledge."[51] His estimation included supervisory personnel. We must "train those Mexicans," the director stated, and "supply them with technical training that will bring them back to skill."[52] The Mission and the railway administration consequently established two training programs whereby Mexican personnel would be sent to the United States to learn from their counterparts. In one program, small groups of managerial employees traveled to observe North American rail operations for periods of three weeks. This program trained at least 86 managerial personnel between 1943 and 1945. A more extensive program was envisioned for up to 5,000 railway workers, each training for six months on U.S. railway lines. Although planners hoped to create a Mexican labor force "competent to institute and follow modern shop practices," the latter program did not succeed.[53] By February 1945, shortly before both training programs ended, only 250 worker trainees had been sent to the United States.[54]

A number of related issues affected the rapid demise of these programs. Dissatisfaction grew among the participating railway personnel, both with conditions in the United States and upon returning to Mexico. In the United States, Mexican workers faced discrimination. Supervisors at the American Refrigeration and Transportation Company, located in St. Louis, Missouri, routinely assigned skilled Mexican railway workers to clean-up duty, which provoked discontent.[55] "We are helpers of everyone," said one Mexican carpenter. "It is all one big mess. . . . They can order us to rivet or work as boilermakers." (However, this carpenter did find the food to be "half-way" satisfying, "plentiful and good.")[56] As the war slowly drew to a close in 1945, U.S. railway employers became less interested in the trainees as well. War industry cutbacks created a larger pool of available American workers seeking employment in the railway industry.[57] Back in Mexico, "dissatisfaction" developed among returning trainees who felt their time in the United States had been "wasted." The railway administration did not employ these trainees in managerial positions or use their newly acquired expertise to train other workers. Mexican managers excused themselves, claiming that the seniority clauses of the collective contract prevented them from using these workers more effectively.[58] However, no organizational system existed to take advantage of the acquired knowledge. Rather than accommodating themselves to take full advantage of their newly trained personnel, the managers simply blamed the workers' collective contract.

The Mission personnel established other programs to advance technical training within Mexico, where the results were more satisfactory despite the design flaws. More than a hundred manuals, demonstrating how to perform a wide range of operations, were distributed. In November 1943, short technical courses began in the larger shops. The Mission even supported several English-language classes, which the Mission director found to be surprisingly "well attended." "It is surprising to me how fast these people pick up our language," he wrote, ignoring the fact that few of his fellow American technicians even cared to learn Spanish.[59] According to one observer, however, the workers often "neglected or ignored" the new techniques and manuals.[60] "I can not see where a single plan has been put into effect permanently," reported another technician in 1944. Workers did not follow the rules prescribed in the locomotive inspection manuals. They "absolutely ignored" the welding manual, and foremen and supervisors did not even possess copies of the manual.[61]

At the root of the overall problem lay the Instruction Department of the Mexican National Railways, which lacked the materials and infrastructure to provide technical training to all its workers. Established in 1909, the Instruction Department provided courses for operating personnel (e.g., engineers, conductors, telegraph operators). In 1944, the sixty workers who were enrolled in departmental courses met in an unused warehouse with ten chairs and no textbooks.[62] Besides the material shortages, the technical training that did exist was too personalized. According to the U.S. technicians, individual instructors examined their own students and rarely failed anyone. Similar deficiencies existed in the training of shop workers. New shop employees received very little training, and seniority rather than achievement determined advancement to second- and first-class positions and to supervisory jobs. The foremen rarely provided instruction. Workers picked up their skills on an ad hoc basis, slowing production and creating unsafe working conditions. The Mission director argued that no one on the Mexican railways would be properly trained unless the administration initiated immediate changes.[63] To overcome the inadequacies, the Mission recommended the expansion of the Instruction Department to encompass all railway employees.

The union wholeheartedly supported the Mission's emphasis on education even though it did not agree with all the Mission director's proposals. Railway workers valued literacy and were respected by their fellow citizens. In the railroading town of Aguascalientes, railway workers were "esteemed" members of the community and held formal offices in the city and state governments. They often led the battle to establish schools in their communities. In Tierra Blanca, an isolated railway center, workers petitioned for federal funding to build a school "to eradicate as much as humanly possible the criminality and barbarity in the region."[64] In 1942, the union petitioned the government to create an Educational Center and technical schools for its members. Moreover, Mexican railway workers, highly skilled craftsmen, were capable of constructing and inventing any part required on a locomotive or car. In 1942 and 1944, for example, workers in Acámbaro constructed two steam engines inexpensively and without outside assistance.[65] The Mission director even acknowledged that the Mexican workmen were "good, conscientious," and "capable of splendid workmanship" even though they worked under adverse conditions.[66]

Partly as a result of the Mission's advocacy, on 1 February 1946 a new technical school opened amid much fanfare at the Buenavista Station in Mexico City. The school incorporated many of the educational techniques used by the U.S. railway companies. Since 75 percent of the maintenance-of-way workers were illiterate as well as unskilled and poorly paid, visual aids such as films and charts would be used along with the oral instruction. The administration hoped to reach additional workers with correspondence courses. Three mobile educational cars were also equipped and put into service. Importantly, the new system included mandatory courses for managerial personnel.[67] The railway union agreed to support advancement based on a combination of merit and seniority partly because the new managerial courses—in theory—would prevent the railway administration from arbitrarily hiring managers without railroad training. In 1945, the railway administration opened technical schools in Monterrey and Aguascalientes, and the workers eagerly embraced the new technical training program.

The Most Intelligent and Influential of All Workers

Although the new educational system represented a long-term victory, officials began to question the U.S. Mission's continued efficacy in Mexico. Food shortages occurred in various parts of Mexico between 1942 and 1944, and critics blamed both the railway workers and the Mission. Strategic war industry goods sat awaiting shipment to the United States. Railway workers complained increasingly of U.S. interference, while mission employees and railway administrators, on the other hand, claimed that the union's collective contract impeded progress. Thwarted in their efforts to "modernize" the railway system and the Mexican workers, the technicians talked increasingly of returning to the United States.[68] Simmering conflict within the ranks of the railway workers further stymied the rehabilitation.

Unity within the Union of Mexican Railway Workers collapsed in 1944. In February, the operating personnel (conductors, engineers, firemen, and brakemen) and the boilermakers seceded from the railway union. These nine thousand workers established the Brotherhood of Operating Personnel and Helpers (hereafter referred to as the *trenistas*) and the Brotherhoods of Boilermakers and Helpers. In 1933, the *trenistas* and boilermakers had supported the creation of one industrywide union representing all railway workers. But they continued to compete with other railroaders for greater representation within the union. They seceded from the union when their common candidate failed to win the heated election for the union's leadership. Only after President Avila Camacho effected a reconciliation, in March 1944, did they agree to support a coalition executive committee.[69] But the *trenistas* and boilermakers continued to press for dominance, and the fragile coalition soon collapsed.

One especially divisive issue concerned the question of wage increases. During the war, inflation soared in Mexico, as it did in many other countries. The cost of living doubled between 1939 and 1944. Following a series of strikes in 1943 (which slowed the rehabilitation projects), union negotiators won an overall 5 percent wage increase. But the *trenistas* remained dissatisfied with so small an increase. An earlier federal law, which classified their jobs as piecework, entitled them to an 18.5 percent pay boost. Labeling union negotiators as "traitors," the *trenistas* demanded their own independent representation.[70] Boilermakers and *trenistas*, after all, earned more than most other workers and paid higher union dues. They expected to be fully represented in all matters concerning their specialties. In seceding from the union, the *trenistas* and boilermakers hoped to negotiate their own future unhindered by the remaining fifty-five thousand railway workers.

However, the federal government, the railway administration, and the Union of Mexican Railway Workers refused to recognize the secession. The government of Avila Camacho advocated labor unity at the same time that it pursued policies of national industrialization. During the 1940s, the government regularly arbitrated labor conflicts, appealing to the workers' patriotism and emphasizing national unity, especially during the war. "Mexico is not a conglomerate of contrary elements . . . [but] a single, indivisible whole, an harmonic machine, a real Nation," Avila Camacho declared in 1940.[71] Mexico's largest unions accepted a no-strike pledge in 1942 and agreed to cooperate with industry for the war's duration (although several, including the railway union, were to deviate from that pledge). In addition, federal labor laws recognized only one union within any given industry so that the Union of Mexican Railway Workers, representing the majority, officially represented all railroaders.

The breach within the railway union, however, led to pitched battles. In March 1944, after management had deducted official union dues from their paychecks, the boilermakers and *trenistas* blocked all railway lines converging on Mexico City. Traffic backed up as far north as Ciudad Juárez on the U.S. border. Sit-down strikes paralyzed rail service throughout Mexico, and boilermakers in Aguascalientes impeded the implementation of Fordism. Locomotive repairs declined 16 percent between April and June 1944, compared with the same period in the previous year. Workers affiliated with the official union countered with their own sit-down strikes. Armed violence occurred in several locals.[72]

As the workers fought among themselves, the rehabilitation projects of the U.S. Railway Mission drew to a standstill, although the Mission director did not consider the union dissension as overly detrimental. The dissident workers, especially the *trenistas*, were the "most intelligent and influential of all workers," and the American director vowed to work with them. In fact, the *trenistas* and boilermakers had sought his counsel when they seceded from the union.[73] The *trenistas* especially had been wholehearted supporters of the rehabilitation project. When workers at Monterrey complained about the interference of U.S. technicians, the local *trenistas* labeled them "fools."[74] They believed that such protests gave all workers a bad name. The *trenistas* and boilermakers considered themselves skilled, professional workers with a long history of union activity. They sought to reestablish their separate interests by seceding from the majority of railway workers. Despite the Mission director's early prediction, the continuing struggle among the workers did indeed undermine the rehabilitation project. The administrators pondered the next move.

Converting the Worker into a Machine

Believing that union factionalism rendered the workers defenseless, the railway management in May 1944 announced sweeping modifications to the workers' collective contract, thereby risking labor's wrath. The government issued decree GG-96. President Avila Camacho had consistently contended that the workers "should not be treated like animals."[75] But the labor strife in the railway industry was impeding industrialization as well as Mexico's wartime trade to the United States. The railway administration, deflecting its own responsibility, advocated greater control over the workers. "*The ones who really manage the railways are the workers themselves through their collective work contracts*," complained a railway administrator to the Mission director, "*and they do it without the least bit of responsibility.*"[76] The Mission director did not have to be convinced. From the outset, the Mission's goals included a drastic modification—if not the complete abrogation—of the collective contract. Decree GG-96 encompassed sweeping contract changes that broadened managerial powers. The Union of Mexican Railway Workers, however, rejected the new decree as "extremist." It "converted the worker into a machine without a sense of his rightful existence," said a union communiqué, "and propelled him into a slave-like state of depression."[77] Decree GG-96 required workers to make all the sacrifices.

Railway workers especially objected to modifications that eroded labor's prerogatives in the workplace and broadened managerial control. A key point of contention concerned modifications to the customary means of ensuring labor discipline. First introduced to the Mexican railway lines in 1909 by the U.S. manager, the "Brown" system governed labor discipline. Workers received demerit marks for infractions such as theft, desertion, working under the influence of alcohol or drugs, insubordination, immorality, and negligence. Each infraction carried a minimum of five demerit points. After accumulating a total of ninety-one demerits, the worker faced dismissal. Merit points for heroic acts and meritorious service could cancel out demerit points. All disciplinary decisions could be appealed to local committees, which were composed of three union and two administration representatives.[78] Workers had always considered the "Brown" system to be fair. Management, on the other hand, demanded greater power to dismiss "recalcitrant" workers, especially now that it was attempting to "modernize" the railways. The union and administration had compromised on this issue in 1942. The merit/demerit system remained intact, but a National Appeals Committee replaced local committees. Representation on the national committee consisted of four appointees from both the railway administration and the union.[79] Labor had already given up some control to managers even before Decree GG-96.

The 1944 decree sought yet again to diminish workers' control within the workplace, eliminating the National Appeals Committee. Decree GG-96 provided for a new process whereby workers appealed disciplinary decisions to management. The total number of demerit points was reduced from ninety-one to sixty.[80] The decree also provided for a more extensive list of infractions. One of the most damaging of the new infractions prohibited the worker from expressing or provoking violence toward supervisors—on the job or off.[81] Of course, the managers would decide what kind of behavior might provoke violence. This stipulation rendered even the workers' private actions and words subject to possible disciplinary action. If the administration succeeded in enforcing these changes, the workers' daily existence would become more precarious and dependent on management.

Secondly, the union opposed management's bid to increase the number of confidential employees.[82] GG-96 would expand the definition of confidential employees to include all administrative, supervisory, fiscal, and vigilance personnel, and even the cooks. Management could also appoint all these new confidential employees without considering experienced union workers. The union argued that extending such powers to management would destroy seniority rights within the workforce. If the worker could not expect to advance to the top of his specialty after twenty or more years, the union asked, why should he continue to work for the railroad? The new decree would undermine all efforts to eliminate nepotism and favoritism in the selection of managerial personnel as well. Administrators would now be able to hire managers completely ignorant of railway operations. Opposing these changes, the union argued that only confidential employees drawn from the union's seniority lists could successfully fulfill the necessary job requirements.[83] Besides, it was well known that the administrators were political appointees and career bureaucrats. Instead of experienced railway men or university-trained professionals, men with political or family connections got the best jobs in the railway administration.[84] Workers understood that an increase in confidential employees diminished their control of the workplace and increased their insecurity.

That was not all. Decree GG-96 also empowered management to transfer personnel to any part of the system without the worker's consent. The union argued that the new rule "gravely eroded the worker's stability, because it threatened his home life and impeded the education of his children."[85] The new stipulation also violated the union's seniority rules. Workers had always been able to request transfers, and senior workers received first pick. The new rule placed workers at the mercy of management and subjected them to arbitrary managerial decisions. Management could use transfers to punish dissident railway workers and to dissipate labor unrest by transferring workers to distant, isolated locations.[86]

These changes envisioned by CG-96 provoked labor rebellion and a wave of strikes throughout the country. In Monterrey, striking workers abandoned thirty locomotives on the tracks and cut telegraph communications and electrical power throughout the city. Local police and federal troops suppressed public demonstrations denouncing both the decree and the national government. U.S. technicians felt the brunt of worker dissatisfaction. In San Luis Potosí, the U.S. consul reported that the "feeling is running high against both the President [Avila Camacho] and the US Railway Mission."[87] Afraid they would be "shunted off on the sidings" or placed in the path of oncoming

A Mexican engine crew on the National Railways, ca. 1946.
(Courtesy of the Fototeca del Instituto Nacional de Antropología e Historia,
Pachuca, Hidalgo)

trains, U.S. technicians stopped traveling in their private train cars.[88] Decree GG-96 also compelled the *trenistas* and boilermakers to make peace and rejoin forces with their fellow workers. The official railway union recognized their right to independent representation within the union in exchange for their cooperation. The railway workers were once again united in resistance, albeit momentarily.

As rail traffic throughout the nation slowed to a trickle, the Mexican government capitulated. Had it not done so, all wartime trade between Mexico and the United States would have been jeopardized. The compromise agreement represented a labor victory. Off-duty activities were not subject to disciplinary actions. Demerit points were reduced to sixty, but a General Committee, with four representatives from both labor and management, would consider appeals. Although the number of confidential employees increased, such positions were clearly defined and would be filled according to the union's seniority lists. Management could, however, reorganize personnel depending on local labor exigencies. All decisions, however, required the union's approval.[89] The workers accepted the compromise but continued to insist that management similarly reform its hiring practices and eliminate abuses: "Management must select supervisors and officials based on their capacity, knowledge, rectitude and their ability to teach their subordinates. . . . Management must also became more responsible and eliminate abuses, favoritism, and nepotism which destroys discipline. Supervisors must have more contact with the actual work, identify with their subordinates, and be just and humane."[90]

The workers successfully resisted the complete abrogation of their collective contract and retained a high degree of control within the workplace. Mexican managers had failed to shift the entire weight of railway modernization onto the backs of the workers. As the war drew to a close, the United States no longer depended so heavily on Mexico for raw goods or migrant workers. One U.S. planner deemed it wise, therefore, to pull out "while [the Mission] still stood out . . . as a generous and valuable expression of friendship."[91] After concluding a few projects in 1946, the Mission withdrew and left the rehabilitation in Mexican hands. The inefficiencies of the Mexican railway industry remained, but the workers prevented themselves from being sole victims of the modernization project from which the state railway managers exempted themselves.

Conclusion

North American technicians and Mexican railway officials had sought to create a "modern," efficient workforce, thereby increasing labor productivity.

Projects initiated during the period of wartime economic cooperation had attempted to promote safer and more hygienic work environments, rules observance, technical training, extra shifts, and serial reparations. The ultimate goal was to increase managerial control in the workplace by making substantial changes, if necessary, to the collective contract.

The workers embraced most portions of the rehabilitation project, but they refused to bear all of the blame for the industry's inadequacies. Managerial incompetence accounted for as many problems as the "evils" of the collective contract. Modernization and contract modifications threatened job stability, increased managerial supervision, undermined labor initiative, increased the workload without commensurate pay, and disrupted seniority. The workers protested and engaged in sit-down strikes. Although divided when decree GG-96 was announced, the workers made up their differences in order to fight from a position of strength. The resulting negotiated compromise broadened the scope of managerial powers, but it also significantly preserved labor's prerogatives. In this case, the railway workers did not seek to shape events at the national level. They neither advocated a change of government nor questioned the arrangement of political power. However, they successfully challenged management within the workplace in order to determine successfully the terms of work.

Subsequent governmental modernization plans pitted labor against management, as contractual conflicts continued into the postwar era. The Alemán administration (1946–52) introduced a distinctly new practice to labor-management relations: the *charrazo*. The railway union, joined by other major industrial unions, established an independent labor confederation to challenge the dominance of the progovernment Confederation of Mexican Workers at the same time that railway workers were mobilizing against another attempt to modify their collective contract. President Miguel Alemán supported the union's secretary-general in an interunion showdown in October 1948. The so-called *charrazo* repressed one faction of the railway workers and imposed new managerial prerogatives, although the workers and their union retained many prerogatives.

Between 1958 and 1982, the railway industry and the struggle for workers' control deteriorated. The government invested inadequately in the railway system and placed most resources into highways that successfully competed against the railways. The workers struggled against low salaries, union corruption, and repression. Roughly twenty-six thousand retired railway workers, most of whom began their railway careers during the 1930s and 1940s, had to battle for their retirement benefits and pensions. After the 1982 economic collapse, when privatization became the dominant government policy, the problems of the retirees began in earnest. In that year, the railway workers, including the retired workers, were incorporated into Mexico's Social Security Administration. That state agency attempted to liquidate all of its future obligations—including retirement pay, medical attention, and paid funeral services—by offering the retired workers a modest onetime payment. The workers refused to renounce their retirement benefits and accept what they considered to be an insultingly low amount. In 1994, the retired workers—now numbering only ten thousand—continued to battle for their retirement benefits against administrative intransigence and corruption.[92]

In the meantime, active railway workers today are confronting a different battle. In 1988, the Salinas administration set in motion the privatization of the state-run enterprise. Privately owned Mexican and Spanish companies have just received concessions to operate seven of the twenty-eight railway shops. On the National Railways, management has implemented new productivity incentives and merit-based job advancement policies. Downsizing began. Between 1990 and 1991, twenty thousand of the ninety-two thousand railway workers "voluntarily" retired in preparation for privatization.[93] Early in 1995, the Mexican government announced that the National Railways would be sold off to the highest bidders in order to repay the nation's international debt. The workers will again face foreign managers in the workplace as the struggle for workers' control continues.

Notes

The author would like to thank Alan Knight for his comments on earlier drafts of this chapter.

1. The Mission reconstructed nineteen hundred miles of track on several lines between the United States and Mexico City as well as southbound lines to the Guatemalan border.

2. H. Hill memo, 10 March 1942, National Archives and Record Service, Washington, D.C., Record Group 59, General Records of the Department of State, State Department Correspondence, 1940–44, Decimal Files (hereafter cited as NAW, RG 59), 812.77/1479.

3. Lorena M. Parlee, "The Impact of United States Railroad Unions on Organized Labor and Government Policy in Mexico," *Hispanic American Historical Review* 64, no. 3 (August 1984): 450.

4. *El Ferrocarrilero*, 20 June 1904, as quoted in Parlee, "Impact of United States Railroad Unions," 456.

5. Javier Sánchez Mejorada quoted in Ferrocarriles Nacionales de México, *Breve*

reseña histórica de los Ferrocarriles Mexicanos (Mexico City, 1987), 46. See also Jonathan C. Brown, "Trabajadores nativos y extranjeros en el México Porfiriano," *Siglo XIX: Cuadernos de historia* 3, no. 9 (May–August 1994): 7–49.

6. G. Messersmith to M. Avila Camacho, 13 August 1942, NAW, RG 59, 812.77/1682.

7. R. Kling to O. M. Stevens, 28 December 1942, National Archives and Record Service, Washington, D.C., Record Group 229, General Records, Office of the Coordinator of Inter-American Affairs, (hereafter cited as NAW, RG 229) entry (hereafter cited as e.) 57, b. 755.

8. Ibid; *Unificación Ferroviaria*, July–August 1943; A. Zimmerman to Stevens, 20 May 1943, National Archives and Record Service, Washington, D.C., Record Group 84, Foreign Service Posts of the Department of State, Correspondence, Mexico City Embassy (hereafter cited as NAW, RG 84), 877, b. 403.

9. Amadeo Betancourt, "Problemas de higiene del trabajo en las industrias de jurisdicción federal," *Trabajo y previsión social* 10 (July 1941): 66.

10. J. Rangel to Avila Camacho, 10 July 1943, Archivo General de la Nación, Mexico City, Ramo de Presidentes-Manual Avila Camacho (hereafter cited as AGN-AC), 513/2-2.

11. *Excélsior*, 27 May 1944; Hill to secretary of state, 25 April 1942, NAW, RG 59, 812.77/1484.

12. Meeting minutes, 15 February 1944, NAW, RG 229, e. 64, b. 848; Waterman to secretary of state, Monterrey, 18 February 1943, NAW, RG 84, 877/800.

13. *Ferronales* 15 (June 1944): 12.

14. W. Busser to secretary of state, 8 December 1942, NAW, RG 84, 877, b. 253.

15. J. Campos to Stevens, 26 March 1943, NAW, RG 229, e. 64, b. 819; Stevens to N. Rockefeller, 19 May 1943, NAW, RG 84, 877, b. 403; Stevens to P. Douglas, 24 December 1943, NAW, RG 229, e. 64, b. 819.

16. Ferrocarriles Nacionales de México, *Series estadísticas, 1930–1987* (Mexico City, 1988), 21, 45; *Ferronales* 15 (June 1944): 10.

17. Secretaría de Economía, *Anuario estadístico de los Estados Unidos Mexicanos, 1942* (Mexico City, 1948), 1302–3 (hereafter cited as *Anuario, 1942*); Secretaría de Economía, *Anuario estadístico de los Estados Unidos Mexicanos, 1943–1945* (Mexico City, 1950), 818–19 (hereafter cited as *Anuario, 1943–1945*).

18. Manuel Sotelo Pallares, Interview with author, Aguascalientes, 7 June 1994.

19. Secretaría de Economía, *Anuario, 1942*, 1302–3, and *Anuario, 1943–1945*, 818–19; V. Campa in M. T. de la Peña, "Integración vial y coordinación de transportes," in *Memoria del Segundo Congreso Mexicano de Ciencias Sociales* (Mexico City, 1946), 2:410–12; *Ferronales* 14 (November 1943): 12; *Ferronales* 18 (May 1947): 33.

20. Luciano Cedillo Vázquez, ¡*Vaaamonos!* (Mexico City, 1979), 73–74; Secretaría de Comunicaciones y Obras Públicas, *Estadísticas de los ferrocarriles y tranvías de concesión federal correspondiente al año de 1944*, 201; n.a. to Avila Camacho, 25 March 1944, AGN-AC, 545.2/15, b. 754, f. 9.

21. Elías Palacios Chaires, "Corrido de la cuadrilla sistemal M-15," printed in *Unificación Ferroviaria*, 1 August 1948.

22. Puebla workers to STFRM, 28 February 1945, NAW, RG 229, e. 63, b. 778.

23. *Excélsior*, 5 August 1944; Helming to Stevens, 7 August 1944, NAW, RG 229, e. 64, b. 778, f. 250. These figures are for the National Railways. The percentages are even higher for the railway industry as a whole. See Secretaría de Comunicaciones y Obras Públicas, *Estadísticas, 1944*, 196; Secretaría de Comunicaciones y Obras Públicas, *Estadísticas de los ferrocarriles y tranvías de concesión federal correspondiente al año 1947* (Mexico City, n.d.), 171.

24. Stevens in Fred Linder, *The United States Railway Mission in Mexico* (Washington, D.C., 1946), 14.

25. "Contracto colectivo celebrado entre el Sindicato de los Trabajadores Ferrocarrileros de la República Mexicana y la Administración de los Ferrocarriles Nacionales de México, abril 1937," *Revista Mexicana del Trabajo* 8 (1937): 264; author unknown, 8 May 1942, Archivo General de la Nación, Mexico City, Secretaría de Trabajo y Previsión Social (hereafter cited as AGN-STPS), 6/513(29)/110.

26. *Ferronales* 15 (June 1944): 12; Stevens to M. Ramírez, 6 January 1943, NAW, RG 84, 877, b. 402.

27. *Ferronales* 15 (January 1944): 1.

28. Ibid., 16 (February 1945): 26–27; E. Bishop to G. Rigby, 10 June 1944, NAW, RG 229, e. 64, b. 837.

29. Author unknown, February 1948, AGN-STPS, 5/106.5/58"48"-2/1 and 2.

30. Emma Yanes Rizo, *Vida y muerte de Fidelita: La novia de Acámbaro* (Mexico City, 1991), 174–75.

31. L. Díaz to Ramírez, 13 May 1943, NAW, RG 229, e. 64, b. 820; P. Suárez to J. Franco, 13 May 1943, NAW, RG 229, e. 69, b. 909.

32. See "Progress Report, 1944," NAW, RG 229, e. 57, b. 793; L. Studer to Messersmith, 8 June 1943, NAW, RG 84, b. 531, b. 403.

33. C. Jordon to secretary of state, San Luis Potosí, 27 February 1943, 30 September 1943, NAW, RG 59, 812.00 San Luis Potosí/195, /202.

34. *El Universal*, 20 December 1943.

35. Meeting minutes, 11 and 15 February 1944, NAW, RG 229, e. 64, b. 848.

36. Messersmith to J. Carrigan, 16 December 1945, 27 March 1946, NAW, RG 84, 812.77/12-1645, /3-2746.

37. *Excélsior*, 26 March 1946.

38. *El Porvenir*, 23 and 24 November 1943; *El Norte*, 24 November 1943; *El Universal*, 30 November 1943; Stevens to R. J. de Camp, 29 March 1944, NAW, RG 84, 877, b. 530.

39. Chihuahua workers to U. Tracy, 31 May 1945, NAW, RG 229, e. 63, b. 797, f. 286.

40. Stevens to Kling, 1 September 1943, NAW, RG 229, e. 57, b. 758.

41. Stevens to staff, 30 June 1943, NAW, RG 229, e. 64, b. 817.

42. Stevens to interpreters, 5 July 1943, NAW, RG 84, 877, b. 404; E. V. Vandercook to interpreters, 10 October 1944, NAW, RG 229, e. 63, b. 806.

43. Jesús Bernal Reyes, interview with author, Aguascalientes, 21 July 1994; Kling to Stevens, 28 December 1942, NAW, RG 229, e. 57, b. 755.

44. I. Foreman to N. Arnold, 7 January 1945, NAW, RG 229, e. 57, b. 911.

45. Stevens to A. Ortíz, 11 April 1944, NAW, RG 229, e. 57, b. 761.

46. Arnold to Stevens, 21 April 1944, NAW, RG 229, e. 64, b. 813.

47. Arnold to Stevens, 24 July 1944, NAW, RG 229, e. 57, b. 762.

48. Kling to Stevens, 11 October 1943, NAW, RG 229, e. 57, b. 759; Stevens to Ortíz, 7 June 1944, NAW, RG 229, e. 64, b. 813.

49. *Unificación Ferroviaria*, 15 July 1944, 1 January 1945.

50. Arnold to Stevens, 21 April 1944, NAW, RG 229, e. 57, b. 761; n.a., "Progress Report, July 1945," NAW, RG 229, e. 57, b. 763; n.a., "Progress Report, November 1945," NAW, RG 229, e. 57, b. 766.

51. Stevens to U.S. Congressional Committee, 13 May 1943, NAW, RG 229, e. 53.

52. Ibid.

53. Linder, *United States Railway Mission*, 62; de Camp to J. Luhrsen, 20 May 1944, NAW, RG 59, 812.77/1995; Stevens to Messersmith, 28 April 1944, NAW, RG 229, e. 64, b. 812.

54. Messersmith to secretary of state, 5 February 1945, NAW, RG 59, 812.77/2-545.

55. J. López to Stevens, April 1944, NAW, RG 229, e. 64, b. 812.

56. Lozano to R. Siller, 20 April 1944, NAW, RG 229, e. 64, b. 812.

57. Author unknown, 21 April 1945, MacLean to J. Carrigan, 30 July 1945, NAW, RG 59, 812.77/4-445, 812.77/7-3045.

58. Messersmith to secretary of state, 25 April 1945, NAW, RG 59, 812.77/4-2545; Busser to Messersmith, 13 July 1945, NAW, RG 84, 877, b. 649.

59. Stevens to de Camp, 12 November 1943, NAW, RG 229, e. 63, b. 802.

60. P. Scanlan to Vandercook, 20 September 1944, NAW, RG 229, e. 66, b. 853.

61. Kling to Stevens, 24 August 1944, NAW, RG 229, e. 69, b. 911.

62. Author unknown, 24 October 1944, NAW, RG 229, e. 68, b. 871.

63. Author unknown to Stevens, 19 April 1944, NAW, RG 229, e. 63, b. 806.

64. Jesús Bernal Reyes, interview; Tierra Blanca workers to M. Avila Camacho, 16 February 1943, AGN-AC, 534.4/22.

65. *Unificación Ferroviaria*, April 1942. For an account of the construction of the two steam locomotives, see Yanes Rizo, *Vida y muerte*.

66. Stevens to Rockefeller, n.d., NAW, RG 84, b. 1.

67. *El Universal*, 8 February 1944; Linder to A. Dawson, 28 February 1946, NAW, RG 229, e. 49, b. 699; Vandercook to de Camp, 24 October 1944, NAW, RG 229, e. 68, b. 871.

68. Bateman to Foreign Office, 13 March 1944, Public Records Office, London, Foreign Office General Correspondence (hereafter cited as FO), 371/38310.

69. *El Popular*, 22 March 1944.

70. *Trenistas* to Avila Camacho, 17 December 1943, 21 January 1944, AGN-AC, 432/75, 432/75-3. The cost of living rose from an index of 100 in 1939 to 121 in 1942 and 198 in 1944.

71. Manuel Avila Camacho quoted in n.a., *Avila Camacho y su ideología: ¡La revolución en marcha!* (Mexico City, 1940), 136.

72. Kling to Stevens, 17 August 1944, NAW, RG 229, e. 63, c. 797; *El Popular*, 4, 5, 7 and 8 March 1944; Foreman to Arnold, 7 January 1945, NAW, RG 229, e. 57, b.911.

73. Stevens to Messersmith, 24 February 1944, NAW, RG 84, 877, b. 530.

74. C. E. McAuliffee to Stevens, 2 December 1943, NAW, RG 84, 877, b. 405.

75. Messersmith to secretary of state, 12 February 1943, NAW, RG 59, 812.504/217.

76. Franco to Stevens, 7 October 1943, NAW, RG 84, 877, b. 405, v. 395.

77. Messersmith to Rockefeller, 15 December 1943, NAW, RG 59, 812.77/1910; *El Popular*, 21 May 1944; Workers to Avila Camacho, May 1944, AGN-AC, 542.2/15.

78. By the turn of the century, most U.S. railway companies used the Brown system. It was implemented in Mexico at the insistence of U.S. workers. During the 1920s, the Mexican workers fought hard for its universal application. Marcelo Rodea, *Historia del movimiento obrero ferrocarrilero en México (1890–1943)* (Mexico City, 1944), 137–40.

79. Messersmith to secretary of state, 28 November 1942, Busser to secretary of state, 8 December 1942, NAW, RG 59, 812.77/1725, 812.77/1737; Ramírez to J. Ibarra, 27 November 1942, NAW, RG 84, 850.4, b. 222; STFRM to Avila Camacho, 9 March 1943, Avila Camacho to STFRM, 15 March 1943, AGN-AC, 413/2-2, 513/2.2; *El Universal*, 6 December 1942.

80. *El Popular*, 6 May 1944; STFRM to Ortíz, 18 May 1944, AGN-AC, 545.2/15.

81. *El Popular*, 6 May 1944.

82. C. Stainer to Messersmith, February 1946, NAW, RG 84, b. 1. In 1946, 994 "confidential" employees worked strictly for the administration and did not pay union dues or belong to the union.

83. STFRM to Ortíz, 18 May 1944, AGN-AC, 545.2/15; *El Popular*, 6 May 1944.

84. See the conclusions of a 1936 Mexican congressional investigation cited in Antonio Vera, *La pesadilla ferrocarrilera mexicana* (Mexico City, 1943), 124–25.

85. *El Popular*, 6 May 1944.

86. STFRM to Ortíz, 18 May 1944. AGN-AC, 545.2/15.

87. Jordon to Messersmith, 13 May 1944, NAW, RG 59, 812.5045/1066.

88. Bateman to Foreign Office, 5 June 1944, FO, 371/38310.

89. "Supplement to GG-96," 5 June 1944, AGN-STPS, 9/200 (03)/223.

90. STFRM to Avila Camacho, 9 March 1943, AGN-AC, 513/2-2.

91. Carrigan to Messersmith, 21 June 1945, NAW, RG 84, 812.77/6-2145.

92. *Proceso*, no. 899 (24 January 1994): 42; *El Heraldo de Aguascalientes*, 5 March 1994; *La Jornada*, 1 July 1993.

93. *La Jornada*, 27 August 1992, 15 August 1994.

CHAPTER FOUR

MAINTAINING UNITY

Railway Workers and the

Guatemalan Revolution

MARC CHRISTIAN McLEOD

Since its abrupt termination in 1954, scholars have tried to understand the essential nature of the "Guatemalan revolution." Recent debate has centered on the agrarian reform program carried out by the administration of Jacobo Arbenz from 1952 to 1954 and its subsequent effects on rural society.[1] Other works have documented the role played by international forces during this period—namely the nefarious activities of the U.S. government, whose Central Intelligence Agency organized the overthrow of the elected Arbenz regime.[2] While also analyzing the role of the United States, the recent study by Piero Gleijeses views the revolutionary decade from the perspective of the Guatemalan actors; yet his account focuses on Arbenz himself and on a few national labor leaders in the Communist Party.[3] The question remains to be answered: What role did labor play in the Guatemalan revolution? And, to the extent that we can ascertain it, what influence did the rank-and-file workers have on the course of their country's history from 1944 to 1954?

The existing historiography holds that a small group of communist labor leaders dominated the Guatemalan workers' movement during the revolution—apparently by manipulating an ignorant or apathetic rank and file. Although a "moderate" group of railway workers resisted communist control of their union for several years, the railroaders eventually were "neutralized" by "Communist tactics and propaganda," according to North American commentators.[4] For more than thirty years, these assumptions have gone unchecked. No study has been made of a single union during this period, includ-

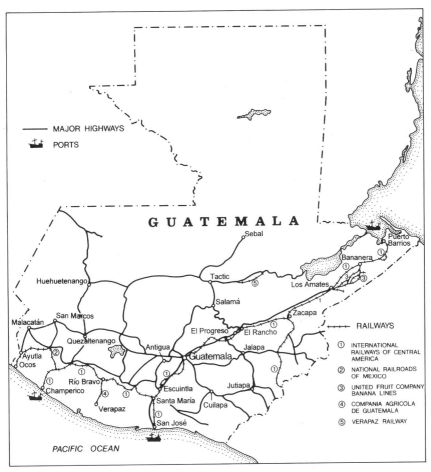

Map 3. *The railways and ports of Guatemala, 1952*

ing that of the railway workers.[5] Yet only by looking closely at internal union dynamics, and the often complex relationship between rank-and-file workers and syndical leaders, can we better understand the nature of the labor movement—and how and why labor influenced and was influenced by the Arévalo and Arbenz governments.

Casting our glance toward Guatemala's railway workers, we see that the rank-and-file *ferrocarrileros* repeatedly sought greater control over their working lives—through wage increases, job security, better working conditions, and control over the work process.[6] Although leaders of the railway union, the Sindicato de Acción y Mejoramiento Ferrocarrilero (SAMF), sometimes acted for ideological and, more likely, nationalistic reasons, they ultimately were responsible to the *samfistas*, as the rank-and-file members were known.

At times, the railway workers even forced the removal of certain national and local union directors. Because they recognized that a unified union offered the best opportunity to achieve their goals, the railroaders waged a constant struggle to maintain unity within the union. Responding to the perceived opening presented by the prolabor governments of Juan José Arévalo and Jacobo Arbenz, the *ferrocarrileros* pressed their own agenda to the level of the state. They also pushed for passage of an agrarian reform law. In so doing, they demonstrated that a desire for national economic development free from foreign control could transcend the cultural and ethnic divisions separating them from rural Guatemalans. Despite being perceived by previous scholars as long-lasting holdouts against communism, the railway workers actually speeded up the pace of change during this period. Thus, in the continuous attempt to extend control over their own lives—through job security, wage increases, better working conditions, and control over the work site—the SAMF rank and file pulled Guatemala along a more revolutionary track.

In the Land of Eternal Tyranny

From independence in 1821 until the eve of revolution in 1944, dictatorial rule characterized the political scene in Guatemala. Just four dictators—Rafael Carrera (1839–65), Justo Rufino Barrios (1871–85), Manuel Estrada Cabrera (1898–1920), and Jorge Ubico (1931–44)—ruled for approximately seventy-five years. The postindependence period also witnessed the integration of Guatemala into the world economy as a coffee and banana exporter.[7] The railroad, incidentally, served as a crucial instrument in this process. Incorporation into the world market involved changes in the social relations of Guatemala. To provide land and labor for large coffee estates, the state passed laws that forced the rural population, consisting primarily of Mayan Indians, off their landholdings and into the rural wage labor force.[8] The middle and urban classes continued to expand during the early twentieth century in conjunction with the growth of the export economy. Brief flirtation with democratic government during the 1920s offered some degree of participation to these sectors in the political life of the country. But the onset of the depression and the precipitous drop in coffee prices on the world market enabled Ubico to step in and begin his period of heavy-handed, brutal rule in 1931. Popular pressure forced Ubico to step down in June 1944 and brought about the fall of his hand-picked successor in October of that year.[9] For the next decade, a period described by one Guatemalan scholar as ten "years of spring in the land of eternal tyranny," Presidents Juan José Arévalo (1945–51) and, especially, Jacobo Arbenz (1951–54) presided over the steady transformation of Guatemalan society.[10]

The early history of the railway workers involved nascent attempts to organize in order to better meet their economic needs.[11] Construction of the railroad itself began in the summer of 1879, when the Guatemala Central Railroad Company, owned by a group of California capitalists, began laying track from Puerto San José to Esquintla. Within the next twenty-five years, a handful of companies oversaw the development of a rail system stretching from Mexico to El Salvador and from the Pacific port of San José to Puerto Barrios on the Atlantic coast. The Guatemala Railway formally consolidated these lines in 1904.[12] One year after the International Railways of Central America (IRCA) assumed control of Guatemala's rail network in April 1912, the railroaders struck for salary increases, albeit unsuccessfully, against their new employer. The discharge of the strike leaders elicited early nationalistic feelings, with an article in the local press calling for the lynching of the "vampires that manage foreign companies."[13] In November 1913, the railroaders formed a mutual aid society.[14] Many *ferrocarrileros* participated in the movement to unseat the dictator Manuel Estrada Cabrera in 1920. Throughout the 1920s, hoping for support from a less repressive state, they continued to seek wage increases and better working conditions, striking four times in the early 1920s to press their demands on the International Railways. From 1931 to 1944, however, the Ubico regime repressed virtually all attempts at worker organization. Only the railway workers managed to maintain a mutual aid society during this period. Then, less than a week after the fall of Ubico, thirty-five *trenistas*, or trainmen, held a general meeting and established statutes for a "true" labor union, the Sindicato de Acción y Mejoramiento Ferrocarrilero (the Union of Railway Worker Action and Improvement, or SAMF). The *ferrocarrileros* would soon take a leading role in the Guatemalan revolution.

Who were the *ferrocarrileros*? Or, stated more pointedly, why study Guatemala's railway workers? First, the industrial census in 1946 identified only 21,234 workers in manufacturing, yet the railroad labor force comprised approximately 5,000 members.[15] Thus, because of their sheer numbers, the *ferrocarrileros* represented more than 20 percent of the country's industrial labor force. More important, the railway workers formed an integral part of Guatemala's "export-production complex." As suggested by Charles Bergquist, we might expect to find that "workers, especially those engaged in production for export, have played a determining role in the modern history of Latin American societies."[16] The railroaders in Guatemala prove to be no exception.

The power of the SAMF stemmed from two main factors: the strategic nature of the railway system and the strong sense of community shared by its members.[17] The smooth functioning of the Guatemalan export economy depended on the transport service provided by the *samfistas*. Of the 850 miles of railway lines in Guatemala, the IRCA controlled and operated 590 of them. The United Fruit Company owned almost all of the remaining track, which connected its plantations at Bananera (near the Atlantic coast) and Tiquisate (on the Pacific coast) with the main IRCA line to Puerto Barrios. The International Railways also owned the pier at this deep water port and operated the terminals at the two other important shipping points, Puerto San José and Champerico (see map 3). Moreover, the IRCA lines ran from San Salvador to the border with Mexico. Thus, Guatemala's rail system served the needs of the entire country and especially, but not merely, the banana company. As the U.S. Central Intelligence Agency noted in 1950, "Few goods can be imported or exported, or moved from one part of the country to the other, without the use of the United Fruit–controlled IRCA of Central America."[18] The *samfistas*, as we shall see, did not hesitate to take advantage of the strategic nature of the railroad industry. Both the Arévalo and Arbenz governments, unwilling and unable to have the transport of essential goods disrupted by labor unrest on the railroads, frequently sided with the SAMF in its disputes with the International Railways.

The existence of an "occupational community" among the railroaders also increased the strength of their union. Railroad workers performed a variety of jobs in many different locations. From a shop mechanic in Guatemala City to a track cleaner near Zacapa, or an engineer on the San José–Esquintla line to a stevedore on the docks of Puerto Barrios, most railway workers affiliated with the SAMF.[19] But how did such a heterogeneous group of individuals find a basis for organization? In identifying the existence of an occupational community among railroad workers in pre-Perón Argentina, Joel Horowitz focuses on their self-perception as an elite, the noneconomic benefits offered by their union, and the closed nature of the workforce.[20] Guatemala's *ferrocarrileros* exhibited the essential characteristics of an occupational community. Most railroaders also shared a common cultural identity as Ladinos (mestizos) in a nation whose population was two-thirds Mayan Indian. Therefore, they found it easy to approach their relationship with the IRCA in a unified fashion through their union. Then, as internal division split the *samfistas* in the early 1950s, the goal of unity—and the attempt to deal with both capital and state as a group—gained more importance than before.

To Watch Over the Interests of the Railroad Workers

In the early years of the Arévalo presidency, the *samfistas* demonstrated the strong belief that they constituted the elite of organized labor. Following the example of the railroaders (and with the active encouragement of the teachers' union, which had formed soon after the SAMF), other workers had organized more than forty labor unions by the end of 1944. These groups formally established the Confederation of Guatemalan Workers. But unity of the labor force did not last. In May 1945, the confederation inaugurated the Escuela Claridad, a school for workers that taught, with the assistance of four members of the Salvadoran Communist Party, labor organization techniques and Marxist-Leninist theory. Dissenting from the focus of Claridad's curriculum and unwilling to share power with the teachers' union, the SAMF resigned from the confederation. Nine other unions soon followed suit. In January 1946, the breakaway unions—representing the majority of the urban industrial proletariat and more than five thousand workers on the Tiquisate plantation of the United Fruit Company—formed a rival labor federation, the Trade Union Federation of Guatemala. Despite repeated overtures and steady progression toward unity, the two labor federations would not formally consolidate until October 1951.

Beginning in the mid-1940s, labor acted virtually alone in lobbying for agrarian reform. The workers called upon the state to expropriate uncultivated land from large estates and to distribute it to rural peasants and wage workers in the form of individual ownership, lifelong usufruct, or cooperative farms. A joint session of the two labor confederations in April 1946 urged labor unity and also vowed to push for agrarian reform.[21] The Second Congress of the Confederation of Guatemalan Workers approved a resolution demanding *reforma agraria* in October of that same year.[22] The *samfista* leadership espoused the cause as well. The First Railroad Convention of Central America and the Caribbean, an October 1946 gathering dominated by the SAMF, identified "the fight against the *latifundistas*" as being of paramount importance. The first point of the railroaders' statement asserted: "The central objective of winning complete national liberation and democracy requires . . . agrarian reform."[23] For the rank-and-file railroaders, however, the primary purpose of their union was to bring them more control over their working lives.

The early SAMF unsuccessfully represented the *ferrocarrileros* in their direct struggle with railroad management over salary demands and other work-related issues. On 2 August 1946, the SAMF presented twelve demands to the International Railways, including that Guatemalan workers, rather than foreigners, be utilized to fill "positions of responsibility"; that regular train crews be allowed to work more than the existing maximum of 208 hours; that extra train crews be guaranteed a minimum of fifteen days' salary for remaining on call; that tickets be collected by auditors rather than conductors; and that the sale of tickets be placed on a commission basis. Clearly, the *samfistas* aspired to greater income and more control over the work site. Yet the IRCA managers refused to comply with their claims. In the face of this intransigence and with no apparent support from the government, the SAMF leaders backed down.[24] Even as late as the middle of 1947, the railway workers were no closer to realizing satisfaction of any of their demands. Unity within the SAMF itself also faced difficulties during the early years of the revolution. Thirty-nine SAMF members resigned from the union in November 1946 to form a rival railroad union. Dissension among the railway workers generated from the suspicion that the SAMF leaders, headed by the charismatic Arturo Morales Cubas, were pilfering union funds and, in general, using their positions for self-serving reasons. "We only want you to watch over the interests of the railroad workers and not to spend the money that we contribute monthly on trips abroad that in no way benefit the workers," wrote one dissenter to the SAMF's executive committee.[25] By the end of 1946, twenty-five more *ferrocarrileros*—mostly from the machine repair shop in Guatemala City—had joined the rival union. According to a U.S. government source, at least five hundred more railroaders, although worried about the possibilities of SAMF retaliation, were also considering such a move.[26]

Yet support for the SAMF leadership remained strong along the line. Fewer than 2 percent of the 5,000 or so *obreros ferroviarios* had split with the union. Moreover, most *samfistas* pursued measures to bring about the dissolution of the rival syndicate. The SAMF local in Esquintla sent a letter bearing more than 130 signatures to the supreme court protesting government authorization of what they termed the "white union."[27] More than 220 workers in Puerto Barrios expressed support for a general strike to force the removal of the dissident laborers, insisting that four foreign managers also leave the railroad. Expressing another concern of the rank and file at the Caribbean port, Alfredo Reyes protested that the union officials had not taken into account the problem of salaries as well.[28] For the leaders of the SAMF, however, the threat to their authority posed by the breakaway syndicate constituted the most pressing concern.

The SAMF directors, in fact, embroiled the IRCA management in the conflict with the rival railroad union. The SAMF threatened a general strike if the company did not terminate employment of the dissident *obreros*. Faced with intransigence, the *samfista* leadership reduced this demand: first, to include only five of the most visible rebel railroaders; then, that the International Railways merely transfer them to posts in neighboring El Salvador. The railroad management refused to concede, so President Arévalo, fearing that "a strike would have very grave consequences for the nation," intervened. The president made clear his position on the dispute: the railway workers "were outside of the law on many different points."[29] Realizing that support from the state would not be forthcoming, the *ferrocarrileros* relented. Only two of the leading union dissidents "voluntarily" resigned from IRCA employment.[30]

Since union activity was not succeeding in satisfying the workers' concerns, it would have made sense for the rank and file to grow sour on the SAMF leadership. Yet morale remained strong. Apparently the railway workers realized that a unified union represented their best chance to elicit concessions from IRCA management. As one *ferrocarrilero* stated at a February 1947 meeting in Zacapa: "It is necessary to demonstrate to the bosses of the company that we are united and always ready to fight for the rights that legally are ours."[31]

To be sure, some rank-and-file *samfistas* attempted to improve their representation within the SAMF. In March 1947, the workers in Puerto San José impeached their local general secretary, who had been absent from several meetings. "In view of the repeated absences by the secretary," said the meeting's minutes, "the decision was made to retire him from the post with all the pleasure with which it was conferred upon him."[32] Two weeks later, a delegate from Esquintla, apparently acting at the behest of the SAMF central executive committee, urged the Pacific port workers to return the former secretary to his post. Rebutted in his attempt, the delegate then tried to call for new elections, to which "all the members said 'NO!, there is no need' for another vote."[33] Against the wishes of the SAMF leadership, the Puerto San José rank and file had taken control of local union affairs. Also in 1947, incidents of individual resistance versus the International Railways took place. In one attempt at sabotage involving the throwing of a railway switch, a passenger train derailed (with no reported injuries).[34] Yet despite sometimes poor union representation, almost all *ferrocarrileros* throughout the country continued to believe that the SAMF would provide them with increased wages, job security, and control over the workplace. Patience paid dividends.

The leadership of the SAMF, acting as directors of the Trade Union Federation of Guatemala and in conjunction with the Confederation of Guatemalan Workers, exhorted Arévalo and some of the more progressive political parties to pass a labor code. As Piero Gleijeses notes, by "using their leverage as the only group that could provide active support as well as votes to the various revolutionary parties, [the workers] achieved significant victories."[35] The new labor code, promulgated on 1 May 1947, provided the Guatemalan working classes with an extensive array of previously unavailable legal rights. The new law confirmed the right to unionize, guaranteed the right to strike, afforded protection from unfair firings, established basic health and safety requirements for the workplace, regulated the employment of women and children, and instituted the forty-eight-hour workweek.[36] Although the SAMF did not act alone in pressing labor's demands on the government, the *ferro-carrileros* lobbied strenuously—primarily through propaganda in the union newspaper—for passage of the labor code. The railway workers certainly bene-fited from the new legal rights bestowed on Guatemala's working population.

The more radical leaders of the SAMF, headed by Manuel Pinto Usaga, soon parlayed the state's support for labor into concessions from the company. Although the Communist Party remained illegal in Guatemala, certain na-tional labor leaders had begun organizing and meeting in secret. A handful of *samfistas*, most notably Pinto Usaga, considered themselves communist as well. Beginning in the second half of 1947, these SAMF leaders stepped up pressure on the railroad to sign a collective contract governing relations be-tween the International Railways and its SAMF employees. They waged an active campaign, characterized by the distribution of massive amounts of propaganda and anti-IRCA literature, to prepare the railway workers for a strike against the company.[37] Threatening to bring the contract dispute before the labor tribunals, the *obreros ferroviarios* were prepared to test the value of the new labor code. The SAMF secretary of propaganda proclaimed: "We will make use of all the rights bestowed upon us by the laws."[38] Moreover, the procommunist SAMF leaders obtained a promise of support from the Con-federation of Guatemalan Workers and the minister of economy and labor in the event of a strike. On 16 February 1948 the railway workers began a series of work stoppages. The *ferrocarrileros* demanded primarily that management answer their proposal for a collective contract. Support for the stoppages came from every department of the rail system.[39] Faced with a SAMF leadership backed by the rank and file as well as by the state, the International Railways relented and, on 5 May 1948, signed the first collective labor contract in Guatemalan history.

The collective contract between the union and the railroad company ad-dressed a multitude of concerns held by the *ferrocarrileros*. Topics included rules governing the hiring and firing of workers; regulation of promotions; salaries, rest days, and vacations; overtime and pay for extra work; time sched-ules; and job descriptions.[40] The *pacto colectivo* put into writing previously understood aspects of management-labor relations and, more important, of-fered the railway workers a greater degree of control over their working lives. As a result, the procommunist leaders of the SAMF enjoyed a clear victory in the June 1948 union elections. The union leaders also elicited wage increases, twenty days of annual vacation, and free travel passes on the railroad from IRCA management in the following year.[41] But communist guidance of the *samfistas* would not last.

The Revolution in Danger

The leftward drift of the SAMF paralleled—and influenced—changes in the national political scene. The assassination of Col. Francisco Arana is a noteworthy case in point.[42] Arana had been one of the military heroes of the October 1944 uprising that ended Guatemala's latest spell of dictatorial rule. Serving as chief of the armed forces for the Arévalo administration, he harbored desires to become president in the elections of November 1950. By 1949, however, Arana faced opposition from the revolutionary parties and the labor movement. He convinced himself that a putsch would be his only path to the presidency.

The actions of the powerful railroad union in particular supported Arana's belief in the need for a *golpe de estado*. The SAMF's political committee, organized in late 1948, had pledged support for Arana's principal opponent, Minister of Defense Jacobo Arbenz, in April 1949. As the presidential election neared, the political committee asserted, "The revolution is in danger; all workers have to vote for Col. Jacobo Arbenz Guzmán."[43] More important, a series of public demonstrations by *ferrocarrileros* responding to their legal battle with the International Railways forced Arana's hand. For more than a year, the union and the company had struggled over the specifics of their collective pact. The management had steadfastly rejected proposed reforms "such as those relating to increase in salaries, those which tend[ed] to place the management of the Company in the hands of the workers, [and] those which contain[ed] the closed shop."[44] Seeking greater income and control over the work process, the *samfistas* sought recourse in the Guatemalan courts. SAMF leaders, backed by other urban unions, repeatedly assembled outside the Palace of Justice, threatening a general strike should the court rule in favor of the company. Accused of manipulating the justice system, one railroader replied, "It's the IRCA boys that can coerce the magistrates, with their money."[45]

The SAMF manifestation reached new heights on 15 July. In their dispute with the company, union leaders remained firm. "We don't want to settle on a friendly basis," they said, "for we could not then be loyal to our comrades." But the *ferrocarrilero* leaders also targeted the U.S. government—not just a U.S. company—for attack. "In Guatemala the Guatemalans give orders and not the *gringos*," proclaimed one SAMF leader. "We don't accept orders from anyone, much less from the Department of State of North America."[46] Already worried about the growing strength of the labor movement, conservative opponents of the Arévalo administration became unnerved by the public demonstrations held by the railroaders.

On 18 July 1949, Colonel Arana ordered President Arévalo to resign. That same day, government supporters killed Arana. In the uprising that followed his death, opposition forces in Guatemala City, composed predominately of military personnel who backed the deceased colonel, attempted to overthrow the government of Arévalo. Civilian volunteers, armed by loyal officers of the armed forces, provided critical support in putting down the rebellion. Many *ferrocarrileros* came to the defense of the government. As a contemporary observer noted, the "SAMF was probably more responsible than any other civilian organization in actively suppressing the military revolt of July, 1949."[47] The U.S. Congress of Industrial Organizations also noted that "the decisive participation of the workers had been an important factor in the triumph of the democratic forces that support[ed] the government of President Arévalo."[48] The railroaders in Esquintla offered financial assistance to union leader José Luis Caceros, who suffered a hand wound when leading more than two hundred *samfistas* during the conflict in the capital.[49] Backing for the elected administration of Arévalo came from throughout the railway lines. This support opened the door for General Arbenz to assume the presidency two years later; it also set the stage for communist labor leaders to move into the national spotlight.

The rise of the Communist Party in Guatemala led to an increase in turmoil within the railroad union. The formation and public appearance of the Guatemalan Communist Party occurred in late 1949. The first issue of the party's weekly paper appeared on 21 June 1950.[50] During this preelection period, the Guatemalan public became aware of the close ties existing between certain top communist leaders and the future president, Jacobo Arbenz. Increased communist influence both in national politics and within the union concerned many *ferrocarrileros*. Some railway workers clearly were moved by deep-felt anticommunist feelings; the majority worried that their relatively high wages and privileged position vis-à-vis the rest of the laboring population would diminish if political turmoil impinged upon Guatemala's agro-export economy. The deteriorating economic position of the railroaders only aggravated their concerns.

By the end of the 1940s, export production—and, hence, railway transport—was declining. The amount of freight carried by the railroad dropped, owing mostly to a decrease in banana shipments. Railroad transport of bananas for export declined from 389.9 million tons in 1947 to only 132.8 million tons in the first half of 1950.[51] While the reduction in freight threatened the job security and income of all railway workers, the stevedores at Puerto Barrios suffered the most. The *samfistas* in Barrios bore the brunt of the drop in banana transport, as the Atlantic port accounted for more than 77 percent of

Guatemala's exports.[52] Dockworkers did not work on salary but, rather, received wages for work actually performed; however, now they were working less and less. Railway laborers also faced a decline in real wages because of the increasing cost of living in the late 1940s. Between January 1943 and August 1950, consumer prices in the capital for twenty-one basic goods had risen by more than 160 percent.[53] Economic pressures threatened to divide the rank and file against each other. In September 1949, mechanics in Esquintla sent a letter to the superintendent of the machine shop, complaining, "The salary they earn is peanuts and doesn't compare to what workers in the same branch in Guatemala [City] earn."[54] Faced with an increasingly uncertain economic future, the rank-and-file *ferrocarrileros* turned to their union for help.

However, the communist leaders of the SAMF had focused their attention elsewhere. As the 1940s came to a close, the SAMF leadership displayed an increasing concern with ideological issues and international matters. From 1948 to mid-1950, the slant of the railroad union newspaper, the *SAMF*, leaned more and more toward the left. Anti-imperialist, anti–United States themes became commonplace.[55] Not surprisingly, the radical *ferrocarrilero* leadership continued calling for land reform. An October 1949 editorial in *SAMF* insisted that "agrarian reform should be a fact."[56] The procommunist SAMF leaders also encouraged the Trade Union Federation of Guatemala's affiliation with the Marxist-oriented Confederation of Workers of Latin America, led by Vicente Lombardo Toledano, and the World Federation of Trade Unions in January 1950. An April article and May Day speech by SAMF leader Manuel Pinto Usaga in 1949 reached an extreme of procommunist, anti–U.S. rhetoric.[57] Such demonstrations of radicalism did not, in and of themselves, alienate the *ferrocarrilero* rank and file from their communist directors. But the railway workers were becoming disillusioned with a leadership that seemed more concerned with promoting the distant notion of international working-class unity over the welfare of the *samfistas* themselves. Events in Puerto Barrios in August 1950 tipped the balance.

In August 1950, 256 members of the Syndicate of Independent Banana Loaders in the Atlantic coast port petitioned the International Railways for a fixed minimum wage. These stevedores who worked non–United Fruit vessels received payment for each bunch that they carried from rail car to ship's hold. Since banana transport had decreased to approximately one-tenth of the volume carried in 1947, these dockworkers were finding themselves in precarious financial straits. Hoping to improve the situation of the independent loaders, the central leadership of the SAMF added their names to the railroad union's list of emergency employees available for handling general cargo passing through the port. The union leaders were opening dock work to nonunion workers, but their names did not remain on the roster for very long. Almost immediately, those SAMF workers already on the docks objected strenuously, and their leaders dropped the plan to assist nonunion workers.[58] At the same time, more than 1,000 workers signed a letter of complaint to the inspector general of labor that IRCA plans for mechanizing the freight-handling system at Barrios would reduce the amount of jobs available to railway workers.[59] Ignoring their leaders' calls to aid the stevedores, the rank-and-file *samfistas* had chosen instead to press their own claims for job security. The *ferro-carrileros* also decided that it was time to change the union leadership.

The expulsion of Pinto Usaga and other communist leaders began at an animated general meeting held in September 1950. Morales Cubas and the more pragmatic leaders of the SAMF accused their more radical counterparts of ignoring the interests of the railroaders. What apparently began as a power struggle between union leaders soon blossomed into a more widespread effort to combat communist influence within the union. It soon became clear that "many persons within the SAMF wish[ed] to rid themselves of a leadership which seem[ed] to be more concerned with international than with union problems."[60] The charges extended into attacks on the most important pro-communist figure, Pinto Usaga. In the course of defending himself, Pinto Usaga engaged in heated debate with members of the Morales Cubas clique. Because "spirits were rather overheated," the local police had to restore order to the meeting. More than seven hundred *samfistas* ultimately signed a letter demanding that three of the *"divisionistas"*—Pinto Usaga not included—be expelled from the IRCA.[61]

The anticommunist backlash had only just begun. In a second special assembly in September, the Commission of Honor and Justice of the SAMF voted to expel Pinto Usaga and the other three important communist leaders from the union. More than three hundred *samfistas* also signed a petition urging that Pinto Usaga also be removed as secretary-general of the Trade Union Federation of Guatemala. In particular, the stevedores in Puerto Barrios, whose economic security was most threatened by the drop in banana transport, lambasted "the traitor" Pinto Usaga and "the puppets" who supported him.[62] Finally, the union requested that the four expelled workers be dismissed by the railroad.[63] Once again, the International Railways found itself embroiled in an internal dispute among the *obreros ferroviarios*. On 4 October, hoping to convince the IRCA to comply with their demand, the workers in the machine shop in the capital initiated a one-hour work stoppage. The number of workers participating in the hour-long strikes grew rapidly over the next few days, reaching more than thirty-five hundred on 7 October. Support for the daily disruptions came from nearly every *samfista*, and consequently the IRCA was prepared to let the inspector general of labor decide the matter. The railway workers rejected the labor tribunal's first decision, which called for three-month suspensions of the four communists without pay.[64] On 19 October, the inspector general proposed that these four workers be discharged from the railroad, with the union and the company sharing the cost of their severance pay. Two days later, the *ferrocarrileros* voted to accept this resolution. Why did the railway workers go to the extreme of launching mass work stoppages to settle an internal union dispute? "It may well be that the great majority of those in revolt against the pro-Communist control were not concerned with it as an undesirable form of society," noted a State Department analyst, "but with it as a distant and poorly understood objective to which the immediate interests of the labor union were being subordinated."[65]

While it is not clear as to who initiated the efforts to expel Pinto Usaga and the other communist leaders, the attempt surely found overwhelming support throughout the entire railway line. The SAMF rank and file had brought about rapid change in the upper echelons of the union hierarchy in order to satisfy their own concerns.

Through Unity and State Support

In the early 1950s, Guatemala's *ferrocarrileros* searched for unity among themselves. As a scholar studying the labor movement in general noted in 1950: "The need for solidarity is urgent."[66] The union leaders' yearning for unity stemmed, in part, from pragmatism. In order to best represent the interests of the rank-and-file railroader—and, thus, remain in a position of power within the SAMF—union directors required worker harmony. The rank and file, for their part, comprehended the advantages of representation by a strong, unified SAMF in pursuing their demands against the railroad. Moreover, recognizing that the rise of an avid nationalist to the presidency offered greater opportunities for positive alliance with the state, Guatemala's *ferrocarrileros* attempted to enlist governmental assistance in their struggle for control. In the Arbenz years, therefore, the railway workers fought simultaneously on two fronts: for internal unity and for external state support.

Although Pinto Usaga and his communist counterparts never regained control of (or even membership in) the SAMF, internal turmoil continued unabated. The *samfistas* remained divided between the Center-Left, or those espousing unification of the entire Guatemalan labor movement and active support for Arbenz's reform program, and the Center-Right, led by Morales Cubas, who felt that the SAMF should remain independent in its quest to improve the lives of the railroaders.[67] Although the Center-Left recognized the importance of solidarity with the labor movement as well as the Arbenz government, it certainly did not espouse the communist beliefs held by the defeated Pinto Usaga faction. Both the Center-Left and Center-Right attempted to depoliticize their images. The SAMF executive committee, through the union newspaper and legal political arm of the organization, the Railroad Political Committee, issued statements proclaiming that the railroad union was neither anticommunist nor communist but democratic.[68] Morales Cubas, who enjoyed a substantial following among the rank and file and maintained control over the SAMF consumer cooperative, asserted, "I am not with the communists, but neither am I with the reactionaries."[69] Such apparently similar messages obscure the extent of the differences racking the SAMF.

Attesting to the level of internecine struggle, the Center-Left union leadership coupled its moderate self-portrayal with a call for *ferrocarrilero* solidarity. Perhaps most telling, in the 28 July 1951 issue of *SAMF*, the usual slogan on the masthead—"For the dignity and defense of the railway worker"—included an additional phrase: "Let's maintain the unity of our conglomerate." Whereas the pages of *SAMF* in the late 1940s were sprinkled with anti-imperialist sayings, exhortations toward syndical unity now covered the union newspaper. "Todos hacia la unidad del SAMF" and "¡Manténgamos la unidad!" appeared frequently. In addition to these public overtures toward worker harmony, the SAMF directors tried to strengthen the democratic nature of their organization. The Center-Left leaders urged all railway workers to attend union meetings and voice their opinions. In September 1951, members of the SAMF central executive committee, insisting that union decisions "must move from below to above," traversed the railway lines in an effort "to ascertain the opinion of each and every one" of the *obreros ferroviarios*.[70] Yet without satisfying the demands and concerns of the *samfistas*, calls for unity and improved communication would have accomplished very little.

Coincidental with the internecine struggle within the SAMF, labor activity by the railway workers increased during the early 1950s as union leaders competed for the allegiance of the rank and file. Not surprisingly, the *ferrocarrileros* turned to the state for help in their conflicts with the International Railways. The first concern of the railroaders after the union purge stemmed from the IRCA plan to put into operation six new diesel locomotives. Imported into the country in April 1950, the new engines were capable of traveling three times as fast as a steam engine and could be operated by only one engineer. The railroaders feared that there was "no doubt that [the diesel locomotives] would cause a scarcity of work, especially among the *trenistas*," and stopped running them at the end of May.[71] Because the company hesitated in reaching an agreement with the *samfistas* over use of the diesel engines, the SAMF sought support directly from President Arévalo. The inspector general of labor ordered the new locomotives to be returned to service but under the following conditions: that no workers be dismissed; that diesel train crews receive a 70 percent salary increase; and that foreign experts in the operation and repair of diesel engines be replaced as soon as Guatemalans were capable of doing the work. In January 1951, a SAMF general assembly voted to accept these conditions. Tired of seeing its $1.5 million investment sitting idle, the International Railways also agreed to these stipulations.[72] With conditions favorable to most of the railway workers, the diesel locomotives began running again in February.

Yet not all *ferrocarrileros* were satisfied with the agreement. More than five hundred conductors and brakemen protested the agreement, as they did not receive the wage increases offered to the firemen and engineers. The unsatisfied trainmen claimed that the new engines pulled a greater number of cars, resulting in a twofold increase in work and responsibilities for all those who worked on the trains. The union leadership blamed the "foreign persons and enemies agitating" among the railroaders.[73] Clearly, however, the complaining *trenistas* needed no instigation. They were acting to satisfy their desire for a higher income commensurate with their increased workload.

Relations between the SAMF and the International Railways did not calm down. In response to the dismissal of seven employees for suspected theft, workers in Puerto Barrios initiated a strike in April 1951. The Barrios *samfistas*, claiming that they were "not disposed to put up with foreigners" who came to their fatherland "to tread on the honor of Guatemalans," called for reinstatement of the fired workers and the removal of three local IRCA managers.[74] The spontaneous strike spread to Zacapa the following day; within two days, a general strike paralyzed the entire railroad. The expanded workers' demands included reinstatement of fifteen recently discharged *samfistas*; dismissal of six IRCA supervisors; compliance with a recent labor court decision awarding extra overtime pay to most *trenistas*; and full pay for strike days not worked. The Guatemalan government, through the mediation of the minister of economy and labor and of President Arbenz himself, urged an end to the strike at the end of April. Bending to government pressure, the IRCA consented to a settlement favorable to the workers.[75]

The April 1951 strike provides an outstanding example of the rank-and-file *ferrocarrileros*' ability to press their demands against the International Railways even to the level of the state. U.S. State Department analysts were only partially correct in asserting that "the lack of importance of the demands" suggested that they did not "reflect the real purpose of the strike," which was to "force President Arbenz to align himself definitely with the leftist labor."[76] After the strike had "spread like dynamite throughout the entire rail system," the SAMF leadership, as well as both labor confederations and at least two political parties supporting the railroaders, did view the conflict as a means to test the new president's commitment to labor.[77] To the railway workers in Barrios who started the strike, however, the issue of worker dismissal—of job security—was of the utmost importance. That foreign managers had ordered the layoffs only heightened their quest for dignity. When additional demands were included, the great majority of *ferrocarrileros* wholeheartedly backed the strike effort. The *samfistas* had struck successfully for greater control over their working lives—job security, wages, and workplace control. At the same time, the SAMF, headed by the Center-Left faction but still racked by internal division, forced Arbenz to commit his support to the labor movement in general.

Two months later, in June 1951, the *ferrocarrileros* once again threatened to strike. The dispute centered on the prolonged disagreement over the amount of overtime pay the IRCA owed its employees. The general assembly over-whelmingly approved a resolution to strike again over the issue of wages. However, the union agreed to call off the strike and allow management to exhaust its recourses in the Guatemalan court system. The *ferrocarrileros'* confidence in the government paid off. On 1 September, the International Railways accepted the Second Labor Court's decision awarding the railway workers overtime pay at their desired rate.[78]

Encouraged by repeated success—and repeated support from the national government—the *samfistas* struck again in November 1951. During most of the month, railway workers throughout the system participated in daily half-hour to hour-long work stoppages. Their demands included reinstatement of twenty-one men discharged for disciplinary reasons and removal of one of the IRCA vice presidents. The *ferrocarrileros* considered the first demand most important. The firing of any IRCA employee threatened the job security of all railroad workers. "We will defend the employment of our associates," one union leader to proclaimed, "so that all *samfistas* can say that 'our work is guaranteed.'"[79] On this occasion, government intervention was less favorable to the workers. The state upheld the dismissals as justified.[80] Nevertheless, throughout 1951, the *ferrocarrileros* had fared well in the struggle with the International Railways.

The SAMF leadership was not so fortunate in maintaining syndical unity. Although the Center-Left faction had won the July 1951 union elections, a number of dissatisfied railroaders challenged the legality of the open ballot vote. At least sixty-five *obreros* resigned from the SAMF in protest.[81] The

Guatemalan railway workers on strike, 1951. (Photo from SAMF *[newspaper of the railway workers' union], 15 December 1951)*

Zacapa *samfistas*, in particular, continued to support the losing candidate, Víctor Merlos, who enjoyed "great popularity among the rank-and-file members of the SAMF because of his fight over the [previous] six years against the controlling group" in the union.[82] Although the Department of Labor confirmed the legality of the elections, grumbling within the SAMF ranks continued. In order to quell the unrest, President Arbenz intervened in August, declaring the vote legal and stipulating that all future elections would employ the secret ballot.[83] Disunity persisted, despite the president's efforts.

In late 1951 and 1952, divisions among the *samfistas* threatened to split the union apart. The most radical members of the SAMF had been purged in late 1950, but many *ferrocarrileros* continued to decry the dangers of communist influence within the union and within society in general. The October 1951 merger of the two national labor federations into the General Confederation of Workers of Guatemala, headed by the openly communist labor leader Víctor Manuel Gutiérrez, concerned many *samfistas*.[84] An increase in labor agitation did not assuage their fears. In just two years—from 1949 to 1951—the number of labor disputes brought before the inspector general of labor by all types of workers had more than doubled, from 4,016 to 8,703 cases.[85] The major Guatemala City daily, *El Imparcial*, had complained that "the recrudescence of workers' strikes" since Arbenz came to power did "not have parallel in [the country's] contemporary history."[86]

Increased social upheaval worried some *samfistas* as well. The SAMF local in Puerto Barrios in 1952 forced the resignation of its secretary-general and the entire executive committee for "subordinating union interests to those of the Communist party."[87] The locals in Barrios, Esquintla, and Zacapa, as well as a substantial number of union members in the capital, temporarily aligned themselves with a rump general executive committee seated in the Atlantic coast port. Sensing widespread support within the SAMF as a whole, the Center-Right group composed of Morales Cubas backers agreed to disband prior to the union elections in June 1952. The perceived need for *ferrocarrilero* fellowship thus remained strong. Despite a low voter turnout for the midterm elections, the Center-Right won easily—1,321 to 720 votes.[88] It seemed poised to play a more prominent role in guiding the *samfistas* in their quest for job security, wage hikes, and work site control. But greed intervened.

The second half of 1952 witnessed the explosive conclusion to the long-running sagas of two SAMF economic endeavors: the Consumer Cooperative and Condetsa. The former, founded in 1945, bought goods wholesale, warehoused them in the capital and elsewhere along the railroad line, and sold them to union members at supposedly discount prices. Condetsa was a former IRCA-owned trucking company, purchased in 1945 by a group composed of railway stockholders. Both organizations were operated by Morales Cubas and the faction opposed to SAMF unification with the rest of the labor movement; both entities had a long history of unreported finances and suspected economic mismanagement, embezzlement, and fraud.[89] Railway workers in Esquintla and, to a lesser extent, in Puerto Barrios had frequently complained about the "poor management" of the cooperative and the high prices it charged.[90] By 1952, suspicion had given way to certainty. Condetsa declared bankruptcy in April 1952. Two months later news spread that more than 100,000 *quetzales* ($100,000) had disappeared from the cooperative. Railroaders throughout the line joined a new group called the United Front of Railroad Forces, which had been formed "to carry out the purification of opportunism in the ranks of the workers [and] to give our vote to the new men who ought to manage our sacred interests so vilely squandered by dishonest directors."[91] In September 1952, the government appointed an intervenor to take over the cooperative and investigate its shady financial past, thus marking the virtual end of Morales Cubas's political career. A public auction of the remaining goods in March 1953 set the stage for the final defeat of the Center-Right faction within the SAMF. A letter to the editor in a March issue of *SAMF* testified to the mood of the *ferrocarrileros*, claiming that Condetsa and the cooperative were "two brothers born under the same evil sign . . . who had been the cause of such severe headaches for more than one *samfista*."[92] Not surprisingly, the June 1953 union elections witnessed the sound defeat of the Morales Cubas slate, 2,008 to 1,024 votes.

After more than two and a half years of serious internal discord, the *ferro-carrileros* finally were able to regroup. Union leadership rested firmly in the hands of the Center-Left—those *samfistas* who urged alliance with the entire labor movement as well as with the state. In large part, the railroaders recognized that their struggle for workers' control depended on the future of the Arbenz administration. "The majority of the *compañeros ferrocarrileros* [are] convinced that our participation in the ranks of the [national labor confederation] is most important," said one SAMF leader, "since with it we help to maintain not only the unity of the working class but also the endurance of the Revolution."[93] For others, the desire to maintain harmony within their occupational community—so as to better pursue their struggle with IRCA management—led to the cessation of intrasyndical conflict. As rank-and-file worker Juan Morales opined after the July 1953 union elections, "It is very beautiful to be totally united. . . . If any difficulty happened in the past it was undoubtedly because [some railroaders] were in a bad mood because of too much sun, but these things happen and one cannot take them very seriously."[94] These sentiments attest to the fact that the *ferrocarrileros* stood united behind their Center-Left directors. Yet within a year, the SAMF leaders themselves would be out of power. In June 1954, the United States government engineered the overthrow of President Arbenz primarily because of the Guatemalan revolution's program of agrarian reform, in which the railway workers played a large part.

The Importunate Need for Agrarian Reform

Support for agrarian reform by the leaders of the railway workers union had increased dramatically in the first half of 1952. Public bulletins and *SAMF* editorials stressed the urgent need for land redistribution.[95] The Center-Left union leadership contended that agrarian reform would create a relatively wealthier peasantry who would consume more, thereby stimulating national industrial production and resulting in increased wages and employment opportunities. Organized labor in general argued for agrarian reform for other reasons as well. Leaders of the General Confederation of Workers of Guatemala hoped that administration of a land reform program would be overseen by their federation, which already had established ties in the countryside, thus strengthening its power on the national political scene. Albeit to a lesser degree, the SAMF leaders also expected similar opportunities.[96] Moreover, land reform and rural organization threatened to erode the power of Guate-

118 • *Marc Christian McLeod* •

mala's landed elites, one of organized labor's strongest political rivals. Decree 900, the Agrarian Reform Law, was proposed by Arbenz in May 1952 and became law in June of that same year.

The *samfistas* specifically, however, had reason to oppose the proposal for land reform. Any decline in export production, such as that threatened by enactment of agrarian reform, would limit opportunities for work on the railroad. Moreover, ethnic differences existed between the *ferrocarrileros* and the intended direct beneficiaries of agrarian reform—the smallholders and wage earners in the countryside. The overwhelmingly Ladino railway workers claimed mixed European-Mayan ancestry, spoke Spanish, and held a world-view oriented toward the urban centers and national life. The campesinos who made up the primarily indigenous rural population, on the other hand, tended to speak a Mayan dialect, wear traditional clothing, and retain close ties to village communities. With an attitude of superiority even toward the rest of the Ladino labor movement, the railroaders must have looked in conde-scension upon the indigenous population concentrated in the highlands of western Guatemala.[97] Why, then, did the rank-and-file railway workers not protest when their leaders repeatedly sang the praises of agrarian reform?

It seems quite plausible that the *ferrocarrileros* also desired agrarian reform to promote increased economic opportunity in the countryside, thus decreas-ing urban migration and reducing competition for scarce industrial jobs. Not surprisingly, the railway workers never publicly expressed this particular rea-son. But by the late 1940s, long-standing vagrancy laws were no longer en-forced by the Arévalo government, thus enabling the rural population to move freely about the country, especially to Guatemala City. Moreover, population growth and years of soil erosion prohibited many campesinos from surviving off the land.[98] Responding to increased rural-to-urban migration, Guatemala's *obreros ferroviarios* may have promoted agrarian reform in order to keep the peasants on the land and to satisfy their own concerns about job security.

More important, however, the railroaders seem to have been motivated by a sense of nationalism. Years of struggle with their U.S. employers, coupled with their recent backing of the Arbenz administration, had convinced most rail-way workers of the need to pursue national economic development indepen-dent of the interests of foreign capitalists. The *ferrocarrileros* displayed a high degree of economic nationalism and even supported construction of a road to Puerto Barrios that would serve as an alternative form of transport free from foreign control yet threaten the critical position of the railway workers in Guatemala's export economy. Most railroaders had come to agree that only through land reform would their country achieve "national liberation and democracy," as their leaders had pronounced back in 1946. The extensive nature of the railroad system, moreover, had brought *ferrocarrileros* into daily contact with rural Guatemala, where campesino organizing in San Marcos and elsewhere must have demonstrated to industrial workers the desirability and feasibility of land redistribution.[99] Indeed, the railway workers advocated agrarian reform to serve their own interests, primarily because their concerns had become linked by the early 1950s with those of the broader national revolution. Yet support for land reform backfired.

By the end of June 1954, the success of the land reform program of the Guatemalan revolution brought about its own demise. In less then two years, the agrarian reform program had expropriated more than one million *manzanas* (one *manzana* equals approximately 1.65 acres) of uncultivated land and had benefited almost half a million Guatemalans, or more than one-sixth of the entire population. Perhaps more important, the law claimed the vast majority of United Fruit's landholdings: 234,000 acres of unworked land at the 295,000-acre Tiquisate plantation and 173,000 acres of idle land at the 253,000-acre Bananera site. Along with the fears engendered by the Cold War, this large-scale expropriation of the fruit company's property ultimately convinced the administration of President Eisenhower to direct the overthrow of the popularly elected Arbenz government. Internal opposition led by large landholders, merchants, the Catholic Church, and some members of the armed forces set the stage for the success of the counterrevolution. With the complicity of these groups angered by Arbenz's prolabor stance and agrarian reform measures, the U.S. government placed Col. Carlos Castillo Armas in power in August 1954. The armed forces have ruled—either directly or, more recently, indirectly—the country ever since. A "culture of fear" in which "violence, torture, and death are the final arbiters," writes Piero Gleijeses, has characterized Guatemalan society.[100] The workers could no longer turn to the state for support; the military again backed the employers.[101]

Conclusion

From 1944 to 1954, however, the *ferrocarrilero* rank and file enjoyed repeated success in struggling with the International Railways. Recognizing the importance of union representation, the railway workers influenced, and sometimes even removed, union leaders. The railroaders did not withstand communist advances only to succumb eventually to communism, as the accepted historiography contends. Rather, in the early 1950s, the railway workers settled on a Center-Left leadership to direct their struggle for control. Yet even under Center-Left leadership, the *ferrocarrileros* raised their struggle into the larger political arena and advanced the revolutionary project of national development. As demonstrated by their actions both before and after Colonel Arana's death in July 1949, the pressure they placed on President Arbenz in April 1951, and their continuous support for agrarian reform, Guatemala's railroad workers increased the pace and extent of social transformation throughout this period. The combined force of the U.S. government and Guatemalan elites in mid-1954, however, prevented the *ferrocarrileros* from halting the derailment of the Guatemalan revolution.

Yet the struggle for workers' control did continue. Immediately after Castillo Armas's coup, the International Railways began a program of "arbitrary, large scale dismissals" of railway workers suspected of "engaging in any sort of union activity."[102] The SAMF remained united, however, and the *ferrocarrileros* still attempted to strike to satisfy their economic concerns. In 1957, the railroaders sought a 50 percent wage increase and other fringe benefits. Nine years later, the *samfistas* tried to strike when the IRCA refused to pay Christmas bonuses that were required by law. Yet in both cases the military intervened to end the strikes.[103] The railway workers no longer could count on support from a prolabor state. Furthermore, the railroaders ceased to be such a critical element in the smooth functioning of the Guatemalan export economy. The strategic nature of the railroad, whose rolling stock and other infrastructure were already in a state of deterioration during the revolution, declined upon completion of the highway to Puerto Barrios in 1959. In the late 1960s, the International Railways sold its weakened holdings to the Guatemalan government. The railway workers have never enjoyed as much control over their working lives as they did during the revolution.

Notes

The author would like to thank Jeffrey L. Gould and Virginia Garrard Burnett for their advice regarding this chapter.

1. See Jim Handy, *Revolution in the Countryside: Rural Conflict and Agrarian Reform in Guatemala, 1944–1954* (Chapel Hill, 1994); Cindy Forster, "The Time of 'Freedom': San Marcos Coffee Workers and the Radicalization of the Guatemalan National Revolution, 1944–1954," *Radical History Review* 58 (Winter 1994): 35–78; Carol Smith, "Local History in Global Context: Social and Economic Transitions in Western Guatemala," *Contemporary Studies in Society and History* 26, no. 2 (1984): 193–228; Edelberto Torres-Rivas, "Crisis y coyuntura crítica: La caída de Arbenz y los contratiempos de la revolución burguesa," *Revista Mexicana de Sociología* 41, no. 1 (January–March 1979): 297–323; Robert Wasserstrom, "Revolution in Guatemala: Peasants and Politics under the Arbenz Government," *Contemporary Studies in Society and History* 17, no. 4 (1975): 443–78.

2. Richard H. Immerman, *The CIA in Guatemala: The Foreign Policy of Intervention* (Austin, 1982); Stephen Schlesinger and Stephen Kinzer, *Bitter Fruit: The Untold Story of the American Coup in Guatemala* (New York, 1982); José M. Aybar de Soto, *Dependency and Intervention: The Case of Guatemala in 1954* (Boulder, Colo., 1978).

3. Piero Gleijeses, *Shattered Hope: The Guatemalan Revolution and the United States, 1944–1954* (Princeton, N.J., 1991).

4. See Ronald M. Schneider, *Communism in Guatemala, 1944–1954*, 2d ed. (1958; New York, 1979), esp. 171–84; Robert J. Alexander, *Communism in Latin America* (New Brunswick, N.J., 1957), 350–64; Daniel James, *Red Design for the Americas: Guatemalan Prelude* (New York, 1954); Edwin Bishop, "The Guatemalan Labor Movement: 1944–1959" (Ph.D. diss., University of Wisconsin, 1959); Archer C. Bush, "Organized Labor in Guatemala, 1944–1949: A Case Study of an Adolescent Labor Movement in an Underdeveloped Country," Colgate University, Latin American Seminar Reports No. 2, 1950; R. L. Woodward Jr., "Octubre: Communist Appeal to the Urban Labor Force of Guatemala, 1950–1953," *Journal of Inter-American Studies* 4, no. 3 (July 1962): 363–74. Significantly, the above scholars are all North Americans writing, with the exception of Bush, on the heels of the overthrow of the Arbenz government in June 1954 and in the midst of the Cold War.

5. Even the most comprehensive general treatment of the labor movement during this period, Asociación de Investigación y Estudios Sociales (ASIES), *Más de 100 años del movimiento obrero urbano en Guatemala*, Tomo II, *El protagonismo sindical en la construcción de la democracia (1944–1954)* (Guatemala City, 1992), 153–54, 230–34, 300–303, only touches on the history of the railway workers in particular and does not address the years after 1951.

6. In subsuming the concept of workers' control of the work process to the broader idea of workers' control over their working lives, I am trying to draw a clear distinction between them. The former refers to "workers' power over the means of production"— or the productive processes—in the more traditional sense. See Antonio Gramsci, "Workers' Control," in *Selections from Political Writings, 1921–1926*, trans. and ed. Quintin Hoare (Minneapolis, 1978), 10–11; Carter Goodrich, "Problems of Workers' Control," *Locomotive Engineers Journal* 57 (May 1923): 365–66, 415; David Montgomery, "Workers' Control of Machine Production in the Nineteenth Century," *Labor History* 17, no. 4 (Fall 1976): 485–509. I use the idea of workers' control over their working lives to refer to the multifaceted struggle—including, but not limited to, the battle for wage increases, job security, better working and housing conditions, and control over the productive processes—versus their employers. The locus of this broader struggle is usually the shop floor or, perhaps more suggestive of the nonfactory setting for most railroad labor, the work site.

7. See Victor Bulmer-Thomas, *La economía política de Centroamérica desde 1920* (San José, 1989), 1–7; Julio Castellanos Cambranes, *Café y campesinos en Guatemala, 1853–1897* (Guatemala City, 1985); David McCreery, "Coffee and Class: The Structure of Development in Liberal Guatemala," *Hispanic American Historical Review* 56, no. 3 (August 1976): 438–60.

8. David McCreery, "Debt Servitude in Rural Guatemala, 1876–1936," *Hispanic American Historical Review* 63, no. 4 (November 1983): 735–59; David McCreery, "An Odious Feudalism: Mandamiento Labor and Commercial Agriculture in Guatemala," *Latin American Perspectives* 13 (Winter 1986): 99–117.

9. Kenneth J. Grieb, *Guatemalan Caudillo: The Regime of Jorge Ubico* (Athens, Ohio, 1979).

10. Luis Cardoza y Aragón, *La Revolución Guatemalteca* (Mexico City, 1955), 9. For a general history of Guatemala, see Carol Smith, ed., *Guatemalan Indians and the State: 1540 to 1988* (Austin, 1990); Jim Handy, *Gift of the Devil: A History of Guatemala* (Toronto, 1984).

11. See Marc Christian McLeod, "Railway Workers in Guatemala, 1944 to 1954" (M.A. thesis, University of Texas at Austin, August 1993), 44–97.

12. McCreery, "Coffee and Class," 442–55; Gerald M. Best, "The Railroads of Guatemala and El Salvador," *Railway and Locomotive Historical Society* 104 (April 1961): 32–36; César Solis, *Los ferrocarriles en Guatemala* (Guatemala, 1952); W. Rodney Long, *Railways of Central America and the West Indies*, U.S. Department of Commerce, Bureau of Foreign and Domestic Commerce, Trade Promotion Series, no. 5 (Washington, D.C., 1925), 2–13.

13. Wilson to secretary of state, 29 April 1913, Records of the Department of State relating to Internal Affairs of Guatemala, Microcopy M-655, Decimal Files, 814.77/39, and article from *La Campaña* (Guatemala City), 19 April 1913, enclosed therein.

14. *Estatutos de la Sociedad de Ahorro y Auxilios Mutuos de los Empleados de los IRCA of Central America* (Guatemala, 1915).

15. Dirección General de Estadística, *Primer censo industrial de Guatemala* (Guatemala City, 1946), 35. Census officials apparently did not consider railway workers to constitute part of the industrial workforce.

16. Charles Bergquist, *Labor in Latin America: Comparative Essays on Chile, Argentina, Venezuela, and Colombia* (Stanford, Calif., 1986), vii, 1–8.

17. Joel Horowitz, "Occupational Community and the Creation of a Self-Styled Elite: Railroad Workers in Argentina," *Americas* 42, no. 1 (1985): 55–58, identifies these two factors as the source of railroad union strength in pre-1940 Argentina.

18. U.S. Central Intelligence Agency, "Report: Guatemala," SR-46, 27 July 1950, *C.I.A. Research Reports: Latin America, 1946–1976* (Frederick, Md.: University Publications of America, 1982), 20. After bailing out a near-bankrupt IRCA in 1936, United Fruit held a 42.6 percent share in the railroad and, in exchange for providing locomotives and rolling stock, enjoyed very favorable rates for the transport of bananas to Puerto Barrios. For more on the complex relationship between IRCA and United Fruit, see Alfonso Bauer Paiz, *Cómo opera el capital yanqui en Centroamérica (El caso de Guatemala)* (Mexico City, 1956), 137–88; Charles David Kepner Jr. and Jay Henry Soothill, *The Banana Empire: A Case Study in Economic Imperialism* (New York, 1935), 154–64; Stacy May and Galo Plaza, *The United Fruit Company in Latin America*, United States Business Performance Abroad, 7th Case Study (Washington, D.C.: National Planning Association, 1958), 165–68.

19. It is worth noting that some of the stevedores in the ports of Barrios (where the United Fruit Company also employed dockworkers) and San José had joined the SAMF, whereas in most other countries stevedores have formed their own unions.

20. Horowitz, "Occupational Community," 55–81.

21. "Proyecto de pacto de acción común y de unidad," 29 April 1946, Guatemalan Documents Collection, 1944–54, Manuscript Division, Library of Congress, Washington, D.C. (hereafter cited as Guatemalan Documents), box 15.

22. Alfredo Guerra-Borges, "Apuntes para una interpretación de la Revolución Guatemalteca y su derrota en 1954," *Anuario de estudios centroamericanos* 14, nos. 1–2 (1988): 113.

23. "Primera Convención Ferroviaria de Centro América y el Caribe," October 1946, Guatemalan Documents, box 45.

24. Thomas Bradshaw, Pres., IRCA, to Robert Newbegin, Department of State, 28 August 1946, National Archives and Record Service, Washington, D.C., Record Group 59, Records of the Department of State Relating to the Internal Affairs of Guatemala, Decimal Files (hereafter cited as State Dept. Decimal Files), 814.504; Hodgman to secretary of state, 29 August 1946, State Dept. Decimal Files, 814.5045.

25. Alfredo González Peralta to SAMF Executive Committee, n.d., Guatemalan Documents, box 45.

26. John Edgar Hoover to Jack D. Neal, Department of State, 13 December 1946, State Dept. Decimal Files, 814.504.

27. Samfistas de Esquintla to Honorable Corte Suprema de Justicia, 14 February 1948, Guatemalan Documents, box 46.

28. "Acta," Puerto Barrios, 12 November 1946, Guatemalan Documents, box 45.

29. "Acta," Puerto San José, 2 December 1946, Guatemalan Documents, box 45.

30. For detailed reporting on the dispute, see Stines to secretary of state, 3, 12, 19, and 27 December 1946, and Memorandum of Conversation, 8 January 1947, State Dept. Decimal Files, 814.5045.

31. "Acta," Zacapa, 1 February 1947, Guatemalan Documents, box 46.

32. "Acta," Puerto San José, 25 March 1947, Guatemalan Documents, box 45.

33. "Acta," Puerto San José, 8 April 1947, Guatemalan Documents, box 45.

34. *New York Times*, 13 August 1947, cited in Bush, "Organized Labor in Guatemala," pt. 3, 62.

35. Gleijeses, *Shattered Hope*, 41.

36. *Diario de Centro América* (Guatemala City), 25, 26 February 1947.

37. *SAMF* (newspaper of the railway workers' union), 30 August, 12 September, 30 December 1947, 19 February 1948; Wells to secretary of state, 10 November 1947, State Dept. Decimal Files, 814.504.

38. César Montenegro Paniagua, "Boletín de Prensa," 2 December 1947, Guatemalan Documents, box 46.

39. Representantes de los departamentos siguientes al FICA, 16 February 1948, Guatemalan Documents, box 46.

40. *Pacto colectivo de condiciones de trabajo celebrado entre el SAMF y la Empresa de los FICA* (Guatemala City, 1948).

41. ASIES, *Más de 100 años,* 200.

42. On the circumstances surrounding Arana's death, see Gleijeses, *Shattered Hope,* 50–71.

43. "Comité Político Ferrocarrilero," Arturo Taracena Flores Collection, Ephemeral Materials, 1944–63, Nettie Lee Benson Latin American Collection, University of Texas at Austin (hereafter cited as ATF), no. 1177, 8 November 1950; see also "Manifiesto de Comité Político Ferrocarrilero," December 1949, and "Comité Político Ferroviario to Jacobo Arbenz Guzmán," 13 November 1950, Guatemalan Documents, box 15.

44. Thomas Bradshaw, president, IRCA, to President Arévalo, 6 July 1949, enclosed in Patterson to secretary of state, 8 July 1949, State Dept. Decimal Files, 814.504.

45. *El Imparcial* (Guatemala City), 28, 29 June 1949; "Boletín de Prensa," 30 June 1949, Guatemalan Documents, box 46.

46. Patterson to secretary of state, 15, 22, 29 July 1949, State Dept. Decimal Files, 814.504; *El Imparcial,* 15 July 1949.

47. Bush, "Organized Labor in Guatemala," pt. 2, 109. See also Bishop, "Guatemalan Labor Movement," 121.

48. Ernst Schwarz, secretary CIO, to José Luis Caceros R., SAMF, 16 September 1949, Guatemalan Documents, box 46.

49. Secretary local, Esquintla, to secretary-general, SAMF, 7 August 1949; Adán Humberto Morales Vielman, secretary-general, SAMF to José Luis Caceros, 12 August 1949, Guatemalan Documents, box 46.

50. For the development of the Communist Party, see Schneider, *Communism in Guatemala,* 55–73.

51. *Boletín de la Dirección General de Estadística* (Guatemala City), no. 11 (April 1951): 29.

52. Calculated from figures in the *Boletín estadístico del Banco de Guatemala* 7, no. 12 (December 1954): 51.

53. *Boletín de la Dirección General de Estadística* (Guatemala City), no. 11 (April 1951): 21.

54. "Acta," Esquintla, 21 September 1949, Guatemalan Documents, box 46.

55. *SAMF,* 1 October, 15 December 1949, 15 January 1950; Steins to Department of State, 20 January 1950, State Dept. Decimal Files, 814.06.

56. *SAMF,* 20 October 1949.

57. Memorandum of Conversation, 5 April 1950, State Dept. Decimal Files, 814.06.

58. Wardlaw to Department of State, 24 August 1950, State Dept. Decimal Files, 814.06.

59. "Boletín de prensa: Atentario proyecto de la IRCA contra los trabajadores de Izabál," 14 August 1950, Guatemalan Documents, box 47; *SAMF,* 31 August 1950.

60. Wardlaw to Department of State, 26 September 1950, State Dept. Decimal Files, 814.062.

61. *SAMF*, 30 September 1950; Wardlaw to Department of State, 26 September 1950, State Dept. Decimal Files, 814.062. For a humorous account of the meeting, as if it were a soccer game, see "Relato subrealista: SAMF vs. Divisionistas," *SAMF*, 30 September 1950.

62. "El SAMF de Puerto Barrios le contesta a los títeres del traidor Pinto," 14 November 1950, Guatemalan Documents, box 47.

63. *SAMF*, 31 October 1950; Wardlaw to Department of State, 29 September 1950, State Dept. Decimal Files, 814.062.

64. "Los bases del SAMF," 14 October 1950, Guatemalan Documents, box 47.

65. Wardlaw to Department of State, 13 October 1950, State Dept. Decimal Files, 814.062. Accounts of the strike(s) are plentiful: *Octubre* (weekly paper of the Guatemalan Communist Party), 1 November 1950; *SAMF*, 31 October 1950; Wardlaw to Department of State, 5, 13, 25 October 1950, State Dept. Decimal Files, 814.062.

66. Bush, "Organized Labor in Guatemala," pt. 3, 50.

67. John D. French, *The Brazilian Workers' ABC: Class Conflict and Alliances in Modern São Paulo* (Chapel Hill, 1992), 144–45, employs characterizations similar to Center-Left and Center-Right in order to move beyond the "simple dichotomy that lumps all nonradicals into one negative reference group." With respect to the SAMF, these terms enable us to differentiate between the "nonmoderate" elements within the railroad union and to avoid the charged, negative terms—"communist," "procommunist," "radical," and "extremist"—traditionally associated with all nonmoderates.

68. El Comité Político Ferroviario, "Manifiesto al pueblo y a los trabajadores de Guatemala: La trayectoria política ferrocarrilera," ATF, no. 1351, February 1951; *SAMF*, 28 July 1951.

69. Arturo Morales Cubas, "A los reaccionarios y a los comunistas," ATF, no. 1560, n.d.

70. *SAMF*, 4 October 1951; *SAMF*, 31 March 1951.

71. Manuel Antonio Morales B., secretary of propaganda, SAMF, to Presidente Arévalo, 3 July 1950, Guatemalan Documents, box 47.

72. Ibid.; *SAMF*, 15 February 1951; Wardlaw to Department of State, 13 February 1951, State Dept. Decimal Files, 814.062.

73. *El Imparcial*, 8, 10 February 1951. For a discussion of how diesel technology impacted upon all categories of workers—and not just engine operators—in the U.S. railroad industry, see Fred Cottrell, *Technological Change and Labor in the Railroad Industry* (Lexington, Mass., 1970), 128–32; *SAMF*, 15 February 1951.

74. El Comité Ejecutivo, "Boletín Informativo," 17 April 1951, Guatemalan Documents, box 48; see also J. Raúl Baily, secretary local Puerto Barrios, to Adán H. Morales V., secretary-general, SAMF, 12 April 1951, Guatemalan Documents, box 48.

75. "Convenio celebrado entre la IRCA y el SAMF que pone fin a la suspensión de labores," n.d., Guatemalan Documents, box 48. Among many State Dept. Decimal File 814.062 dispatches see Wells to Department of State, Incoming Telegram (InTel), 20 April 1951; Schoenfeld to Department of State, InTel, 26 April 1951; and Wardlaw to

Department of State, 27 April, 8 May 1951. See also the coverage in *El Imparcial*, 17–30 April 1951.

76. Wardlaw to Department of State, 26 November 1951, State Dept. Decimal Files, 814.06.

77. *Octubre*, 27 April 1951.

78. *SAMF*, 13 September 1951; *El Imparcial*, 12 June 1951; Wardlaw to Department of State, 18 June 1951, State Dept. Decimal Files, 814.062; *Octubre*, 20 June 1951.

79. *SAMF*, 5 January 1952.

80. *SAMF*, 15 December 1951, 5 January 1952; Wardlaw to Department of State, 31 March 1952, State Dept. Decimal Files, 814.06. See almost daily coverage in *El Imparcial*, 7 November–3 December 1951.

81. "Renunciantes del 6 de julio de 1951 en adelante," July 1951, Guatemalan Documents, box 49.

82. Wardlaw to Department of State, 21 June 1951, State Dept. Decimal Files, 814.062; "Acta #165," Zacapa, 12 July 1951, Guatemalan Documents, box 49.

83. José Abel Recinos Sandóval, Jefe del DAT, to Obreros Ferroviarios, n.d., Guatemalan Documents, box 49; Wardlaw to Department of State, 28 December 1951, State Dept. Decimal Files, 814.06.

84. ASIES, *Más de 100 años*, 300–303.

85. Bush, "Organized Labor in Guatemala," pt. 2, 24.

86. *El Imparcial*, 9 June 1951.

87. Wardlaw to Department of State, 22 April 1952, State Dept. Decimal Files, 814.06.

88. *SAMF*, 26 July 1952.

89. *El Imparcial*, 19, 24 January 1951.

90. Manuel Antonio Morales B. to Clodoveo Santos, Puerto Barrios, 9 October 1949, Guatemalan Documents, box 46; "Acta #144," Esquintla, 18 April 1950, Guatemalan Documents, box 47; "Acta #154," Esquintla, 6 January 1951, and Executive Committee Esquintla to Adán H. Morales Vielman, secretary-general, SAMF, 8 January 1951, Guatemalan Documents, box 48.

91. Frente Unico de Fuerzas Ferrocarrileras, to Compañeros Ferrocarrileros Coop-erativistas de Puerto Barrios, 1 October 1952, Guatemalan Documents, box 51; "Acta #6," Puerto San José, 25 August 1952, Guatemalan Documents, box 47.

92. *SAMF*, 14 March 1953. See also Wardlaw to Department of State, 23 July 1952, State Dept. Decimal Files, 814.06; *SAMF*, 24 December 1952, 11 June 1953.

93. Rolando A. Calderón B., SAMF, to Víctor Manuel Gutiérrez, secretary-general, Confederación General de Trabajadores de Guatemala, 29 November 1952, Guatemalan Documents, box 51.

94. "Acta #206," Zacapa, 23 July 1953, Guatemalan Documents, box 52.

95. "La impostergable necesidad de la Reforma Agraria," *SAMF*, 9 February 1952; "Manifiesto del SAMF," 22 April 1952, Guatemalan Documents, box 50; *SAMF*, 23 June 1953.

96. Secretary-general, SAMF to secretary local Mazatenango, n.d., Guatemalan Documents, box 50.

97. For more on the railway workers and ethnicity, see McLeod, "Railway Workers in Guatemala," 29–38. On the issue of West Indian laborers in Puerto Barrios, see 66–70, 168–69.

98. René Arturo Orellano G., *Guatemala: Migraciones internas en Guatemala, 1950–1964* (Guatemala City, 1974); McCreery, "Debt Servitude in Rural Guatemala," 759; Gleijeses, *Shattered Hope*, 46.

99. See Forster, "Time of 'Freedom,'" 35–78.

100. Piero Gleijeses, "Politics and Culture in Guatemala," Center for Political Studies, Institute for Social Research, University of Michigan, 1988, 1. See also Matthew Carr, "Guatemala: State of Terror," *Race and Class* 33, no. 1 (July–September 1991): 31–56.

101. For post-1954 Guatemala in general, see Susanne Jonas, *The Battle for Guatemala: Rebels, Death Squads, and U.S. Power* (Boulder, Colo., 1991). On state terrorism and the labor movement in particular, see Deborah Levenson-Estrada, *Trade Unionists against Terror: Guatemala City, 1954–1985* (Chapel Hill, 1994).

102. Vallon to Department of State, 20 August 1954, State Dept. Decimal Files, 814.06.

103. *New York Times*, 28, 30 November 1957; 23, 24 December 1966.

CHAPTER FIVE

AS YOU SOW, SO SHALL YOU REAP

Argentine Labor and the

Railway Nationalization

MARÍA CELINA TUOZZO

The study of the relationship between labor and capital in the British-owned railway companies in Argentina from 1930 to 1948 reveals an ongoing struggle that had the workplace as its principal terrain of conflict. This chapter's focus on labor processes and workplace relations questions the stereotype of the workers as irrational actors, uncritically obeying the commands of their populist leader.[1] By changing the perspective of the analysis, this study also seeks to revise the highly baroque and exotic imagery of the Argentine railway nationalization as a demagogic and sentimental concession of the caudillo, Juan Domingo Perón, to the xenophobic masses. Argentine workers and their employers have always been engaged in an occasionally fierce, customarily subtle, but always constant struggle over control of the shop floor. Studying the workplace raises new questions. What was it like to work for the British railway companies? How did their work shape the experience of railroaders? How did the workers transform their work? Why did they unanimously support the state's buying of the British railways despite knowing of the system's deterioration and decay?

When dealing with the workers' experience in the workplace, the scholar needs to inquire about management. It is imperative to introduce the employers into the analysis, lest the scenery assumes an unreal appearance, as if workers were struggling only against phantoms.[2] Therefore, this chapter also analyzes the managerial structure of the British-owned railway system. How did management-labor relations evolve? How did the average railroader relate to the supervisors and foremen? Who had the authority to rule the workers,

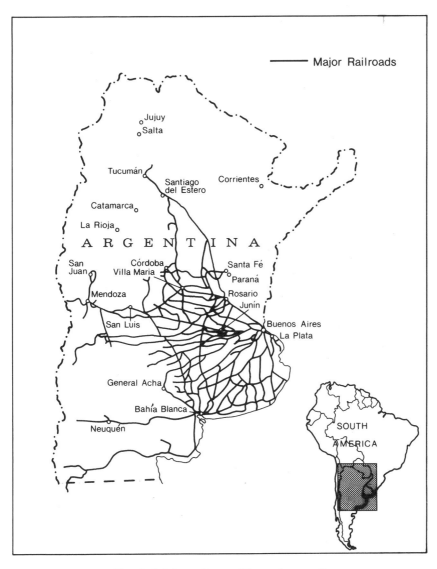

Map 4. *Major railways of Argentina, 1948*

and how did they use it? How did the companies organize their decision-making processes?

This chapter's concentration on the historical dynamics of the workers' resistance and daily struggles does not diminish the significance of the structural context. After all, it was the general breakdown of the Argentine railway industry that precipitated the workplace struggle between capital and labor. Technical stagnation had set in following the First World War and had intensified during the 1920s. Renovation of railway technology, however, required huge investments, and few British enterprises had the necessary capital. Argentina, therefore, partook of a worldwide phenomenon. Following the depression, one nation-state after another commenced taking over the privately owned railways. The rail companies yielded to the state, which presumably had greater resources to undertake the technical innovations.[3] For this reason, Argentina took over the railways from the British in 1948.

In the Argentine case, however, the workers played a central role in the process of nationalization. From 1930 onward, workers confronted a managerial policy focused mainly on annulling the work rules and eroding labor's prerogatives. The British companies did not attempt to undertake technological innovations or to adopt management cutbacks in response to stagnation and decay in the industry. The directors instead chose to enact a repressive labor policy. Their objective was to enhance the companies' efficiency solely by raising the workers' productivity. In other words, the companies "modernized" by intensifying labor's efforts, by expanding the hours of work, and by dismissing redundant workers. The companies also had the support of the Argentine state—at least until the rise of Perón. The British owners did not decide to sell the railways to the Argentine state until Perón came to power in 1946.

In their places of work, railroaders resisted the companies' policy of scapegoating workers for an industry in crisis. They decided that their employers were not to compensate themselves for decreasing rail revenues by squeezing more from labor. When the Peronist state nationalized the railways in 1948, the workers supported the government's decision. Labor's long-standing opposition to management's changes in the work rules was one of the factors that finally convinced the British companies to sell out to the Argentine government.[4]

A Disposition of Extreme Violence

The railway network's geographical pattern in Argentina—spreading principally throughout the fertile Pampas region—followed the agrarian determinants of Argentine economic development beginning in the late nineteenth century. The evolution of the railway companies paralleled Argentina's successful insertion into the world market. Beginning in the 1880s, livestock and cereal production founded a dynamic export economy in which Argentina participated in the international division of labor influenced by Great Britain. The latter provided manufactured products. This import-export economic model relied on an alliance between Argentina's landowners and the British capitalists who developed the nation's rail network, the commercial system, and the meat-processing industry. Connecting the productive sectors to Buenos Aires, the country's principal port and capital city, the rail network was symptomatic of Argentina's dependence on the export of its agricultural and cattle products and of its need to import British capital, technology, and materials to be able to export them. Argentina's railways did not form an integrated system. Rather, they were built like the spokes of a wheel, attached to the hub of Buenos Aires. Each spoke consisted of a different British railway company, headquartered in London.[5]

British railway construction in Argentina ended in the mid-1910s, during a critical political period in which the first democratically elected government replaced the conservative regime that had strongly supported the railway companies. While the popular Radical Party was in power, from 1916 to 1930, the workers initiated their most important struggles for the enforcement of work rules. These rules governed how work was accomplished on the shop floor, protected the workers, and restrained the companies from wielding arbitrary power at the grassroots level. Two unions led the resistance. Founded in 1887, the Locomotive Fraternity (La Fraternidad) constituted the craft union of the engineers and firemen. The nonlocomotive workers did not have their organization until 1922, when they formed the highly centralized Railway Union (Unión Ferroviaria), culminating a long process in which numerous predecessors had failed.[6] The Radical Party governments had been more responsive to workers' demands than the conservatives had been.

Argentina's fledging democracy did not survive the crisis of the international economy, however. In 1930, a military coup returned political rule to the conservative landed elite. Once again, the railway companies could rely on the government's support in order to cut wages and ignore the protests and demands of labor. Fraudulent elections from 1930 to 1943 protected Argentina's contradiction between economic advancement and political regression. During the 1930s, Argentines industrialized while the government remained unresponsive to much of the middle class and especially to labor. There accumulated a number of popular demands, in the meantime, that the neoconservative government refused to address.[7] This situation would give rise to the polemical sociopolitical phenomenon of Peronism beginning in 1943, when a second coup led by a different faction of the military constrained the landed elite's domination of the Argentine state. Through his position within the military junta, Col. Juan Domingo Perón ultimately constructed a powerful alliance with various sectors of Argentine society, notably the working class. The railway workers supported Perón's Labor Party, which won the 1946 presidential election. Two years later, President Perón nationalized the British-owned railways.

A dispute between the Pacific Railway Company and its workers at the Mendoza repair shops in 1934 spotlights the kinds of conflicts agitating labor relations in the rail industry prior to the nationalization. The episode started at the assembling section of the railway shop. A second-class fitter named Statti deliberately violated the work rules while acting under the protection of the shop floor authorities—the section's supervisor, Fossa, and the shop foreman.[8] The union's delegate, another fitter named Franks, and the rest of the fitters in his crew complained to the local grievance committee, the union's institution in charge of processing workplace claims. The grievance committee informed the company of Statti's behavior. On the following day, the shop foreman appointed Statti as crew chief, a promotion specifically violating the seniority rules. His fellow workers were outraged. The revolt that followed involved more than a hundred shop workers, who were joined in the work stoppages by their peers from other sections. Union representatives demanded that the head of the Mendoza shop, DeMarchi, expel Statti from the shop's section, and the workers rejected several compromises proposed by the company. The union's executive board and the company's manager could not agree on a solution, because the conflict at the Mendoza shops involved critical issues in the management-labor relationship.

The issue of workplace supervision was at stake in the conflict. Statti could violate the work rules with impunity because he counted on the supervisor's patronage. When jobs were scarce during the depression, the crew's members took turns missing a day of work without pay so that no one would have to be fired. The supervisor had the power to choose who was to miss the day. Consequently, Statti never left. "This example clearly shows the supervisor's favoritism and arbitrary use of power," exclaimed the Railway Union's general secretary, José Domenech. "In obvious violation of the seniority agreements, workers with more years of railway service than Statti had had to leave."[9] Statti violated other work rules such as the shop's organizational chart. By prior agreement between the the company and the local union, locomotive repair was to take place outside the shop so that the workers did not have to inhale the dust produced by the maintenance. But Statti performed his repair duties indoors, annoying his fellow workers, who also felt under pressure to do the same. The managers at the Mendoza shop protected Statti's transgressions and, temporarily, appointed him to a supervisory position. "Statti, [as] a second class fitter of the assembling section replaced the supervisor during one of his absences," Domenech complained.[10] The appointment clearly disregarded other workers who had more skill and years of service than Statti.

The violation of work rules and seniority by Statti and the shop's management constituted critical issues for the workers. Work rules restricted the employers' actions and maintained the balance of power on the shop floor. "Without work rules," asserted the Railway Union, "a deterioration of the workers' living conditions" would inevitably follow.[11] The seniority system should have prevented the supervisor from favoring Statti or any other compliant worker. According to the rules of promotion, the supervisor should have dismissed Statti from the crew when jobs were scarce, and first-class fitters with more experience and skill should have been selected as supervisor ahead of Statti.

To enforce the company's control, foremen regularly established a network of relationships within the workplace. Statti was part of one such network, and he accepted unfair privileges so that he might later become a supervisor. There were other cases of men who, like Statti, received arbitrary favors, disrupting the precarious harmony of the workplace.[12] Because they represented the company, foremen were isolated, unless they were able to establish a network of "loyal" workers on the shop floor who replaced them in their temporary absences and, eventually, filled their vacancies. Who were these "loyalists"? Why did Statti choose to ally himself with the supervisor, thus gaining the enmity of his peers? Domenech accused Statti of looking for a swift promotion.[13]

The transmission of knowledge aided the foremen in setting up their networks. Supervising the fitters' crew required specific training in and knowledge of the locomotives' internal mechanisms. The first-class fitters at the Mendoza shop could not be promoted to supervisors because the section's foreman refused to teach them the necessary duties. "At the Mendoza shop," Domenech explained, "the first-class fitters do not know the supervisor's duties because they were never taught, which management does on purpose so as to favor a particular man." Statti "was the supervisor's friend and [consequently] the only one who knew the locomotives' mechanism and, therefore, the only worker capable" of being promoted.[14] Through the selective transmission of knowledge, the supervisors had ensured that the new foreman was to be a compliant loyalist. The shop's boss, DeMarchi, stubbornly repeated that "the workers at Mendoza refused to be reasonable," opposing the company's management and appealing instead to the union and the railroaders' community.[15]

In opposition to the foremen's network, the union tried to maintain balance in the workplace by enforcing work rules that curtailed the foremen's power. The Railway Union delegate in the assembling section, Franks, was responsible for the observance and enforcement of the work rules. Agreements signed between the managers of the Mendoza railway shop and the union's local grievance committee concerning the shop's sanitary condition established that, after washing their hands, workers had to pour the remaining water into buckets. One day, the shop's boss "happened to pass by" and noticed spilled water on the floor. He immediately summoned the union delegate to admonish him for the infraction. Through his own network of workers, Franks discovered that Statti and the section's supervisor had caused the incident. The union local reprimanded Statti, who rejected union discipline because he had the support of the shop bosses. Therefore, the local Railway Union officers voted to expel Statti.[16]

Yet Statti represented the foreman's power within the workplace. The union's attempt to restrain him precipitated a confrontation with the shop's authority. Ultimately, the struggle at the shop floor level pitted the union delegate against the supervisor and foremen. Union delegate Franks relied on a different authority than the foremen, as his was the product of the union's legitimacy among the workers. The Mendoza shop boss, DeMarchi, defended his subordinates and attempted to prevent Franks from monitoring "the section's misdemeanors," as this was the supervisor's task.[17] Furthermore, De-Marchi accused Franks of abusing his power by persecuting Statti, the latter of whom claimed that Franks had been mistreating him out of personal animosity.[18] DeMarchi and his foremen continued to pester Franks. The local union board denounced the shop's supervisors for disregarding Franks's authority as the union delegate. It claimed that whenever Franks approached them with the workers' complaints, the shop's authorities dismissed him in a debasing manner. Shop workers from the traction and traffic sections joined protesters from the assembling section. At one point, hundreds of shop workers marched on the offices of the shop's boss, DeMarchi, who recoiled at their "threats, stunning attitudes, and outrageous shouts."[19] DeMarchi called for a truce in order to await the arrival of chief engineer Kimberley, head of the company's mechanical department.[20]

The workers' reaction against the foremen's policy of favoritism and work rules' violation was overpowering. By favoring particular workers, the foremen and supervisors of the Mendoza shops violated the work rules and ignored the workers' grievances. This behavior provoked other workers and precipitated their reaction. Statti's appointment as temporary supervisor, a status that the union claimed he did not merit, was a clear violation of the seniority agreements and exhibited the protection and patronage with which the shop's authorities favored him. Even the local grievance committee admitted that it could do nothing to control the workers' rage. In what could have been a tactic to build consensus, the grievance committee relinquished its authority over the matter to the union's local assembly. "We do not decide anymore, now the assembly is in charge," the grievance committee explained to

DeMarchi. When chief engineer Kimberley finally arrived, he offered to restore peace by removing both Statti and Franks from the assembling section. But the assembly rejected the removal of Franks.[21]

The workers' opposition to compromise eventually involved the highest hierarchies of both the company and union. The company's manager, Mervyn F. Ryan, met with the Railway Union national executive board, led by José Domenech. This was not their first encounter. They had confronted each other in Rosario during the fierce railway struggle of 1917, when Ryan was manager of the Central Argentine Railways and Domenech one of the shop's local union delegates. They were still fighting the same struggle: the workers' efforts to enforce work rules restricting the managers' abuse of power.[22] To satisfy the shop workers at Mendoza, Domenech demanded the removal of Statti from the assembling section. Ryan disagreed. If the manager had given in, he would have removed a key element of the foremen's workplace network. Ryan actually wanted to remove union delegate Franks from the shop because "he [had] tried to solve the workers' problems instead of leaving the matter to the supervisors."[23] Ryan conceived the conflict as "the clash of two different interests, the local grievance committee's and the company's."[24] The company manager made clear that the issue at stake was the power to appoint the shop's authorities. "If the company removes Statti," Ryan said, "then, the company is resigning its authority to appoint supervisors and foremen." In contrast, the workers demanded respect for the work rules, including the seniority system of promotion. The Railway Union wanted to observe the seniority system in which the first-class officials with more years of service had the right to be promoted and become shop supervisors. "Chief Engineer Kimberley thinks he can appoint the man he chooses," said Domenech, "but I do not think that is correct."[25] At the heart of this shop floor conflict was the power to appoint its authority figures and whether the company's loyalists would override the workers' representatives.

The Railway Authorities Are Themselves to Blame

The Mendoza confrontation also illustrates another of the principal factors in the confrontation between railroad workers and employers: the inefficient administration of the British railway companies.[26] The underlying cause for the deterioration of these enterprises had been their decrepit organizational structure. The general manager served as the nucleus of the general administration and the British company's major authority in Argentina. He answered to the directors back in England. Under the general manager came the heads of the different operational departments: traffic and running of the trains;

construction and maintenance of the road beds; the workshops for the design, construction, and maintenance of locomotives and rolling stock; and finally storekeeping.[27] The departmental structure was already an old-fashioned way of organizing a railway enterprise. Its critics pointed to the prevalence of narrow viewpoints that contributed to uncooperative and antagonistic attitudes among the department heads. In fact, by 1927, all but one company in Great Britain had replaced the archaic departmental system of organization.[28]

An additional discrepancy plagued the railway system in Argentina: no department was in charge of labor management. It was left to the general administration, which had multifarious other responsibilities besides coordinating labor policies. Therefore, none of the labor-management relationships could be framed within clear rules and regulations, and none of the several British railway companies maintained consistent companywide labor policies.[29] The manager of each department and of each local installation managed the workers according to his own principles and criteria. This situation resulted either in the foreman's abuse of power in the workplace, as the Mendoza case showed, or in "an anarchic atmosphere" in which neglect, arbitrariness, and personal criteria prevailed.[30] The labor situation in the British railways was unpleasant, and the rank and file lived in a constant state of insecurity and agitation "that obstructed mutual understanding [between] labor and capital," as one observer noted.[31]

A wide gulf separated the administrative and technical authorities of the British railways from the workers. Following the Mendoza rebellion and during labor negotiations at Buenos Aires, a union executive reproached De-Marchi, the Mendoza shop's boss, for his "ignorance of the shop's situation." DeMarchi admitted his lack of contact with the shop floor he supervised.[32] When the shop workers protested, DeMarchi was unable to make a decision. He was bewildered by the general reaction and waited for the decision of the head of the mechanical department. In truth, DeMarchi lacked the authority to resolve any labor issue.[33] But DeMarchi was no exception. When departmental head Kimberley arrived, he also refused to make a final agreement with the shop workers and left the labor problem to manager Ryan. According to a report on the British railways submitted to the minister of public works, Kimberley and DeMarchi represented the situation of the rest of the technical and administrative staffs of the railways. From the heads of departments to the local officer, they all lacked "authority and ability."[34]

In this atmosphere of managerial anarchy, arbitrary appointment of staff was not rare—particularly in the case of administrative personnel. There existed "privileges, castes, and 'untouchables,' in other words, personnel under the protection of influential supervisors," who enjoyed "luxuries" and "ease," one report stated.[35] A contemporary writer naively identified these untouchables. "It is abundantly clear that the British workers constitute the companies' favorite employees as they perform the most prestigious tasks," he wrote. "However, they duly deserve their colleagues' high respect, affection and admiration."[36] The companies favored the British employees, who dominated the "important technical positions . . . throughout the country, to say nothing of the managing staffs in Buenos Aires." According to the British ambassador, the railways were employing nearly 2,000 British citizens at the outbreak of the Second World War.[37] The company's policy of placing British subjects in the highest positions necessarily affected the majority of the workers who were non-British. Of the other railway employees, 49,516 were Argentines, 19,515 were Italians, and 12,062 were Spaniards.[38] The tension between British and non-British employees was not the only ongoing ethnic conflict. Although it is beyond the scope of this study, it is important to mention that tensions existed between Argentine citizens and immigrants and between the unskilled rural migrants and the skilled urban workers.

After the nationalization of the railways in 1948, most workers openly expressed their hostility toward the British employees. These feelings existed beforehand, as a revealing episode suggests. When the Argentine and British governments reached a final agreement concerning the nationalization of the railways in February 1947, the contract guaranteed "the present conditions and assurances of work" to the British subjects."[39] The bulk of the workers, however, resisted this measure. The Argentine secretary of state confessed to a British director that the British employees might have to be replaced. It was a matter of psychology, said the Argentine official. "The pressure from the mass of the staff to be managed by Argentines, and no longer by Britishers, was overwhelming."[40] An ingrained ethnic tension underlay the unending confrontation between workers and British employers.

Ethnic discrimination in the designation of managers and heads of departments also affected the companies' decision-making process regarding labor. These enterprises were highly centralized. Even resident general managers such as Ryan were not the ultimate sources of authority on any matter, labor included. The companies' hierarchical structure snared the managers in a relationship of subordination to the boards of directors in London. "It is well known that no major decision can be taken without reference to London," the companies' directors acknowledged in 1944, "and this has unfortunately undermined the prestige of the managers."[41] Years earlier, the managers' power had been curtailed. In 1936, the London directors forbade the resident managers to negotiate directly with the Argentine government. The reason was that the local railway committees, some of whose members were Argentine citizens, had been dealing with the government in conflict with the general managers. Consequently, a "dual control" existed within the Argentine railway system, an ambiguous situation that was never resolved so long as the British remained owners.[42] Labor relations in the British companies affected several different levels of the companies' hierarchy. But at its apex, only the board of directors ruled on labor matters.

The workers were conscious of the administrative centralization of the companies' decisions. In 1934, while negotiating the Mendoza conflict with the general manager of the Pacific Railways, the Railway Union denounced the company's arbitrary labor policy. The management had been persecuting workers through the systematic violation of the work rules, according to the Railway Union. The company had adamantly opposed the local grievance committee's "efforts to balance the relationships between the managers and the staff."[43] Similarly, the Railway Union criticized the company for allowing bureaucratic procedures that hindered the communication between workers and managers, intensifying their lack of contact.[44] According to the union, the company's violations and abuse of labor were Ryan's responsibility. The general manager had enforced "an attitude of persecution and vengeance," said Domenech, and the workers had to "fulfill their duties in a constant state of anxiety and dread."[45] In general, it was the centralized organizational structure of the British railway companies that engendered the deepest obstacles.

The centralized structure of the British railway companies encountered severe criticism not only from the workers. Its toughest detractor was the British government. In the mid-1930s, the companies' directors asked the British government to assist them in dealing with the Argentine government.[46] The British Foreign Office promised diplomatic support yet also suggested an administrative and financial reorganization. The companies obliged partially in their 1935 merger of the Southern and Western Railways. This reorganization was the boards' last such attempt. By 1943, the Foreign Office was still trying to find "ways to persuade, or even force, these companies to increase their efficiency": "The criticism of their present organization which has reached us is such that H[is] M[ajesty's] G[overnment] would be unwilling to make representations to the Argentine Government or to assist them in any other way until they have reorganised themselves in a manner which H[is] M[ajesty's] G[overnment] considers adequate to meet that criticism."[47] The Foreign Office clearly held the directors responsible for failing to reorganize the British-owned railways in Argentina. "The railways are running inefficiently. . . . It does not seem that any improvement is possible so long as the existing railway organization is allowed to continue," observed one British diplomat. "The railway authorities are themselves to blame at any rate in part for the state of affairs that has been allowed to arise."[48]

The British government believed that the solution to the crisis of the British-owned railways in Argentina depended on the human factor. In contrast to the directors' viewpoint, however, the Foreign Office did not target the workers but the directors themselves. Diplomats often referred to the "idleness and inefficiency of the railway boards in London."[49] On behalf of the Foreign Office, one diplomat suggested to a railway director, John Montague Eddy of the Southern and Pacific Railway companies, that he and all his "reactionary" colleagues ought to resign. "The boards should be reconstituted bringing in fresh blood from outside [so that] the dead wood could be cut out," the diplomat concluded.[50] Other government officials expressed similar opinions. "The trouble of the boards," explained another diplomat, "was not in quantity, but in quality. 9 of the 21 directors had been professional railway men in Argentina, 2 more had been railway executives in this country. To promote so many executives on retirement to the boards of railway companies was seldom a success." Concluded the first diplomat, "His Majesty's Government had a clear locus standi for informing the railway companies that they should set their house in order. . . . No doubt by getting rid of the stale and reactionary ex-manager clique."[51]

A brief analysis of the careers of four directors illustrates what the Foreign Office meant by "professional railway men" and how they were compounding the companies' problems. The principal directors of the railway boards were also members of the London Committee of the British Argentine Railways. It was composed of the chairmen of each of the four companies. They were James Alfred Goudge of the Buenos Aires and Pacific Railways, J. M. Eddy of the Buenos Aires Great Southern and Buenos Aires Western Railways, Follet Holt of the Entre Ríos Railways, and Howard Williams of the Central Argentine Railways. These men certainly did not represent "fresh blood." They averaged seventy years of age and had shared successful careers as engineers in Argentina's railways at the turn of the century. Goudge had been manager of the Buenos Aires and Pacific Railways from 1900 to 1913. Holt had become general manager of the Buenos Aires and Rosario Railways in 1889. Williams joined the Central Argentine Railway as its general manager in 1920, later being promoted to director and chairman. Having joined the Argentine railways at the beginning of the century, Eddy eventually had become the general manager of the Buenos Aires Great Southern. By the end of the 1930s, he acted as director of the Buenos Aires and Pacific Railways and chairman of the Southern and Buenos Aires Western Railway.[52]

These directors had known only the railway business. They served as managers or chief engineers during the golden age, when Argentine revenues and rate freights had been high and the government looked askance on labor unions. These directors were not aware that things had changed in the worldwide depression, especially for the railway industry. British diplomats were amazed at their "lack of an appreciation of the true nature of the dangers in which these companies now [stood]" and referred to them as "tired, bewildered, and disillusioned old men [among whom] defeatism, like an infection, [had] spread throughout."[53] Having spent their whole lives in the service of the railways, the directors had "no wide experience and political influence." They visualized themselves as ill-used benefactors of Argentine development.[54] "The Directors regard everything in their garden as lovely," said one diplomat, "and will not listen to any complaints of extravagance or inefficiency."[55]

The directors' conservative *mentalité* prevented them from confronting the acute railway crisis. From 1929 to 1939, freight transportation had declined by one-half, and total railway profits had decreased more than 40 percent.[56] The main cause of the crisis was the rapid progress of road construction. Growing automotive transport reduced railway receipts by diverting cargo and forcing the continual reduction of railway freight tariffs.[57] A profound modernization of the operating equipment constituted perhaps the best way to respond to the technological challenge. However, since at least 1933, the companies' directors had completely suspended capital investment in rolling stock, installations, and tracks.[58] "The question that is involved," wrote one of the directors, "is one of enabling us to keep our services . . . at a proper level of efficiency but also to enable us to be in a position when it is possible to obtain new and up-to-date material, to have the funds available to re-equip our railways."[59] The directors responded to the crisis by relying on the conservative Argentine government of the 1930s.[60]

Rejecting Reform of the Work Rules

Rather than improving railway services, from the depression until the nationalization of the Argentine railway industry, the British directors resorted to petitioning the Argentine state. They repeatedly requested protection against the growing motorcar competition, they sought the prolongation of the Mitre Law exempting the rail companies from paying taxes, and they requested the government's permission to raise freight rates and passenger fares.[61] The neo-conservative governments of the 1930s, although closely linked with British interests, did not always comply with the companies' petitions. The British ambassador himself attempted to explain the conservative governments' ambivalence. "It must be borne in mind," he wrote, "that most of the landowners who constitute the real governing classes here, are bound to have small personal grievances [i.e., poor services and high freight charges] against the particular railways which they may use."[62] The state, therefore, resisted the railway interests on many propositions—except on labor issues.

From 1930 to 1943, the companies managed to maintain an unalterable labor policy originating from the increasing depreciation of the railway equipment and from the decline in revenues. The directors tried to raise workers' productivity in order to compensate for the companies' technological stagnation and increasing decay. To do so, they needed the state's support to violate and annul the work rules sanctioned by the previous Radical governments. The 1930 military coup, which reestablished a series of neoconservative governments closely tied to employers' interests, came none too soon to help the companies face the incipient railway crisis. During the depression, as the companies themselves recalled later, "traffic had fallen off to such an extent that the railway companies were in a position to dismiss some 6000 employees who had become surplus."[63] Discipline and repression shook workplace relations. One of the military government's first measures was to repeal the eight-hour workday that had been legislated just before the coup.[64] However, the Railway Union leaders, who had experienced the repression of the 1910s, had learned that it was wiser to resort to the state than to press their demands through strikes. They appealed to a unique figure, Eduardo F. Maglione, head of the National Labor Department. Within the military government, Maglione represented a corporativist trend more favorable toward labor organizations. Thanks to Maglione's intervention, a new labor regulation in 1931 reapplied the eight-hour law to the railway industry. The companies demanded the regulation's withdrawal.[65] A series of bitter labor disputes followed, ultimately bringing defeat to the workers.

Apparently, the neoconservative government had decided to support the foreign owners. "[In 1933,] it was understood that the Argentine Government would express their thanks [to the British railway companies] in a practical manner," recounted a British diplomatic document, "by settling the labor situation."[66] Similarly, the directors asserted that "the only practical method of dealing with the railways on an equitable basis would be . . . to modify the labour conditions in order to enable the Companies to lower their working costs." These modifications concerned not only salaries but also work rules. "Certain readjustments of regulations are now under consideration," the company reported, "[which] will lead to a greater flexibility in the use of labour."[67] A Presidential Award by Gen. Juan B. Justo—elected in fraudulent elections—allowed the companies to cut wages as long as they promised not to lay off any more workers. The wage cuts were to be considered temporary retentions (or contributions) that the companies were to return to the workers when their economic situation improved.[68] The Railway Union attempted to give General Justo's decree a different interpretation, in order to make it acceptable to the dissatisfied rank and file. Among other promises, the labor leaders assured the railway workers that the Justo decree would not "abolish the work rule and the seniority system."[69]

In August 1935, however, the Argentine government again came out on the side of the employers. It issued a decree modifying the existing work rules so that the companies could extend and intensify the working day, the ultimate goal of which was to raise labor productivity. "The companies' influence in higher circles has prevailed," concluded the two railway unions.[70] The unions complained that the new decree was intended to worsen working conditions by modifying "the working hours and rests." The decree of 1935 also enforced new, tougher work rules favorable to employers.[71] As the rank and file had feared, the government decree enabled the companies to modify the 1931 work regulation and ignore the eight-hour day. In fact, the 1935 decree institutionalized the companies' violation of work rules. The Mendoza conflict within the Pacific Railway Company certainly was no exception to the ongoing struggle. Other British rail companies, emboldened by the government, also modified the rules at their workplaces. The Western Railway Company established a commission to "study the modification of the work rules affecting the railway stations, and . . . reforms in the seniority program."[72] The union knew that this commission intended to eliminate jobs, reorganize work, and enforce a new distribution of workers' duties. A month later, the Railway Union warned that "various companies were modifying the seniority system," a work rule governing promotions and job security, which had been in force since 1925.[73]

What unions and workers resented most, however, was the extension of the working day. Their letters to political authorities always began with the key issue of working time, because the new decree had enforced "the increase of the working day with the consequent decrease of partial and weekly rests."[74] The railway unions even considered calling a general strike in reaction to the 1935 decree. Although they ultimately gave up the idea, for it meant a "fight against both the companies and the government," railway workers did not renounce future actions "to recover what [had] been so unfairly deprived from [them]."[75]

The companies had argued that the eight-hour working day could not be applied to the railways. Given the singular nature of the railroads, the working day endured frequent interruptions during which workers did not perform any tasks. Thus, the British employers differentiated the average industrial job, considered an uninterrupted labor process, from the railway job. The latter was now defined as an "intermittent occupation" (*trabajo intermitente*).[76] It involved two different concepts, according to the companies. The first component, "productive time" (*tiempo efectivo*), amounted to eight hours dedicated entirely to productive work for the companies. Second, the workers' "personal time" added up to two hours for breakfast and lunch, one hour for sanitary needs, and one hour for traveling.[77] The companies rejected the eight-hour day because it had included the four-hour interruption that workers utilized in satisfying their own needs—and not the companies'. To guarantee a productive time of eight hours, therefore, the 1935 decree extended the working day to twelve hours. The concept of railroad work as an "intermittent occupation" enabled the companies to justify the extension of the working day in the railway business.

Based on the crucial concept of "productive time," the 1935 decree endowed the companies with the right to extend the working times of both day and night shifts. The extension was particularly dramatic in the case of the engineers and firemen. Because the train operators spent most of their time moving throughout the geographically scattered industry, the companies had had difficulties controlling their time. The companies arrived at a solution. Engineers, firemen, and conductors had their earnings determined by a combination of kilometers traveled and daily rates of pay—a rule known as the dual system of wage payment. Since 1917, the number of kilometers run had defined the operating workers' working day. The 1935 decree, however, increased the day's work by extending the maximum beyond the standard 350 kilometers per day. In addition, the companies reduced the rest periods of train crews.[78]

All in all, the government decrees of 1934 and 1935 supported the companies' labor policy of increasing productivity and tipped the balance of power at the workplace in favor of the supervisors. The unions proved to be well aware of the situation. "Through the work rules, the unions [had] achieved the public authorities' recognition of the workers' right to have regulated working hours and rest periods . . . so that the worker is not exposed to the supervisor's arbitrary decision," said labor leaders.[79] The new decrees, however, ignored the unions' claims and deprived them of their control over work time. Now the supervisors could arbitrarily order the workers when to work, subjecting the workers' timetable to daily modifications. Similarly, the supervisors could modify the timetables so as to distinguish between the working hours and the rest intervals. They could also add extra time and extend the shifts.[80] Even the operating crews suffered the increased authority of the supervisors. The engineer who had managed to complete his daily work ahead of time now had to fulfill the supervisor's extra assignments. Workers not only had to run the trains but also had to stay at the terminals and in the yards, performing other duties assigned by supervisors.[81]

The 1935 decree also suppressed previous rules that had restricted the supervisors' authority within the workplace. The new work regulations gave the supervisors the right to force the workers to perform operations beyond their occupational jurisdiction. Particular categories of workers wished to monopolize the performance of certain tasks in the interests of safety and shop floor integrity.[82] Railway workers also suffered the nullification of the diagrams. According to the railway unions, the diagrams had established carefully defined job descriptions as well as each task's duration, thus preventing misinterpretations. A diagrammed working day detailed the tasks to be performed and the times they were to be performed. The diagrams especially protected station agents and shed workers from abuse. Now the supervisors could call them from home to work at any time or even extend their working hours at whim.[83]

In opposition to the companies' concepts of intermittent occupation and productive time, the unions formulated their own definition of the working day. They considered the eight-hour day applicable to the railway industry, despite the varied and peculiar labor processes involved. The unions rejected the distinction between "productive time" and "workers' personal time." Instead, they referred to the eight hours as "time of permanence," because they were under the company's supervision.[84] The following example illustrates the workers' conflicting definition of the working day. On one occasion, because of a technical malfunction in the railroad tracks, the foreman summoned a skilled shop worker to repair them. He spent two hours performing routine work at the shop, four hours getting to the location of the track he had to repair, one hour fixing the damage, and five hours waiting for the train to take him back to his shop. His working day thus had been extended to fifteen hours, but the company refused to pay the worker's traveling time. Basing their argument on the concept of "time of permanence," the shop worker and the union demanded that the company pay him for the twelve hours he spent working and traveling to reach the damaged spot and return to his shop. Although not productive in a direct way, the worker's traveling time was necessary in order to fulfill the assigned task. The worker's travel, after all, had been done in the line of duty.[85]

The workers became incensed that the 1935 decree cast aside the unions' definitions and interpretations of the working day. However, leaders of the two railway unions tried to control a rank-and-file outburst. "It is important to maintain our self-possession and common sense," said one Railway Union communiqué. "[We are] exhorting our comrades to keep calm and await our next dispatch."[86] The executive boards of both the Railway Union and the Locomotive Fraternity cautioned the union locals against precipitous actions. "The only thing we ask of the different railway locals is to read carefully this memo and wait for further news," the boards ordered.[87] The rank and file, nevertheless, resisted the enforcement of the 1935 decree. Against the executive boards' instructions, a large number of local meetings involving Railway Union and Locomotive Fraternity members took place. These assemblies called for resistance against the enforcement of the new decree and created local committees to organize direct actions against the companies. Various union locals also demanded that the executive boards summon an extraordinary general assembly.[88]

To avoid losing their rank-and-file followers, labor leaders claimed to understand and share the feelings of unrest among the workers. "In considering the problem," they wrote, "the boards and the locals do not disagree; on the contrary, we are in accord in condemning the new working conditions."[89] The union directors reminded the locals of the bitter experiences in the 1910s, when decentralized direct actions against the companies led to violence and failure. "Our only objective is to prevent the unions from committing a damaging mistake," the union leaders explained in order to justify their threats.[90] The national leadership rejected the locals' petition to summon an extraordinary general assembly. The Railway Union, led by its general secretary, José Domenech, did not believe that direct action against the companies would be effective. He instead resorted to politics, repeatedly petitioning President Justo and the Congress to annul the decree.[91] Domenech condemned the rebellious locals, disqualified the rank and file's procedures, and threatened to intervene in the agitating locals and dismiss the troublemakers.[92]

The first serious suggestion for the nationalization of the railway industry came up during this intensive labor struggle. Repeated stoppages by laborers demanding better conditions and higher wages obstructed several railway lines in 1936. At the end of the year, President Justo announced that his government would gradually acquire the railway network. Public opinion supported Justo. One of the main arguments that convinced Justo to buy the railways was the uncompromising state of affairs between workers and companies. He complained of the growing difficulty in finding "a reasonable solution to the differences" between the railway workers and the British owners.[93] Already in 1936, the opposition of the workers to the companies' control of the workplace was leading the government to consider nationalizing the British-owned railways in Argentina. It is illuminating that President Justo, a conservative military man, engineer, and landowner closely tied to British interests, was the first one to suggest the government's purchase of the railways. He had been motivated by the companies' failure to manage labor together with their lack of reinvestment and their poor performance. The labor-capital confrontation in the workplaces continued, even though the 1935 decree had swayed the balance of forces in favor of the companies.

The railway directors, therefore, would not yet agree to sell to the Argentine government. They depended on the uncertain developments of Argentine politics to impose their policy of economizing at the expense of labor.[94] As late as February 1943, they had asked the British government—not the Argentine— to become a shareholder of a new enterprise that would monopolize Argentine transport. A month later came the response. "His Majesty's Government had no intention of becoming a shareholder of the proposed coordination of road, rail and air transport."[95] The most satisfactory remedy, from its point of view, responded the Foreign Office, "would be an orderly and immediate transfer of the railways to Argentine ownership [but] the Argentines don't want this." And it firmly added: "Tell the railway directors that they must expect nothing from His Majesty's Government beyond diplomatic support."[96]

In 1943, when another military coup brought an end to the era of neoconservative governments, the directors faced a new situation they had not expected. An "obscuring of the Argentine political situation" followed the coup. The Foreign Office's assessment of March 1943, regarding the directors' "lack of an appreciation of the true nature of the dangers in which these companies now [stood]," proved to be prophetic.[97] As soon as Colonel Perón assumed the leadership of the National Department of Labor in October, he chose the railway unions as the main beneficiaries of his political projects and granted them major concessions.[98] The companies' managers took the state's interference in labor affairs very seriously. General manager Ryan of the Pacific Railways wrote, "Peron is in charge of the . . . new Secretariat [of Labor and] has more authority even than the Ministers. In fact [he is a] dictator." Ryan accused Colonel Perón of conspiring with the railway unions. "Decrees are being issued forcing the railways to grant concessions which we have stood out against in the past." These decrees involved additional expense to the railways. "We are in for a spell of strict totalitarian government in this country," Ryan concluded dramatically.[99] The companies' authorities in Argentina began to fear an expropriation. "When any action is threatened to control the railways, you will have to advise verbally (not in writing) all the responsible and loyal staff," the owners warned in top secret memos. "Some trustworthy men of each department should conform and carry out (au courant) with all that takes place. . . . Remove all private documents and correspondence secretly and any document which might be distorted to our detriments. Please advise all managers verbally."[100]

Despite these forebodings from the British management in Argentina, the directors in London were not unduly alarmed by the 1943 coup. The Argentine junta at first appeared willing to compromise. For example, the government in June 1944 had ordered the companies to hand over to the Labor Secretariat their share of the rate increases of March 1942. The sum amounted to 64 million pesos. The secretariat proposed applying these funds to raising wages and compensating workers for past wage retentions. After three months of difficult negotiations, however, the Argentine government gave way. It actually reimbursed the companies for the return of these funds.[101] No wonder some directors were not yet convinced they would have to sell. In fact, they even entertained the plan of monopolizing Argentina's entire transport system.

Not until 1946 and Perón's election to the presidency did the directors finally resolve to transfer the railways. Two government measures seem to have made them change their minds. A Road Transport Bill in 1946 proposed to prohibit subsidiaries of railway companies from participating in Argentina's highway transportation industry. "This [transport bill] is *fait accompli* however deplorable," lamented Director Forres of the Central Argentine Railways to J. M. Eddy of the Southern and Pacific Railways. But more damaging to the companies than the transport bill was the second measure: the possible annulment of the 1935 decree. "Far more menacing to our interests," one British director informed another, "is [the] labour regulation decree which can be signed by present executive power in spite of fact that it is entirely contrary to undertakings given to you by Peron that labour costs would not be increased before 1947. Decree would cost companies more than 15 million pesos per annum."[102]

The workplace struggle became, once again, the crux of the British companies' relationship to the state and to the Argentine public.[103] Since 1944, General manager Ryan had been warning the directors that the new military government was considering suspension of the procompany decree of 1935.[104] Indeed, before President-elect Perón was inaugurated, the military government did ratify a new labor decree in April 1946. It is difficult to ascertain whether the government really intended to enforce it. As one of the railway executives reported, "Peron's remarks [to the British railway managers were] that these measures will never be implemented," said one manager. "If, however, Peron is sincere, he might have some difficulty in bringing his wilder supporters into line."[105] Even if Perón had no intention of enforcing the new decree, the managers feared the rank and file's power to enforce it at the

Argentine railway workers, ca. 1948.
(Courtesy of the Archivo General de la Nación, Buenos Aires)

workplace. The new decree annulled the 1935 labor regulation, resurrecting the eight-hour day and the rest of the work rules won by labor prior to the military coup of 1930. In May 1946, the Foreign Office reported that "M. Eddy [had] stated that after consultation with the full boards of the railways concerned he was authorised by them to inform [the British government] officially that the [directors had] unanimously [decided] to accept" that the railways should be sold.[106] In other words, the owners had given up their efforts to rationalize the operations of the railways solely by requiring the workers to bear the costs. The Argentine railway workers, at long last, had successfully resisted these plans.

Conclusion

The workplace struggle that occurred at the Pacific Railways' shops at Mendoza illustrates how Argentine workers responded to violations of work rules by their British employers. The workers' will to resist, to maintain some autonomy, and to create new areas of control in the workplace had depended on their deep commitment to the work rules. These work rules and practices traditionally had restricted management's authority. Some of the most significant work rules included the seniority program, which provided security of employment to those with the longest service, eliminating favoritism and discrimination; the occupational jurisdiction, in which each task was performed by a specific category of worker; and the enforcement of "carefully worked-out job descriptions."[107] As demonstrated in the Argentine railway industry, workplace struggle could range from conflict between workers and the foremen's network, to the rank and file's challenge to union leadership, and to labor mobilizations against the companies. The railway workers' resistance, however, did not end with the state's concessions. Perón satisfied the accumulated labor demands, and the railway workers certainly responded to his policies in a favorable way. Yet they did not passively await the state's measures but mobilized to press their demands on the companies, on the unions, and on Perón himself. In fact, labor unrest in the railways continued from 1943 to 1945.[108]

This worker resistance had been motivated by the unwillingness and inability of the companies to revive the railways in any other manner. The British boards of directors, dominated by older men of rather limited vision, had decided against meeting the railway crisis through technological renovation and capital reinvestments. They did not even wish to streamline the managerial organization of their companies. The British owners had intended only to make labor pay for increased efficiencies. For this, they had relied on the assistance of the Argentine government in disciplining the workforce, getting it to accept longer hours and diluted work rules. But the military coup of 1943 had upset these plans. Supported by workers themselves, Col. Juan Perón developed new labor policies that enhanced workers' control over the workplace. That control had been under attack, although the workers were never vanquished even by the pre-Perón alliance between management and the state.

In his June 1946 inaugural address, President Perón promised to assure Argentina's economic independence from foreign powers. The statement coincided with the arrival of a British trade mission to negotiate, among other issues, the selling of the railways. A month later, the Railway Union delegates proclaimed at their general assembly that the nationalization of the railways constituted one of their highest priorities. As it celebrated the end of British ownership, the Locomotive Fraternity declared suggestively: "As you sow, so shall you reap."[109] For once, every sector involved—the Argentine state, the directors, the British Foreign Office, the unions, and the workers—seemed to agree on the need to nationalize the railways. Amid this harmony, however, the railway workers still retained their own agenda.

They continued to strike despite Perón's popularity among workers and his election as president. Ryan, now chairman of the railway managers conference, "told the Secretary [of Labour] that 25 unauthorised stoppages had occurred" from 1945 to 1946.[110] Apparently, the local labor leaders were attempting to discredit their own national union leaders, who had lost prestige "in the eyes of the men."[111] Just four days after Perón's assumption to the presidency, railway workers walked out on strike to force the companies to pay them the Christmas bonus (*aguinaldo*) of one month's wages.[112] The workers not only opposed the directives of their union but Perón's too, for the new president himself had stated that the decree authorizing the bonuses did not apply to the railway industry. Nonetheless, the mobilization continued. As Ryan reminded the union leaders, "The President had told the [workers] only a few days ago that the Christmas bonus presented a difficult matter." Union leaders "acknowledged this but said that the men [believed] that they were entitled to it and that neither the President of the Republic, nor they as heads of the Union, nor the Companies could now get this out of the men's heads. Unless they got it, there would be general railway stoppage."[113] Rank-and-file unrest continued throughout July 1946, the same month in which the union's assembly voted in favor of the railway nationalization. Moreover, labor unrest went on until 1948, throughout the whole negotiation of the railway's sale.[114]

In fact, once the British-owned railways had become Argentine property in 1948, the workers' resistance continued. The same railroaders who had supported the nationalization also opposed Perón's efforts to rationalize production and increase productivity on the lines.[115] The opposition of the workers to rationalization forced the state to approve a new labor regulation that favored the railway workers. The unpopular executive board of the Railway Union also was forced to resign. In 1955, the military government that overthrew Perón tried to modify these regulations and summoned the railway unions to discuss the matter. Because the unions opposed any reform, the military government cautiously abandoned the effort. The democratic government of Arturo Frondizi in 1962 also tried to reform the working rules on the national railways, leading to a dramatic strike known as the "railroad battle." The railroad battle is still raging.

Nowadays, more than forty-five years later, President Carlos Saúl Menem, a Peronist, wishes to sell the railways back to private capital, according to his economic program of privatizing all state companies. Opposition among the railway workers has grown, along with that of most other public employee unions. In January 1990, Menem signed two critical decrees establishing, among other measures, the layoff of fifteen hundred workers. Paradoxically, the banners of higher rationality and efficiency justified this decision, just as they had once justified the nationalization of the railways. Meanwhile, the workers continue to resist by organizing massive railway strikes that, from time to time, paralyze Buenos Aires, its populated suburbs, and the country's interior. It is the same resistance they have been mounting for nearly a century.

Notes

The author wishes to thank Joel Horowitz, Torcuato S. Di Tella, Paul Goodwin Jr., and Rodney Anderson for their helpful comments.

1. Social historians of Latin America are moving beyond the assumed passivity of the working class. Among others are Elizabeth Jelín, *La protesta obrera* (Buenos Aires, 1974); Joel Horowitz, *Argentine Unions, the State, and the Rise of Peron, 1930–1945* (Berkeley, 1990); Daniel James, "Rationalisation and Working Class Response: The Context and Limits of Factory Floor Activity in Argentina," *Journal of Latin American Studies* 13 (1981): 375–402; Samuel Bailey, *Movimiento obrero, nacionalismo y política en la Argentina* (Buenos Aires, 1986); Juan Carlos Torre, ed., *La formación del sindicalismo peronista* (Buenos Aires, 1988).

2. Howard F. Gospel, "Managerial Structures and Strategies: An Introduction," in *Managerial Strategies and Industrial Relations*, ed. Howard F. Gospel and Craig R. Litter (London, 1983), 1–24.

3. Honorio Roigt, *Presente y futuro de los ferrocarriles argentinos* (Buenos Aires, 1956), 30–35. For more information on technological innovation in the railway industry and its social and political aspects, see Fred Cottrell, *Technological Change and Labor in the Railroad Industry* (Lexington, Mass., 1970).

4. The nationalization process, however, is complex, and labor was one of the many variables involved. Specific studies on the Argentine workers and Perón's nationalization policies rarely focus on the shop floor. In contrast, they stress the economic, political, and ideological dimensions. See Bailey, *Movimiento obrero*; Hiroshi Matsushita, *Movimiento obrero argentino: Sus proyecciones en los orígenes del peronismo* (Buenos Aires, 1983).

5. For more detailed studies of Argentine development, see Eduardo P. Archetti et al., *Latin America* (London, 1987); Charles Bergquist, *Labor in Latin America: Comparative Essays on Chile, Argentina, Venezuela, and Colombia* (Stanford, 1986); Torcuato S. Di Tella, *Latin American Politics* (Austin, 1989). See especially Paul B. Goodwin Jr., *Los ferrocarriles británicos y la Unión Cívica Radical, 1916–1930* (Buenos Aires, 1974); Paul B. Goodwin Jr., "The Politics of Rate-making: The British-owned Railways and the Unión Cívica Radical, 1921–1928," *Journal of Latin American Studies* 6 (November 1974): 257–87.

6. *Confederación General del Trabajo: Anuario* (Buenos Aires, 1948), Fundación Simón Rodríguez Archive, Buenos Aires. See also Heidi Goldberg, "Railroad Unionization in Argentina, 1912–1929" (Ph.D. diss., Yale University, 1979); Alfredo López, *Historia del movimiento social y la clase obrera argentina* (Buenos Aires, 1971), 217.

7. Miguel Murmís and Juan Carlos Portantiero, eds., *Estudios sobre los orígenes del peronismo*, 4th ed. (Buenos Aires, 1974); Juan Carlos Torre, *La vieja guardia sindical y Perón: Sobre los orígenes del peronismo* (Buenos Aires, 1990).

8. Circular Parcial (hereafter cited as CP) of the Unión Ferroviaria (hereafter cited as UF) 14, "Reunión especial efectuada en la oficina del Señor Ing. Mecánico Divisional Mendoza, el 12 de marzo de 1935 a las 9.00 horas," 30 March 1935, UF Archive (hereafter cited as Reunión Mendoza).

9. Ibid.

10. CP UF 14, "Reunión realizada en la gerencia del Ferrocarril Buenos Aires al Pacífico el día 15 de marzo de 1935 entre los señores representantes de la empresa y de la UF. Sesión Tarde," 30 March 1935, UF Archive (hereafter cited as Reunión Gerencia B).

11. Circular General (hereafter cited as CG) UF 6, "Coordinación de los medios de transporte," 18 June 1935, UF Archive.

12. CP UF 14, "Reunión Mendoza."

13. CP UF 14, "Reunión Gerencia B."

14. Ibid.

15. Ibid.

16. CP UF 14, "Reunión Mendoza."

17. Ibid.

18. CP UF 14, "Reunión Gerencia B."

19. CP UF 14, "Reunión Mendoza."

20. CP UF 14, "Reunión Gerencia B."

21. Ibid.

22. On the 1917 strike, see Goldberg, "Railroad Unionization in Argentina," 20, 41, 65, 105–7.

23. CP UF 14, "Reunión Mendoza."

24. CP UF 14, "Reunión Gerencia B." Interestingly, Ryan did not interpret the conflict at Mendoza as a confrontation between the union and the company. He understood that the Railway Union's executive board had to discipline the workers; his and Domenech's concepts of discipline, however, were not the same.

25. Ibid.

26. J. V. Perowne, "Minutes," 13 April 1943, Public Record Office, London, Foreign Office General Correspondence (hereafter cited as FO), 371/33533. This document includes a summary of Noni's reports to Argentina's Ministry of Public Works and the General Railway Board on 15 November 1940. The aforementioned report identified the "defects in administration" as primarily responsible for the financial and bureaucratic hardships.

27. Instituto de Estudios Económicos del Transporte, *Estadística de los ferrocarriles argentinos* (Buenos Aires, 1946), 26–28; United States Bureau of Foreign and Domestic Commerce, Transportation Division, Foreign Railway Section, *World Survey of Foreign Railways* (Washington, 1937), 1–5.

28. T. Bernard Hare, *British Railway Operation* (London, 1927), 136–48.

29. Juan Ronald, *El problema de los ferrocarriles argentinos* (Buenos Aires, 1945), 30–37, 41–49. Juan B. Chitti, "Influencia del bienestar de los obreos y empleados en el rendimiento de la explotación," in VI Congreso Panamericano de Ferrocarriles, *Memorias* (Bogotá, 1948), 876–80.

30. Efraim Oscar Schmied, "Aplicación del taylorismo en los ferrocarriles," in VI Congreso Panamericano de Ferrocarriles, *Memorias*, 857–75.

31. Ibid., 858; Juan Ronald, *Los ferrocarriles particulares en la Argentina: Problemas de orden administrativo y sus relaciones con el personal* (Buenos Aires, 1942), 12, 19, 22, 29, 32.

32. CP UF 14, "Reunión Mendoza"; CP UF 14, "Reunión Gerencia."

33. CP UF 14, "Reunión Gerencia B."

34. Perowne, "Minutes," 13 April 1943.

35. Ronald, *Ferrocarriles particulares*, 54, 60, 64, 65.

36. F. Z. Castro Domínguez, *Política ferroviaria argentina* (Buenos Aires, 1945), 85.

37. David Kelly to Perowne, Buenos Aires, 24 March 1943, FO, 371/33533.

38. Dirección de Publicidad Ferroviaria, *Los ferrocarriles particulares en la Argentina* (Buenos Aires, 1938), 39.

39. Embassy to Foreign Office, Buenos Aires, 12 February 1947, FO, 371/61133; Miranda to Eddy, Buenos Aires, 17 May 1947, FO, 371/61133.

40. Embassy to Foreign Office, "Record of Conversation," Buenos Aires, 11 August 1948, FO, 371/68110.

41. M. J. Eddy, Forres, and H. C. Drayton to Foreign Office, London, 1944, FO, 371/37686.

42. Ibid.

43. CP UF 14, "Reunión realizada en la gerencia del Ferrocarril Buenos Aires al Pacífico el día 15 de marzo de 1935 entre los señores representantes de la empresa y de la UF. Sesión Mañana," 30 March 1935, UF Archive (hereafter cited as Reunión Gerencia A).

44. Ibid.

45. UF Executive Board to Manuel García Torre, general director of the General Railway Board, Buenos Aires, 22 March 1935, CP UF 14, UF Archive.

46. Winthrop Wright, *British-Owned Railways in Argentina* (Austin, 1974), 143 n. 13.

47. Foreign Office, "Minutes," London, March 1943, FO, 371/33533. Underlined in text. A month later the argument was reiterated: "Draft Note of a Meeting Held at the Treasury on April 14th to Consider the Position of the British Railways in Argentina," London, April 1943, FO, 371/33533.

48. Foreign Office, "Report," London, 22 January 1943, FO, 371/51799.

49. Perowne, "Minutes," 13 April 1943.

50. Perowne to H. E. Young, London, 20 March 1943, FO, 371/33533.

51. Perowne, "Minutes," 13 April 1943.

52. *Who's Who: An Annual Biographical Dictionary* (London, 1941), 948, 1244, 1536, 1566.

53. E. Mather Jackson, "Minutes," London, 29 March 1943, FO, 371/33533.

54. David Kelly's comment as His Majesty's Ambassador to Argentina in Foreign Office, "Report of Meeting to Discuss the British-Owned Railways in Argentina," London, 19 January 1943, FO, 371/51799.

55. Foreign Office, "Report," 22 January 1943.

56. The volume of cargo that the railways transported in 1929 diminished year by year, from 51,513,705 tons in 1929 to 40,658,696 in 1938, although this trend changed by the early 1940s. For complete figures on railroad traffic, see Instituto de Estudios Económicos del Transporte, "El Ferrocarril Argentino de capital privado en los últimos once años 1928–1939," in IV Congreso Sudamericano de Ferrocarriles, *Memorias* (Bogotá, 1941), 594; Instituto de Estudios Económicos del Transporte, *Estadística de los ferrocarriles argentinos* (Buenos Aires, 1946), 19; Ernesto Soares, *Los ferrocarriles argentinos* (Buenos Aires, 1940), 8, 11; Horowitz, *Argentine Unions*, 47.

57. Board Directors to the Foreign Office, London, 1938, FO, 118/685. Despite this contemporary diagnosis, the effect of automotive competition on the railway finances is a contested matter; for instance, one of the major arguments is that it was only on short hauls that trucks were a major threat.

58. Juan Manuel Santa Cruz, *Ferrocarriles argentinos* (Santa Fe, Argentina, 1966), 45–49; G. E. Leguizamón et al. to Dr. Salvador Oria, Argentine minister of public works, Buenos Aires, 19 January 1943, FO, 371/51799. Concerning the railway stock, by the 1940s, 50 percent of the locomotives were more than fifty years old, 22 percent were twenty-five years old, 10 percent were twenty years old. Only 7 percent of the locomotives were bought within the previous decade. Roigt, *Presente y futuro*, 46–47. This policy continued, and a year later, when confronted with the new government's "big programme of road building in execution and in prospect," the companies responded with a modest project of equipment renewals. Eddy, Forres, and Drayton to Foreign Office, 1944.

59. Eddy to M. A. Carcano, London, 7 December 1942, FO, 371/51799.

60. The companies also resorted to the Foreign Office's support as already mentioned. Yet the the Foreign Office's position concerning the reorganization of the companies' administrative and financial structure weakened the link between the companies and the British government. In 1944, Argentina's new political situation forced the Foreign Office to intervene more actively. Despite this, the companies never yielded to the Foreign Office's reorganization demands, and the four boards of directors never merged and were never renewed. In 1946, after the publishing of the Road Transport Bill and the Labor Regulation Decree, the directors finally agreed to sell and left all negotiations in the hands of the Foreign Office. "The Railway Boards in London, after various futile attempts at negotiation with the Argentine authorities, have now agreed among themselves that the only solution . . . is to sell out. . . . The futile character of past negotiation by the Railway Directors . . . [has] convinced the Treasury that H. M. Government ought to take charge of further discussions for the disposal of the railways, *the Directors coming in as advisers only*." Perowne to Foreign Office, London, 18 April 1946, FO, 371/51804; author's underlining.

61. Esmond Ovey to Alexander Cadogan, Buenos Aires, October 1938, FO, 118/685.

62. David Victor Kelly to Anthony Eden, Buenos Aires, 4 December 1942, FO, 371/51799.

63. Foreign Office, "Report: Antecedents of Argentine Government's Demand For Payment Of 64 Million Pesos (Decree 3/6/1944)," London, 25 July 1944, FO, 371/37687.

64. For more information on Law 11544, see David Tamarin, *The Argentine Labor Movement, 1930–1945: A Study in the Origins of Peronism* (Albuquerque, 1985), 105.

65. Horowitz, *Argentine Unions*, 69; Tamarin, *Argentine Labor Movement*, 105; Matsushita, *Movimiento obrero argentino*, 127.

66. Davidson to Ovey, London, October 1938, FO, 118/685.

67. Stephen H. M. Killik, *Manual of Argentine Railways: Twenty-fifth Annual Issue* (London, 1930), 6.

68. Foreign Office, "Report: Antecedents of Argentine Government's Demand."

69. Article 8 of Justo's decree permitted the companies to modify the 1931 labor regulation in order to maximize labor productivity by extending the working day. Circular Conjunta (hereafter cited as CC), UF and La Fraternidad (hereafter cited as LF), 2, 28 January 1935, UF Archive.

70. CC UF and LF, 7, 16 August 1935, UF Archive.

71. The unions' executive boards to M. García Torre, Buenos Aires, 10 September 1935; CC UF and LF, 9, 31 October 1935, UF Archive.

72. CP UF, 3, 30 January 1935, UF Archive.

73. CG UF, 3, 7 February 1935, UF Archive.

74. Ibid.

75. CC UF and LF, 9, 31 October 1935, UF Archive.

76. Pedro F. Prado, *Leyes y decretos de Trabajo y Previsión* (Buenos Aires, 1949), 559.

77. Ronald, *El problema de los ferrocarriles*, 109–10.

78. Unions' executive boards to General Railway Board, 10 September 1935, CC UF and LF, 9, 31 October 1935, UF Archive, articles 2, 4, 12, 21, 39, 41.

79. Ibid., article 1.

80. Ibid., articles 6, 7, 8, 9, 11.

81. Ibid., article 40.

82. Ibid., article 10.

83. Ibid., article 47.

84. Prado, *Leyes y decretos*, 559.

85. Ronald, *El problema de los ferrocarriles*, 102. Ronald does not clarify how this particular conflict came to an end.

86. CC UF and LF, 10, 5 December 1935, UF Archive.

87. Ibid., 2–3.

88. Ibid., 1, 5, 10.

89. Ibid., 3.

90. Ibid., 2, 5.

91. The executive board's failure in confronting the 1935 decree had as counterpart a bitter internal struggle between the secretary, José Domenech, and the prior leader, Antonio Tramonti. Their confrontation attained its climax when Domenech's faction

took by force the headquarters of the General Labor Confederation (or Confederación General del Trabajo) led by Tramonti and his followers. The labor coup took place in December 1935 when the Railway Union's board had drawn the memo threatening to replace the leadership of the disobedient locals. It remains a problem to differentiate one conflict from the other. Tamarin, *Argentine Labor Movement*, 126; Matsushita, *Movimiento obrero argentino*, 174.

92. CC UF and LF, 10, 5 December 1935, UF Archive.

93. As quoted in Wright, *British-Owned Railways*, 208. Justo's decision founded a consensus favoring the nationalization together with the railway workers and the British government. Internal and external factors—especially the Second World War—would affect the immediate applicability of the project. However, even at this early date the directors stood alone in their opposition. Although highly disregarded by their own government, the British directors counted on the crucial support of the shareholders: "However astonishing it might be, these boards have had the complete confidence of the shareholders in bad times as well as good." Foreign Office, "Report," 22 January 1943.

94. See especially Tamarin, *Argentine Labor Movement*, and Matsushita, *Movimiento obrero argentino*. "By 1937 the internal conflict had been papered over. . . . The railway unions demanded to go back to the 1931 contracts"; Horowitz, *Argentine Unions*, 112. In two decrees of March 1942, the neoconservative government of President Castillo put an end to the *laudo* retentions and authorized increases of passenger and freight tariffs of 5 and 10 percent to compensate the companies. H. M. Chargé d'Affaires to Anthony Eden, Buenos Aires, 28 January 1943, FO, 371/51799; G. E. Leguizamón, F. Garaycochea, A. N. Matienzo, and F. A. Bottomley to Dr. Salvador Oria, Buenos Aires, 19 January 1943, FO, 371/51799. These measures responded to the workers' mobilization, especially the strikes of February 1942; *La Prensa* (Buenos Aires), 25, 26, 27, 28 February 1942; *Review of the River Plate* (Buenos Aires), 27 February 1942. The suspension of the retentions did not solve the rank-and-file unrest, which was manifested in the rise of communist leaders within the railway unions and the defeat of the union leadership in the elections of 1943. See Horowitz, *Argentine Unions*, 113, 163, 165. The military coup of 1943 and the intervention of the railway unions interrupted the course of these events.

95. David Kelly to Foreign Office, Buenos Aires, 2 April 1943, FO, 371/33533; Foreign Office to British Embassy at Buenos Aires, London, 4 May 1943, FO, 371/33533.

96. Foreign Office, "Minutes, the Argentine Railways," London, 15 April 1943, FO, 371/33533.

97. Perowne, "Minutes, Argentine Railway," London, 24 June 1943, FO, 371/33534; Perowne, "Minutes, British-Owned Argentine Railways," London, 29 March 1943, FO, 371/33533.

98. For further studies on early Peronism, see Torre, *La formación del sindicalismo peronista*; Tamarin, *Argentine Labor Movement*; Matsushita, *Movimiento obrero argentino*; Horowitz, *Argentine Unions*; Murmís and Portantiero, *Estudios sobre los*

orígenes del peronismo; Manuel Mora y Araujo and Ignacio Llorente, eds., *El voto peronista* (Buenos Aires, 1980); Torcuato S. Di Tella, "Working-Class Organizations and Politics in Argentina," *Latin American Research Review* 16 (February 1981): 47–51; Hugo del Campo, *Sindicalismo y peronismo* (Buenos Aires, 1983); Joel Horowitz, "The Impact of Pre-1943 Labor Union Traditions on Peronism," *Journal of Latin American Studies* 15 (May 1983): 101–16.

99. Ryan to Goudge, Buenos Aires, 28 January 1944, FO, 371/37686.

100. Goudge to Ryan, London, 28 July 1944, FO, 371/37687.

101. Shuckburgh to Hadow, Buenos Aires, 30 October 1944, FO, 371/37689.

102. Lord Forres to Sir Montague Eddy, Buenos Aires, 31 March 1946, FO, 371/37689.

103. On 20 March 1944, the railway workers mounted a big demonstration to demand, among other things, that the government replace the members of the National Railway Board because of its antilabor and anti-Argentine attitude favoring the British employers; *La Prensa*, 21 March 1944.

104. Ryan to Goudge, Buenos Aires, 28 January 1944.

105. Noble to Foreign Office, Buenos Aires, 10 May 1946, FO, 371/51804. As from 1944, the railway unions denounced the British employers for disobeying the decrees; *La Prensa*, 5 October, 11, 12 December 1944. The Twenty-first UF General Assembly made a public denunciation of this situation as a justification for the unrest among the rank and file; *El obrero ferroviario*, January 1947.

106. Foreign Office, "Minutes," London, 14 May 1946, FO, 371/51804.

107. Morris Aaron Horowitz, *Manpower Utilization in the Railroad Industry* (Boston, 1960), 50; Robert Gomberg, "The Work Rules Problem in the Transportation Industries," and Russell S. Bauder, "The Railroad Work Rules Controversy in Perspective," in *American Transportation Research Forum: Third Annual Meeting* (Pittsburgh, 1962), 72, 63–71.

108. For the mobilization against the companies and the "suicidal" attacks against the Labor Secretariat, see *La Prensa*, 22, 29 October, November 1944; the various manifestations against Perón and the UF leaders throughout 1945 included the foundation of an anti-Peronist Comando Ferroviario and the Locomotive Fraternity leaving the General Labor Conference; *La Prensa*, 1, 2, 14, 19, 21, 28 August, 6, 7, 16 September, 13 October 1945.

109. *La Fraternidad* (Buenos Aires), no. 857, 20 February 1947, 97.

110. British Embassy at Buenos Aires to Foreign Office, Buenos Aires, 11 June 1946, FO, 371/51805.

111. Railway Board to British Argentine Railway Council, Buenos Aires, 18 June 1946, FO, 371/51805.

112. Railway Board to British Argentine Railway Council, Buenos Aires, 8 June 1946, FO, 371/51805.

113. Railway Board to British Argentine Railway Council, Buenos Aires, 18 June 1946, FO, 371/51805.

114. For accounts of the 1947 and 1948 strikes, see Labour Attaché to Foreign Office, Buenos Aires, 30 April 1947, FO, 371/61136; Labour Attaché to Foreign Office, Buenos Aires, August 1947, FO, 371/61136; *Financial Times* (London), 22, 24, 25 November 1947.

115. For a study of Perón's policy of rationalization in the railway industry and the following labor unrest, see María Celina Tuozzo, "Labor and State in the Nationalization of the Argentine Railway Industry," MS, in author's possession, 1989.

CHAPTER SIX

TOPICS NOT SUITABLE
FOR PROPAGANDA

Working-Class Resistance

under Peronism

MICHAEL SNODGRASS

The emergence of Peronism as a social and political movement in Argentina (ca. 1943–55) primarily
depended on Juan Domingo Perón's ability to negotiate the consent of the
working class, whose integration into the political arena paralleled his own
rise to power. That process began after a 1943 military coup toppled a government largely devoted to maintaining the interests of the nation's landed oligarchy and their political allies. Perón, then a colonel in the Argentine army, was
placed in charge of the Labor Department, a position from which, by 1945, he
had emerged as the de facto leader of the ruling junta. A broad series of social
reforms garnered him the support of the nation's working classes. Perón's
subsequent victory in the 1946 presidential elections then consolidated this
alliance between labor and the populist leader.

As president from 1946 to 1955, Perón maintained official commitments to
both harmonious class relations and industrial growth, which often produced
contradictory tendencies. On one level, Perón advocated national industrial
development and promoted policies favoring domestic capital. He promised
to control labor for the industrialists. On the other hand, Perón maintained
his popular appeal by identifying himself—both practically and symbolically—with working-class aspirations. His government encouraged unionization and enhanced workers' control on the shop floor. Perón's public speeches
reinforced traditional cultural antagonisms between the "people" and the
"elite" in order to perpetuate labor's allegiance. However, the steady industrialization of Argentina required the containment of the very rank-and-file

combativeness that such top-down appeals legitimized. Here is where the labor movement sometimes worked at cross-purposes to the industrialization schemes of Perón's government. The workers perceived Peronism as a means of advancing and defending their class interests. Those interests often conflicted with the political and economic objectives of the Peronist elite. During Perón's term in office, this contradictory wedding of social justice and industrial growth created inevitable antagonisms between the rank-and-file workers and their political leaders.

Focusing on the rank and file's actions and attitudes, this chapter analyzes how and why the workers' vision of the Peronist movement came into conflict with the official Peronism espoused by the government. The capacity of the Perón regime to cultivate working-class support during the 1940s derived from its practical commitment to *justicia social*. Social reformism, in turn, depended on sustained economic growth. Economic expansion had been possible following World War II, when Argentina remained a leading agricultural exporter while postwar European agriculture recovered slowly. However, during the latter years of the Perón regime (1949–55), economic decay gradually undermined those social conquests that workers had gained by government decree from 1943 to 1945 and by their own strike activity from 1946 to 1948. Recessionary pressures during the early 1950s led the Peronist government to impose economic austerity and to repress rank-and-file dissent. The process weakened the hegemonic link between Perón and the Argentine workers. Nonetheless, *peronismo* remained—at the grassroots level—a firm source of political identity and the basis of a working-class culture of resistance well after Perón's fall in 1955.

A Prelude to Peronism

What had been possible politically and socially in the the era of Juan Perón had depended on the previous transformation of Argentina from a primarily agricultural society to an industrial one. The 1930s witnessed fundamental changes in the economic infrastructure and social makeup of urban Argentina. The nation embarked on a period of rapid industrialization and massive urban growth.[1] Migrants from the nation's rural interior settled in the industrial enclaves of Argentina's cities, supplementing southern and eastern European immigrants as a source of cheap, unskilled labor. The newcomers worked as factory operatives in the textile and metallurgical sectors. Others labored in the booming construction trades or in the immense meatpacking plants that supplied Europe with Argentine beef. Although the economy expanded, the workers lived in crowded neighborhoods strained by housing shortages, and their wages shrank. Most industrial laborers suffered arbitrary treatment by employers while the government stood by unwilling to enforce existing labor codes.[2] Meanwhile, the electoral fraud and corruption among civilian politicians, which gave title to the 1930s as the "infamous decade," denied the working class an effective voice in the political arena. Workers thus organized unions as the principal means of advancing their class interests.

By the early 1940s, 20 percent of Argentine workers held union cards, a high level of unionism compared with most Latin American countries. Given their strategic bargaining power in an economy historically dependent on agricultural exports, the railroad workers organized the nation's most powerful union. They alone constituted more than one-third of the union members affiliated with the General Labor Confederation (the Confederación General del Trabajo, or CGT). After 1935, communist labor activists began aggressively organizing the less skilled workers in labor-intensive industries such as meatpacking and construction. They also carried their union drive to the rural sector, achieving limited success in the notoriously exploitative sugar industry of Tucumán province. Communist-led organizing efforts accounted for more than 90 percent of new union members during the period from 1936 to 1943.[3] Under communist leadership, unions outside the transportation sector began asserting influence in the labor movement.

Though lacking a coherent policy toward unions, the Argentine state had always sought stable labor relations. The growth in union membership and a rash of strikes during the mid-1930s forced the government to recognize the workers' potentially disruptive power. In a prelude to Perón's own tactics, governments during the 1930s selectively arbitrated labor relations. Powerful organizations such as the Railroaders' Union benefited from the favorable mediation of the Department of Labor. In return, some union leaders deliberately limited their field of operations to economic concerns so as not to become politically disruptive or to provoke government repression. Communist militants, on the other hand, consistently tied union activities to the broader political struggle against fascism. Their unions thus received the unfavorable attention of the police, who harassed labor activists, prohibited union meetings, and arrested striking workers.[4] The anticommunist repression peaked in 1942. So did factionalism among union leaders, a hallmark of the labor movement since the founding of the CGT in 1930. A negotiated truce between leaders of the Railroaders' Union and the government led the communists and socialists to pull their unions out of the labor central. They organized the dissident confederation called the CGT No. 2. Coming only months before the 1943 military coup, the split of the CGT into two ideological camps would facilitate Perón's capacity to bring organized labor under state control.

The experiences of Argentina's workers during the "infamous decade" helped shape their subsequent perceptions of Peronism. Political exclusion, union repression or indifference, and declining standards of living during a period of general prosperity tended to alienate the workers from the established political system. Few laborers enjoyed the material advances won by the well-organized railroad workers. Indeed, the majority remained unorganized. But the struggles initiated by a minority of labor activists helped instill a common desire to realize social justice through collective action. It became increasingly evident to all that the state largely determined the outcome of worker activism.

The 17th of October

The 1943 military coup responded to the growing inflexibility and lack of consensus within the ruling classes but profoundly transformed labor's relationship with the Argentine state. The military's intervention generated working-class expectations for social reform as well as general anxieties over the neofascist leanings of some of its leaders. A relatively unknown but politically astute colonel, Juan Domingo Perón, gained appointment as head of the Department of Labor. During hundreds of meetings with union delegations, visits to factories, and tours of working-class neighborhoods, Colonel Perón addressed the issues confronted by workers on a daily basis.[5] That he often did so in a language particular to Argentina's lower classes enhanced his popular appeal. Recognizing the potential political strength of the working class, Perón used his official portfolio to mediate a growing number of labor conflicts. The Labor Department enforced existing labor legislation and negotiated collective agreements that established industrial wage scales and improved working conditions on a national level. To soften the effects of wartime inflation on the working class, the state lowered fares on public transport, froze rents, and set controls on food prices.[6] While these reforms quickly garnered the allegiance of most rank-and-file laborers, many union leaders regarded Perón's larger designs with suspicion.

Labor-state relations in the emerging Argentina of Juan Perón involved a shifting balance between the government's concessions to rank-and-file demands and its progressive undermining of organized labor's capacity to act autonomously. As a means of institutionalizing labor's support, Colonel Perón sought to organize workers into state-controlled unions and to eliminate antimilitarist dissent from the labor movement. The military government escalated the repression of communists as well as other labor leaders who refused to collaborate with Colonel Perón. New unions emerged, and established ones were reorganized under the leadership of Peronist sympathizers. Most important, however, Perón's ability to identify himself symbolically and practically with working-class social aspirations earned him the loyalty of the rank-and-file workers.

In the meantime, by 1945, middle-class demands for replacing the junta with an elected government and its support for the Allied war cause increasingly divided Argentine society. The Argentine military junta had been notoriously sympathetic toward Germany during World War II. At the same time, Colonel Perón was appointed vice president of the junta and emerged as the most visible figure within the military government. He also became the target of a growing middle-class opposition movement. The anti-Peronist forces identified the fascistic tendencies of the military government—from anti-Semitism and anticommunism to the jailing of students and attacks on the press—with a series of prolabor initiatives that reversed the declining material conditions of the urban and rural working classes. Ideological schisms thus began to polarize Argentine society generally along class lines. An opposition movement led mainly by elites and the urban middle class united in opposition against the military government and its largely working-class base of support.[7]

As the opposition movement gained momentum, its street demonstrations and rallies implicitly carried an increasingly antilabor content. In September, more than two hundred thousand Argentines marched from the wealthy Barrio Norte district to central Buenos Aires, demanding a return to constitutional government. Many carried banners denouncing the *chusma*, a pejorative term referring to the working-class "mob." That led one observer to notice the increasingly "classist . . . and anti-popular content" of the anti-Peronist coalition.[8] For those benefiting most from state interventionism, the industrial workers, the opposition movement signified a return to the recent past. Two years of state-sponsored social and labor reforms had united the majority of workers in support of Perón's vision of a "new Argentina." Yet the growing vigor of the opposition movement divided the military government. A massive demonstration in September 1945 precipitated an aborted coup within the military and forced the resignations of several members of the ruling junta. On 9 October, a coalition of military officers demanded the resignation of Vice President Perón. The ouster of Perón was followed several days later by his arrest and imprisonment by the junta, seemingly ending his mercurial rise to power.[9] Obviously, the military junta was attempting to renounce its previously close association with Argentine labor in order to gain greater respectability with Argentine elites and the middle class.

Argentine workers thought that Perón's arrest would annul the social reforms and reverse the material gains they had just won. They consequently resumed the struggle two days after his arrest. On 15 October, sugar workers struck in the northwest provinces of Salta and Tucumán, while others protested in the streets of Berisso, a meatpacking community some thirty miles south of the nation's capital. Additional labor mobilizations occurred in the industrial suburbs of Buenos Aires and in the river port of Rosario. The capital itself remained quiet.[10] Later that day, the military officials who had imprisoned Perón promised to maintain his reforms. Workers continued to agitate nonetheless. Sensing the inevitability of a large-scale popular mobilization, the General Labor Confederation called a nationwide general strike for the 18th.[11] But Argentine workers already had taken to the streets, without reference to union orders, the day before.

The mobilization of workers that occurred on 17 October 1945 shook the social and political foundations of Argentina. Early on that morning, protesters began jamming Avenida Mitre in Avellaneda, the sprawling industrial suburb just south of Buenos Aires. Marching behind improvised banners, they forced shopkeepers to close their businesses and filled the air with "vivas" to Perón. At the same moment, sugar workers were converging on downtown Tucumán from the surrounding mills. Likewise, protesters emerged from suburban industrial zones and congregated in the cities of Córdoba, Rosario, and La Plata. They agitated for Perón's release and attacked sites symbolic of elite culture: the Jockey Club, university buildings (and students), the offices of the nation's leading banks, and daily newspapers.[12] The most striking display of rank-and-file solidarity with Perón occurred in Buenos Aires. Hundreds of thousands of working-class men, women, and children festively converged on the elegant avenues of the city before reaching the Plaza de Mayo, the political hub of the nation. Never before in this status-conscious nation had the workers so directly defied their ostensible social superiors—the middle class and the elites—and the military authorities.

Throughout the day, the name of Perón echoed through the plaza and the narrow streets adjoining it. Portraits of Perón and banners identifying union and community affiliations bobbed above the heads of protesters. By nightfall, the open plaza fronting the Casa Rosada swelled with Peronist workers using rolled newspapers as torches. The new military junta debated its options, ultimately deciding that the increasingly impatient workers would depart peacefully only after hearing from Perón himself. He was released from custody. As the night progressed, various labor leaders spoke to the amassed workers over a sustained chorus of "PE-RÓN, PE-RÓN!" Finally, at eleven in the evening, Perón appeared on the balcony of the Casa Rosada and addressed his supporters.

The workers had won. Four months later, national elections would confirm that support for Perón's vision of a "new Argentina" ran far deeper than the two hundred thousand to three hundred thousand supporters present at his return to the political arena.[13] Perón's nationalist and developmentalist programs appealed to sectors of the middle class, and his promise to return religion to the public school curriculum won the vote of devout Catholics. For workers, however, Perón's election legitimized labor's historical struggle for better living and working conditions. They interpreted the electoral victory of 1946 as their own and continued to mobilize to expand their social conquests.

Discipline, Hierarchy, Respect

The 1946 elections consolidated a relationship of mutual dependency between labor and the Perón regime. In return for their political support, Perón promised social justice to the workers. Another official tenet of Peronism, however, emphasized economic development along nationalist lines. The Perón regime believed that harmonious class relations would encourage industrial growth. Peronist authorities thus sought to centralize the labor movement in order to limit union autonomy, thereby (they believed) disciplining the rank and file and preventing costly labor disputes. Yet even Perón himself recognized that "no one can preserve or impose discipline until he has first instituted justice."[14] At the same time that the Perón regime asserted greater control over the labor movement, workers continued to pressure the government to meet its commitment to social justice.

The process of integrating workers into Peronist-led unions accelerated after the 1946 elections. During the next four years, the Perón regime broadened its control over the structure and leadership of the nation's principal labor federation. The government intervened in the internal affairs of established unions, replacing dissident leaders with Peronist sympathizers. The General Labor Confederation evolved into a virtual appendage of the state and became the administrator of government policies for the labor movement. State-sponsored organizing drives incorporated the unorganized industrial workforce and previously unaffiliated unions into the ranks of the powerful labor central. Membership of the General Labor Confederation multiplied rapidly. Between 1945 and 1950, the number of unionized wage earners in Argentina jumped from roughly one-half million to more than two million. By 1950, an estimated 50 to 70 percent of the workers in most manufacturing sectors carried union cards.[15] Seen from the top down, this organizing process institutionalized the political muscle displayed by the working class in the

1946 elections. From a grassroots perspective, however, unionization galvanized a rank-and-file commitment to improve living and working conditions beyond the levels conceded by the state prior to the 17 October mobilization.

The post–World War II expansion of industrial output provided the rank-and-file workers with the bargaining power necessary to realize their own aspirations. Europe's devastation and the conversion of North American factories to wartime production briefly protected Argentine industry from foreign competition. The Peronists inherited an economy growing at an annual rate of nearly 10 percent between 1945 and 1949. Industrial production rose 26 percent, and despite a resumption of foreign immigration, employment levels increased 13 percent over the same period. Workers seized on these favorable economic conditions and struck in record numbers from 1946 to 1948.[16] They no longer feared unemployment. They also anticipated Perón's tolerance. Furthermore, the strengthening of industrial unions gave Argentine workers the collective muscle necessary to confront employers through direct action.

The state's gradual elimination of non-Peronist union leaders did not end rank-and-file militancy. Working out of its headquarters in Buenos Aires, the CGT came to dominate the Argentine labor movement by the late 1940s. The repression of rival union leaders and the labor central's unquestionable capacity to deliver the economic goods guaranteed its power. Yet its dominance did not remain unchallenged, even within the CGT fold. Provincial union leaders in Córdoba and Bahía Blanca vigorously protested the appointment of outsiders as regional CGT delegates. The question of regional autonomy fueled strikes by commercial workers in Santa Fe and the Provincial Workers' Federation of Corrientes.[17] The radical labor activists who played such a crucial role in the pre-Peronist union movement also acted within the CGT unions. Many communists considered Peronism "progressive" for its vision of creating a single, unified labor central. They thus followed orders emanating from Moscow and disbanded their organizations to "bore from within" the Peronist unions.[18] One communist activist noted how these "real" labor leaders "worked quietly" in their union locals in order to "educate" the Peronists.[19] However, the CGT knew of their intentions. The official Peronist newspaper, *El Laborista*, cautioned Peronist union leaders to remain vigilant of communist infiltration.[20] The relationship between these dissidents and rank-and-file workers remains difficult to uncover. But continuous government efforts to stifle militancy in industries such as meatpacking and the metal trades—sectors with a history of radical labor activism—suggest that this militant minority played an active role in promoting a degree of independence and combativity within their union locals.

Workers proved particularly combative in those sectors with a history of union activism. The importance of chilled beef to Argentina's export economy led the Perón regime to intervene early in the meat workers' unions in order to "impose discipline." Authorities had purged communist leaders from the national federation prior to 1946. Peronist sympathizers assumed control of the rapidly growing meat workers' unions. But the communists, in their own effort to maintain working-class unity, disbanded their locals and encouraged the rank and file to affiliate with the Peronist unions.[21] The union locals, organized at the factory level, maintained an exceptional degree of independence from the national federation. The clandestine character of their activity complicates the historian's task of determining the subsequent activities of the communists. But sustained rank-and-file militancy forced the Perón regime to continue intervening in the affairs of union locals, especially those where the communists had been most successful prior to the emergence of Peronism.

The meat workers struck sporadically throughout the late 1940s despite government efforts to appease rank-and-file demands. Perón ended a two-month strike in 1946 by intervening directly. The resulting collective contract imposed by the state proved the most favorable to date for the meat workers. Yet the packing plants' efforts to fire union activists led workers to return only reluctantly. In Avellaneda, where five plants employed some thirty thousand laborers, the strike remained effective; union militants blocked access to the packing houses. The Avellaneda strike ended only after police arrested the alleged leaders and closed union locals.[22] Still, wildcat strikes continued to plague this vital industry because employers refused to comply with the contract. Their attitude provoked rank-and-file militancy and further government interventions. The CGT justified the 1948 intervention of a former communist stronghold in Avellaneda, the "La Blanca" plant, as a means of inhibiting "disturbances of an organic nature . . . that seriously compromise the unity and discipline that should reign in all organized sectors of work."[23] The government achieved this objective of forging "unity and discipline" only gradually. State control of unions and the repression of dissident leaders did not imply the containment of rank-and-file insurgency.

The conflicts in the meat industry demonstrate well the mutually dependent relationship between rank-and-file workers and the Perón regime. Workers struck to translate Peronist promises of social justice into concrete deeds. Not all strikes enjoyed the immediate sanction of the Peronist authorities. Some were declared illegal. Although many union leaders lost their positions when the CGT removed them from their locals, the rank and file essentially emerged victorious during these early years of the Perón government. Conservative estimates indicate that, between 1945 and 1948, real wages for skilled and unskilled workers rose 22 and 30 percent, respectively. More important, the percentage of national income earned by blue-collar workers grew from approximately 40 to 50 percent. The majority of industrial laborers enjoyed workers' compensation, maternity leave, paid vacations, and protection from arbitrary dismissal.[24] At the shop floor level, workers gained greater autonomy relative to management. New contracts guaranteed employers' recognition of the right of union delegates to oversee working conditions, job demarcation, and labor mobility on the factory floor.[25] The rank and file willingly sacrificed union autonomy for these concrete improvements in their daily lives.

The imposition of collaborationist leaders did not incapacitate the rank and file from agitating and redefining *peronismo* on its own terms, and worker protest placed the Perón regime in many politically embarrassing situations. A mid-1947 strike by Buenos Aires' garbage collectors revealed the divergent perceptions of workers and their ostensible allies within the Peronist movement. The government had removed the leaders of the socialist-affiliated Municipal Workers' Union in 1944. Three years later, in March 1947, the Peronist union bosses resigned in protest over the government's failure to increase wages.[26] Soon thereafter, the sanitation workers struck when the city of Buenos Aires fired several of their colleagues for selling "goods" collected on their routes.[27] The workers argued that junk dealing was a necessary supplement to their minimum wages. The strike spread quickly to nearby suburbs. After several days, two-foot-high piles of refuse clogged the streets of downtown Buenos Aires. Despite the hardships imposed on city residents, one observer noted how the strikers garnered "considerable public sympathy" once their meager salaries became known. The government declared the strike illegal, claiming that it entailed no conflict with "capital." However, the chief of police of Buenos Aires resigned when ordered by Perón to repress the strike.[28] Perón responded by ordering soldiers from nearby barracks to start collecting the city's trash. Meanwhile, the CGT began recruiting replacement workers.

After a week, the Department of Labor declared its intention of forming an investigative committee to study the workers' demands. Authorities simultaneously threatened mass dismissals for those refusing to resume work. But on the same day, Perón greeted an enthusiastic gathering of strikers from the balcony of the Casa Rosada and promised to resolve the conflict quickly. Juan Queraltó, a leader of a right-wing nationalist organization allied with the Peronists, addressed a similar rally of suburban workers. They emphatically shouted him down with calls of "We don't care about nationalism!" and "What are we, Peronists or nationalists?" The strike concluded with the reinstatement of all workers and the announcement of new wage scales. The CGT immediately claimed responsibility for the workers' triumph, while the gov-

ernment appointed new intervenors in an effort to quell the municipal workers' combativity. Two years later, however, this union would still be considered
among the "unreconstructed rebels" within the Peronist labor movement.[29]

The garbage collectors' strike revealed clearly how the workers' own perceptions of Peronism departed from that of the nonlaboring elements within
the multiclass Peronist coalition. It also suggests that the Perón regime's control of the labor movement remained fragile. The rank and file's capacity to
act autonomously remained firm. So did Perón's ability to preserve his reputation as the champion of the working class. Despite his secret orders to break
the strike, he continued to promise a favorable resolution. Thus can one
understand his enthusiastic reception by the strikers compared with the quick
dismissal of his nationalist ally. As with the earlier conflicts in the meat industry, Perón maintained his reputation intact by delivering the economic goods
to the rank and file. In large measure, Argentina's postwar economic boom
established the structural parameters within which labor-state relations co-
alesced. In 1948, however, that foundation began to weaken.

Workers in many industrial sectors continued to agitate despite the reversal
of Argentina's economic fortunes. In late 1948, a North American correspon-
dent reported that the rising cost of living was sowing dissension within the
labor movement.[30] A manifesto released by the General Labor Confederation
confirmed the depth of unrest. The labor central's hierarchy condemned
slowdown movements, high absenteeism, and shop floor sabotage carried out
by its own members. The CGT's directive further reflected the Peronist authorities' incomplete control over the rank and file. It is difficult to gauge the
depth of shop floor resistance. But its emergence corresponded with an increased number of wildcat strikes.[31] In November 1948, the CGT declared a
bakers' strike illegal as mounted police broke up a gathering of workers demonstrating in the Plaza de Mayo.[32] The economic downturn hardened the
state's resolve to repress labor unrest, particularly in sectors such as the heavily
subsidized food industries.

Recessionary pressures struck the northwest provinces particularly hard. In
Tucumán, the bankruptcy of a sugar mill in January 1949 put three thousand
laborers out of work. Later that year, in November, the Sugar Workers' Federation struck for higher wages.[33] The union timed the action to coincide with
the beginning of the sugar harvest. Within days, more than one hundred
thousand cane cutters, drivers, and mill workers at twenty-eight mills walked
out, paralyzing the industry. The CGT declared the strike illegal. Police jailed
hundreds of militants, closed union locals, and issued arrest orders for labor
leaders escaping detention. But union locals continued to meet clandestinely.
By mid-November, police contingents surrounded the mills to protect those

Striking Argentine workers, 1951.
(Courtesy of the Archivo General de la Nación, Buenos Aires)

workers who chose—increasingly—to return to work. Strikers resisted longer in those mills where "Communist elements were numerous."[34] Late in the month, police arrested twenty delegates of "autonomous" unions in the city of Tucumán as they were discussing plans for a general strike in support of the sugar workers. The Sugar Workers' Federation lifted the strike on the 28th after authorities promised to release detained workers and boost wages by 60 percent. The Peronist congressional bloc subsequently expelled three deputies from Tucumán for denouncing the CGT's strikebreaking tactics. The Sugar Workers' Federation would remain under control of the national labor central until the Perón regime collapsed in 1955.

The strike in the sugar industry was but one manifestation of a broader expression of working-class discontent, the emergence of which coincided with the end of Argentina's economic boom. The sudden appearance of "spiraling prices, consumer goods shortages, and an aggravated housing deficiency" was undermining labor's previous conquests.[35] The number of strikes escalated. Several months before the sugar strike, 120,000 construction workers had walked off the job in protest of the government's failure to approve wage hikes.[36] In the meat industry, 70,000 workers struck to protest employers' efforts to reassert control over the shop floor. The state declared the strike illegal, and the workers returned after a week. The CGT arrested the union leaders and replaced them with a rival faction willing to eliminate the advances made in job security and working conditions earlier in the decade.[37] The rank and file also expressed its disillusionment outside the workplace. One eyewitness characterized the traditional celebration of "Loyalty Day"— the Peronist holiday marking the 17 October mobilization—as "something less substantial than the noisy, multitudinous affair of years past." Only one-half of the 100,000 workers issued free transport passes by the CGT made the journey from the provinces to the capital. Most of those arriving allegedly spent the day sightseeing rather than expressing their loyalty in the Plaza de Mayo. The observer noted emphatically that the poor attendance did not reflect a "waning of Perón's popularity." He simply concluded that, for the workers, "there really [wasn't] too much to shout about."[38]

On a symbolic level, the most significant industrial conflict of the period involved the railroad workers. The wages of these workers, traditionally among the highest, began declining after the Perón regime nationalized the industry in 1948. To cut operating expenses, the government laid off some seventeen thousand workers. In late 1950, thousands of the lowest-paid railroaders carried out a series of wildcat strikes—led by dissident leaders. The industry was paralyzed. The state responded to the "national emergency" by drafting the striking workers into the civil defense corps and placing the railroads under military jurisdiction.[39] Police arrested thousands of workers and removed the leaders of numerous union locals. Ultimately, the state gave in to the striking railroaders, bringing their wages in line with those of other skilled workers and abandoning efforts to reduce the number of personnel.[40] But the means used to break the wildcat strikes revealed that Perón had reversed his earlier policy of accommodating labor. Ironically, one of Perón's first speeches to union workers, back in January 1944, had come before the Rosario railroaders. On that occasion, Perón declared that the "cohesion and strength" of the military made it the ideal model for organized labor. By 1951, however, Perón apparently concluded that only the deployment of the army could instill a sense of "discipline . . . hierarchy and respect" within the insurgent rank and file.[41]

Drastic Solutions of the Past

As the Argentine economy declined during the late 1940s and early 1950s, the state hardened its authoritarian impulse vis-à-vis the labor movement. Yet popular support for Perón still depended on the government's capacity to maintain a prominent role for the working class within Argentine political and social life. For this reason, the government often capitulated to the workers' demands after repressing their strikes. Furthermore, labor's support for Perón did not merely reflect an exchange of political loyalty for economic goods. Workers also identified their interests with Peronism for less tangible reasons. Perón's speeches constantly reiterated the enhanced social status of workers in the "new Argentina." The language of Peronism juxtaposed the distance between the "infamous decade" and the Peronist present. The workers' support for Perón, according to CGT head Eduardo Vuletich, derived not merely from the provision of material benefits. Rather, working-class loyalty reflected their gratitude for "the dignity . . . that the oligarchy always denied [them]."[42] Government propaganda reinforced the link between President Perón and social reformism. Working-class housing projects bore names such as "Presidente Perón" and "Evita." Highly visible reminders that "Perón Fulfills" and "Evita Dignifies" adorned new public buildings and parks. Portraits of Juan Perón and his wife, Eva Duarte de Perón, hung from classroom walls; they even adorned the front of city buses.[43] The historian faces a difficult task in weighing the effects of these propagandistic images on working-class consciousness against the more concrete experience of economic degradation and the state's repression of worker protest.

The Perón regime certainly remained capable of mobilizing popular support at election time. The creation of a network of Peronist political clubs in working-class neighborhoods aided the task. So did the government's 1947 decision to grant women the franchise. Perhaps owing to the prominent political role of Perón's wife, Evita, women proved to be more ardent supporters of Perón than men. In late 1951, they helped elect Perón for a second presidential term.[44] It was none too soon. Within a year, a full-blown recession eroded working-class living standards and crippled labor's capacity to sustain the material advances won during the mid-1940s.

The recession may be traced to a decline in traditional agricultural exports after the close of the Second World War. Increased internal consumption and severe droughts in 1951 and 1952 further exacerbated the declining exportation of foodstuffs.[45] The resulting depletion of foreign exchange reserves undermined Argentina's capacity to import the capital goods and raw materials it needed for sustained manufacturing growth. By 1952, industrial production had fallen to a level near that of 1946. The nation's gross domestic product, which had grown 25 percent during the three years of 1945–48, increased by only 14 percent over the seven years before 1955. Rising food prices caused inflation to skyrocket from under 4 percent per annum (in 1947) to more than 40 percent (in 1952). Although social benefits and improved working conditions remained intact, inflationary pressures were really eroding workers' earnings.[46] The Perón regime responded to the crisis with an economic austerity program. It froze workers' wages in two-year contracts while attempting to curb inflation through price controls. In the long run, the austerity program proved as effective in stabilizing prices as at controlling wages. In 1954, inflation returned to the 4 percent level.[47]

Figures and percentages, however, do not reveal the totality of human experience. Acute shortages of meat, rising costs of other basic commodities, and long lines at the markets reflected a real decline in the living standards of all working-class families. Early in 1952, an Anglo-Argentine business journal reported that the typical four-member family of a *porteño* laborer could scarcely afford the barest necessities.[48] Survival depended on the regularity of employment. Yet the economic crisis dealt a harsh blow to several labor-intensive industrial sectors. Falling consumer demand, for example, slowed textile production. In 1952, the number of hours worked in the mills dropped 25 percent between March and November alone. Overall, an estimated forty thousand textile workers suffered layoffs during the year. The same period witnessed the dismissal of twenty-five thousand meat workers.[49] The curtailment of public works projects and a decline in private construction forced layoffs in the metal and building trades as well. Labor demand would continue falling until 1954.

The strategic bargaining power enjoyed by organized labor during the mid-1940s now declined along with the economy. Workers were unable to resist the wage freezes and layoffs, and employers attempted to subvert earlier labor conquests. The state also abandoned its commitment to mediating industrial conflicts on behalf of the working class. Perón himself declared that workers could raise their own standards of living through increased productivity and that they should no longer depend on the "drastic solutions of the past."[50] Henceforward, the government was to withdraw from labor disputes. The secretary-general of the General Labor Confederation publicly supported this new policy, declaring that Perón "should not be involved in a purely domestic matter between employer and employee."[51] This policy reversal coincided with industrialists' efforts to rationalize the production process by raising the workers' output.

An active commitment to industrial growth was, from the outset, a basic component of "official" Peronism. In 1952, a recession year, promoting labor productivity took priority over the government's support of working-class interests and of social justice. The Perón regime organized a series of Productivity Congresses in which union leaders met with employers to negotiate worker productivity. Argentine industrialists lacked the capital to introduce technological innovations and refurbish worn machinery in their factories. They therefore sought to raise production levels by increasing output per worker. Owners first attempted—with the tacit approval of the state—to raise labor productivity by implementing a series of incentive schemes and speedups. The workers resisted. In those industries in which bonus systems existed, they struggled against employers' efforts to reduce the time allocated for the fulfillment of a particular task. After all, one crucial achievement of the strikes of the mid-1940s, one historian notes, had been "the [worker's] ability to earn a good wage without being subjected to inhuman pressures within the production process."[52] Although inflation was eroding their wages, workers remained committed to the ideal of higher hourly rates as the principal means of reestablishing their standard of living.

The recession made the contradictions of "official" Peronism transparent. The state could no longer maintain its commitment to sustained industrialization at the same moment that it delivered on its promises of social justice for the workers. The government's abandonment of the "drastic solutions of the past" effectively permitted industrialists to restructure labor relations without the threat of state intervention. Rank-and-file resistance prevented that transformation. Despite the erosion of their bargaining power, Argentine workers clung tenaciously to *their* interpretation of Peronism. They also directly limited the extent to which industrial growth would proceed at *their* expense.

Matters for the Police

The year 1952 marked a watershed in relations between the rank and file and the Perón regime. The recession had undermined the dramatic material conquests of the mid-1940s. Growing unemployment and the state's abandonment of its policy of mediation had eroded labor's bargaining power. Combined with the social consequences of economic decay, Eva Perón's death cast a shadow over the Peronist movement. Evita had symbolized the Perón regime's active commitment to championing the rights of the working classes. Although myth has obscured her historical role, individual laborers perceived Evita as the Peronist official most sympathetic toward the working-class community.[53] Her death weakened the paternalistic (or maternalistic?) bonds between the state and the workers. Evita's passing coincided with a hardening of the government's authoritarian response to popular protest.

Working-class disaffection with Peronist discipline and the labor hierarchy emerged with clarity after the state adopted economic austerity. But economic as well as political determinants forced workers to employ means other than the strike to express their discontent. For one thing, declining bargaining power limited the possibility of a strike's successful outcome. Furthermore, by 1952, the risks inherent to collective action outweighed the potential benefits. Given the heightened level of political repression, dissident labor leaders held a vested interest in avoiding explicit displays of insubordination.[54]

Several instances of intimidation announced the dire consequences of direct action. A strike in a Pirelli tire plant, launched during the renegotiation of two-year wage contracts, lasted an hour before police declared it illegal and jailed the organizers. Twenty workers in the Cantábrica metal works factory staged a wildcat strike for higher wages. They were fired without indemnity and blacklisted.[55] The repression of "dissidents" occasionally assumed more violent proportions. Reportedly arrested for seditious talk, a metallurgical worker died under detention in a Buenos Aires police station. The secretary-general of a local CGT union also died under similar circumstances in the northern province of Misiones. In both cases, efforts by Radical Party congressional deputies to form investigative committees failed. "These are matters for the police to handle," declared the president of the Peronist bloc.[56] Indeed they were, for the maintenance of order within the social base of Peronism knew no boundaries. Peronist labor leaders clearly faced greater repercussions for dissident activities than rank-and-file workers engaging in wildcat strikes. But even the threat of blacklisting remained a powerful deterrent to all but the most militant workers during a period of growing unemployment.

Rank-and-file workers in Buenos Aires consequently employed alternative means of resistance to express their diminished confidence in the Peronist hierarchy. In September 1952, immediately after the imposition of wage freezes, CGT secretary-general Juan Espejo entered a Buenos Aires soccer stadium and met a chorus of sixty thousand whistling spectators. Soon thereafter, workers gathered in the Plaza de Mayo to celebrate the 17th of October Peronist holiday. They again greeted Espejo's appearance with a round of catcalls and jeers. He resigned immediately, citing the clear "indication that the working class [was] no longer satisfied with the actions of the directors of the labor central." The executive committee of the CGT refused to accept his resignation. But a large group of rank-and-file workers had congregated outside the CGT's massive downtown headquarters. Upon hearing of Espejo's apparent reinstatement, a delegation of *porteño* metal workers loudly voiced their angry disapproval. Only then did the Peronist union bureaucrats reconsider and accept the resignation of the discredited labor leader.[57]

Workers also created subtler and less visible forms of resistance. A clandestine paper issued by dissident Peronist railroaders criticized Perón's unfulfilled promise to reinstate workers dismissed during the 1950–51 strikes. The tract also condemned the imposition of union bureaucrats "qualified only by their influence in a certain political sector [and] completely ignorant of matters related to the railroad industry."[58] Another underground newspaper circulating among Buenos Aires' port workers sarcastically questioned Perón's commitment to his supporters. "[Of] course you don't care about [their material condition] because the topic would not be suitable for a partisan speech," it warned, "much less for propaganda."[59] The dissident longshoremen noted the divergence between the language of Peronism and working-class reality. Whether voiced in the plazas and stadiums or through the clandestine press, these protests reflected a growing working-class alienation from the Peronist hierarchy—and this from railroaders, who had been among Perón's earliest supporters.[60] After the 1950–51 wildcat strikes, they joined the vanguard of workers' dissidence. Those railway strikes had foreshadowed the emerging antagonisms between the labor hierarchy and the rank and file as both leaders and followers articulated *peronismo* in a manner congruent with their separate interests.

The recession exposed the Perón regime's long-term inability to sustain manufacturing growth while promoting working-class interests. That contradiction forced labor leaders into a quandary. While workers continued to agitate for higher wages to combat inflation, their union representatives faced exhortations from above to limit rank-and-file demands. Throughout Perón's ten-year regime, leaders from all levels of the labor movement lost their positions for refusing to act within the parameters set by the state. Yet these leaders' unresponsiveness to rank-and-file grievances generated pressures from below and, as in the case of CGT-head Juan Espejo, occasionally resulted in their forced resignation by popular demand.

During the recession, workers employed their own grassroots interpretation of *peronismo* to legitimize a culture of resistance. When the two-year contracts that froze wages neared expiration, workers carried their struggle from the shop floor, plazas, and clandestine press into an open confrontation with employers and the Peronist hierarchy. The months preceding the 1954 renegotiation of collective wage contracts witnessed an upsurge of working-class militancy. Bitter intraunion factionalism emerged. When port workers in Buenos Aires' Barracas district—one of a handful of unions still affiliated with the anarchists—struck for higher wages, they received support from several Peronist unions active on the *porteño* docks. Authorities immediately intervened in the internal affairs of the CGT-affiliated locals and expelled their leaders.[61] In September 1953, violence erupted when a leader of the Buenos Aires municipal workers' union opposed demands for wage hikes. The same issue precipitated gunshots at a meeting of power-and-light workers in the capital. In both cases, the union leaders upholding the government's austerity measures were also Peronist congressional deputies.[62]

Although economic imperatives generated the conflicts, the Perón regime chose to emphasize ideological motives as the underlying cause. The government initiated a renewal of anticommunist purges within the labor movement. In Buenos Aires, authorities expelled scores of bakers and port workers from their Peronist unions. The Metal Workers' Union established new statutes forbidding discrimination against anyone except "him who accepts the directives or ideology of the Communist Party."[63] As mentioned above, the Perón regime remained vigilant after the communists ordered their ranks to enter Peronist unions during the mid-1940s, and the state's fear of working-class insurgency in the 1950s led authorities to resurrect the specter of communist agitation. James Scott suggests, however, that those most likely to challenge the status quo directly are the ones who take the dominant ideology seriously. If so, union authorities had "most to fear from those . . . among whom the institutions of hegemony [had] been most successful."[64] In Argentina of the mid-1950s, they were the Peronist rank and file. Arresting "foreign agitators" (as authorities called the dissidents) belied the genuine cause of the emerging labor conflicts: rank-and-file Peronist demands for higher wages. The recession of the early 1950s had crippled the state's capacity to maintain the material components of *peronismo*. But workers nevertheless retained a healthy commitment to the ideal of decent living standards through high hourly wage rates. When the expectations inherent to their grassroots interpretation of Peronism failed to materialize, workers who were partisans of Perón were the first to resist.

State authorities feared that higher wages would trigger another round of inflation. Although collective contracts expired early in 1954, the government delayed negotiations until after the April congressional and state elections. Electoral results confirmed the political muscle of Peronism yet masked the increasing conflicts within the movement. Tensions escalated. The General Labor Confederation officially called for a 15 percent wage hike to bring workers' salaries in line with the rising cost of living. Unions objected because the proposal was too low. The metal workers, for example, demanded a 40 percent wage hike.[65] Workers pressed their claims through the largest series of strikes and slowdown movements since the industrial unrest of 1948. By May, an estimated three hundred thousand *porteño* workers from numerous sectors were engaging in collective action. The strikes spread through industries such as textiles, shoes, metals, chemicals, urban transport, cement, and the ports. Milk shortages became severe and cigarettes nonexistent.[66] CGT officials denounced the strikes as unproductive and condemned the use of sabotage on the shop floor. By mid-1954, most unions had accepted wage increases along the lines of the CGT's proposed 15 percent. Within a year, however, inflation would again reduce workers' purchasing power to 1944 levels. Meanwhile, the traditional May Day celebration in the Plaza de Mayo suffered its lowest turnout since Perón had come to power.[67]

Workers in most industrial sectors accepted the new contracts with uncharacteristic resignation. Others protested. In Buenos Aires, police used tear gas to break up a demonstration by hundreds of rubber workers.[68] Forming one of the largest and most militant of the Peronist unions, the metal workers reacted violently to their leaders' announcement of a new contract allocating 12 to 25 percent wage hikes (in contrast to the union's demand of 40 percent). A melee in the union's headquarters left three workers dead and forty-eight injured. Violence soon spread to the industrial suburbs of Buenos Aires, where the government ordered police to protect stricken plants. In the suburb of Morón, a Peronist municipal deputy appeared at a factory to urge workers to end their wildcat strike. The ensuing violence resulted in additional fatalities. Other working-class neighborhoods experienced similar pitched battles as workers agitated in the streets surrounding their factories. In an effort to break the strike, Peronist authorities arrested dozens of union leaders. They blamed the factional conflict on communist agitators and ordered the deportation of several foreign-born activists as "undesirables." Rank-and-file discontent, however, remained strong. A week after the metal workers' strike officially ended, more than fifty thousand workers continued wildcat stoppages. Government officials eventually acknowledged six working-class deaths as a result of the conflict; union sources, however, claimed that more than one hundred workers had lost their lives in this struggle for higher wages.[69] In those working-class communities forming the front line of resistance, the industrial unrest registered as more than an economic setback, for the government's response forced the rank and file even to rethink their allegiance to Perón.

Since the mid-1940s, *peronismo* had meant more for Argentine workers than a series of social reforms and institutional structures through which improved living and working conditions were channeled. Peronism also signified a process in which workers created a social movement and reinforced a well-established culture of resistance. The means they themselves had per-fected included mass mobilizations, strikes, and shop floor struggles. Those experiences established new standards and rights, transforming rank-and-file consciousness. New perceptions of the state, of unions, and of the limits of employers' authority on the shop floor, in turn, guided the rank and file in defense of its collective interests. After 1948, state-sponsored strikebreaking, union interventionism, economic austerity measures, and the government's repressive response to industrial unrest all exposed Perón's weakened commit-ment to social justice. The government's devotion to industrial growth enticed Perón to neutralize the state's role in mediating labor-capital conflicts, forcing workers to confront employers directly. They now possessed the organiza-tional structures and collective consciousness to do so. But workers could no longer count on the state's support. The totality of these processes weakened the hegemonic link between Perón and the rank and file. More important, the experience of struggle strengthened the workers' commitment and capacity to defend their class interests against subsequent threats either from employers or from the state.

Cinco por Uno

Late 1954 witnessed a resurgence of large-scale civil unrest in Argentina. Uni-versity students and the church emerged as the focal points of middle-class (as distinct from working-class) opposition to Peronist authoritarianism. In Octo-ber, a university strike spread nationwide. Hundreds of students faced arrest, and violence in La Plata resulted in the death of a law student.[70] The same period witnessed the emergence of state anticlericalism. The Catholic hier-archy had initially supported Perón in 1946 after he reestablished compulsory religious instruction in the public schools. Church leaders withdrew their backing during the early 1950s after Perón accused the church of attempting to undermine Peronist control of labor unions. Perón's indictment of the organiz-ing activities of Catholic Action, a church-based social activist movement, was based on fact as well as historical precedent. A labor leader active in the textile industry during the 1930s noted how Catholic organizers had worked in collu-sion with the mill owners to dissuade workers from joining his socialist-led union. The early 1950s witnessed a renewal of Catholic Action's proselytizing efforts within the working-class community.[71] The government saw this action as a threat to Peronist hegemony in labor affairs and reversed its education policy and ended subsidies to Catholic schools. The state-controlled press became vehemently anticlerical in 1954. When authorities began arresting priests and closing churches in November, they inadvertently broadened civil opposition beyond the more visible resistance of the students to include large numbers of middle-class Catholics.[72]

Events transpired rapidly in 1955, the year of Perón's fall. In May, the government announced its intention to introduce a constitutional amendment legally separating the church and the state. The jailing of priests continued. On 11 June, during the traditional Corpus Christi parade, a hundred thousand largely middle-class protesters conducted a silent demonstration through the streets of central Buenos Aires. Perón's excommunication stripped the papal seal of approval from Peronism and led the General Labor Confederation to organize a rally in support of the deportation of two clergymen for antigovernment agitation.[73] The labor demonstration ended in tragedy. On 16 June, as thousands of Peronist workers gathered in the Plaza de Mayo, rebel military officers from the navy and air force mutinied against the Perón regime. Air force warplanes swung low over the gathering of defenseless workers in the open plaza, bombing and strafing until at least 156 workers were killed and scores injured. Loyal officers thwarted the coup by storming the nearby naval headquarters with the aid of armed civilians. In the aftermath, crowds of Peronist loyalists sacked several churches near the plaza.[74]

Rather than employ the rebel officers' bloody offensive against workers to mobilize the rank and file, Perón capitulated to the mutineers' demands. He removed the most vocal anticlerical officials from his cabinet. Perón then declared an end to the "revolution" and promised to continue his term in office as the "president of all Argentines." The truce failed. A reinvigorated opposition emerged in a series of highly visible street demonstrations, as rumors spread of the president's imminent resignation. However, Perón caught the public unaware in a speech characterized as a "virtual declaration of civil war." "The watchword for every *peronista*," warned Perón, "is to answer one violent act with another . . . and whenever one of us falls, five of them will fall."[75] The government imposed a state of siege, and the "cinco por uno" speech fueled rumors that the workers were being armed to defend *peronismo*. Two weeks later, Gen. Eduardo Lonardi launched the "Revolución Libertadora," a coup meant to conclude the Perón regime's "destruction of the culture and economy [of Argentina]."[76] Perón resigned passively. In stark contrast to his arrest in October 1945, Argentine military officers now stood united in their opposition to the populist leader.

The General Labor Confederation initially responded to the 1955 coup with a broadcast over state radio calling on workers to mobilize in a struggle against the rebel military forces. Small contingents of workers attempted

Middle-class opponents celebrating the fall of Perón, 1955.
(Courtesy of the Archivo General de la Nación, Buenos Aires)

to enter Buenos Aires from outlying industrial districts. Soldiers fired on them, and their resistance collapsed. Perón's sudden capitulation prompted the labor central to reverse its ill-advised call to arms, now urging instead that workers remain calm. The CGT even denounced "some groups who [were] trying to create disturbances."[77] There would be no repeat of the 17 October mobilization in 1955. On a pragmatic level, the military's immediate occupation of the industrial suburbs of Buenos Aires precluded any efforts to mobilize en masse. Furthermore, the bombing of the Plaza de Mayo several months earlier demonstrated the risks inherent to collective resistance. In Rosario, however, heavy street fighting between workers and soldiers continued. Transport workers, meat packers, and cereal mill workers erected barricades and controlled the city center for a week. Only the military's physical occupation of Rosario ended the open defiance of the workers against the so-called Revolución Libertadora.[78] Yet the Rosario workers' fierce resistance had proved to be an exception to an overall pattern of rank-and-file passivity.

Conclusion

In 1945, Argentine workers identified Perón with their social and material aspirations. They struggled throughout the mid-1940s to realize those goals. During the 1950s, however, the rank and file experienced the partial reversal of their achievements. Falling wages, intraunion factionalism, and the state's repression of labor dissent led the rank and file to perceive Perón differently in 1955 than in 1945. Although the "Revolución Libertadora" promised no loosening of state repression, the workers were no longer willing to sacrifice mightily to save Perón.

The ouster of Perón did not, however, imply the fall of *peronismo*, for the Argentine working class remained committed to the grassroots movement bearing his name. Throughout the Perón regime, workers had waged a constant struggle with Peronist authorities over the articulation of the ideals of *peronismo*. The fall of Perón, therefore, did not carry the devastating consequences implicit in the remark of one Peronist that "[the workers] didn't know how to reply. . . . They were the sons of a paternalistic government and their father had left them. . . . They were like orphans."[79] In fact, Argentine workers had reached maturity with the 17 October mobilization in 1945. The mass strike activity of the mid-1940s, when rank-and-file insurgency forced a bottom-up interpretation of *peronismo* on Perón, signaled their passage into adulthood. During the early 1950s, Perón's authoritarian effort to bring the family budget under control led the working class to leave home.

Nonetheless, despite the family feuds within Peronism, Perón's fall from power and the military government's subsequent effort to undermine Peronist leadership in the unions resulted in labor's vigorous and united defense of the family honor. Daniel James's account of the post-1955 working-class experience in Argentina, *Resistance and Integration*, demonstrates the depths to which the workers remained committed to the ideals of *peronismo*. General Lonardi, as president, attempted to forge a conciliatory relationship with Peronist unions, but he was abruptly forced to resign in November 1955. The new hard-line military government then tried to impose industrial rationalization on the shop floor. It forcibly dismissed thousands of Peronist activists from CGT unions, a tactic achieving only partial success. By mid-1956, a "new generation of militants with little or no formal experience" had organized a semiclandestine resistance movement on the shop floor and within the working-class community. That mobilization eventually resulted in renewed strike activity and the widespread employment of graffiti, pamphleteering, and sabotage as a means of expressing the Peronist culture of resistance.[80] These were the genuine "orphans" of Perón. The new generation of labor militants struggled in defiance of a repressive state to defend the rights demanded and won by the working class from the "paternalistic government" of Juan Perón.

The Peronist resistance broadened during the 1960s to include disaffected middle-class students and the urban guerrilla group called the Montoneros. Popular protests eventually led the military to capitulate. In 1973, Juan Perón returned from exile to reassume the presidency. But by then, Perón was an elderly figurehead. His command over the factious family of Peronists was weaker than ever. Following his death in office, his widow, María Estela Martínez de Perón (Isabel), assumed the presidency. She could neither control inflation, nor reverse the industrial paralysis, nor defuse the violent conflicts between the Left and Right within her own Peronist Party. The military coup of 1976 ushered in the Dirty War, in which the armed forces attempted once and for all, with state terror, to "cleanse" Argentina of "dissidents," Peronist or otherwise. Many labor leaders were singled out for arbitrary arrests, torture, and summary execution. Then the military government discredited itself with economic mismanagement, human rights' abuses, and a disastrous war with Great Britain over the Malvinas (Falkland) Islands. Labor agitation in 1982 helped return a civilian regime to power. Six years later, the rank and file still identified with the party of Perón, helping to elect another Peronist, Carlos Saúl Menem, as president. These same workers, however, soon discovered that Menem's brand of *peronismo* places greater emphasis on labor productivity than on social justice. They are standing by for the IMF-style economic austerity policies to bring about the structural conditions conducive to a renewal of the struggle for workers' control.

Notes

The author would like to thank Joel Horowitz for his helpful comments.

1. During the two-year period 1935–37, Argentine industrial growth nearly equaled that of the previous two decades. The industrial workforce expanded from roughly 430,000 (1935) to more than 1 million (1946) in a nation of 16 million persons. The

population of Greater Buenos Aires, home to more than 70 percent of these workers, grew from 3.4 million to 4.7 million persons between 1935 and 1947. See David Tamarin, *The Argentine Labor Movement, 1930–1945: A Study in the Origins of Peronism* (Albuquerque, 1985), 23; Hugo del Campo, *Sindicalismo y peronismo: Los comienzos de un vínculo perdurable* (Buenos Aires, 1983), 38–40.

2. Joel Horowitz, *Argentine Unions, the State, and the Rise of Peron, 1930–1945* (Berkeley, 1990), 32–35; Tamarin, *Argentine Labor Movement*, 24–33.

3. Tamarin, *Argentine Labor Movement*, 150–68; Charles Bergquist, *Labor in Latin America: Comparative Essays on Chile, Argentina, Venezuela, and Colombia* (Stanford, 1986), 144–67.

4. Horowitz, *Argentine Unions*, 99–100; José Peter, *Crónicas proletarias* (Buenos Aires, 1968), 147–48; Juan Carlos Torre, *La vieja guardia sindical y Perón* (Buenos Aires, 1990), 99–100. Horowitz notes that the growing intransigence of employers increased unions' dependency on the mediatory services of the Department of Labor.

5. For an exemplary description of the impact of Perón's early visit to the industrial enclave of Avellaneda, see Adriana Raga, "Workers, Neighbors, and Citizens: A Study of an Argentine Industrial Town, 1930–1945" (Ph.D. diss., Yale University, 1988).

6. Horowitz, *Argentine Unions*, 149–50; Tamarin, *Argentine Labor Movement*, 176–92; David Rock, *Argentina: 1516–1987, desde la colonización española hasta Raúl Alfonsín* (Madrid, 1985), 343.

7. The ideological ambiguity of Peronism often blurred the class divisions between Peronist sympathizers and the opposition. Perón's economic nationalism thus attracted middle-class supporters while the protofascist traits of the military junta drove socialist workers into the opposition camp.

8. Félix Luna, *El '45: Crónica de un año decisivo* (Buenos Aires, 1969), 94–102.

9. Ibid., 208–11.

10. *La Nación* (Buenos Aires), 16 October 1945.

11. For historical analyses on the emergence of Peronism, the role of the CGT, and the social origins of the workers involved in the 17 October movement, see Juan Carlos Torre, "La CGT y el 17 de octubre de 1945," *Todo es historia* 9, no. 105 (1976): 70–90; Gino Germani, "El rol de los obreros y de los migrantes internos en los orígenes del peronismo," *Desarrollo económico* 13, no. 51 (1975): 435–88; Miguel Murmís and Juan Carlos Portantiero, "El movimiento obrero en los orígenes del peronismo," in *Estudios sobre los orígenes del peronismo*, ed. Murmís and Portantiero, 2 vols. (Buenos Aires, 1971), 1:59–126.

12. On the methods of protest and their symbolic implications, see Daniel James, "October 17th and 18th: Mass Protest, Peronism, and the Argentine Working Class," *Journal of Social History* 21, no. 3 (1988): 441–61.

13. See *La Nación; La Prensa* (Buenos Aires), 18 October 1954.

14. Juan Domingo Perón, *El pueblo quiere saber de que se trata* (Buenos Aires, 1944), 161. Perón made this statement—explaining why Peronism would prevent communism—during a 1944 speech to members of Buenos Aires' stock exchange.

15. By 1948, the metal and textile workers' unions each numbered more than one hundred thousand members. Unions in the food-processing and transportation industries totaled in excess of three hundred thousand members. See Louise Doyon, "El crecimiento sindical bajo el peronismo," in *La formación del sindicalismo peronista*, ed. Juan Carlos Torre (Buenos Aires, 1988), 174–78.

16. Bergquist, *Labor in Latin America*, 177; Carlos Díaz Alejandro, *Essays on the Economic History of the Argentine Republic* (New Haven, 1970), 125; *Review of the River Plate* (Buenos Aires), 10 October 1950; Louise Doyon, "Conflictos obreros durante el régimen peronista," in Torre, *La formación del sindicalismo peronista*, 259–60.

17. Watkins to State Department, 4 March 1947, United States Department of State Records, Record Group 59, Argentina: Internal Affairs, 1945–49 (hereafter cited as SD), 835.504/3-447.

18. For many workers associated with the radical unions of the 1930s, the decision to affiliate with a Peronist union became a matter of economic compulsion during the 1940s. In June 1947, laborers in the river port of Rosario struck to protest government efforts to mechanize the handling of cargo. The regional CGT ordered the port workers, long associated with the anarchist-oriented Regional Federation of Argentine Workers, either to join the Peronist union or to relinquish their work cards. Waltrous to State Department, 8 July 1947, SD, 835.504/8-747.

19. Waltrous interview with anonymous union leader in Waltrous to State Department, 13 September 1946, SD, 835.504/9-1346.

20. Cited in Waltrous to State Department, 13 September 1946, SD, 835.504/9-1346.

21. See Peter, *Crónicas proletarias*.

22. Bergquist, *Labor in Latin America*, 172; *La Prensa*, 14–20 November 1946.

23. *El Trabajador de la Carne* (Buenos Aires), May 1948.

24. Díaz Alejandro, *Essays on the Economic History*, 125. Daniel James concludes that industrial workers' real wages rose by 53 percent. Daniel James, *Resistance and Integration: Peronism and the Argentine Working Class, 1946–1976* (Cambridge, England, 1988), 11; Rock, *Argentina*, 331–32.

25. James, *Resistance and Integration*, 56–57.

26. Doyon, "Conflictos obreros durante el régimen peronista," 240. Leaders of this well-organized union sharply opposed Perón after the 1943 coup. By 1947, the organization remained under executive control by government (as opposed to CGT) authorities. Waltrous to State Department, 7 July 1947, SD, 835.504/7-747.

27. Unless otherwise indicated, details of the strike gleaned from *La Prensa*, 30 May–7 June 1947.

28. Waltrous to State Department, 7 July 1947, SD, 835.504/7-747.

29. Vallon to State Department, 20 December 1949, SD, 835.504/12-2049.

30. *New York Times*, 26 December 1948.

31. CGT document quoted in *Review of the River Plate*, 2 July 1948.

32. *New York Times*, 26 December 1948.

33. *La Prensa*, 18 October 1949. Unless otherwise indicated, information on the strike has been obtained from *La Prensa*, 15 November–3 December 1949.

34. Vallon to State Department, 20 December 1949, SD, 835.504/12-2049.

35. Vallon to State Department, 23 November 1949, SD, 835.504/11-2349.

36. *New York Times*, 2 August 1949.

37. Doyon, "Conflictos obreros durante el régimen peronista," 248–49; Bergquist, *Labor in Latin America*, 174–82; Vallon to State Department, 20 December 1949, SD, 835.504/12-2049.

38. Vallon to State Department, 23 November 1949, SD, 835.504/11-2349.

39. *New York Times*, 28 January 1951; Andrea Spears, "Labor's Response to Centralization and Rationalization: The Argentine Railway Strikes, 1950–1951," Texas Papers on Latin America (Austin, No. 90-05), 13.

40. Doyon, "Conflictos obreros durante el régimen peronista," 250–51.

41. Perón's speech cited in Del Campo, *Sindicalismo y peronismo*, 139.

42. *La Nación*, 16 April 1953.

43. *El Trabajador de la Carne*, February 1951; James Bruce, *Those Perplexing Argentines* (New York, 1953), 290.

44. See Robert Potash, *The Army and Politics in Argentina, 1945–1962* (Stanford, 1980), 91.

45. Both Peronist agricultural policies and the international economic boycott directed covertly by the United States acted to decrease the exportation of Argentine foodstuffs to European markets. See Carlos Escudé, *Gran Bretaña, Estados Unidos y la declinación argentina, 1942–1949* (Buenos Aires, 1983). See also David Rock, "The Survival and Restoration of Peronism," in *Argentina in the Twentieth Century*, ed. Rock (London, 1975), 190; Paul Lewis, *The Crisis of Argentine Capitalism* (Chapel Hill, 1990), 193. Foreign currency reserves, which Argentina accumulated during the war, directly financed the government's purchase of the foreign-owned public utilities and transportation, including the railroads (1948), all of which pleased Perón's nationalist supporters. More important, hard currency also purchased the machinery necessary to sustain industrialization and to bankroll higher wages and social benefits for the urban working class.

46. Díaz Alejandro, *Essays on the Economic History*, 110, 122. In 1952, average real wages for unskilled workers in Buenos Aires stood 21 percent below the 1949 average. See figures compiled by *Review of the River Plate*, 6 November 1954.

47. Juan Carlos Torre and Liliana de Riz, "Argentina since 1946," in *The Cambridge History of Latin America*, edited by Leslie Bethell (Cambridge, England, 1991), 81.

48. *Review of the River Plate*, 8 January 1952.

49. Ibid., 20 February 1953; *New York Times*, 4 October 1952; *El Plata* (Montevideo), 13 December 1952.

50. *El Plata*, 13 April 1954. "Today, as always," Perón declared, "our motto is: Produce! . . . Produce! . . . Produce!"

51. *Review of the River Plate,* 21 May 1954.

52. Daniel James, "Rationalisation and Working Class Response: The Context and Limits of Factory Floor Activity in Argentina," *Journal of Latin American Studies* 13 (1981): 383–84.

53. See especially Marysa Navarro, *Evita* (Buenos Aires, 1981).

54. A state of siege had been in effect since an aborted military coup in late 1951.

55. *El Plata,* 13 September 1953, 12 January 1954.

56. Ibid., 7 August 1953, 9 March 1954.

57. *La Capital,* 23 October 1952; *New York Times,* 24 October 1952; *Review of the River Plate,* 31 October 1952.

58. *El Plata,* 28 October 1954.

59. *New York Times,* 12 April 1953.

60. Among the first unions to embrace Perón, the railroaders of Rosario held one of the earliest Peronist labor rallies, in January 1944. The union's leader, José Domenech, dubbed Perón "Argentina's #1 Worker." Within a short time, however, Domenech joined many communists and socialists within the Unión Ferroviaria leadership in opposing Perón. Joel Horowitz comments that the continued existence of a cadre of respected dissident leaders facilitated the railroaders' 1950–51 mobilization against state budget cuts. See *New York Times,* 14 September 1945; Horowitz, *Argentine Unions,* 194.

61. *El Plata,* 17 February 1953.

62. Ibid., 18 September 1953.

63. *New York Times,* 25 September, 14 December 1953.

64. James Scott, *Domination and the Arts of Resistance: Hidden Transcripts* (New Haven, 1990), 106–7.

65. *El Plata,* 15 March 1954; *New York Times,* 11 April 1954.

66. *New York Times,* 4 May 1954.

67. Bergquist, *Labor in Latin America,* 176; *El Plata,* l June 1954.

68. *New York Times,* 8 June 1954.

69. Ibid., 8 to 11 June 1954; *El Plata,* 9 June 1954.

70. *El Plata,* 22 October 1954.

71. Luis Bonilla, interview from Proyecto Historia Oral del Instituto Torcuato di Tella, Buenos Aires, 1971; David Rochford, "In Search of a Popular Mission: The Argentine Catholic Church under Juan Domingo Perón, 1946–1955," MS, University of Texas at Austin, 1992, 19.

72. Rock, *Argentina,* 391–93; Torre and de Riz, "Argentina since 1946," 90–91.

73. Rock, *Argentina,* 393.

74. *New York Times,* 17 June 1955.

75. Torre and de Riz, "Argentina since 1946," 91–92.

76. "Primer mensaje del general Eduardo Lonardi," 17 September 1955, quoted in *Medio siglo de proclamas militares,* ed. Horacio Verbitsky (Buenos Aires, 1988), 60–62. See also Potash, *Army and Politics in Argentina.*

77. *New York Times*, 19–21 September 1955.

78. Ibid., 25 September 1955; James, *Resistance and Integration*, 50.

79. Alberto Belloni quoted in James, *Resistance and Integration*, 43.

80. James, "Rationalization and Working Class Response," 390–92; James, *Resistance and Integration*, 76–88.

CHAPTER SEVEN

THERE SHOULD
BE DIGNITY

São Paulo's Women Textile

Workers and the "Strike

of 300,000"

JOEL WOLFE

L ocal and foreign commentators often cited São Paulo, Brazil, in the early 1950s as "Latin America's Number One Boom City." A reporter for *U.S. News and World Report* wrote that the city gave "the impression of a kind of Chicago rising in Brazil's tropical interior."[1] The ongoing industrial expansion that led to such descriptions often had an adverse affect on Paulistano workers. ("Paulistano/a" refers to someone from the city of São Paulo; "Paulistas" are people from the state of São Paulo.) Textile entrepreneurs, whose mills constituted the largest sector of the city's economy in terms of workers employed and industrial output, instituted a series of productivity measures in the late 1940s and early 1950s that dramatically altered life on the shop floor. The introduction of new automated spinning and weaving equipment in many of the city's mills affected all Paulistano textile workers. Even factories without the new machinery changed work regimes in order to remain competitive.

São Paulo's textile workers were not passive observers of these important changes. As they had in the past, they organized on the shop floor to push for changes in the work regimes. They did so because they felt they were losing control over their lives within the mills. At the same time, Paulistano textile workers pushed for wages that would be commensurate with the increases in their workloads because prices for food and other goods rose rapidly during this period of economic expansion. The changes on the shop floor and the ris-

Map 5. *São Paulo state, Brazil, 1953*

ing prices for food and other goods in the city's markets most directly affected São Paulo's women workers. They were the majority of textile workers, as well as the individuals most often responsible for the maintenance of working-class households. The unions that ostensibly represented these women, however, were controlled by men who demonstrated little interest in the concerns of the female rank and file.

This situation left women textile workers to their own forms of organizing within their factories, which eventually led to one of Brazil's largest and most effective strike movements: In March and April 1953, some three hundred thousand industrial workers struck in unison to force their bosses to grant improved wages and work conditions. The strike was initiated and run by a mix of women's and men's independent factory commissions along with their formal unions. The workers stayed out for five weeks and only returned once all their demands had been met. In other words, they carried out a large-scale, unified, and effective general strike. These women's organizing and protest activities in the early 1950s not only succeeded in gaining work and wage concessions from employers, but they also succeeded in taking control of the closed, state-run unions out of the hands of unrepresentative labor bureaucrats and giving it to male and female activists with close ties to the rank and file. Moreover, São Paulo's women textile workers—through both their actions and the example they set—led an industrywide worker insurgence that forced employers and labor leaders throughout the city to grant levels of worker control on the shop floor and in the unions that had never before existed in Brazil. This process also involved politics. São Paulo's industrial workers, led by the city's women textile workers, managed to push the national political leader Getúlio Vargas from simply voicing populist promises to actually delivering proworker policies.

Running All Day Long

As in many other countries, the textile industry led the way in Brazil's industrial development. The Brazilian textile industry, much like that in the United States, depended on female labor. Beginning in the first years of the twentieth century, girls (often as young as ten and twelve years old) migrated from the rural sector to work in the textile mills.[2] Specific gender ideologies about young women and their value in the labor market encouraged mill owners to develop work regimes divided by sex. (It is important to distinguish between *gender* and *sex*. *Gender* refers to a set of ideas about the appropriate behavior for men and women. Accordingly, gender ideologies can change. *Sex* is a biological distinction that refers to men and women.) The foremen would be male and spinners and weavers overwhelmingly female. This division of labor developed because most Brazilians believed that young women were naturally dexterous and that they would only work for a short period in the mills before marrying and having children. Because their skills were considered innate and their presence in the labor market temporary, mill owners looked on these girls as ideal, inexpensive workers for the textile factories. Girls' dexterity was, of course, learned in the home by practicing domestic labor such as sewing, which was deemed "women's work." The belief in women's natural dexterity reveals several important facets of the gender ideology at work in Brazil. First, people conflated quite a few unrelated tasks, such as sewing at home and operating power looms in textile mills. In addition, women's skills were only seen as preparing them for specific female work. The belief in their natural dexterity did not lead to calls for training women as surgeons, for example.

The daughters of Italian immigrant coffee workers who migrated to the city of São Paulo did so under the supervision of family or extended kin (*paisani*). (*Paisani* is an Italian term for people who are not blood relations but who make up an extended kin group by virtue of having the same village origins. This kin connection was particularly important among Italian immigrants to Brazil, Argentina, and the United States.) These young women often gained employment in the mills through these connections. The workforce in many factories, therefore, not only shared experiences on the shop floor and in the city; they were often relatives and *paisani*. Working together further strengthened the bonds of solidarity these women workers felt.

The mills and other large industrial establishments did not employ only immigrant women. Men also worked in the mills, but often in higher-paying positions such as mechanics and foremen. Afro-Brazilians, who faced a great deal of discrimination in employment in the city of São Paulo, eventually gained access to industrial employment in the 1930s. People of color did not have extensive industrial employment in São Paulo, though, until the mid-1950s, when tens of thousands of migrants from Brazil's northeast traveled from that impoverished region to the country's economically dynamic south, especially the state of São Paulo. In the final analysis, although industrial establishments in the city of São Paulo hired both men and women of all ethnic backgrounds, women dominated employment in the textile mills in the first half of the twentieth century.[3] It is also important to note that women in São Paulo tended to hold industrial jobs throughout their lives; this work was not restricted to their youth.[4]

It is far beyond the scope of this essay to recount the long history of women's relations with the male-dominated union structure in São Paulo. Still, a few basic components of this relationship need to be mentioned. Women had always made up the majority of São Paulo's textile workers but remained a tiny minority within the various unions that sought to represent the mills. From the city's first major labor upheaval—the great General Strike of 1917—through the 1920s and early 1930s, women workers organized their own independent factory commissions that bargained for improved wages and conditions. Their activism actually put them in a leadership position within the workers' movement, and during these years women combined their activism with male anarchists' politics. The result was a distinct anarcho-syndicalist ideology that defined São Paulo's labor movement into the 1930s.[5]

Getúlio Vargas (the president and dictator from 1930 to 1945 and then president again in 1951–54) established a corporatist industrial relations system in the 1930s and 1940s that profoundly altered the evolving relationship between the rank and file and labor activists. Vargas sought to put himself in the center of labor relations. He would act as a benevolent "father of the poor" on behalf of the country's workers. Institutionally, the state would control all Brazilian unions. This system led to the establishment of small, closed, and clearly unrepresentative *sindicatos*. Unions more often than not served the interests of the state and industrialists; these government-controlled *sindicatos* worked to increase productivity and to silence rank-and-file activists who sought better conditions and higher pay. During Vargas's Estado Novo dictatorship (1937–45), these unions—which had been planned as a cornerstone in the corporatist system—had few members overall, and few of these were women.[6] Consistently fewer than 3 percent of São Paulo's textile workers became formal members of the union. This number is even more startling given the fact that *all* workers paid a union tax whether or not they decided to become formal members by paying additional dues.[7]

Vargas's corporatist framework led to the creation of a new type of labor leader whose survival depended more on the continued support of the Ministry of Labor than on that of the workers. Sometime in the late 1930s, the rank and file in São Paulo began to deride these representatives of the state by labeling them *pelegos*. A *pelego* is literally a sheepskin horse blanket. Workers opposed to the government-controlled union structure applied this term to the co-opted leaders. The analogy consisted of the working class as the horse, the industrial bourgeoisie as the rider, and the *pelego* as the saddlelike blanket that cushions the ride for the elites.

All Paulistano workers—but especially the women—maintained their own independent factory commissions in the face of this government intervention in the 1930s and 1940s. Workers had practiced such local, informal organizing since the first decade of the twentieth century. Moreover, the initial weakness and later compromises made by the Communist Party (Partido Comunisto do Brasil, or PCB)[8] encouraged workers to maintain their independent institutions.[9] These independent commissions remained important after Vargas's ouster, for the "republic" that followed Gen. Eurico Gaspar Dutra's election in 1945 to the presidency actually brought intensified government repression of the workers' movement.[10]

Workers' commissions had done much more than simply bargain with bosses. Workers used these informal institutions to coordinate many of their survival and resistance strategies. They even collectively petitioned Vargas for his personal intervention in work and neighborhood issues. The commissions also worked with sympathetic unionists during strikes. In the Textile Workers' Union, for example, non-*pelego* members helped the rank and file push the *pelegos* to support their wage and other demands. Vargas's return to power in January 1951—this time as the elected "populist" president—provided São Paulo's women textile workers with the opportunity to use a variety of institutions and strategies in their ongoing conflicts with their employers and their union's *pelegos*.

Throughout the late 1940s and early 1950s, São Paulo's industrialists intensified the program of rationalizing production they had begun in the late 1940s. Mill owners continued to install automated spinning and weaving equipment and to create work regimes that would limit workers' independence on the shop floor. Managers carefully timed everything from the number of minutes weavers spent to produce a meter of cloth to how long a worker spent in the bathroom. Both Dutra and Vargas encouraged the importation of capital equipment. Their governments geared exchange rate policies to limit some imports (e.g., consumer goods) and to encourage the entry of others (e.g., machinery and other capital goods) for industrial production.[11] The rationalization, however, was uneven. A 1953 study by São Paulo's Industrial Training Service found that only four mills in the city were completely equipped with the latest automated weaving and spinning machinery. At the same time, 35 percent of all Paulistano looms were automated because many firms had to mix the new machines with the old. Those mills that did not have any automated equipment were forced to change their work regimes in order to keep pace. There was no distinction between large and small factories; some of each installed the new automated equipment. All in all, productivity per weaver rose 80 percent from 1949 to 1959 as a result of the changes owners forced on work regimes.[12] Such an increase in overall productivity meant that the rationalization program affected, directly or indirectly, all the city's textile workers.

São Paulo's textile workers experienced this rationalization program through speedups, increases in the number of looms and spindles they had to tend, and an increased frequency of accidents. Their memories of these changes remain bitter. Mill laborer João Bonifácio recalled that the new spinning machinery had an automatic shutoff that any flaw in the thread might trigger: "What I remember is how tired we would get running around fixing the thread and restarting machines. Before the automated machines came we worked hard, but afterward we would just run around the spinning room. We just kept running all day long." Luís Firmino also remembered that bosses changed both work loads and piece rates after they installed the new looms.[13] Diolinda Nascimento hated the new machines. "I was a weaver, 'first class.' But once the new looms came, I spent more time running up and down aisles switching machines on and off than I did weaving," Nascimento reminisced. "I was still a weaver, 'first class,' but all I did was run around with the new looms."[14]

Many other weavers and spinners resented losing control over the work process when bosses installed the automated equipment. They also had to cope with increasingly harsh work regimes and decreasing real incomes. In response, the rank and file filed thousands of petitions (*processos*) through their union to force changes on the shop floor and to protect the piece-rate system. Although the union won many of these *processos*, filing them was time consuming. Each *processo* usually dealt with only one worker or shift of workers.[15] In November and December 1952, the Textile Workers' Union pressed bosses to give their workers a Christmas bonus as a sort of payment for all the changes the workers had been experiencing. Apparently, some mills granted the bonuses, but no industrywide policy was adopted.[16]

Shortages in raw materials for São Paulo's factories, as well as problems maintaining a steady supply of electricity in the city, allowed industrialists early in 1953 to shorten or stagger work shifts.[17] Mill owners who were installing automated machinery took advantage of the opportunity to fire any "redundant" employees. Those factories with new looms or spindles intensified work regimes while they decreased the length of each shift. That is, with the rationing of electricity in the city, textile workers had fewer hours of work per shift (and in some cases, fewer shifts), so they had to increase their piece-rate wages by speeding up their work pace. The shortage of electricity played a key role in the rationalization of production. It also adversely affected mill workers whose shifts—and therefore wages—decreased substantially.[18] Industrialists had begun the rationalization program when the city's unions were in the hands of *pelegos* and the federal industrial relations system operated to stifle workers' demands. In the midst of this rationalization program, however, the national political landscape changed dramatically. So did industrial relations in São Paulo.

A Free and Vigorous Union Movement

The Dutra years had been hard ones for São Paulo's industrial working class. The city's industrialists had been utilizing the full power of the national and state governments to further their goals, while *pelegos* maintained a tight grip on workers' unions. Throughout this period, however, Getúlio Vargas publicly fashioned himself the defender of Brazilian workers' rights. As Vargas's opponents dismantled the Estado Novo in 1945 and 1946, the former dictator began to position himself as the workers' benefactor in Brazil's "New Republic." He told workers he would be "a representative of the popular will."[19] As early as 1947, Vargas campaigned for popular backing in the 1950 presidential election. He moved to solidify his working-class support by criticizing Dutra's version of "capitalist democracy." In its place, Vargas called for the establishment of a "socialist democracy, the democracy of the workers." He told an audience in Rio de Janeiro: "If I am elected on October 3, as I take office the people will climb the steps of Catete [the presidential palace] with me. And they will remain with me in power."[20]

Brazil's working people clearly favored Vargas over all other politicians. A public opinion survey conducted in São Paulo one month before the election revealed that 83 percent of people classified as working class or poor supported Vargas. A survey conducted among Rio's workers (79 percent of whom supported the former dictator) detailed their dissatisfaction with President Dutra's economic management. Not surprisingly, 86 percent of the respondents called on the government to regulate wages and rents more fairly; 58 percent favored government control of corporate profits.[21] These polls apparently reflected workers' actual hopes and beliefs. On 3 October, they gave Vargas a landslide victory with 48.7 percent of the vote in a presidential election with two other candidates.[22]

Even though Vargas represented many different things to his diverse constituency—several of São Paulo's leading industrialists, for example, had helped finance his 1950 presidential campaign—workers wasted little time in pressing their own agenda.[23] They hoped that Vargas would support their claims in general and, at the same time, lessen Ministry of Labor control of their unions. One week after the election, while Dutra was still in office, men and women workers at the Santa Celina mill in São Paulo used their factory commissions without union support to strike for 50 percent wage increases overall. They especially demanded improvements in women's wages so that they would earn equal pay for equal work. The police broke up the strike. But the factory's managers understood that the political atmosphere was changing and promised quick action on wage "readjustments."[24] By late November, São Paulo's workers began pushing their employers for Christmas bonuses. They demanded this extra pay as compensation for the wage squeeze they had been experiencing since 1947. Once again, the city's workers—especially women in the mills—relied on their factory commissions to bargain for higher wages and improved conditions. The *pelegos* who continued to control the industrial unions contributed very little.[25]

Textile workers began to look to the union elections scheduled for late 1950 and early 1951 as yet another opportunity in their struggle to improve wages and factory conditions. Their experiences with sympathetic members of union directorates in 1945 and 1946 had demonstrated that the *sindicatos* could help workers in wage and other disputes. Besides, Vargas promised during his presidential campaign that he would lessen the federal government's control over the unions. Even before Vargas's January 1951 inauguration, the Ministry of Labor loosened its grip on union affairs. Some state governments even permitted communists and other opposition candidates to run in the upcoming union elections.

These changes brought mixed results to São Paulo's main industrial unions. After Vargas's election, hundreds of factory commission members joined the Textile Workers' Union in order to participate in the election of a new directorate. Unfortunately for them, voting requirements (e.g., the prerequisite of twenty-six months of full union membership under the terms of the 1943 Consolidated Labor Laws) severely restricted the total number of voters. Just 4 percent of the 100,325 textile workers in the city actually elected the new directorate. Not surprisingly, union stalwarts chose those candidates with close ties to the Ministry of Labor. Joaquim Teixeira won as president, João Ferri as first secretary, and Antônio Mendes Brazão as treasurer.[26] Notwithstanding his close cooperation with the Ministry of Labor, Teixeira knew he would have to fight for wage hikes to satisfy workers' high expectations. He immediately negotiated new wage rates with mill owners and government officials. At the same time, women workers used their independent factory commissions to hold talks on hours and wage scales with the Têxtil Assid Nassif and other firms. Teixeira used the factory commissions' negotiations to manipulate industrialists' fears of wildcat strikes. He convinced owners that granting some concessions, such as changes in the absenteeism clause, would ensure labor peace. This clause, which was imposed during the early stages of the rationalization process, allowed employers to void wage increases if workers did not maintain near perfect attendance. Rescinding the absenteeism clauses from their work contracts therefore became one of the workers' primary demands in the early 1950s.[27]

Textile workers throughout the city supported the union's demands, but women workers felt they did not go far enough. Women weavers and spinners continued to earn about 68 percent of men's wages for the same jobs.[28] Glória Salviano recalled how she and her *companheiras* complained to each other that they never seemed to earn the same wages men did. "The union wasn't going to upset the men by demanding we get increases," she said. "After all, most of the union was men." Hermínia Lorenzi dos Santos agreed: "We knew we had to do something ourselves to get men's wages, so we went in our commissions to talk to the bosses about increases."[29] Irene de Oliveira, who was only fourteen years old when she began in the mills in 1951, remembered that women textile workers aggressively pushed for increased wages because they knew they would succeed. "The factories were going all night back then, with lots of girls, like me, on the night shifts," Oliveira recalled. "The foremen needed all the skilled weavers they could get, and we knew it, so we told them we would strike if we didn't get increases."[30] Indeed, strikes run by factory commissions without any ties to the Textile Workers' Union succeeded in gaining wage increases in 1951 and 1952.[31]

Vargas had encouraged factory commissions' activities by loosening the Ministry of Labor's control over the unions and by changing the overall tone of relations between the federal government and workers' organizations. Although many *pelegos* retained leadership positions, unions throughout Brazil elected mildly reformist directorates like those chosen by São Paulo's Textile Workers' Union. Vargas's minister of labor, Danton Coelho, said the federal government would not intervene in unions because "the Brazilian worker [was] mature and ready for a free and vigorous union movement."[32] And the ways in which Vargas changed the federal government's role in São Paulo received enthusiastic support from the city's workers. Union leaders had complained to Coelho and Vargas that the State Department of Labor was nothing more than a tool of the city's industrialists. Its inspection service ignored workers' complaints. It also provided employers with the names of individuals who had filed "confidential" grievances. In May, therefore, Vargas announced that the federal government would again manage industrial relations in São Paulo. The state's industrialists would not again appoint labor officials, as they had during the Dutra administration.[33]

Even though Vargas had met some of his campaign promises, São Paulo's industrial workers already had a good understanding of the limited value of politicians' promises. The brutal repression of the Estado Novo—under Vargas's leadership—lay less than ten years in the past. And both President Dutra and Adhemar de Barros, São Paulo's governor, had recently reneged on guarantees of support for labor's cause. Odete Pasquini, a lifelong weaver, summed up the workers' relationship with politicians when she said, "We were very important people when the elections were coming, but after we elected them, they didn't remember anything."[34] So, São Paulo's workers pressured Vargas to meet his most recent promises. They responded to his May Day address by joining the city's main industrial unions (especially the Textile Workers' and Metalworkers' unions) at a rate of more than five hundred people per month in May and June 1951. Factory commissions took Vargas at his word. They pressed their bosses for wage increases that met inflation. Women textile workers also pushed for an increase in the minimum wage, which in 1951 was only worth half its 1944 value.[35] That is, they pressured Vargas to translate his populist rhetoric into populist policies.

Textile and other industrial workers took advantage of two separate but highly significant developments in their drive for control on the shop floor. First, industry was booming, and there was a clear shortage of labor in the factories. The São Paulo Federation of Industries complained that its members' establishments could not find enough "skilled" operatives. Workers bragged to each other that they could always change jobs if their bosses did not increase their pay. According to Diolinda Nascimento, "A foreman would do almost anything to keep a good worker. . . . There weren't enough girls available for all the looms, so the foreman would say, 'please tell your girlfriends, sisters, neighbors, anyone that we have work for them here.' "[36] The second development that helped workers was the transfer of the Regional Labor Delegacy from state to federal control. Although Vargas stripped the Paulista state government of its authority, he did not staff the São Paulo office. Instead, he ordered Enio Lepage, a Ministry of Labor official in the state of Paraná, to assume control of all wage negotiations in São Paulo.[37]

Workers quickly turned this weak governmental presence to their advantage by opening direct negotiations with employers, thereby ignoring the elaborate corporatist labor structure. The city's textile workers continued to rely first on their commissions. But they increasingly coordinated their activities with sympathetic unionists. The union had been negotiating for an increase over the last general wage accord from 1948. In September 1951, the directorate listened to the demands from women in the various factory commissions and agreed to support the goals of the rank and file.[38] The directorate and membership next elected a separate strike committee (composed of factory commission leaders, many of whom were women) to handle the negotiations. The directorate lobbied Ministry of Labor officials in Rio for help with their union's demands.[39]

In the midst of these negotiations and facing steadily increasing popular pressure, Getúlio Vargas met one of his May Day promises. He raised the minimum wage for all Brazilian workers for the first time since 1943. The increase brought the minimum wage to the same level (after being adjusted for inflation) it had been in 1944.[40] The increase, announced by Vargas on Christmas Eve, embodied the complex relationship that was developing between the president and São Paulo's industrial workers. He clearly hoped to position himself as the benefactor of the working class. But Vargas responded to the strikes by saying, "We don't need strikes or calls for extreme measures. . . . You can be sure that the solutions to your problems are being handled by the government."[41] In the final analysis, however, workers' activism and militancy had clearly forced the president's hand. Vargas was no longer the "father of the poor"; he was now just another politician beholden to an important and active constituency.

The textile strike of 1951 had brought mixed results. On one hand, the strikers ended up accepting the 25 percent increase (which represented only a slight increase over the new minimum wage, especially for women workers) and the abolition of all absenteeism clauses. On the other hand, this strike movement led to a new division of labor within the union. Directorate members took on roles as lobbyists with the Ministry of Labor, while the factory commissions ran the strike movement through a committee elected by the rank and file.[42] The December 1951 strike was the first time in the history of São Paulo's textile industry that the rank and file directed the union's activities. This new union openness took on a further significance, given the fact that more than 65 percent of the city's textile workers were women.[43] That is, the union finally bargained for the actual demands put forward by the majority of the rank and file; it did not push for an end to women's night work and other so-called protective measures opposed by the female majority.[44] At last, the Textile Workers' Union had become a real representation of São Paulo's industrial working class.

The relationship between São Paulo's textile workers and their union activists had been complex and confrontational since the 1910s. Although women workers were at ease within their own informal institutions (e.g., the factory commissions), they faced an entrenched male leadership in the union. These male unionists, at their best, had been paternalistic; at their worst, they had demonized women as opponents of the labor movement. The rank and file's activism in the 1951 strikes offered a new path for the Textile Workers' Union. São

Paulo's industrial workers—especially women in the textile mills—confronted a possible watershed in their relations with unionists, bosses, and the state.

Striking for Dignity

By 1952, factory commission members, reformist union activists, and young members of the Communist Party had recognized the importance of bringing grassroots leaders into the formal union structures.[45] They realized that the election of central committees to coordinate the activities of the commissions and the unions proved to be an effective strategy for mediating internal conflicts. The Textile Workers' Union, therefore, institutionalized the factory commissions. Its leaders and rank-and-file members created a series of standing committees to represent the factory commissions.[46]

Within the Textile Workers' Union, the salary committee and strike committee quickly became the two most important institutions beyond the directorate. At first, only the most active factory commission members, who were also formal members of the union, were encouraged by Teixeira and other directorate members to work on these committees. Those activists soon pressured the directorate. At a general assembly, they voted to allow factory commission members who were not formal union members to participate in these new committees.[47] Many of these committees came to be dominated by women workers. Maria Pavone remembered that the women on the salary committee sometimes seemed to be running the general assemblies in 1952 and 1953. "We wouldn't pay attention to the official union business, budgets, number of *processos* filed, that sort of thing. We waited for the report of the salary committee, and once they got going nobody paid attention to the directorate."[48]

Early in 1952, São Paulo's textile workers tested their new union structure. Factory commissions and union committees coordinated their activities in the push for higher wages. Workers struck Tecelagem Aziz Nader mill on 3 January to force their bosses to increase pay levels. By 12 January, an estimated seven thousand workers from six more mills in the city had struck. With the union lobbying the Ministry of Labor and the factory commissions coordinating their activities with the union, the mill owners had few options other than settling with the workers or bracing for a general textile strike. They chose to meet the workers' demands, and the strikers returned to the mills on 16 January. But some mill owners attempted to pay wages below the agreed-upon scale. The coordinated action of the factory commissions and the union brought a quick settlement. Employers met their obligations and paid the proper wages.[49]

The United States labor attaché in São Paulo reported on the extraordinary success of the factory commissions. He noted that most industrialists seemed to prefer direct negotiations with the commissions over using the labor courts. The diplomat speculated that the reasons for this change were the speed with which disputes could be settled through direct negotiations, the desire of employers to pay wages that would keep up with the rising cost of living (although this does not explain why industrialists tried to renege on the agreements from December 1951), and the continued apprehension they had about sending wage disputes to Enio Lepage, the federal labor delegate in Paraná.[50] There was one key factor the American attaché failed to report. The unity of purpose between the rank and file and the union leadership clearly had altered the calculus of São Paulo's industrial relations.

Vargas took note of these developments among the very people he considered his strongest supporters.[51] On May Day 1952, he placed himself on the side of the rank and file in their struggles with entrenched *pelegos*. He apologized for the past role the Ministry of Labor had played in supporting the *pelegos*. He pledged his assistance to help the rank and file in their struggles to rid their unions of corrupt leaders and then added a criticism of politicians that many workers themselves had articulated. Vargas told Brazil's workers they should not be "at the mercy of those who only [remembered them] on the eve of election day."[52] In October, his minister of labor, José de Segadas Vianna, continued these admissions by telling the pro-Vargas newspaper *Ú Hora* that corruption in the unions had been an open secret since the Estado Novo. He assured Brazilians that the Ministry of Labor would do all it could to help workers expel the corrupt unionists.[53] Vargas followed these denunciations by abolishing once and for all the "ideological certification" for election to union office (which had kept radicals and communists from assuming leadership positions) and by calling for a thorough reorganization of the labor ministry.[54]

Ultimately, Vargas was denouncing the very industrial relations system he himself had foisted on Brazil. He tried to obscure this fact, pushing for reforms of the union structure and offering new benefits to workers. Vargas had given up trying to coerce or gently persuade Brazil's workers into a government-manipulated union structure.[55] That is, Vargas finally abandoned the corporatist policies he, as dictator, had so forcefully introduced during the 1930s. His new perspective stemmed from more than a just a desire to be remembered as a democratic politician. By refusing to join *pelego*-run unions, by independent organizing and protesting, and by communicating directly with Vargas, Brazilian workers had demonstrated that they would not be manipulated by the corporatist government structure.[56]

São Paulo's textile workers continued to reveal their deep distrust of the official union structure and its representatives. The rank and file in the Textile Workers' Union worked with young Communist Party and factory commission activists to expel *pelegos* through popular votes in general assemblies. Borrowing the terminology of the Estado Novo dictatorship and Dutra's crackdown on labor, the workers declared corrupt unionists from the past directorates to be *cassados* (i.e., they lost their political rights within the union).[57] In August 1952, the rank and file elected outspoken critics of *peleguismo* to fill vacancies on the directorate. They chose Nelson Rusticci first secretary, Carlos Pinto Ferreira second secretary, and Luís Firmino de Lima librarian. All three men had ties to the salary and strike committees. Luís Firmino had also been an activist in the young wing of the Communist Party.[58] This election took on even greater significance when, after Joaquim Teixeira died in December, the rank and file elevated Rusticci to the presidency of the union.[59]

The city's textile workers did not elect any women from the commissions to the directorate at this time. Although women from the factory commissions influenced the activities of the salary and strike committees, they could not gain access to the highest union positions. The directorate, challenged by women's activism in the commissions, sought to limit their power within the union. The failure to include women in leadership positions demonstrates the limits of the open unions. Women had a greater voice than they had had in the past, but they were still denied access to power. After these elections, the city's textile workers continued to push forward the opening of their union. Women workers took such actions because by the early 1950s they had accumulated a vast set of experiences that persuaded them that they could trust only their own institutions. Moreover, the shifting position of the federal government toward labor since the early 1940s provided factory commission members from throughout the city with various opportunities to meet (sometimes in jail and sometimes in open union general assemblies). They began to map out new strategies. Vargas's latest stance favoring free and open *sindicatos* hastened the rise of factory commission members to positions of authority. This development, in turn, helped to bring about Brazil's most important labor action since the 1917 General Strike.

São Paulo's industrial workers had faced rationalization schemes and economic recessions in the past, but they had never before had well-integrated factory commissions and unions to organize against these changes. The situation changed in 1953. Not only had the rank and file in the Textile Workers' Union gained de facto control of union policies through the strike and salary committees, but they had also—with the acquiescence of the federal government—replaced *pelegos* with opposition activists. The process continued. In February 1953, the city's metalworkers elected as their president Remo Forli, whose union career had begun as an opposition activist from the commissions. This election coincided with a coordinating movement among factory commission members from the textile and metallurgy establishments in the Mooca neighborhood. According to Conrado de Papa, the entire effort to build formal ties between activists from the two unions was initiated during this period of open unions. "I guess it was the proximity of the mills to the metals shops," Papa said. "Besides, a lot of the guys I worked with had started out in the textile factories, and they still knew the factory commission people in the mills."[60]

Leaders of the salary committees of the Textile and Metalworkers' unions agreed formally to coordinate their wage demands. The union directorates accepted this proposal, for they had worked together in their push for Christmas 1952 bonuses. Local Communist Party activists, such as Luís Firmino, helped to coordinate the two union strategies, but the party itself played little or no role in the emerging strike movement.[61] Indeed, as factory commissions throughout the city met to discuss what tactics they would use against their employers, who were overwhelmingly Brazilians, the Communist Party newspaper, *Imprensa Popular*, blamed "United States imperialism" for the problems in São Paulo's factories.[62] The party leadership thus revealed just how out of touch it was with daily struggles of the city's workers.

The salary committee in the Textile Workers' Union had gathered information on wages and the cost of living and then demanded of the Textile Industrialists' Association a 60 percent wage increase for all weavers and spinners.[63] The mill owners stalled. Consequently, the strike committee decided to hold a march from the union's headquarters to the Textile Industrialists' Association. On 10 March, an estimated sixty thousand textile workers paraded down the Avenida Rangel Pestana, through the Praça da Sé, across the downtown to Anhangabaú. The mobilization of so many workers clearly unnerved mill owners. A Ministry of Labor official even referred to the peaceful march as "a cunning form of agitation."[64] The mill owners still refused to increase wages, however.

Similar salary committees in unions representing bank workers, furniture makers, glass makers, and printers contacted committee activists from the Textile and Metalworkers' unions to coordinate citywide salary demands. On 18 March, workers from all six unions held a rally in the Praça da Sé. They demanded increased wages and action by Governor Lucas Nogueira Garcez to lower the prices of foodstuffs in the city's markets. With no increases offered by their bosses, factory commissions from several textile mills decided to strike on Monday, 23 March 1953. Women from commissions in the Brás and Mooca mills agreed they would begin work in the morning and strike after their lunch break. While workers from hundreds of factories and small shops ate their lunches, women from commissions called on all their *companheiros* and *companheiras* to join the walkout. Diolinda Nascimento recalled how women from the Matarazzo mill spread news of the walkout: "They didn't have a hard time convincing us [i.e., other women] to join them, but some of the men in the mills, who received higher salaries, didn't want to strike. I remember one man arguing with a group of girls from the commission. He wouldn't strike, so they cornered him, and a big fight broke out. Finally, one girl took off her shoe and started beating the guy in the head."[65]

On Wednesday, 25 March, general assemblies of the Textile and Metalworkers' unions decided to call strikes in their two industries. Textile workers still wanted a 60 percent increase, and metalworkers sought a wage hike of up to 50 percent. Although both union directorates sanctioned these walkouts, the strike committees actually coordinated their activities in the Clube Piratininga (a social and sports club) in Mooca, rather than at one of the two unions' headquarters. The commission activists were now working with the unions, but they still maintained some distance from the formal *sindicato* structure by organizing in Mooca rather than in a union headquarters.[66] They created the Central Strike Committee that coordinated day-to-day activities and received reports directly from the factory commissions. Operating outside the formal *sindicato* structure, weavers were finally able to put in a woman textile worker, Mariana Galgaitez, as one of the directors. Young girls' and adult women's factory commissions dealt almost exclusively with Galgaitez. The result was a strike of more than one hundred thousand textile and metallurgical workers run by the Central Strike Committee. The committee declared that neither the textile nor metallurgical workers would end the strike until all the demands of both had been met.[67]

Soon, furniture makers and glassworkers joined the strike movement. By early April, some 300,000 industrial workers in São Paulo (which had a population of about 2.2 million people in 1950) were on strike. Owners of paper and candy factories quickly granted their workers increases of between 10 and 20 percent in order to keep them from joining.[68] These developments, however, did not speed the settlement of the textile and metallurgical workers' wage disputes. In fact, mounted city police and the state political police began to attack peaceful picketers. They beat the striking men and women in order, they said, to keep the factories open. The United States consul in São Paulo telegrammed to the embassy in Rio that the police even attacked a peaceful march, calling on Governor Nogueira Garcez for assistance. "Crowds onlookers dispersed by mounted police, tear gas, fire hoses. . . . Reinforced police on alert patrolling affected areas. Situation disquieting," the consul reported.[69] These attacks were part of the Ministry of Labor's opposition to the strike movement. Enio Lepage urged workers to return to their factories and ordered the state political police to prevent any "unauthorized" workers' meetings. Vargas's minister of labor, Segadas Vianna, blamed the strike on "outside agitators," suggesting the police crack down harder.[70]

The federal government's opposition only strengthened the position of factory commission activists who were running the Central Strike Committee, for the union directorates could not accomplish much by lobbying Ministry of Labor officials.[71] Union leaders had better luck with Governor Nogueira Garcez. The Paulista governor worked with the Regional Labor Tribunal to put forward an offer of a 23 percent wage increase for all the strikers. Although a few unionists wanted to accept this, both the rank and file and industrialists rejected it. Four unions' strike committees representing textiles, metals, furniture making, and glassworking, in the meantime, formed the Inter-Union Unity Pact. They announced publicly that no one union's workers would return to work until all the strikers had settled.[72]

The city's industrialists at first reacted to the simultaneous walkouts with bravado and threats. At a rancorous meeting in State Federation of Industries' headquarters, mill owners complained bitterly that the strike was nothing more than a "communist plot." They admitted that the cost of living had increased at least by 23 percent since the last pay hike, but they pledged not to offer any new wages.[73] As the meeting wore on, owners of several metalworking shops acknowledged that they had, in fact, offered their workers 20 and 23 percent increases that strikers turned down. The Federation of Industries president Antônio Devisate assured members that a favorable ruling from the Regional Labor Tribunal would force workers back to the factories. He predicted that employers would have the right to fire those who refused to end the strike.[74]

São Paulo's factory districts soon developed the look and atmosphere of a battlefield. Mounted police attacked peaceful marches by picketers, and the state's political police set up machine gun nests near factories. On 9 April, more than four thousand workers clashed with police in Mooca. Hundreds were wounded, and many were beaten and dragged off to jail. Factory commission members and union leaders moved to settle the strike as quickly as possible. Nelson Rusticci of the Textile Workers' Union negotiated with the governor to limit police attacks.[75] Commission members maintained pickets and collected strike funds. "We all helped out during the strike, cooking and taking care of children," Hermínia Lorenzi dos Santos recalled. "We didn't have a lot of money, but there was always a way, by borrowing from relatives in the interior, that sort of thing." Maria Pavone added, "The strike was hard, but we knew we could win. Sure we all helped out, because during a strike, at work, [and] in your home you should have dignity. In everything, there should be dignity, and that's what we were fighting for."[76]

Soon after the clash in Mooca, the Regional Labor Tribunal proposed a 32 percent increase of the wages for all metalworkers in the city. A general assembly of thousands of metalworkers met at the Mooca racetrack the next day and overwhelmingly rejected the offer. They said they would accept such an increase once it was also offered to their fellow workers in textiles, glass, and furniture making. Representatives of the unions then went to Rio to try to convince Vargas that he should support their demands. With Brás, Mooca, Ipiranga, and other factory districts in the city paralyzed by the strike, the Regional Labor Tribunal offered textile workers a 32 percent wage increase. When this same rate was offered to glass and furniture workers, a second assembly of strikers at the Mooca racetrack voted unanimously to accept the increase and return to work—but only after all jailed strikers were freed.[77] The unity among textile, metallurgical, glass, and furniture workers stood in stark contrast to the disarray of the industrialists. The latter had attempted only piecemeal and uncoordinated concessions in a vain effort to divide the workers.

The strike leaders prepared a memorial thanking Governor Nogueira Garcez for his help in settling the walkout and then continued with the final list of demands from the rank and file: All prisoners were to be freed, no factory commission leaders should be fired, and the 32 percent pay increase was to be codified in a two-year contract that could be renegotiated after one year.[78] The Central Strike Committee initiated a march of twenty thousand workers to the governor's palace demanding the release of their fellow strikers from the city's jails. By this time, many strikers were so frustrated they actually attacked the police along the route. "We gave everyone special instructions to remain peaceful," Luís Firmino said, "but a lot of the women were so fed up with the police that they cornered a few of them and beat them!" Ultimately, the march achieved its goal; the police released jailed strikers, and the city's industrial workers returned to work on 23 April, more than six weeks after textile workers had initiated the strike.[79]

The "Strike of the 300,000," as it quickly became known, was the culmination of years of grassroots worker organizing. The rank and file's factory commissions operated in opposition to their bosses' rationalization and wage policies and against the closed unions run by *pelegos*. A series of conjunctural factors also helped to bring about the strike. Industrial production was booming, and factory owners felt they faced shortages of workers. Then, responding to popular political pressure, Vargas loosened the government's control of the unions. The new political atmosphere of the early 1950s convinced grassroots leaders to maintain their own commissions as autonomous entities. At the same time, however, they sought to institutionalize their power through salary and strike committees. This process opened São Paulo's unions. In the case of the Textile Workers' Union, the strike finally provided the female majority with the opportunity to direct policy. The more open and representative unions and the unity among the four striking unions created a powerful and assertive workers' movement unlike anything that had previously existed in Brazil.

Conclusion

São Paulo's industrial workers managed to establish a high degree of control on the shop floor and in their formerly closed unions through direct confrontations with employers and entrenched *pelegos*. Two key factors facilitated this worker movement. First, the city's women workers called upon their tradition of independently organizing against the deteriorating conditions engendered by the rationalization of production. Women had made up the majority of the textile industry's labor force since the beginning of the twentieth century. Yet they had never had access to power within the various unions that sought to represent textile workers. Women also made up between 30 and 40 percent of the workers in the clothing, chemical, and food-processing industries. Because they had been denied access to power within the union structure, São Paulo's women factory workers developed their own shop floor organizations, the commissions. Male workers soon adopted the commission structure, which they also used to bargain directly with employers for increased control on the shop floor and for higher wages. This legacy of independent organizing that flowed from women's experiences proved to be an important component in the success of the "Strike of the 300,000."

The other key factor was the political situation. Vargas returned to power in the early 1950s, promising to represent Brazilian workers in their struggles with employers. Through their organizing and protest activities as well as through direct appeals, Paulistano workers cajoled Vargas into meeting his promises. They convinced him to raise the minimum wage, remove Ministry of Labor controls, and allow rank-and-file insurgents to gain control over the state-sponsored *sindicatos*. That is, by pressing their demands beyond their employers, São Paulo's industrial workers—led by women in the textile sector—not only regained some control over the productive process on the shop floor but also moved the president from simply mouthing populist platitudes to implementing populist policies. São Paulo's women textile workers were far from being passive victims of the changes brought on by rationalization.

The strike affected both local union and national politics over the course of the 1950s. Rank-and-file textile workers—especially women—continued to gain power within their *sindicato*. Other industrial unions in São Paulo also experienced a political opening. Paulistano unionists in the aftermath of the strike were often characterized as labor independents—not *pelegos* or communists.[80] The cross-union solidarity of this era went on to have a long-term impact on labor politics in Brazil. Activists from these unions, along with members of the Bankworkers' Union, went on to found the Inter-Union Department of Statistics and Socioeconomic Studies in 1955. This independent labor group studied working-class wages and the cost of living and helped coordinate union activities throughout the city. Its statistics became an important tool in all future wage negotiations. This group continued to play an important role as a voice for labor throughout Brazil during the military dictatorship (1964–85) and during the transition to civilian rule in the 1980s.[81]

The strike and the ongoing labor activism it ushered in also affected national politics. Vargas replaced Segadas Vianna with João (Jango) Goulart as minister of labor in June 1953. Since Vargas created the post in 1930, the minister of labor had been either neutral or pro-industry in labor disputes. Goulart (who went on to serve as vice president, and then as president was deposed by the military in 1964) was Brazil's first openly prolabor minister of labor. Vargas further courted labor with a series of increases in the minimum wage, including a 100 percent increase in May 1954. The popular effervescence of the "Strike of the 300,000" and the labor activism that followed was, however, too much for Vargas. Brazilian workers forced him to meet the populist promises he had been making for more than a decade. Such a pro-worker stance alienated Vargas's elite and military backers, and when the president could no longer juggle the competing claims of his diverse constituency, he killed himself, on 24 August 1954. In a way, Vargas's suicide was a product of the populism that the "Strike of the 300,000" helped usher in. Vargas had come to power planning to be the "father of the poor," but workers were not willing to follow blindly a paternalistic figure. São Paulo's and other cities' workers looked at Vargas as just another politician who had promised more than he could deliver.[82] In the final analysis, Brazilian workers proved they would no longer be mobilized "from above." These workers instead demanded their rights within Brazilian society.[83]

Notes

The author thanks Jeanne Boydston, Mike Conniff, Mike Jimenez, Florencia Mallon, Tom Skidmore, and Steve Stern for their helpful comments on the various incarnations of this chapter.

1. See *U.S. News and World Report*, 10 August 1951, and *Time*, 21 January 1952.
2. For a thorough account of the development of Brazil's textile industry, see Stan-

ley J. Stein, *The Brazilian Cotton Manufacture: Textile Enterprise in an Underdeveloped Area, 1850–1950* (Cambridge, Mass., 1957). For an account of industrialization in São Paulo, see Warren Dean, *The Industrialization of São Paulo, 1880–1945* (Austin, 1969). On labor in Paulista rural sectors, especially the coffee economy, see Thomas H. Holloway, *Immigrants on the Land: Coffee and Society in São Paulo, 1886–1934* (Chapel Hill, 1980); Verena Stolcke, *Coffee Planters, Workers, and Wives: Class Conflict and Gender Relations on São Paulo Plantations, 1850–1980* (New York, 1988).

3. The best account of discrimination faced by Afro-Brazilians and how they eventually gained employment in industrial establishments in the 1930s and 1940s is George Reid Andrews, *Blacks and Whites in São Paulo, Brazil, 1888–1988* (Madison, Wis., 1991). On women's industrial employment, see Eva Alterman Blay, *Trabalho domesticado: A mulher na indústria paulista* (São Paulo, 1978), 135–92.

4. A high turnover rate within textile mills has led some to believe that female industrial employment was temporary, but a closer examination of employment practices reveals that women often used labor mobility to bid up their wages. See Joel Wolfe, *Working Women, Working Men: São Paulo and the Rise of Brazil's Industrial Working Class, 1900–1955* (Durham, N.C., 1993), chap. 6.

5. Women and men workers' organizing and protest activities during the 1910s and 1920s are detailed in Joel Wolfe, "Anarchist Ideology, Worker Practice: The 1917 General Strike and the Formation of São Paulo's Working Class," *Hispanic American Historical Review* 71 (November 1991): 809–46. The late 1920s and early 1930s are analyzed in Wolfe, *Working Women, Working Men*, chap. 2. Anarcho-syndicalism is an ideology that combines the antistatism of anarchism with calls to organize workers into unions. These unions would serve as the basis for popular class participation in politics.

6. Although Vargas formally established the Estado Novo in November 1937, the federal government had begun an authoritarian crackdown on Paulista labor activists as early as 1935.

7. The membership figures are from the internal records of the Textile Workers' Union. See Wolfe, *Working Women, Working Men*, chaps. 3 and 4. The Metalworkers' Union, which represented an industry that was almost exclusively male, had a higher density of membership, but still fewer than 5 percent of the workers in this industry were *sindicalizados*.

8. During the early days of the Estado Novo, the small and weak Paulista PCB was decimated by Vargas's brutal repression. During the war, the party's leadership, following Moscow's Popular Front strategy, aligned itself with the regime, which had sent troops to fight in Europe. After the war, the PCB made alliances with "progressive" members of the national bourgeoisie and even maintained a no-strike pledge under the "Tighten Your Belt" campaign. Young members of the PCB opposed these national policies and worked with members of the factory commissions, but the national party continued to articulate policies that estranged it from the rank and file. See Wolfe, *Working Women, Working Men*, chaps. 4 and 5.

For works that posit a larger role for the PCB, see Ricardo Maranhão, *Sindicato e de-*

mocratização: Brasil, 1945–1950 (São Paulo, 1979); and John D. French, "Workers and the Rise of Adhemarista Populism in São Paulo, 1945–1947," *Hispanic American Historical Review* 68 (February 1988): 1–43; "Industrial Workers and the Birth of the Populist Republic in Brazil, 1945–1946," *Latin American Perspectives* 16 (Fall 1989): 5–27; John D. French and Mary Lynn Pedersen, "Women and Working-Class Mobilization in Postwar São Paulo, 1945–1948," *Latin American Research Review* 24 (Fall 1989): 99–125.

9. For an interesting historical and theoretical perspective on the importance of such independent popular class organizing and how it is often hidden from both the dominant classes and later scholars, see James Scott, *Domination and the Arts of Resistance: Hidden Transcripts* (New Haven, 1990). On women's independent political institutions, see Estelle Freedman, "Separatism as Strategy: Female Institution Building and American Feminism, 1870–1930," *Feminist Studies* 5 (Fall 1979): 512–29.

10. The Dutra regime is analyzed well in Thomas E. Skidmore, *Politics in Brazil, 1930–1964: An Experiment in Democracy* (New York, 1967), 48–80. One reason behind Dutra's crackdown on labor was that São Paulo's industrialists sought to rationalize production, especially in the textile mills. Dutra supported industrialists so much that he appointed the vice president of São Paulo's Federation of Industries, Morvan Dias de Figueiredo, Brazil's minister of labor.

11. See Werner Baer, *The Brazilian Economy; Growth and Development*, 2d ed. (New York, 1983), 68; and Skidmore, *Politics in Brazil*, 91–97.

12. Arquivo do Serviço Nacional de Aprendizagem Industrial (hereafter cited as SENAI) and Institute of Inter-American Affairs, "Estado de indústria têxtil e necessidades de treinamento," 1953, SENAI, São Paulo, 25–26; United Nations, Economic Commission for Latin America, *Labor Productivity of the Cotton Textile Industry in Five Latin American Countries* (New York, 1951), 17–20; Estanislau Fischlowitz, "Manpower Problems in Brazil," *International Labour Review* 79 (April 1959): 398–405; Flávio Rabelo Versiani, "Technical Change, Equipment Replacement, and Labor Absorption: The Case of the Brazilian Textile Industry" (Ph.D. diss., Vanderbilt University, 1971), 105–30.

13. Interview, João Bonifácio, São Paulo, 3 September 1987; interview, Luís Firmino de Lima, São Paulo, 1 September 1987.

14. Interview, Diolinda Nascimento, São Paulo, 2 September 1987.

15. Interview, João Bonifácio, São Paulo, 3 September 1987; interview, Luís Firmino de Lima, São Paulo, 1 September 1987; interview, Irene de Oliveira, São Paulo, 11 August 1987; interview, Assumpta Bianchi, São Paulo, 10 August 1987. See also Márcia Mendes de Almeida, "O Sindicato dos Têxteis em São Paulo: História, 1933–1957" (tese de mestrado, Universidade de São Paulo, 1981), 163–64, 185. One reliable estimate by a prolabor statistical agency put the increase of the cost of living from 1948 to 1953 at 62 percent. See Arquivo do Departamento Intersindical de Estatística e Estados Sócio-Econômicos (hereafter cited as DIEESE), "Inflação," 1957, São Paulo, GCN-68.

16. Sindicato de Indústria de Fiação e Tecelagem em Geral (hereafter cited as SIFTG), *Circular*, no. 3441, 24 November 1952.

17. *O Estado de São Paulo*, 5 December 1952; *A Gazeta*, 5 December 1952; *Folha da*

Manhã, 7 March, 10 March, 11 March 1952; SIFTG, *Circular*, no. 3394, 22 July 1952; no. 3395, 25 July 1952; no. 3485, 31 March 1953; no. 3486, 31 March 1953; Federação das Indústria do Estado de São Paulo (hereafter cited as FIESP), Reunião Semanal, 18 March 1953.

18. Scholars of this period have pointed out that the power shortages helped to bring on the strike, but they fail to note how rationing of electricity fit in with the rationalization program for the mills. See José Álvaro Moisés, *Greve de massa a crise política; Estudo da greve dos 300 mil em São Paulo, 1953–1954* (São Paulo, 1978); Timothy Harding, "The Political History of Organized Labor in Brazil," (Ph.D. diss., Stanford University, 1973), 257–61.

19. Quoted in Skidmore, *Politics in Brazil*, 52.

20. Quoted in ibid., 79.

21. Arquivo de Instituto Brasileiro de Opinião Pública e Estatística (hereafter cited as IBOPE), *Pesquisas Especiais* 9, São Paulo (6–15 September 1950); *Pesquisas especiais* 9, Rio de Janeiro (September 1950).

22. On the 1950 election, see Skidmore, *Politics in Brazil*, 73–80, and John W. F. Dulles, *Vargas of Brazil; A Political Biography* (Austin, 1967), 292–99. Eduardo Gomes of the União Democrático Nacional received 29.7 percent of the vote, and Christian Machado of the Partido Social Democrático received 21.5 percent.

23. For a list of industrialists who helped fund the campaign, see Arquivo do Getúlio Vargas (hereafter cited as AGV), 50.08.09.00/52, Centro de Pesquisa e Documentação (hereafter cited as CPDOC), Fundição Getúlio Vargas (hereafter cited as FGV). See also AGV, 48.11.30/2, CPDOC, FGV. See also Maria Celina Soares D'Araújo, *O segundo governo Vargas, 1951–1954: Democracia, partidos, e crise política* (Rio de Janeiro, 1982), 17–80.

24. Interview, Hermínia Lorenzi dos Santos, São Paulo, 12 August 1987; interview, Glória Salviano, São Paulo, 14 August 1987; "Labor Conditions in the São Paulo Consular District," October 1950, 17 November 1950, São Paulo (hereafter cited as SP) Post 560, Record Group (hereafter cited as RG) 84, United States National Archives (hereafter cited as NA).

25. Interview, Hermento Mendes Dantas, São Paulo, SP, 14 September 1987; "Labor Conditions in the São Paulo Consular District," November 1950, 13 December 1950, SP Post 560, RG 84, NA; "Labor Conditions in the São Paulo Consular District," December 1950, 23 January 1951, SP Post 560, RG 84, NA; Sindicato dos Metalúrgico de São Paulo (hereafter cited as SMSP), Assembléia Geral, 24 March 1950; *O Metalúrgico*, June 1950.

26. "Labor Conditions in the São Paulo Consular District," October 1950, 17 November 1950, SP Post 560, RG 84, NA; Mendes de Almeida, "O Sindicato dos Têxteis em São Paulo," 241.

27. Sindicato dos Trabalhadores na Indústria de Fiação e Tecelagem de São Paulo (hereafter cited as STIFTSP), Reunião de Directoria, 16 November, 5 December 1950, 3 April 1951; "Labor Conditions in the São Paulo Consular District," First Quarter 1951, 26 April 1951, SP Post 560, RG 84, NA.

28. *Conjunctura Econômico* (December 1949): 37.

29. Interview, Glória Salviano, São Paulo, 14 August 1987; interview, Hermínia Lorenzi dos Santos, São Paulo, 12 August 1987.

30. Interview, Irene de Oliveira, São Paulo, 11 August 1987.

31. Interview, Luís Firmino de Lima, São Paulo, 1 September 1987; interview, Enrique de Lima, São Paulo, 2 September 1987; interview, Diolinda Nascimento, São Paulo, 2 September 1987. Strikes waged by the factory commissions are detailed below.

32. Quoted in Harding, "Political History of Organized Labor in Brazil," 243.

33. SP to Rio, 8 May 1951, SP Post 560, RG 84, NA; "Labor Conditions for the São Paulo Consular District for the Second Quarter of 1951," 19 July 1951, RG 89, NA. Since the conclusion of the 1932 civil war, Getúlio Vargas had allowed Paulista industrialists to manage the State Department of Labor. This body frequently overruled the federal Ministry of Labor in the state during the 1930s and 1940s.

34. Interview, Odete Pasquini, São Paulo, 17 September 1987.

35. "Labor Conditions in the São Paulo Consular District for the Second Quarter of 1951," 19 July 1951, SP Post 560, RG 84, NA; interview, Herminia Lorenzi dos Santos, São Paulo, 12 August 1987; interview, Glória Salviano, São Paulo, 14 August 1987; interview, Conrado de Papa, Osasco, SP, 23 September 1987. For specifics on the cost of living and the value of the minimum wage, see Seiti Kaneko Endo and Heron Carlos Esvael do Carmo, *Breve histórico do índice de preços ao consumidor no município de São Paulo* (São Paulo, 1987), 17; DIEESE, "Objectivos e caraterísticas do Plano Cruzado III," Arqivo do DIEESE.

36. Interview, Diolinda Nascimento, São Paulo, 2 September 1987. See also FIESP, *Relatório* 1 (1951): 86.

37. "Labor Conditions in the São Paulo Consular District for the Third Quarter of 1951," 5 October 1951, SP Post 560, RG 84, NA.

38. Interview, João Bonifácio, São Paulo, 3 September 1987; interview, Luís Firmino de Lima, São Paulo, 7 August 1987; interview, Odete Pasquini, São Paulo, 17 September 1987; SIFTG, *Circular*, no. 3341, 17 January 1952.

39. *Folha da Manhã*, 18 December, 19 December, 20 December 1951; SIFTG, *Circular*, no. 3341, 17 January 1952; interview, Maria Pavone, São Paulo, 12 August 1987; interview, Laura Machado, Osasco, SP, 8 September 1987; interview, Angela Neto, São Paulo, 8 August 1987.

40. For a comparison of the real value of the minimum wage, see Endo and Esvael do Carmo, *Breve histórico do índice de preços ao consumidor no município de São Paulo*, 17.

41. *Folha da Manhã*, 25 December 1951.

42. *Folha da Manhã*, 21 December, 25 December 1951; SIFTG, *Circular*, no. 3342, 18 January 1952; interview, João Bonifácio, São Paulo, 10 August 1987; interview, Hermínia Lorenzi dos Santos, São Paulo, 12 August 1987.

43. SENAI Report, "Distribution of Industry and Labor in the State and City of São Paulo," translated and reproduced in Memo, 26 September 1951, SP Post 560, RG 84, NA.

44. In the past, male unionists had sought to protect women workers from long

shifts, night work, and so forth, but the women opposed these measures because they limited their ability to work when and where they wanted. See Wolfe, "Anarchist Ideology, Worker Practice," 826–28. For the same process in Argentina, see Marysa Navarro, "Hidden, Silent, and Anonymous: Women Workers in the Argentine Trade Union Movement," in *The World of Women's Trade Unionism: Comparative Historical Essays*, ed. Norbert C. Soldon (Westport, Conn., 1985), 171–72.

45. There were important divisions between young communist activists who concentrated their energies on union and work issues and the PCB leadership, which remained out of touch with working-class issues.

46. Interview, Hermento Mendes Dantas, São Paulo, 14 September 1987; interview, Roberto Unger, Osasco, SP, 23 September 1987; interview, Carlos Heubel Sobrinho, Osasco, SP, 23 September 1987; interview, João Bonifácio, São Paulo, 10 August 1987; interview, Hermínia Lorenzi dos Santos, São Paulo, 12 August 1987. The Metalworkers' Union also created formal committees from its factory commissions.

47. STIFTSP, Assembléia Geral, 16 December 1951; interview, João Bonifácio, São Paulo, 10 August 1987; interview, Hermínia Lorenzi dos Santos, São Paulo, 12 August 1987; Mendes de Almeida, "O Sindicato dos Têxteis em São Paulo," 224–25.

48. Interview, Maria Pavone, São Paulo, 12 August 1987. See also Mendes de Almeida, "O Sindicato dos Têxteis em São Paulo," 224–25.

49. *Folha da Manhã*, 6 February, 9 February, 10 February, 12 February 1952; "Labor Conditions in the São Paulo Consular District for the First Quarter of 1952," 24 May 1952, SP Post 560, RG 84, NA.

50. "Labor Conditions in the São Paulo Consular District for the First Quarter of 1952," 24 May 1952, SP Post 560, RG 84, NA.

51. For a careful analysis of Vargas's complex and shifting relations among his enemies and allies at this time, see Skidmore, *Politics in Brazil*, 100–112. A poll conducted by IBOPE for *Última Hora* found that Brazil's working class (including workers interviewed in São Paulo, Campinas, and Riberão Preto) supported and trusted Vargas more than any other politician. See IBOPE, *Pesquisas especiais*, vol. 11, May–June 1952. Vargas read reports from various government agencies concerning labor activities in São Paulo. See, for example, Cyro Riopardense Rezende, Chefe de Polícia, DFSP to Ministry of Labor, 13 February 1952, AGV, 52.02.13, Confid., CPDOC, FGV; José Segadas Vianna to Lourival Fontes, 7 April 1952, AGV, 52.04.07/1, CPDOC, FGV.

52. Quoted in Harding, "Political History of Organized Labor in Brazil," 251. A popular character on a long-running radio show in the 1940s and 1950s used to make similar comments about the limited utility of elections. See Valter Krausche's biography of the samba musician and actor Adoniran Barbosa, *Adoniran Barbosa: Pelas ruas da cidade* (São Paulo, 1985), 34–47.

53. *Última Hora*, 8 October 1952.

54. *O Metalúrgico*, August 1952; Mendes de Almeida, "O Sindicato dos Têxteis em São Paulo," 201.

55. At the same time he was criticizing *pelegos*, Vargas pushed for the implementa-

tion of the long-forgotten profit-sharing provisions in the 1946 constitution, improved government inspection of factories, and an increase in social services for workers. For details of these measures, see FIESP, *Relatório*, 1952, vol. 4, 5–48; "Labor Conditions in the São Paulo Consular District for the Second Quarter of 1952," 1 August 1952, SP Post 560, RG 84, NA.

56. See Wolfe, *Working Women, Working Men*, chaps. 3–5, for workers' independent letters and petitions to Vargas and for an analysis of Vargas's failure in the 1930s and early 1940s to convince workers to participate in the formal corporatist structure.

57. STIFTSP, Assembléia Geral, 27 January 1952.

58. Ibid., 26 August 1952; interviews, Luís Firmino de Lima, São Paulo, 7 August, 1 September 1987. See also Mendes de Almeida, "O Sindicato dos Têxteis em São Paulo," 240–43.

59. STIFTSP, Reunião de Diretoria, 9 December 1952; *Última Hora*, 9 January 1953; interview, Luís Firmino de Lima, São Paulo, 7 August 1987; interview, João Bonifácio, São Paulo, 3 September 1987.

60. Interview, Conrado de Papa, Osasco, SP, 23 September 1987.

61. Ibid.; interview, Hermento Mendes Dantas, 14 September 1987; interview, João Bonifácio, São Paulo, 3 September 1987; interview, Luís Firmino de Lima, São Paulo, 1 September 1987.

62. *Imprensa Popular*, 5 March, 11 March, 12 March, 13 March, 19 March 1953. For works that posit a leading role for the PCB in the strike, see Moisés, *Greve de massa*, 123–52; Moisés, "Brazil: New Questions on 'The Strike of the 300 Thousand' in São Paulo (1953)," paper presented for the workshop "Urban Working-Class Culture and Social Protest in Latin America," Woodrow Wilson International Center for Scholars, Washington, D.C., 1978, 13, 30–34.

63. Interview, Maria Pavone, São Paulo, 12 August 1987; interview, João Bonifácio, São Paulo, 10 August 1987; interview, Hermínia Lorenzi dos Santos, São Paulo, 12 August 1987; SIFTG, *Circular*, no. 3471, 22 January 1953; no. 3476, 20 February 1953.

64. *Folha da Manhã*, 11 March 1953; interview, João Bonifácio, São Paulo, 10 August 1987; interview, Hermínia Lorenzi dos Santos, São Paulo, 12 August 1987; interview, Maria Pavone, São Paulo, 12 August 1987.

65. Interview, Diolinda Nascimento, São Paulo, 2 September 1987; *Folha da Manhã*, 19 March 1953.

66. *Folha da Manhã*, 26 March, 27 March 1953; telegram, SP to Rio, 20 March 1953, SP Post 560.2, RG 84, NA; interview, Conrado de Papa, Osasco, SP, 23 September 1987; interview, Diolinda Nascimento, São Paulo, 2 September 1953. The Textile Workers' Union is still headquartered in Brás, the Metalworkers' Union in the Centro. These sources also seem to indicate that while the union directorates participated in the strikes, they had initially opposed the walkouts.

67. *Folha da Manhã*, 27 March, 28 March 1953; interview, Luís Firmino de Lima, São Paulo, 7 August 1987; interview, Antônio Ciaveletto, São Paulo, 3 September 1987; interview, Hermínia Lorenzi dos Santos, São Paulo, 12 August 1987; interview, Maria Pavone, São Paulo, 12 August 1987.

68. *Folha da Manhã*, 31 March, 2 April 1953; telegram, SP to Rio, 31 March 1953, Rio Post 560.2, RG 84, NA. Bank workers and printers do not seem to have formally struck for higher wages at this time.

69. Telegram, SP to Rio, 31 March 1953 (afternoon), Rio Post 560.2, RG 84, NA. See also *Folha da Manhã*, 31 March 1953. See also *Folha da Manhã*, 2 April 1953, for details of a police raid on the headquarters of the State Commission for the Fight against Food Shortages.

70. *Folha da Manhã*, 26 March, 29 March, 31 March, 1 April, 7 April, 8 April 1953.

71. *Folha da Manhã*, 29 March, 1 April 1953; interview, Luís Firmino de Lima, São Paulo, 7 August 1987; interview, Antônio Ciaveletto, São Paulo, 3 September 1987; interview, Hermínia Lorenzi dos Santos, São Paulo, 12 August 1987.

72. *Folha da Manhã*, 3 April, 4 April, 7 April 1953; interview, Luís Firmino de Lima, São Paulo, SP, 7 August 1987. Because the *bancários* and *gráficos* were not formally on strike, they did not join the pact at this time.

73. FIESP, Reunião Semanal, 8 April 1953.

74. Ibid.

75. *Folha da Manhã*, 10 April 1953; STIFTSP, Reunião de Diretoria, 9 April 1953.

76. Interview, Hermínia Lorenzi dos Santos, São Paulo, 12 August 1987; interview, Maria Pavone, São Paulo, 12 August 1987.

77. *Folha da Manhã*, 11 April, 12 April, 14 April, 15 April, 16 April, 17 April, 18 April 1953; interview, Conrado de Papa, Osasco, SP, 23 September 1987; interview, João Bonifácio, São Paulo, 3 September 1987.

78. *Diário de São Paulo*, 18 April 1953.

79. *Folha da Manhã*, 19 April, 21 April, 22 April, 23 April 1953; *Folha da Tarde*, 20 April 1953; *O Estado de São Paulo*, 24 April 1953; *Última Hora*, 24 April 1953; interview, Luís Firmino de Lima, São Paulo, 7 August 1987.

80. See Robert J. Alexander, "Brazilian 'Tenentismo,'" *Hispanic American Historical Review* 36 (May 1956): 240; Ruth Berins Collier and David Collier, *Shaping the Political Arena: Critical Junctures, the Labor Movement, and Regime Dynamics in Latin America* (Princeton, 1991), 549.

81. On the founding of the Inter-Union Department of Statistics and Socioeconomic Studies, see Wolfe, *Working Women, Working Men*, chap. 6. See Margaret E. Keck, *The Workers' Party and Democracy in Brazil* (New Haven, 1992), 63–64, 75, 170–71, for its role in the 1970s and 1980s.

82. An excellent account of Brazilian politics leading up to Vargas's suicide is Skidmore, *Politics in Brazil*, 112–42. See also Soares D'Araújo, *O segundo governo Vargas*. On dockworkers in Rio and their relationship to Vargas at this time, see Dennis Linhares Barsted, *Medição de Forças: O movimento grevista de 1953 e a época dos operários navais* (Rio de Janeiro, 1982).

83. For an analytical account of the ongoing labor activism up until the 1964 military *golpe*, see Collier and Collier, *Shaping the Political Arena*, 380–402, 546–55.

CHAPTER EIGHT

STRUGGLING FOR EMANCIPATION

Tungsten Miners and the

Bolivian Revolution

ANDREW BOEGER

Years of struggle to exert control over their lives fostered the capacity of Bolivia's mineworkers to influence the course of national politics. Working in an industry subject to the whims of the international market and living in remote communities owned by their employers shaped their struggle for control in three fundamental ways. First, these factors forced the workers to address a wide variety of issues. Second, they spurred them to devise creatively an array of tactics and strategies to counter the overwhelming power of the mining companies. Third, the vagaries of international markets and the power of the employers made the workers temper their struggle for control with efforts to achieve job security. An examination of the workers at one mining community, Chojlla (pronounced CHOK'ya), permits an intimate analysis of the relationship between local labor struggles, the economic structure, and national politics.

Chojlla's geographical isolation obliged the workers to confront the company on many different fronts. Like workers in other settings, the Chojlla mineworkers fought to improve their wages and working conditions. However, since they felt the company's presence in many other aspects of their lives, the miners were forced to extend their efforts into many areas that urban workers did not. The company owned and operated the local hospital, the elementary school, and most important, the company store. The company paid for the local constabulary and owned the homes of the workers. The company literally owned the soil on which the employees walked and under which most of them worked—and more than a few of them were buried. Everywhere

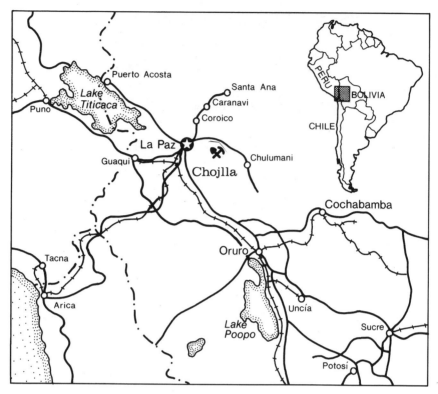

Map 6. *The Chojlla Tungsten Mine of Bolivia, 1952*

workers went in Chojlla, they faced the property—and the power—of their employer, the International Mining Company. No wonder, then, that their struggle for control involved so many issues and took so many different forms.

Ever changing market conditions and the prevailing presence of the company forced the Chojlla miners to be creative in their efforts to control their workplace and their community. Only during the last four of the sixteen years under consideration (1940–56) did both economic and political factors allow workers to make real gains through collective bargaining. The miners of Chojlla had organized and joined with miners across the country to bring to power a regime favorable to their interests.

But even before the Bolivian national revolution of 1952, the Chojlla mineworkers had devised two strategies that served as adjuncts to the collective bargaining process. First, workers sought on an individual basis to have a voice in their workplace and their community through informal acts of resistance. These ranged from fights with supervisors to simple absenteeism. Second, the Chojlla workers actively recruited allies among individuals and organizations outside their community, including miners at other companies, and political and labor organizations. By building these alliances, the Chojlla workers sought to offset the power of their employer. The national workers' movement they helped create allowed the Chojlla miners to influence the direction of national politics and defeat a repressive political order. With the triumph of the 1952 revolution, in which they played an active role, the mineworkers were poised to exert unprecedented control over their lives.

Protecting Their Health

The weakening of the Bolivian mining industry during the depression and the Chaco War with Paraguay (1932–35) created conditions that enabled workers and peasants to break down Bolivia's elite-dominated political order. Mining, especially tin mining, steadily rose in economic importance starting in the 1890s. By 1929, mining exports accounted for 94.18 percent of Bolivia's export earnings.[1] The depression dealt the tin mining industry a blow from which it never recovered. Tin prices and production fell dramatically.[2] Even high world demand for Bolivian tin during World War II did not totally revive the industry, and tin production never again reached the 1929 level.[3] New barriers to production emerged. It became more difficult to extract the ores, which were of increasingly lower purity. The large mining companies such as Patiño Mines encountered a labor shortage, and finally, no longer confident that they could control the political environment, the large mining companies ceased making the investments necessary to maintain productivity.[4] By the end of the 1930s, the "tin barons" found their grip on their workers and on Bolivian society starting to slip.

Popular discontent and nationalist sentiment rose after the disastrous Chaco War, and much of both were directed against the mining "superstate," as the mining companies came to be called. The Toro and Busch governments of the late 1930s tried to harness the growing militancy of the miners and other workers for their nationalist political project. The Busch administration proposed a comprehensive labor code and attempted to force the mining companies to sell all their foreign earnings to the Central Bank at a discounted rate. The Busch government fell in 1939 before it could implement these reforms.[5] For the next four years, conservative governments tried unsuccessfully to hold back the rising tide of nationalism and worker organization. The tragic massacre at Patiño's Catavi mine on 21 December 1942 exemplified the desperate and brutal measures the government was willing to take to serve the interests of the mining companies: Army troops opened fire on a crowd of eight thousand women, men, and children, killing scores. Opposition politicians of the Revolutionary Nationalist Movement (Movimiento Nacionalista Revolucionario, or MNR) loudly denounced the Catavi massacre, using it to whip up popular opposition to the regime.[6] Consequently, in December 1943, a nationalist military faction led by Col. Gualberto Villarroel seized power in alliance with the MNR. The regime enacted and enforced some new labor reforms.[7] Seeking to strengthen its support among the workers, the MNR organized the founding congress of the Miners' Federation (Federación Sindical de Trabajadores Mineros de Bolivia, or FSTMB) in June 1944. The miners voted as a block for both independent and MNR candidates in local and national elections.[8] But the Villarroel-MNR government fell in 1946.

Over the next six years, the mining companies successfully enlisted the help of the state in their fight against the miners' organization, but they could not contain the MNR and the labor movement. The MNR presidential candidate, Víctor Paz Estenssoro, bolstered by support from the miners, won a clear-cut victory in the 1951 elections. However, a military takeover prevented him from taking office. Its failure to gain power via the ballot box obliged the party to seek the armed support of the mining proletariat. Fueled by years of subjugation, low wages, and repression, the miners seized arms from army and police garrisons and surrounded La Paz and Oruro. In just three days—from 9 April to 12 April 1952—they drove the old regime from power. The miners used their votes, their guns, and their organizational strength to transform what might have been just another coup into a social revolution.

The United States, in the meantime, had needed Bolivian tungsten to make weapons of war. While small amounts were used in peacetime electronics, far more tungsten was needed for the production of jet aircraft, armor-piercing projectiles, and tool steel for war industries.[9] The importance of Bolivian tungsten increased when other suppliers, most notably China, could not or would not provide an adequate supply. Demand for the mineral peaked during World War II. In 1944, Bolivia provided 47.32 percent of all U.S. imports of tungsten.[10] At the end of the war, U.S. imports of Bolivian tungsten dropped by nearly 70 percent. In 1949, growing Cold War hostilities and the takeover of China by Mao Tse-tung's Red Army once again made Bolivia an important supplier of tungsten to the United States.

The Chojlla mine, located ninety kilometers by road from La Paz, actually got its start as a result of the high demand for tungsten created by World War I. Some of Bolivia's richest and largest tungsten deposits in the form of wolframite were discovered mixed with tin ores in the Yanacachi district of the Sud Yungas Province of the department of La Paz.[11] It is rumored among the miners and peasants of the area that a violent rock slide exposed the ores to view.[12] In 1914, the locals sold their rights to the Zalles family, who owned several hundred hectares of land nearby and were engaged in the primitive exploitation of a handful of small tin and tungsten mines.[13] The W. R. Grace Company, already engaged in the import-export business in Bolivia, was eager to profit from the World War I mineral boom. On 1 July 1918, Grace entered into a partnership with the Zalles and a few foreign investors to form the International Mining Company (IMCO). Grace held the majority interest.[14] Foreign demand, foreign capital, and rich tungsten ore deposits led to the creation of the Chojlla mine.

The Great Depression of 1929 plunged the Bolivian mining industry into a crisis. In 1932, the Zalles sold their interests to the Grace Company, which sought to modernize and rationalize production.[15] While roughly half of Bolivia's tungsten production was refined using primitive hand-grinding methods, U.S. investment capital outfitted the Chojlla mine with a high-capacity mill made in Europe. The company also constructed worker housing "that [left] nothing to be desired," according to a local government official.[16] Increased demand caused by World War II stimulated production, and in 1940 Chojlla, together with smaller IMCO mines, produced a monthly average of fifty tons of wolframite and thirty tons of tin. Most of the time, 40 percent of the mine's production was tin and the remaining 60 percent tungsten. The company's Chojlla and Enramada mines employed about 525 workers.[17] To a large extent, the ebb and flow of world demand set the parameters within which the miners shaped their lives at Chojlla.

Who were the miners of Chojlla?[18] The majority—perhaps as many as 80 percent—came to Chojlla as first-generation miners from Aymara peasant communities in the Department of La Paz. Although some came from the Yungas region near the mine, more came from the higher-elevation communities of the Altiplano, especially those near Lake Titicaca. There agrarian conflict raged with greater intensity, and the labor supply was higher. Many of the new workers heard about job opportunities at Chojlla from friends and family members. Up until the mid-1940s, labor contractors attracted additional workers to the mine with cash advances and promises. This system of labor recruitment, known as the *reenganche*, seems to have been fraught with problems. Some people say that for roughly every thirty workers recruited in this way, only one would remain at the mine for more than a month. Faced with the demands and dangers of work underground and the low pay, many took what was left of their cash advance and fled. The vast number of personnel files stamped in red ink "escaped" remain a mute witness to the unpleasant realities of life at the mine.

Each and every day, the International Mining Company met strong resistance from the workers as it tried to shape a reliable and well-disciplined

labor force. Those who toiled extracting ore inside the mine caused the greatest number of problems. Available documents indicate that these workers,
younger and more recently arrived from the peasant communities than those
who worked elsewhere, attempted to exert control over the workplace in three
ways. They refused to work with supervisors who mistreated them; they ignored the time card system set up by the company; and they sometimes simply
did not show up for work. Supervisor Benigno Aldunate, for example, was
forced to quit when a group of workers informed him that they would no
longer work with him because of his abuses.[19] In November 1948, the company attempted to crack down on those who ignored the time card system by
barring from the mine all who did not present their time cards to their supervisors.[20] This management tactic worked for a while. Absenteeism probably
posed the biggest discipline problem to the managers, and there seemed to be
little they could do about it. Jenaro Humérez was so shocked that he was fired
for three consecutive absences that he wrote to the union's general secretary.[21]
In 1951, the company posted notices about the number of workers who did not
show up each day. For example, on 8 October twenty-nine people did not
report to work, twenty-two of them from the interior mine. On 17 October
twenty-five people were absent, thirteen of whom worked inside the mine.[22]
One worker explained that his colleagues sought to protect their health by
staying home from work when they felt ill.[23] This assertion is borne out by
more complete data on absenteeism for the post-1952 period analyzed below.
Through their daily resistance, the rank and file made their work situation
more tolerable. Upon this base of worker resistance, union leaders sought to
build institutions that would challenge the power of the mining companies
while preserving the production of the mines.

Waging a Fruitless Struggle

Ties to labor and political organizations outside their community during the
favorable political climate of the Villarroel/MNR government enabled the
Chojlla workers to establish their union. No one sought to disrupt production,
however. Previously, the company had effectively squelched efforts at unionization.[24] A delegation of representatives from the MNR-dominated Unionized Labor Federation of La Paz presided over the *gran asamblea* of workers
that formally founded the union on 29 March 1944.[25] Two days later, the
union sent a letter to the section supervisors of the mine, asking them to allow
all nonessential personnel to leave their posts to attend a union meeting on a
Sunday afternoon. The letter called for the mass meeting to be held on the

soccer field, to enable, "all workers and employees . . . to become familiar with the ends pursued [by the union] and give their names in order to swell the ranks of the organized and disciplined proletariat."[26] By scheduling the meeting on a Sunday and by leaving a few workers on duty, the union leaders hoped to increase attendance without disturbing the work schedule.

Immediately following the establishment of the union, labor leaders began to build what proved to be a very important relationship with the MNR. La Paz attorney Federico Alvarez Plata served as the union's connection to the party. Alvarez Plata was in many respects typical of the young, college-educated middle-class men and women who became MNR activists once Villarroel took power. The son of hacienda owners from a nearby town, he completed his legal education at the Universidad Mayor de San Andrés in La Paz in 1942. Alvarez Plata held an official position in the government of the Department of La Paz, which he owed to his MNR affiliation.[27] Barely three days after the its founding in March 1944, the union wrote Alvarez Plata asking him to serve as its legal representative "in protests [*reclamos*], requests, controversies, administrative formalities, etc. etc, before the Ministry of Labor and similar bodies, as well as in matters involving the courts of this district." The letter makes no mention of Alvarez Plata's MNR connections and political influence as the basis for his selection. Instead, union officials stressed his "unquestionable expertise in Mining Legislation."[28] Through this political alliance, the Chojlla miners sought both to protect and to exercise their right to organize.

What accounts for the Chojlla union's support for Alvarez Plata and the MNR? First, the union needed legal representation and political influence to deal with the vagaries of Bolivian labor law and the bureaucracy that enforced it. Secondly, the leadership was convinced that favorable intervention of the state was necessary to the long-term survival of their jobs. Who better to serve the union in both capacities than a young, energetic lawyer who was also an activist of the party in power and a departmental government official? Alvarez Plata did not disappoint. He used his influence with MNR congressional deputy (and future president) Hernán Siles Zuazo to secure legal recognition of the union by the Ministry of Labor.[29] Under Bolivian law, the union could do nothing without this bureaucratic formality. The union also called upon Alvarez Plata to represent individual union members before various government bodies. For example, in December 1945 the union requested that he help mineworker Manuel Aliaga Palabra obtain his social security benefits.[30] The La Paz lawyer also used his influence to get the Ministry of Labor to donate furniture and office supplies to the union. Finally, Alvarez Plata personally donated a quantity of books to the union, which formed "the solid base of [its] future library."[31] Alvarez Plata's legal knowledge, personal influence, and access to resources helped the union grow and represent its membership.

In return for his help, the Chojlla union provided political backing for Alvarez Plata. As did miners elsewhere in Bolivia, the workers of the Chojlla mine provided crucial electoral support to the MNR during the 1940s. One of the first organized activities of the newly formed union was to support the MNR in the elections for Congress scheduled for the summer of 1944. First, the leadership petitioned to have either Chojlla or nearby Yanacachi declared a polling place. In a letter to the minister of government, the union's executive committee argued that the prospect of traveling the fifty kilometers "of bad roads and many difficulties" to the nearest polling place, Chulumani, discouraged the some one thousand voters in Chojlla and the additional two hundred voters in Yanacachi and Villa Aspiazu from actually voting.[32] "We see an urgent need for you to concern yourself with getting a Supreme Decree [to make Yanacachi an electoral district]," union leaders wrote Alvarez Plata. It was the only way to get the mineworkers to the voting booths and "obtain the victory of the Nationalist Revolutionary Movement."[33] Alvarez Plata was happy to comply, as the union and the local committee of the MNR had proclaimed him their Sud Yungas congressional candidate two days earlier, "in recognition of services . . . lent [to] the working class."[34] His efforts on this occasion failed, however. Chojlla was not recognized as an electoral district until 16 October 1945.[35]

The Chojlla miners did not limit themselves to bureaucratic maneuvers and paper endorsements to express their political will. They encouraged other unions in the area to collaborate with the MNR. "Let's take advantage of this opportunity, comrades," the *chojlleños* urged other miners, "to come to a mutual understanding, and make a common cause in the upcoming elections to bring to the supreme command of the nation an element that supports us and not elements that see us as *cannon fodder*."[36] And when rumors spread that Alvarez Plata had resigned his candidacy, the union's leadership actively fought what it saw as a deliberate misinformation campaign directed by the mine owners.[37] Despite the efforts of the Chojlla union, Alvarez Plata did not win the congressional election in 1944. His defeat can be attributed in part to Chojlla's failure to become an electoral district. Faced with the prospect of a long and uncomfortable trip to Chulumani, many of Alvarez Plata's supporters stayed home on election day. The electoral failure of 1944, nevertheless, served to heighten the political consciousness of the workers, which they needed to survive what was about to befall them.

The vertical drop in U.S. demand for tungsten at the end of World War II cost many workers their jobs at Chojlla. Although 1944 was a boom year for Bolivian tungsten, it also marked the beginning of a crisis. Most Bolivian tungsten producers ceased operations. The International Mining Company managed to stay open but was forced to reduce production. In April 1945, the company fired one hundred workers, nearly a fifth of its workforce.[38] The company issued another round of ninety-day dismissal notices at the end of October. Union general secretary Cristóbal Rivas received one of those notices.[39]

In the face of the layoffs, union leaders pressured their MNR allies in the government to intervene. On 9 November 1945, General Secretary Rivas announced to the membership that the union board was setting aside a pending list of worker demands until its leaders met with government officials. Rivas promised that the union would do all it could to preserve everyone's job. He urged the membership to keep working and avoid acts of sabotage.[40] Fortunately for Rivas and his fellow workers, the MNR authorities and President Villarroel recognized the political importance of the union. They intervened in favor of the workers. At their meeting with government officials, the union representatives learned that the government planned to annul the company's letters dismissing the Chojlla workers. The government also lifted taxes on tungsten exports to keep the mines open. Despite these measures, the union delegates warned that the future of the mine was uncertain. "The tungsten mines might last from a few months to a few years, or they might close within two or three days," they said, "because the good intentions of the heads of State are not enough, nor is the good will of the companies, nor the workers' enthusiasm for their jobs; what truly matters is that there is a price and a market for this metal."[41]

Despite the union's pessimism, employment at Chojlla did not drop significantly for a decade. In 1947, roughly seven hundred workers were employed at the mine; in 1951, some eight hundred workers were employed at Chojlla.[42] But the leaders became discredited in the process. Many workers, especially those who toiled inside the mine, interpreted the leadership's efforts to discipline the workers in order to keep the mine open as a betrayal.[43] Thus, what seems in retrospect to have been a successful effort to preserve jobs hardly seemed a victory to those who carried it out.

Ties with the MNR allowed the Chojlla workers to organize their union and preserve their livelihood. However, organization initially did little to enhance the workers' control over their community and their jobs. The company, bolstered by economic factors, continued to hold their jobs hostage and deny them any significant concessions. From 1946 to 1952, the International Mining Company essentially succeeded in ignoring the demands of the workers. Much of the rank and file grew increasingly disenchanted with the union leadership. Union leaders, therefore, spared no effort to build horizontal ties with other unions and offered support to the Miners' Federation. Since the company owned and controlled everything in the camp, worker complaints addressed a variety of issues: the company hospital, the company store, wages, shortages of tools and supplies, child care, working conditions, and inadequate lighting in the camp.[44]

But the company store seems to have generated most of the grievances voiced by union leaders to management. Key problems included insufficient supplies of goods, the treatment of workers by store personnel, and the quality of the merchandise. On one occasion, the union presented the store administrator with a loaf of bread accompanied by a note, "As you will be able to see and appreciate, this case is most curious," the note stated, "because while trying to eat this bread during the night, nobody could see that it contained an entire mouse."[45] This is but one of the more graphic examples of a litany of worker complaints about the company store.

Although racial and ethnic aspects can be seen in all the conflicts between the predominately "white" management and the "Indian" miners, nowhere are they more evident than in the conflict over coca. The leaf from which cocaine can be derived, coca held great cultural importance for the miners. Their use of the leaf symbolized their continuing ties with the peasantry and their indigenous identity.[46] Miners started each work shift talking together while filling their mouths with the leaf; sharing this small pleasure provided a context for miners to strengthen their ties to one another. Not only did the miners seek to ensure the help and protection of each other with this ritual; they also made a daily offering of coca to the guardian spirit of the mine, *el tío*, to ensure that he would not work against them.[47] Miners chewed coca for its mild stimulant effect, to stave off hunger, and to filter somewhat the dust that filled the air of the mine. In the words of one miner, "Without coca, the workers of the mine cannot work." Shortages of good coca in the company store particularly angered workers, particularly because the surrounding Yungas region supplied nearly all Bolivian domestic consumption.[48] But the penny-pinching managers bought coca only when prices were low and then in very large quantities. When stored, the coca leaf would lose the color and flavor preferred by the workers. The managers were not "Indians" and did not chew coca; thus they failed to understand these subtleties. Only after the workers voiced these complaints on various occasions did the administration stop stocking such large quantities of the leaf.[49] Unlike many other worker gripes, the administration did take steps to address the coca issue. It realized that coca was closely tied to getting the miners to be productive.

The company administration, on the other hand, generally dismissed griev-

*Miners sharing coca and camaraderie underground at the Chojlla mine,
1992. (Courtesy of Andrew Boeger)*

ances about the company store and told workers to wait. In one instance,
union leaders complained about shortages of sugar, rice, meat, and bread.
The fact that many workers had large families at Chojlla magnified the se-
riousness of the problem.[50] Management's response typifies the way the company treated all worker grievances in the years before the revolution. The
chief administrator counseled patience. He denied that a shortage of sugar
existed and deflected the blame for other shortages. No fresh meat and flour
could be found in all of Bolivia, he stated, but the company was trying to buy
dried meat (*charqui* and *chalona*, traditional Andean foods) as replacements.
The administrator went on to blame the workers themselves for aggravating
the shortages, claiming that workers had sold "several hundred pounds" of
basic foods for a profit in La Paz. Fortunately, he announced, more rice would
be arriving "in a few more days."[51] In the meantime, the workers were to wait.

The inability of the union to force major concessions from the company
during the years before the revolution caused considerable discontent. Many
workers became convinced that the union had no chance of ever becoming a

vehicle for workers' control. At one point in 1948, the Chojlla union's general secretary urged Miners' Federation leader Juan Lechín to come to Chojlla to help resolve "several complaints with the company, especially those regarding the provision of vital supplies in the company store." The union leader pointed out that the Chojlla union had "in every instance demonstrated its loyal compliance" to federation directives. The local union's failure to wrest major improvements from the company had created, he continued, "an extraordinary pessimism in this district on the part of the fellow-workers": "They don't attend the meetings which are called. . . . Grievances brought before the company aren't backed up by the mass [of workers], which is to say that this is a fruitless struggle."[52] Operating in isolation, the Chojlla union had been unable to counter the power of the International Mining Company. Union leaders became convinced that, only with the help of the federation and miners in other districts, would they be able to achieve a modicum of control over their jobs and their lives. Time would prove them correct.

Preventing Capitalists from Destroying the Unions

Necessity forced the Chojlla miners to build ties with the Miners' Federation and with unions in other mining centers. Alvarez Plata succeeded in getting the International Mining Company to grant an eight-day leave to two union leaders so they could represent Chojlla at the federation's founding convention in 1944.[53] The Chojlla union came to play an important role in the federation. At its second congress in 1945, the Chojlla delegates presented eight motions for the assembly's approval. These proposals addressed a variety of unfair practices of the mining companies, from the use of blacklists to unjustified firings.[54] As time went on, the Miners' Federation became more important to the Chojlla miners than the MNR.

Union congresses, and less formally, intraunion soccer tournaments, allowed the Chojlla workers to develop horizontal ties with miners in other districts. The Chojlla union regularly exchanged information with other miners' unions about wages, company store prices, and changes in union leadership. For example, in 1944, the Llallagua miners' union, one of the largest and most powerful in the country, informed the Chojlla union's general secretary of the results of internal union elections. Instead of the usual "sincerely" or "fraternally yours," the Llallagua union leaders closed their letter: "hoping for the most ample cooperation of you and yours in the struggle for the social and economic emancipation of the proletarian class."[55] Ideology was diffused from one mining center to another along with more practical knowledge. In 1945, the Chojlla union leadership wrote twelve other unions requesting data on wages and company store prices. The *chojlleños*, not to be outdone, closed their request with a revealing flourish: "We hope that your Proletarian Institution, the cornerstone of National Security, keeps alive the hope for a brighter future."[56] Their frustrations at countering the power of their employer had convinced the Chojlla leaders that a better future would be had only through uniting with miners all across the country.

The Miners' Federation came to be the primary means by which the Chojlla union leadership sought to influence national politics. A Chojlla representative, Felipe Bernal, was elected to the executive board of the federation.[57] In the October 1946 congressional elections, the Chojlla union shifted its loyalties from the MNR by endorsing the federation-backed candidate (a Trotskyist) to represent the Sud Yungas province. Alvarez Plata of the MNR won the election anyway.[58] The union did not actively support the MNR again until 1951. After the Villarroel-MNR government fell in 1946, the union's participation in the nationalist struggle against the mining companies was channeled through the federation.

The union leadership's commitment to the Miners' Federation resulted in the union's first and only strike before 1952. The strike attempted to counter the frontal assault mounted against the federation by Patiño Mines, the largest mining company in Bolivia. Early in September 1947, in response to rising union militancy, the Patiño company fired its entire workforce of some seventy-five hundred persons. It then rehired all but four hundred workers, whom it judged to be disruptive agitators. The dismissals effectively destroyed, temporarily, the largest and traditionally most militant unions of the Miners' Federation. Although the firings violated Bolivian labor law, they were carried out with the support of the Ministry of Labor and the armed forces.[59] The Miners' Federation fought back. It called for a general strike of all miners, in an effort to restore four hundred workers to their jobs.[60]

The strike call of the Miners' Federation elicited a quick response from the Chojlla union. At a ten A.M. executive board meeting on 16 September 1947, a messenger named Manjón read a communiqué from the Miners' Federation calling for "a strike of unlimited duration in support of the *compañeros* in Catavi and other important points." Manjón assured the leaders that the strike would last only three days. Hugo Durán moved to declare an immediate strike "in view of the fact that the miners' union of Chojlla [was] affiliated with the FSTMB." But everyone agreed on the need for a general assembly to decide the issue. At a general assembly that very afternoon, the union membership voted to strike.[61]

While involving the rank and file in the decision to strike, union leaders took measures to ensure that strike activities would not damage the mine's productive capability. Some feared worker sabotage. On the evening of the 16th, Manjón helped the executive board organize a union security squad (*policía sindical*) to "keep an eye on the installations and avoid any violence on the part of the *compañeros*." The leadership also decided that the mine watchmen should continue to work, along with workers in the electric plant and the hospital.[62] The leadership wished to continue the pumps removing water from the depths of the mine, thereby avoiding costly water damage. Determined to support the Miners' Federation strike, the union's directorate was equally committed to keeping the mine open in the long run.

The lack of communications from the outside world in general and the Miners' Federation in particular led the leadership to organize a general assembly on 19 September. Expecting the strike to last only three days, the leadership was uncertain what to do, since they had received no further information from the federation. The membership, however, decided to remain on strike until the federation sent instructions to the contrary. One worker said that although he initially opposed the strike, he now supported it. "[A] few more days of striking aren't going to make us die from hunger," said another. One member of the executive board supported continuing the strike: "We must always prevent the capitalists from destroying the unions."[63] But the national government cooperated with the owners. It had prevented the strike call from spreading by cutting postal and telegraphic communications to the mining camps. The minister of labor also claimed that only two miners' unions had heeded the strike call. However, La Paz newspapers were quoting a federation official as saying that the strike had closed six mines, among them Chojlla.[64] The government clearly felt threatened, declaring a state of siege on 18 September.[65] Isolated from news of national events, the workers of Chojlla were left to ponder their commitment to the federation.

On the sixth day of the 1947 strike, without word from the federation, the executive board of the Chojlla union again called for a general membership meeting. Some of the leaders were completely disillusioned. One called the strike "pure romanticism."[66] Some members echoed this sentiment, saying that "fathers of families want[ed] to go back to work." But other leaders invoked the memory of the 1942 Catavi massacre to remind the workers of the importance of the struggle against the mining elite. When the issue was finally put to vote, "those who wanted to return to work were very few."[67] The *chojlleños* actually stayed out on strike several days after Juan Lechín, executive secretary of the federation, had called an end to the strike.[68] But in the end, the Bolivian mining strike of 1947 failed. Not until the triumph of the revolution would a special decree reinstate the victims of the mass firings to their jobs. Unlike their involvement with the MNR when that party held power, the

Chojlla workers' involvement with the Miners' Federation brought few immediate benefits.

A strategic alliance between the Miners' Federation and the MNR proved key to the victory of the 1952 national revolution. The Chojlla workers joined with other miners in the mass mobilization that swept representatives of the mining oligarchy from power. The union had voted for the MNR in the 1951 elections, and approximately ten workers from Chojlla lost their lives in the insurrection of April 1952 when the military tried to prevent the MNR from taking office. The union supported the revolution with donations of supplies, money, and medical care.[69] However, little evidence of direct contact between the party and the Chojlla union exists in the union archive. Evidently, the union's support for the revolution was for the most part funneled through the Miners' Federation.

End of the Era of Good Understanding

The 1952 Bolivian revolution held different meanings for the different social groups that had brought it about. The urban middle-class leaders of the MNR sought power both for their personal benefit and to enact from above a few mild reforms for Bolivia's economic modernization. They wanted to exert control over the mining companies as a means to generate the revenues needed for their development project.[70] The miners similarly wanted Bolivia to develop. For them, however, the first step was to resolve their long-standing grievances with their employers. This could be accomplished only by greater control over their workplaces and their communities. After 12 April the power of the miners' militias went unchallenged, because the army had disintegrated during the rebellion. Pressure from below, primarily from the miners but increasingly with the support of other sectors of the working class and the peasantry, obliged the reformers to become revolutionaries. The politicians of the MNR were forced to broaden the scope of reform.

The newly formed Bolivian Workers' Central (the Central Obrera Boliviana, or COB) exercised what came to be called cogovernment with the MNR. The COB obliged the government to appoint Miners' Federation leader Juan Lechín as minister of mines and petroleum, factory workers' leader Germán Butrón as minister of labor, and Ñuflo Chávez as minister of peasant affairs. Unrelenting pressure from the miners then moved the government to nationalize the three largest mining companies in October 1952. The central state assumed ownership of the mining companies, thus eliminating the most dangerous threat to the political survival of the regime, namely the power of the mine owners. At the same time, the government gained control of the primary source of revenue in the country. The workers now gained control over the workplaces. Labor representatives joined the board of directors of the newly formed Bolivian Mining Corporation and participated in management decisions at the local level. The enactment of universal suffrage increased the size of the electorate from 200,000 to 1.6 million voters. The following year, widespread turmoil in the countryside also induced the government to initiate a wide-scale agrarian reform program. Pressure from below was forcing the MNR to convert its political revolution into a social revolution.

From the outset, it became clear that Chojlla would not be nationalized. The text of the nationalization decree made no mention of the roughly twenty medium-sized mining companies. Nor did the *chojlleños* push for the nationalization of the International Mining Company. Politically and economically, workers realized that the nationalization of companies wholly owned by U.S. capital would have created serious international problems for the nascent revolutionary state. The three big mining companies, which were nationalized, were not foreign owned. Only the Patiño enterprise had a significant number of U.S. investors, and American diplomats insisted that the Bolivian government compensate the Patiño shareholders. Since nearly all Bolivian tin and many other minerals were consumed in the United States, the Bolivians found themselves in a weak bargaining position.[71] Nationalization of Chojlla and other U.S.-owned enterprises would have invoked further international pressure. But the realities of postwar hemispheric politics did not dampen the militancy of the Chojlla miners.

The insurrectionary victory rekindled the hope of the Chojlla workers for greater control through collective action. In June 1952, the union presented a long list of demands to the International Mining Company that touched upon several key issues: the need for better wages, greater production bonuses, more housing, adequate provisioning and better prices at the company store, extra vacation time for underground workers, and improved health care. The company professed shock at the new militancy of the workers. "The Company deeply appreciates the cordial relations that always have existed in this mining center," the management said. "And just as deeply, we feel that there exists the danger of losing all the good understanding for which we have struggled to protect for so long."[72]

The traditional "good understanding" was in greater danger than the administration realized. Aware of the new political situation and their role in bringing it about, the rank and file decided the time had come to replace traditional paternalism with worker control. "We want to know the concrete result of the list of demands presented to the Internacional [*sic*] Minig [*sic*]

Co. by our Board," a group of workers informed their union leaders. "Otherwise, we will enter into a sit-down strike 24 hrs. after presenting this document to the Board." Approximately two hundred workers signed the petition, and another twenty or so indicated their assent with their thumbprints.[73] This mass action resulted in high-level negotiations in La Paz between management and the union. No less an authority than Juan Lechín, head of the Miners' Federation and newly appointed minister of mines and petroleum, assisted the negotiations. Available documents do not indicate the outcome, but the manner by which the Chojlla rank and file brought about the negotiations set the tone of company-labor relations for the next several years. Clearly, the era of "good understanding" (as the company saw it) or "total pessimism" (as workers called it) had come to an end. The *chojlleños* now wanted to reap the harvest of their years cultivating political change.

Realizing their new power, the Chojlla miners clamored to union meetings and harangued their union leaders and shop stewards to resolve long-standing problems. One exasperated union leader proposed including shop stewards in negotiations "so that some of the big-mouthed fellow-workers realize that it is not easy to get anything [out of the company] and that [the workers] in fact control their leaders."[74] Even though the Chojlla workers voiced many different demands, the company store became the focus of discontent. The disruption of food production resulting from agrarian conflict, speculation, and complex rules for currency exchange made it difficult for the company to keep its stores adequately stocked. Company store personnel were also regarded as corrupt and abusive. Most important, the company store directly impinged upon the daily lives of the women. Most of its shoppers were women.

Just as aware as men of the opportunities brought about by the revolution, women also pressed their age-old grievances. Only the words of men were recorded in the minutes of union meetings and in union correspondence, but often women's outrage at the treatment they received in company stores can be discerned. Asked if women faced many problems in the company store, a retired union leader said, "Always! And they always complained about them, too."[75] A shop steward told the local union board of one disagreeable incident. When the "wife of Flores" asked for an advance in her meat ration, two store clerks snarled, "For you there isn't shit!" The union asked the company to fire these two and increase the size of the company store staff to provide "better service for the workers as well as for the wives of same."[76] The store's accountant subsequently was the subject of numerous complaints voiced by "the wives of workers and [white-collar] employees" for "mistreatment and violence." The union demanded his transfer to a different post.[77]

How did the union respond to the constant complaints of the rank and file about conditions in the company store? As they did before the revolution, union officials presented the administration with specific written demands. Many workers complained about shortages of meat, soap, coffee, and cigarettes and other items "of vital necessity," leading union leaders to "request a report" from the administration.[78] Before the revolution, the administration usually responded by counseling patience and pleading that it was unable for various reasons to meet the workers' demands. Now, however, increased worker militancy in the revolutionary context enabled the union to force the company to allow them greater control in managing the company store. Instead of merely requesting a report from the local mine officials, a delegation of union leaders pushed their demands with officials in the company headquarters in La Paz. A union leader traveled to La Paz every fifteen or thirty days. "Together with the man in charge of purchases," the union representative helped purchase items for the company store. Two union officials now supervised the storage and distribution of the coca in the company store.[79]

However, the union's new participation in the management of the company store did not immediately resolve all of the workers' grievances. Only two weeks after the union won the right to control store purchases, union leaders threatened a twenty-four-hour strike because of the "serious inattention" on the part of the company to shortages. "I have never had to suffer such a serious insult," replied the chief administrator. "If this is any indication of the impatience and lack of understanding that you will have in the future when many and diverse problems will have to be solved . . . I am disposed to leave this great responsibility to someone who perhaps will serve you better." But the administrator had lost the control over the workers. "We will increase the milk, soap, and oil rations, and orders to that effect will be given today, and steps are being taken to correct other shortages," he conceded. "Furthermore, the quality of the bread will be improved today, and even though costs went up, we won't increase the price."[80] Although they had made a breakthrough, this did not prevent the *chojlleños* from resorting to direct action to enforce their control.

The success of collective action after the revolution did not mean that the Chojlla workers had abandoned their traditional means of individual resistance. Many workers continued to practice absenteeism, in particular to safeguard their health and in general to preserve a sense of individual control over their lives. Copies of company documents indicate that unexcused absences accounted for approximately half of all absences. Furthermore, the majority of those workers whose names appeared on the lists of the habitually absent spent at least one of those days in the hospital.[81] Illness seems to have caused a fair number of the absences from work. This would serve to corroborate what the miners said about absenteeism: that it was a means by which the workers sought to protect their health.

However, the administrators of the Chojlla mine believed worker absenteeism was a major impediment to production. Its prevalence led them to devise several schemes to eliminate it. Company officials attributed the high number of absences not to health concerns but to lack of discipline and moral defects. The traditional racist view of the Indian as a lazy, coca-chewing drunk no doubt shaped this interpretation.[82] One means by which the company attempted to boost production and crack down on absenteeism was by offering the workers a production bonus. This bonus would be distributed among all the workers in the mine if a certain quantity of mineral was extracted and processed. However, the company offered the production bonus on the condition that union leaders help reduce the number of absences. In January 1954, the union sent out a memorandum to all workers on the list of the habitually absent. Since all workers will gain "a production bonus," the letter explained, "the habitually absent, by slowing down production, place this benefit in jeopardy." The union will not try to prevent the company from firing the habitually absent, it said, "since this would signify going against the interests of the majority."[83] However, further evidence suggests that, beyond sending out the occasional memo, the union never wholeheartedly transformed itself into an enforcer of time discipline. Union leaders did not relish being involved in the firings of workers. No available documents indicate that the union assented to the firing of a worker for excessive absences. On one occasion, the company tried to punish workers by depriving them of part of their paid vacations. The union obtained the intervention of the Ministry of Labor to stop the company from taking this action against absentees.[84] They may have exhorted the habitually absent to change their ways, but union leaders did not cooperate with company schemes to reduce worker absences.

The union assented to the firing of workers in a few instances, but these had nothing to do with absenteeism. In one case, the union succeeded in dismissing a worker who had been accused of rape.[85] In another, union leaders assented to the firing of two hospital orderlies who, after repeated warnings, had come to work drunk, but the shop stewards objected and forced them to rescind that decision.[86] Perhaps the stewards had stronger personal ties to workers, prompting them to question the action of the higher-ranking union officials. When worker misconduct truly threatened the safety and security of the workers and the community, however, union leaders did not hesitate to intervene.

The lack of cooperation from the Chojlla union obliged company officials to take different measures to reduce absenteeism. They reinstated a time card system for the control of attendance. They deprived workers of their right to buy in the company store on the days they were absent. They changed the pay system so that workers with high numbers of unexcused absences would be deprived of bonuses, and habitually absent workers were not allowed to make extra money by working on special overtime projects and on Sundays.[87] Union assent to these measures implied that the interests of habitually absent individuals were sacrificed when they "went against the interests of the majority." However, union leaders avoided involvement in the firings of these workers and always sought less severe measures. Local labor leaders sought to shift the blame for low production from the workers, habitually absent or not.

The union leadership was, in fact, eager to help increase production at Chojlla. But it identified shortages of tools and materials, insufficient personnel, and poor supervision as posing the greater barriers to production. Union leaders in 1953 pinpointed personnel shortages and an insufficiency of tools as hampering the workers' efforts to boost production. More workers could not be hired because no housing could be found for them, according to one union leader.[88] Nor was management spared its share of blame. The union's general secretary complained about the "disorganization, indiscipline, and unwillingness to work" on the part of the company's supervisors. "It is impossible to accept, that while we ask the workers to do the humanly possible to make life better in Chojlla . . . the bosses are the first to provide examples of indiscipline [and] disorganization, [and] that they go about fighting amongst one another," he told the company.[89] Reflecting the point of view of the rank and file, union leaders traced the roots of production deficiencies not to worker absenteeism but to the employers' disorganization.

Conclusion

The degree of control exerted by the miners of Chojlla after the 1952 revolution was due to a confluence of factors. Since the United States badly needed their tungsten, they could openly and militantly demand concessions from the company without fear of jeopardizing their jobs. The world economic and political situation, over which they had slight influence, put them in a good bargaining position. Tungsten markets had begun to improve well before the 1952 insurrectionary victory. But the *chojlleños* could not immediately share in their rebounding prosperity until their efforts to change the national political context had borne fruit. Only when the years spent building the MNR and, more important, the Miners' Federation finally unleashed a social revolution could the Chojlla miners demand and receive more control and more economic benefits from the International Mining Company. Without their own agency—their years of struggle—they would have gained nothing from the increased production and profitability of their employer.

Dire necessity, not some mystic revolutionary destiny, compelled the Chojlla workers to stand with other miners in the movement to transform Bolivia. Alone, the power of the company overwhelmed them. With the help of the MNR, the Chojlla miners began to build a union that allowed them to have greater control over their workplace and their community. By supporting the MNR in the 1940s, the union succeeded in obtaining government intervention that prevented the company from firing them and took further steps to ensure their jobs. But their employer still found it possible to refuse to accede to the workers' demands. Consequently, the Chojlla miners built ever stronger ties to workers in other mining centers. They exchanged information and ideas with other unions, participated in union congresses, and supported federation-approved politicians. Most dramatically, they struck for six days in 1947 and supported the armed struggle that brought about the Bolivian revolution of 1952. The Chojlla miners did not engage in these activities merely to be oppositional. They built a national union movement because it was their only hope to counter the power of the International Mining Company.

When their organizing efforts finally destroyed the political order that had held them down for so long, the Chojlla miners stridently demanded more control over their jobs and their community. They wrested control of the company store from the management. No longer would they permit the company to pin all of the blame on them for deficiencies in production. They forced the company to acknowledge that management and supply problems imposed limits to production, not just worker absenteeism. The revolution they helped bring about finally allowed them to demand the fair treatment they felt they deserved.

After 1956, political and economic factors turned against the Bolivian miners. United States demand for Bolivian tungsten diminished, and the International Mining Company lost the market for its production. As a result, roughly three-fifths of the Chojlla workers lost their jobs in 1957. Tungsten mines across Bolivia closed down. Workers in mines producing other minerals also found their jobs in jeopardy, but more for political reasons. The MNR government of President Hernán Siles Zuazo, elected in 1956 with the backing of labor, imposed a monetary stabilization program that dramatically reduced the standard of living of workers. Among other measures, the low prices in company stores were eliminated. Although the leaders of the labor movement and the Miners' Federation initially supported the stabilization program, the rise in company store prices soon caused the rank and file to oppose the government. Siles aggravated the situation by attempting to foster rivalries within the Miners' Federation and the Bolivian Workers' Central. The ruling coalition soon deteriorated into various factions, paving the way for a U.S.-backed military takeover.

New forms of repression occurred after November 1964, when a reconstituted army under Gen. René Barrientos Otuño seized power. The Miners' Federation initially supported the coup, but within six months Barrientos showed his true colors. He announced major wage cuts for the miners and sent troops to occupy the mining centers. The army stationed one hundred troops at Chojlla and imprisoned two hundred workers. In other mining centers, the military again perpetrated horrible massacres to subdue the workers. The economic situation of the mines did improve, but the policies of the governments, with one brief exception, remained antilabor until 1982. Thus the miners did not share in the new prosperity of the mines. Through the 1980s, runaway inflation, a new stabilization program, and the evaporation of world demand for Bolivian minerals, especially tin, resulted in massive layoffs of miners and the closing of many mines. Today what remains of the Bolivian mining proletariat struggles as it did before 1950, while building alliances that in the long run will offset the power of international capital. Only then will the miners of Bolivia again wield the control they enjoyed immediately following the revolution.

Notes

A grant from the Tinker Foundation enabled me to conduct preliminary research in Bolivia; a Fulbright grant allowed me to continue my research. I also wish to express my gratitude to the staffs of the Sistema de Documentación e Información Sindical, the International Mining Company, the Archivo de La Paz, and the libraries of the Universidad Mayor de San Andrés and the Asociación Nacional de Mineros Medianos (all in La Paz, Bolivia), as well as the subjects of my interviews. Thanks are also due Alan Knight and Erick Langer, who read and criticized earlier drafts of this chapter.

1. Walter Gómez D'Angelo, *La minería en el desarrollo económico de Bolivia, 1900–1970* (La Paz, 1978), 32, 209.

2. *Minería Boliviana* (La Paz) 9, no. 64 (May–June 1957): 12; Gómez, *La minería en el desarrollo*, 65–66.

3. Gómez, *La minería en el desarrollo*, 85; *Minería Boliviana* 9, no. 64 (May–June 1957): 12.

4. David J. Fox, "Bolivian Mining, a Crisis in the Making," in *Miners and Mining in the Americas*, ed. Thomas Greaves and William Culver (Manchester, England, 1985), 111; Gómez, *La minería en el desarrollo*, 33, 93; Manuel Contreras, "La mano de obra

en la minería estañífera: Aspectos cuantitativos, c. 1935–1945," unpublished manuscript presented at the V Meeting of Bolivian Studies, Cochabamba, 18–22 January 1989, 5–8; Luis Peñaloza Cordero, *Nueva historia económica de Bolivia*, vol. 6, *El estaño* (La Paz, 1985), 30, 43–45.

5. James M. Malloy, *Bolivia: The Uncompleted Revolution* (Pittsburgh, 1970), 86–94; Peñaloza, *Nueva historia económica de Bolivia*, 109.

6. Martin J. Kyne, *Report to the CIO on Labor Conditions in Bolivia* (Washington, D.C., 1943), 25–31; Guillermo Lora, *A History of the Bolivian Labour Movement, 1848–1971*, ed. Laurence Whitehead and trans. Christine Whitehead (Cambridge, England, 1977), 221–22; Jerry W. Knudson, "The Impact of the Catavi Mine Massacre of 1942 on Bolivian Politics and Bolivian National Opinion," *Americas* 26, no. 3 (1970): 254–76; Gustavo Rodríguez Ostria, *El socavón y el sindicato* (La Paz, 1991), 110–22.

7. Herbert S. Klein, *Parties and Political Change in Bolivia, 1880–1952* (Cambridge, England, 1969), 357–68; *Leyes sociales de Bolivia sancionados por la Honorable Convención Nacional de 1944 y promulgadas por el gobierno Villarroel* (La Paz, 1946), 23–97; Luis Peñaloza Cordero, *Historia del movimiento nacionalista revolucionario, 1941–1952* (La Paz, 1963), 77.

8. Steven S. Volk, "Class, Union, Party: The Development of a Revolutionary Union Movement in Bolivia (1905–1952)," *Science and Society* 39, no. 2 (Summer 1975): 188–89; Lora, *History of the Bolivian Labour Movement*, 237; Laurence Whitehead, "Miners as Voters: The Electoral Process in Bolivia's Mining Camps," *Journal of Latin American Studies* 13, no. 2 (November 1981): 313-17; Peñaloza, *Historia del movimiento*, 67–68.

9. U.S. Department of Commerce, *Materials Survey: Tungsten* (Washington, D.C.: United States Government Printing Office, 1956), 1:3.

10. Ibid., 6:2.

11. Federico Ahlfeld, *Los yacimientos minerales de Bolivia*, 2d ed. (La Paz, 1954), 111–12.

12. Alfonso Aparicio Saavedra, interview with author, La Paz, 20 July 1989.

13. Rosendo y Gregorio Viscarra Heredía, *Guía general de Bolivia* (La Paz, 1918), 65; "Proyecto granito, Mina Chojlla de International Mining Company, S.A." (internal company document, 1988), Archivo de la Chojlla, Chojlla, Bolivia, 26.

14. Manuel Contreras and Mario Napoleón Pacheco, *Medio siglo de minería mediana en Bolivia, 1939–1989* (La Paz, 1989), 58; Lenox H. Rand and Edward B. Sturgis, *The Mines Handbook*, vol. 18 (Suffern, N.Y., 1931), 2814.

15. Rand and Sturgis, *Mines Handbook*, 2815; Alfonso Aparicio Saavedra interview.

16. H. L. Dotson, "Concentrating Tungsten Ore By Hand in Bolivia," *Engineering and Mining Journal* 142, no. 2 (1942): n.p.; George D. Bellows, "Chojlla Mine: Unusual in Geologic Features," *Engineering and Mining Journal* 148, no. 3 (1947): 68; Humberto Chopitea Alvarez to Enrique Alcoreza P., Chulumani, 5 January 1941, Archivo de La Paz, La Paz, Correspondencia de la Prefectura, caja 124.

17. Federico Ahlfeld, *Los yacimientos minerales de Bolivia* (La Paz, 1941), 137; Bellows, "Chojlla Mine," 68; Secretario General, Sindicato Minero de La Chojlla (here-

after cited as SMCh), to the Administrador General de la Empresa, Chojlla, 12 December 1944, Archivo del Sindicato Mixto de Trabajadores Mineros de La Chojlla, located in the Sistema de Documentación e Información Sindical, La Paz, (hereafter cited as ASMCh); survey conducted by the Depto. de Sindicalización of the Ministerio de Trabajo y Previsión Social, ca. November 1945, ASMCh.

18. This most basic of questions is one of the most difficult to answer, owing largely to limitations imposed by the sources. What is presented here is based upon data taken from a sample of fifty personnel files and supplemented with insights garnered from interviews with former and current workers at the mine.

19. Secretario General (hereafter cited as Sec. Gral.), SMCh, to Administrador General (hereafter cited as Adm. Gral.), IMCO, Mina Chojlla, 27 October 1945, ASMCh; Adm. Gral. IMCO to Sec. Gral., SMCh, Chojlla, 29 October 1945, ASMCh.

20. Superintendente de la Mina to "Todos los Obreros del Interior de la Mina," Chojlla, 28 September 1948, ASMCh; Superintendente de la Mina to "Mayordomos, Capataces y Polvorineros," Chojlla, 28 November 1948, ASMCh.

21. Jenaro Humérez to Sec. Gral. SMCh, Chojlla, 6 June 1944, ASMCh.

22. "Recopilación de Obreros Faltones," for 8, 17 October 1951, Chojlla, ASMCh.

23. Guillermo Dalence, interview with author, La Paz, 20 July 1992.

24. Mario León Heredia, interview with author, Chojlla, 4 August 1989.

25. "Acta de Fundación del Sindicato Minero de La Chojlla," Chojlla, 29 March 1944, ASMCh.

26. "Aviso a los Camaradas Jefes de Sección," from Jorge Sologuren and Rosendo Azcui, Chojlla, 31 March 1944, ASMCh.

27. *Quién es quién en Bolivia* (La Paz, 1959), 17–18; Salinas Aramayo to Subprefecto, La Paz, 23 September 1938, caja 1221, Correspondencia de la Prefectura, Archivo de La Paz, La Paz, Bolivia. Once the MNR-led revolution triumphed in April 1952, Alvarez Plata reaped the benefits of his years of party activism. President Víctor Paz Estenssoro named him minister of economy. See Ecege, *Así lucharon los hombres del MNR* (La Paz, ca. 1953), 14.

28. Hugo Quisbert Cusicanqui to Federico Alvarez Plata, La Paz, 2 April 1944, ASMCh. The rank and file ratified Alvarez Plata's position as the union's legal representative at a general assembly three months later. See "Asamblea General," 22 June 1944, ASMCh.

29. Sec. Gral. and Sec. Rels., SMCh to Hernán Siles Zuazo, Mina Chojlla, 27 March 1945, ASMCh.

30. Comite Ejecutivo, SMCh, to Alvarez Plata, Chojlla, 18 December 1945, ASMCh.

31. Sec. Rels. and Sec. Gral., SMCh to Alvarez Plata, Mina Chojlla, 28 April 1944, 12 December 1945, ASMCh.

32. Comité Ejecutivo, SMCh, to the Ministro de Estado en el Despacho de Gobierno, Chojlla, 24 April 1944, ASMCh.

33. Sec. Gral. and Sec. Rels., SMCh to Alvarez Plata, Mina Chojlla, 28 April 1944, ASMCh.

34. Comite Ejecutivo, SMCh to Alvarez Plata, Chojlla, 26 April 1944, ASMCh.

35. Sec. Gral. and Sec. Rels., SMCh to Ministro de Gobierno, La Paz, 27 March 1951, ASMCh.

36. Comité Ejecutivo, SMCh, to the Sec. Gral. del Sindicato de Mineros de Urania, Chojlla, 20 April 1944, ASMCh.

37. Comité Ejecutivo, SMCh to Alvarez Plata, Chojlla, 7 June 1944, ASMCh.

38. *La Calle* (La Paz), 10 April 1945.

39. Presidente, IMCO to Cristóbal Rivas, La Paz, 31 October 1945, ASMCh.

40. Sec. Gral., SMCh, to "Camaradas," Chojlla, 9 November 1945, ASMCh.

41. Sec. Gral., SMCh, to the Adm. Gen., Chojlla, 20 November 1945; "Informe de la delegación del Sindicato Minero de Chojlla, sobre las gestiones planteadas ante el Supremo Gobierno, con motivo del paro de las minas de wolfram," Chojlla, 27 November 1945, ASMCh.

42. "Sesión de directorio," 22 September 1947, ASMCh; Sec. Gral. and Sec. Rels., SMCh, to Ministro de Gobierno, Justicia, e Inmigración, La Paz, 27 March 1951, ASMCh.

43. Sec. Gral., SMCh, to Lechín, Chojlla, 30 November 1945, ASMCh.

44. C. Rivas and J. Salomón to Adm. Gral. IMCO, Mina Chojlla, 27 February 1945, Inspector General de Trabajo to Gerente, IMCO, La Paz, 7 May 1946, Sec. Gral. Int. and Sec. de Hacienda to Adm. Gral. IMCO, Mina Chojlla, 13 August 1948, William D. Lord to Directores del SMCh, Chojlla, 13 November 1951, ASMCh.

45. Cristóbal Rivas and Juan Salamanca to Adm. Gral. IMCO, Mina Chojlla, 28 March 1945, ASMCh.

46. For more on the use of coca by the miners, see June Nash, *We Eat the Mines and the Mines Eat Us: Dependency and Exploitation in Bolivian Tin Mines* (New York, 1979), 198–200; Domitila Barrios de Chungara as told to Moema Viezzar, "*Si me permiten hablar": Testimonio de Domitila, una mujer de las minas de Bolivia*, 4th ed. (Mexico City, 1979), 26–27. The latter book is also available in English translation.

47. This is based upon personal observation and interviews. It is impossible to say how this ritual might have changed over the years; miners I spoke with assured me "it has always been this way."

48. Shop steward, El Barco and Santa Ana sections, to Cristóbal Rivas, Chojlla, ca. 1945, ASMCh.

49. Sec. Gral. and Sec. Rels., SMCh, to G. Bellows, Mina Chojlla, 18 February 1948, G. Bellows to Sec. Gral., SMCh, Chojlla, 19 February 1948, ASMCh.

50. Rivas and Salamanca to Adm. Gral. IMCO, Mina Chojlla, 25 November 1944, ASMCh.

51. George D. Bellows to Rivas and Salamanca, Chojlla, 25 November 1944, ASMCh.

52. Sec. Gral., SMCh to Lechín, Mina Chojlla, 12 November 1948, ASMCh.

53. Alvarez Plata to Jorge Sologuren, La Paz, 5 June 1944; Sec. Gral. and Sec. Rels., SMCh, to Sec. Gral. del Sindicato de Mineros de Huanuni, Chojlla, 6 June 1944; Augustín Barcelli, *Medio siglo de luchas sindicales revolucionarias en Bolivia, 1905–1955* (La Paz, 1956), 165.

54. "Ponencias que presentan los delegados del Sindicato Minero de la Chojlla y Anexos, al Segundo Congreso de Sindicatos Mineros de Bolivia, a efectuarse en la ciudad de Potosí," Potosí, July 1945, ASMCh.

55. Serafín Rodríguez and Junio Cadimo to Sec. Gral., SMCh, Llallagua, 22 August 1944, ASMCh. Llallagua was in the heart of the Patiño mining empire.

56. Salamanca and Rivas to Sec. Gral. del Sindicato Minero, 2 May 1945, ASMCh.

57. Barcelli, *Medio siglo de luchas sindicales*, 236.

58. "Gran Asamblea," Chojlla, 28 November 1946, ASMCh; *Quién es quién en Bolivia*, 17–18; Whitehead, "Miners as Voters," 338–39.

59. Roberto Querejazu Calvo, *Llallagua: Historia de una montaña*, 3d ed. (La Paz, 1984), 326–27; Barcelli, *Medio siglo de luchas sindicales*, 201–4; Lora, *History of the Bolivian Labour Movement*, 260–64; Peñaloza, *Historia del movimiento*, 137; June Nash, "Conflicto industrial en los Andes: Los mineros bolivianos del estaño," *Estudios Andinos* 4, no. 2 (1976): 230–34. A valuable set of documents is presented along with the Patiño Mining Company's perspective in Patiño Mines and Enterprises Consolidated (Inc.), *Los conflictos sociales en 1947: I. Documentos; II. Notas finales por el Dr. José E. Rivera* (La Paz, 1948).

60. *El Diario* (La Paz), 16 September 1947.

61. "Sesión de Directorio," 16 September 1947, ASMCh.

62. Ibid.

63. "Asamblea General Extraordinaria," 19 September 1947, ASMCh.

64. *El Diario*, 18 September 1947.

65. Lora, *History of the Bolivian Labour Movement*, 263–64; *El Diario*, 19 September 1947.

66. "Sesión de Directorio," 22 September 1947, ASMCh.

67. "Asamblea General," 22 September 1947, ASMCh.

68. *El Diario*, 23 September 1947; "Credencial," Chojlla, 24 September 1947, ASMCh.

69. SMCh, "Proclamación," 3 May 1951, ASMCh; Alfonso Aparicio Saavedra interview; Prefect of the Department of Oruro to SMCh, Oruro, ca. late April 1952, ASMCh.

70. James M. Malloy, "Revolutionary Politics," in *Beyond the Revolution: Bolivia since 1952*, ed. Malloy and Richard S. Thorn (Pittsburgh, 1971), 111–18. For the history of the MNR, its ideology, and its leadership, see Christopher Mitchell, *The Legacy of Populism in Bolivia* (New York, 1977); Charles H. Weston Jr., "An Ideology of Modernization: The Case of the Bolivian MNR," *Journal of Inter-American Studies* 10, no. 1 (January 1968): 85–101; Peñaloza, *Historia del Movimiento*; Subsecretaría de Prensa, Informaciones y Cultura, Departamento de Comunicaciones, *El libro blanco de la independencia económica de Bolivia* (La Paz, 1952). I would like to thank James Dunkerly for bringing the last source to my attention.

71. Kenneth Lehman, "U.S. Foreign Aid and Revolutionary Nationalism in Bolivia, 1952–1964: The Pragmatics of a Patron-Client Relationship" (Ph.D. diss., University of Texas at Austin, 1992), 183–93, 288–325.

72. "Propuesta de la empresa 'International Mining Co.,' para la solución del pliego de peticiones presentado por el 'Sindicato Mixto de Trabajadores de la Mina Chojlla,'" Chojlla, ca. 26 June 1952, ASMCh; "Respuesta a la propuesta hecha por la empresa International Mining Company, Minas Yungas, al pliego de peticiones del Sindicato Mixto de Trabajadores Mineros de la Chojlla," 27 June 1952, ASMCh.

73. "Los Compañeros Sindicalizados Mixtos de La Chojlla," Chojlla, 30 June 1952, ASMCh.

74. Hugo Pedregal and Jaime Burgos, "Acta de la sesión del directorio," Chojlla, 4 September 1953, ASMCh.

75. Manuel Tola, interview with Miriam Aguilar, La Paz, 4 August 1992.

76. "Acta," Chojlla, 16 May 1953, ASMCh.

77. Remberto Quintanilla to Pedro Horna, Chojlla, 16 November 1954, ASMCh.

78. Alberto Tórrez and Jaime Burgos, "Acta de la asamblea del día 2 de April de 1953," Chojlla, 2 April 1953, ASMCh.

79. Alberto Tórrez and Jaime Burgos, "Acta de la sesión de directorio efectuada el día 26/4/53," Chojlla, 26 April 1953, ASMCh; Sec. Gral. and Sec. de Turno, SMCh, to Pedro Horna Moreno, Chojlla, 6 July 1954, ASMCh.

80. William D. Lord, Chojlla, 16 May 1953, ASMCh.

81. Mark Nofthaft, "Nómina de obreros inasistentes a trabajo en la sección interior mina," Chojlla, 29 December 1953; Nofthaft, "Nómina de obreros de interior mina que tienen asistencia *MALA*," Chojlla, June 1954; Nofthaft to SMCh, Chojlla, 1 February 1955, ASMCh.

82. This view is graphically expressed in mining industry journals of the period. For example, see G. V. Bilbao La Vieja, "El problema del obrero minero y los salarios," *Minería Boliviana* 1, no. 12 (November 1944): 31–37.

83. Renato Ayaviri Velasco and Víctor Criales to Nestor Cossío, Chojlla, 19 January 1954; Velasco and Criales to Superintendente de la Mina, Chojlla, 19 January 1954, ASMCh.

84. Lord to Jefe de Oficina Tiempo, Jefes de Sección, Chojlla, 22 January 1953; Inspector de Trabajo to Gerente IMCO, La Paz, 17 June 1953, ASMCh.

85. Tórrez and Criales to Lord, Chojlla, 5 May 1953; Lord to Tórrez, Chojlla, 8 May 1953, ASMCh.

86. Manuel Andrade M. to Alejandro Zegarra, Chojlla, 9 March 1955; Andrade M. to Zembrana, Chojlla, 9 March 1955; Pedregal to Adm. Hospital, 31 March 1955, ASMCh.

87. Nofthaft to Jefes de la Mina, Chojlla, 1 February 1955; Nofthaft to Jefes de Sección, Chojlla, 9 August 1955; Gerente IMCO to SMCh, La Paz, 29 November 1955; Joseph L. George to Francisco del Castillo, Chojlla, 29 September 1956; George to SMCh, Chojlla, 9 October 1956; Gerente IMCO to SMCh, La Paz, 2 December 1956, ASMCh.

88. Pedregal and Burgos, "Acta de la sesión del directorio," Chojlla, 4 September 1953, ASMCh.

89. Pedregal to Lord, Chojlla, 4 September 1953, ASMCh.

CHAPTER NINE

CONTINUING TO BE PEASANTS

Union Militancy among Peruvian Miners

JOSH DeWIND

B etween 1969 and 1971, miners in the Peruvian Andes engaged in an unprecedented series of strikes. The mines of the U.S.-based Cerro de Pasco Corporation were affected most. From these strikes, the corporation lost three times more production days than during the entire previous decade. The unions led the miners in demanding not only significant improvements in wages and working conditions but also the nationalization of the mines. The mineworkers fought for their demands through hard bargaining with both the company and the Peruvian government, intermittent and sustained work stoppages, *marchas de sacrificio* on the capital, confrontations with the police, and the kidnapping of company officials.

The Peruvian government had long cooperated with the company in controlling the union activities of the miners, having sent in troops to repress strikes on several occasions. However, the state's relations with the company became uncertain in October 1968, when the Peruvian military took over the government in a bloodless coup d'état and initiated a "revolution" that it characterized as "neither capitalist nor socialist." The military junta intended to promote Peru's industrialization, which the generals believed had been blocked by the agrarian elite that had long dominated Peruvian politics. The government wanted political support for its reforms from popular sectors such as the mineworkers. But it also expected increased foreign investment in mining to provide the foreign exchange earnings necessary to implement its plans for economic development. The rash of strikes during this period inconvenienced this government program. As the miners' strikes continued into 1971, the military found it increasingly difficult to balance its relations with labor and the company.

Why did the miners so strenuously challenge the conditions of their labor at this point in Peru's history? The government, the company, and the leftist organizations supporting the miners offered political explanations to answer this question. For example, Peru's self-proclaimed "revolutionary government" of Gen. Juan Velasco Alvarado, the junta's president, accused left-wing agitators of promoting the strikes to create political chaos, subverting the government reforms. Officials of the Cerro de Pasco Corporation agreed that leftist agitators were to blame but saw their company rather than the government as the major target. Leftist organizers believed that, through conflicts with both the company and the government, they had brought the miners to recognize and act on their latent proletarian interests. The demand for nationalization of the mines was introduced by this leftist leadership. These political explanations of the strikes are based on two assumptions: first, that the miners used their strikes to influence national political developments; and second, that these political goals reflected their economic interests as a "proletariat," meaning that they had become a free labor force separated from agricultural lands and dependent on wage labor for their livelihoods.

In fact, the miners were far from being a homogeneous proletariat. This author's research and observation at the mining camps of the Cerro de Pasco Corporation in 1969 and 1970 revealed that some miners were indeed landless wage laborers. The large majority, however, still maintained ties to the land and were involved to varying degrees in agricultural production. Further, a large majority of the miners planned on working in the mines for only a limited period of time, after which they expected to have accumulated savings, skills, and contacts that would enable them to pursue self-employment either in agriculture or in some other economic enterprise outside mining. How, then, are we to interpret and understand the strikes and militancy of the miners? If the miners were not entirely a proletariat pursuing their class interests, what exactly were their social and economic interests? How were their interests and goals reflected in the strikes? If the miners were looking forward to escaping from mining employment, to what extent were they interested in taking control of their workplaces?

Two long-term processes influenced the miners: the mechanization of mining production and the commercialization of the agricultural economy. Beginning in the early decades of the century, the company had employed unskilled and temporary peasants, but subsequent industrialization of mineral production forced it to create a more skilled and stable labor force. Miners

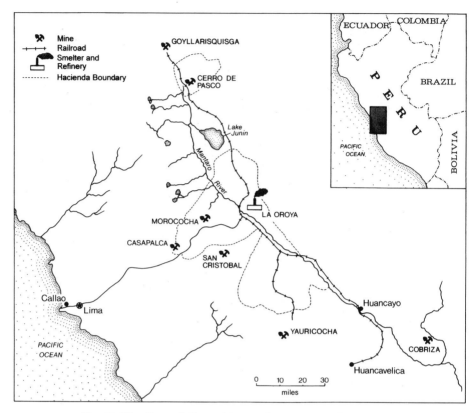

Map 7. *The Cerro de Pasco Mining Corporation of Peru, 1968*

became increasingly dependent on wages to satisfy their family's consumption needs. The commercialization of subsistence agriculture, spurred in part by wages brought back from the mines, simultaneously forced additional peasants to enter the wage labor market. But commercialization also created new opportunities for self-employment in farming, merchandising, skilled trades, and other market-oriented enterprises. By accumulating savings, learning skills, and establishing networks that they would need to become independent, workers used employment in the mines to enter such enterprises.

Ironically, the working-class ideology and revolutionary goals promoted by leftist organizers and union leaders aided many mineworkers in fighting collectively to pursue largely individual, petite bourgeois aspirations. Why did they strike? The transformation of the industrial-rural nexus, the workers' attempts to meet their consumption needs, their integration of mine employment with peasant agriculture, and their taking advantage of new economic opportunities—all these things formed the interests of the mineworkers and directed their participation in the strikes. The miners never committed themselves as a working class to the nationalization of the mines. Their militancy reflected resistance against proletarianization more than their pursuit of proletarian interests.

Wages Insufficient for "Elemental Civilization"

Historically, market competition and the depletion of mineral deposits have stimulated the industrialization of the international mining industry. Metal producers have introduced increasingly productive technologies in order to reduce costs and increase profits. As they have depleted the richest and simplest ores, mine owners have had to introduce new mechanical and chemical processes in order to exploit the lower-grade and more complex ores that remain. This process of progressive industrialization altered work requirements and, in the case of Peru, transformed the nature of mine labor.[1] At the beginning of the century, most miners were peasants who worked in the mines only temporarily. They depended on their own production of agricultural goods as their major source of sustenance, using wage labor to supplement their consumption either by purchasing manufactures that they could not make for themselves or by acquiring lands and animals. In the 1960s, when most miners were working at the mines throughout the year, their purchasing power depended on mine wages. Many of those still tied to the land also earned income from commercialized farming. Mine wages were often used to accumulate savings that would eventually enable mineworkers to leave the mines to become self-employed.

With nearly sixteen thousand employees, the Cerro de Pasco Corporation was the largest employer in Peru. "The company," as it was referred to in the Sierra, where its mines were located, had begun operations in 1902 with financing from prominent North American businessmen and financiers. Throughout the next three decades, the company consolidated ownership of claims in six major mineral regions of central Peru and integrated them into a single enterprise. The new industrial technology that made this integration possible included compressed air drills, automatic scoops, elevators, railroads, a hydroelectric power grid, mineral crushing and concentration plants, and in 1920 a central smelter and refinery.

Some of the company's most important advances in mineral extraction took place after 1950. By the 1970s, the most highly mechanized mines were in the town of Cerro de Pasco, which had been mined since Spanish colonization, and in Cobriza, the corporation's newest mine. The company introduced open pit extraction at Cerro de Pasco in 1956. With this method, vast quantities of ore were dug out of a large, open pit by huge earth-moving machines and gigantic trucks. This method of extraction avoided the slower and more costly drilling, blasting, and transporting of ore underground. In Cobriza, where the mantlelike shape of the mineral deposit would not permit open-pit mining, the company introduced "trackless mining," the most highly mechanized underground mining technique in Latin America. Trackless mining replaced underground rails and trains with diesel-powered loaders and scoops that drove into oversized mining tunnels. This new system provided speed and mobility. Also in Cobriza, miners utilized a raise-bore machine that, operated by two men, could quickly cut smooth-sided ore chutes and connecting shafts between levels of the mine. This machine could accomplish in three weeks what the older system of drilling and blasting required eight months to complete.[2]

Reducing low-grade ores after their extraction from the mines became a long and complex industrial process. The company introduced flotation, one of the most productive innovations in ore treatment, in the 1930s. This process mixed pulverized ores with water and chemicals in order to separate minerals from waste material and to separate different types of minerals from one another. Workers prepared ore for flotation by grinding it to a fine powder in rock crushers and ball or rod mills. After flotation at the mine sites, concentrated ores containing copper, lead, zinc, silver, gold, and other metals were shipped to the large central plant in La Oroya for smelting and electrolytic refining. The finished mineral products then passed by rail to the coastal port of Callao for export primarily to Europe and the United States.[3]

The progressive industrialization and shift from labor-intensive to capital-intensive mining transformed the company's labor system. In the late 1960s, the company employed roughly the same number of wage laborers, or *obreros*, as it had in the late 1920s. But the Cerro de Pasco Corporation was now producing twice as much copper, lead, silver, gold, and zinc. The new technology that permitted this substantial increase in productivity also required an increasingly sophisticated and stable labor force. By the 1970s, specially trained drill operators, vehicle drivers, laboratory assistants, plumbers, mechanics, electricians, and welders had replaced the unskilled peasants who worked in the mines at the beginning of the century. Mineworkers now understood the basic principles of the combustion engine, air compressors, chemistry, electric circuitry, and metallurgy. Workers who could develop the requisite skills were difficult to find and train and were costly to replace. Consequently, the company sought to reduce employee turnover and to retain workers in its employ for as long as possible.[4]

Not only had the workers' stability and skills been transformed, so too had their patterns of investment. When the Cerro de Pasco Corporation began mining in Peru, the available labor force consisted of peasant workers who were primarily engaged in subsistence agriculture. Their wearing of home-made clothing marked them as *indios* in the eyes of the rural elite, who wore commercially manufactured clothing. For peasants, labor in the mines was a means of acquiring those goods and agricultural resources, such as metal tools or land, that they could not produce for themselves or acquire through barter. Because of their dependence on agriculture, the peasants tried to avoid em-ployment in the mines at times when they would be needed in their villages. Peasants sought to avoid the mines when it was time to plant or harvest crops, celebrate important saints' days, or perform other village social obligations. The resulting fluctuations in the labor supply were problematic for the com-pany, and, particularly at harvest times, the Cerro de Pasco Corporation had to curtail production.[5] Nevertheless, the company benefited from the work-ers' rural ties. The workers' access to agricultural produce enabled the com-pany to keep wages well below the level that the company would have needed to sustain full-time workers.

In the early days of mining, the company established wage levels and tried to control the seasonal flow of workers through a debt labor system known as *enganche* (the hook). Company-commissioned *enganchedores* (labor contrac-tors known literally as "hookers") advanced loans to peasants who had to repay them by working in the mines.[6] The company set mine wages so low that workers were often unable to pay for their living expenses in the mines or repay their *enganche* debts.[7] As an investigator for the International Labor Organization reported in 1938, "The wages of the mineworkers show them-selves to be absolutely insufficient to permit a standard of living adequate for a most elemental civilization." He found that most miners reduced their expen-diture of wages on living expenses in the mines by consuming their own agricultural products.[8] The amount of food that miners could bring from their villages to the camps determined how long they would have to work in the mines before they could repay their *enganche* debts.

The susceptibility of Andean peasants to *enganche* derived from an increas-ing need for cash created by the gradual commercialization of land, labor, and products of subsistence agriculture. Population growth in central Peru forced families to divide their lands into increasingly smaller holdings. The division of land into subsistence plots that were too small to support individual households stimulated a market for the sale and purchase of lands.[9] Peasants who sought cash to buy new land turned to the *enganchedores* in order to seek work in the mines. Temporary labor in the mining sector infused increasing amounts of cash into village market, promoted the further commercialization of the local economy, introduced market price inflation, and helped to make migration to the mines a self-perpetuating process.[10]

As the commercialization of traditional subsistence agriculture drove increasing numbers of peasants to seek wage employment, the recruitment of mineworkers through *enganche* became less necessary. A visitor to the mines in the 1920s reported that roughly half the labor force consisted of *enganchados*, "hooked ones," as contracted workers were known. The others had contracted directly with the company.[11] By contrast, the company in the 1940s hired most of its workers directly, although it occasionally still resorted to *enganche*.[12] The number of workers seeking mine employment in the 1950s had increased to the extent that the company became quite selective about whom it would hire. Between the 1920s and the 1950s, the company was able to hire increasing numbers of the relatively long term workers it needed to operate the more sophisticated technology in the mines and at the La Oroya smelter—at wages that were 25 to 50 percent higher.[13]

Year-round rather than seasonal employment in the mines altered the miners' domestic economies. Workers who remained for long periods in the mines tended to bring their families to live with them. Although most miners did not have to sever their ties with their peasant villages, having their families in the mining camps meant that they could no longer as easily grow foods to supply their consumption needs. Unlike the *enganchados* of the past, most of the long-term miners now had to rely on their mine wages to purchase whatever they and their families consumed. But always, the miners' dependence on market consumption grew more quickly than their wages, a condition raising workers' ire.

Full-Time Employment and "Keeping the Women Happy"

In addition to teaching job skills to new workers, the company sought to instruct them about the social conduct it thought was proper in the mining camps. A picture on the first page of a worker orientation manual provided to supervisors illustrated the company's image of a typical new recruit. It showed a slightly stooped, poor peasant descending from the mountains to the La Oroya smelter, carrying his belongings over his shoulder in a woolen blanket and wearing a rumpled hat, patched jacket, homemade knee pants, and leather thong sandals. Although few workers hired by the company actually fit this image, the lifestyle of some miners certainly reflected rural origins. They slept on pallets instead of beds, acquired little furniture, raised animals indoors, stored vegetables in the toilets, did not bathe frequently, and often invited relatives to live with them. Company officials sought incessantly to change these "Indian" customs among their workers. In aiding the miners to adapt to camp life, however, the company inadvertently taught them to aspire to a way of life based on expanded consumption that could only be attained with higher wages.

Following the Second World War, the Cerro de Pasco Corporation took advantage of the increasing availability of workers to become more selective about whom it would hire in order to create a permanent, skilled workforce. The hiring criteria, which were primarily educational, medical, and political, also brought about a cultural transformation in the workers and virtually eliminated *indios* from employment—a change reinforced by the semiurban lifestyle of the mining camps. The most important general requirement that the company set for all workers was the ability to speak, read, and write Spanish. By the late 1960s, the vast majority of new miners being hired had completed primary school; nearly half had begun or completed secondary school. As a result, most miners were able to read not only the company's work orders, bulletins, and safety regulations but also comic books, newspapers, and union fliers.[14]

Because the company was obligated by labor laws and the *convenio colectivo* (the union contract) to provide its workers with extensive free medical care, it required all job applicants to pass a medical examination. Anyone who needed dental work, who showed a serious lung ailment (silicosis from previous mine labor and tuberculosis are common in Peru's central highlands), or who had a physical handicap would not be hired. Most of the applicants whom the company rejected had failed the medical examination. Political requirements were numerous and included clearance by the police to show lack of a criminal record; presentation of tax and social security identity cards; proof of military service to be sure that an applicant was over twenty years of age and would not be conscripted in midemployment; and a check against the company "black list," which included a large number of known political organizers and militant unionists. The application of these selective criteria resulted in the hiring of a group of workers who were culturally and, to some extent, racially different from those hired earlier in the century.

In the 1960s, company officials identified the miners they were hiring as *cholos* and mestizos, terms referring to people of Indian and mixed Indian-European ancestry respectively. These groups differed from the *indio* peasants, many of whom were hired as *enganchados* earlier in the century, by their speaking Spanish, wearing modern dress, and practicing Catholicism. In the mining camps, the term *indio* was usually employed either to insult or to disparage a worker. Occasionally, however, some workers identified themselves with militant pride as *indios* in order to associate themselves with the Inca civilization and against the urban elite of Spanish ancestry or against the company and foreign bosses. The constitution of a workforce of workers identified as *cholos* or mestizos reflected the company's hiring of workers who had become integrated into the commercialized rural economy.[15]

Despite the general upgrading of the miners' educational level, most newly hired workers lacked the specific skills that the company needed. Therefore, the company introduced its first training course for workers in 1954 at the La Oroya smelter. By 1970, the Personnel and Training Department annually was offering more than three hundred courses to nearly 4,500 out of its 13,700 *obreros*.[16] In Cobriza, the company's new and most highly mechanized underground mine, approximately one-fifth of all miners participated in training courses each year. Some courses taught basic principles of mathematics, electricity, or combustion that were useful for a variety of jobs. Others prepared workers to perform specific tasks such as maintaining heavy machinery or operating rock crushers and pneumatic drills. Many of company's courses taught skills that workers could transfer to occupations outside the mines.

Moreover, the company hired social workers to supervise the miners and their families in daily camp life. Social workers focused on the miners' use of company housing and their spending habits. The social workers strove to reduce the company's costs in maintaining housing and providing social services and to teach the miners and their families how to live within the limits of their wages. The nature of this social engineering is indicated in an annual report of the Cobriza social workers. "Special effort has been made to teach [workers' families] the housing regulations," said the report, "to avoid the raising of domestic animals and the eternal problem of visitors (relatives and villagers) who generally create situations of a moral character."[17]

Because the men were away at work, the main burden of a family's adaptation to camp life—including dealing with social workers—fell to the women, for whom the most difficult problem was making ends meet on a miner's wages. The social workers' courses taught the women practical and money-saving skills. They learned to cook on kerosene stoves and to combine industrially processed foods, such as noodles, instant coffee, gelatin, bleached flour, and canned fruit, into a nutritious diet. As the clothing worn in the mining camps was store-bought, sewing courses taught the women how to save money by making similar clothes at home. The social workers also taught women how to furnish and keep their homes. Their suggestions ranged from purchasing furniture to decorating the home "properly" with calendar pictures. Social workers frequently intervened in family disputes that threatened the camp's tranquillity. They advised the husbands and wives regarding the proper male and female roles in a nuclear family, the obligation of fathers to support their children, and the right of wives to share their husband's earnings or to have a voice in determining how they should be spent.

These interventions by social workers often met resistance—not the least because some social goals became impossible to achieve. The women usually understood the principles of a full diet quickly enough, but they could not afford to buy sufficient meat for the entire family. Sewing may have meant saving money, but it added significantly to the women's work. The purchase of home furnishings required considerable savings, which took many years to accumulate. That the social workers rated 72 percent of the miners' homes in all of the camps as an unacceptable "third class" was less an indication of the workers' "low cultural level" than of the inadequate purchasing power of their wages.

Another reason why the company's social work program backfired concerned its goals. From the start, the miners and their wives perceived the social workers to be serving the interests of the company rather than their families. "The point is to keep the women happy," said one North American administrator. "Otherwise on some rainy day, they'll corner their husbands and take their complaints out on them. Then the husbands will go get drunk and when they get together like that, they go on strike and blame everything on the company."[18] But rather than make the women happy, the social work program humiliated them. It made them feel as though their rural way of life was inferior. Then it frustrated them by teaching them to need and want more than they actually could afford to buy. The increasing pressure on the women resulted in frustration and anger, motivating them to form *comités de damas* (women's groups that paralleled the men's unions). Later, women would prove more militant and aggressive than the men.

In addition, to increase labor stability and cut housing costs, the company began to sell houses to the miners. At the Cerro de Pasco mine, only 40 percent of the miners lived in company housing; the rest rented quarters within the adjacent city. When the company began to purchase and tear down these old urban dwellings to make way for an expansion of open-pit mining in the late 1960s, the government required the company to build a new city nearby and relocate the residents. The miners were forced to buy these new homes through a lease-purchase program.[19] Although the program might have reduced the company's expenses in maintaining the camps, the housing purchases also added to the miners' need for higher pay.

In their strikes between 1969 and 1971, workers complained that they were finding it more and more difficult to live on their wages. The company tried to discredit this claim by pointing out that wages over the previous fifteen years had risen more than the cost of living. Although the company's contention may have been correct, its argument failed to take into account the fact that the workers had become increasingly dependent on market consumption and needed to buy more from the market than ever before. Ironically, the company's attempt to create a stable, economically independent, and socially adjusted labor force had only increased the difficulties and frustrations of living on the company's wages. The company misunderstood that it was actually accomplishing more to provoke strikes than to create labor peace.

Collective Militancy without Working-Class Consciousness

Interested in more than just raising their income and standard of living in the camps, most miners aspired to greater personal independence possible only with self-employment. While working in the mines, many miners sought savings, skills, and networks that would eventually enable them to escape the industrial discipline imposed by the company and to avoid their permanent proletarianization. Paradoxically, while the miners' long-term economic strategies and their ongoing ties to a commercialized rural economy increased their motivation to engage in strikes, these economic interests also detracted from the miners' proletarian identity and the likelihood of their embracing a working-class political ideology.

How workers used the resources available to them in the mines varied according to their ties to agriculture and communal obligations, education, skills, and wages. For some, mine labor provided the means to return to an agricultural way of life. As in the past, a few miners sought only to obtain savings that would enable them to continue as subsistence agriculturists. They used their savings to make supplementary purchases such as land, animals, tools, or a tin roof for their house or to meet extraordinary or occasional expenses such as paying medical or funeral bills or buying school uniforms for their children.[20] Other workers used their wages to begin commercial farming. Going into partnership with family members or fellow villagers, the miners provided funds to purchase seeds and hire peons, while their partners oversaw the work and marketed the crops. By combining and reinvesting agricultural and mining incomes, miners sought over the years to accumulate savings sufficient to purchase better or larger lands, perhaps with irrigation or farm machinery, that would support their full-time return to agriculture.

A large number of workers also saw mining as a means of attaining savings, skills, and contacts that would enable them to escape agriculture and practice trade or begin commercial ventures. The skills that workers learned in the mines as drivers, mechanics, electricians, and carpenters could be transferred to private businesses. Drivers saved their wages, hoping to make the down payment on a truck so they could hire out as *transportistas*. Some workers used their ties with the company to obtain contracts for hauling lumber to the mines or ore concentrates to La Oroya. With savings, mechanics could open garages, and carpenters and electricians could become construction contractors. Just as often, miners invested their savings in a marketing enterprise. Beginning on a small scale, they purchased household goods, special clothing, or novelty items to sell in the mining camps. Others aspired to obtaining leases on stores within the mine camps and to extending their commercial ventures elsewhere.

Finally, a large number of workers, mostly young bachelors, used mine work to finance their education on both secondary and university levels. Some workers alternated years in school with years in the mining camps. Others paired with family members and took turns financing each other's education. These educational interludes exposed miners to radical social perspectives, inspiring some student miners to take an active role in union leadership.

For the most part, workers who came to the mines as short-term earners had little incentive to become involved in union activities. Because their stays in the mines were limited, they tended to endure rather than seek to improve their working and living conditions. Strikes caused them to lose income and delay their departure from the mines more than they might speed the accumulation of savings. However, the Cerro de Pasco Corporation actively promoted labor stability, lengthening the miners' stay on the job, and the employer's pressures significantly altered workers' calculation of the potential benefits from strikes. The miners' average length of employment grew during the 1950s and 1960s. According to company records, the annual turnover rate among *obreros* was down to 30 percent in 1958. By 1969, it had dropped to 20 percent, indicating that miners on average were staying at the mines for five years.[21] The company's monthly newsletter often commemorated workers' tenth, fifteenth, and occasionally twentieth or twenty-fifth anniversaries of employment. For these workers, wage increases won through a strike would more than repay the wages lost—even if the strike was prolonged. They also took greater interest in the quality of company housing, medical care, and schools.

Miners seeking to accumulate savings chose between two ways to raise their wage levels. First, if their supervisors approved, workers could obtain three or more promotions within their basic job categories. The company's general practice in the 1960s was to promote one out of four or five of its workers each year, raising wages between 5 and 10 percent.[22] Second, workers might also try to win an across-the-board wage increase through the unions' annual re-

negotiation of wage rates. Workers advocating strikes to obtain higher contracted wages might jeopardize promotions. Then again, a successful strike
might gain them a larger wage increase than promotions offered. In the
calculations of workers who, in the long run, wanted to leave the mines,
militant opposition rather than collaboration with the company became a
potentially beneficial strategy.

The increasing stabilization of the workforce reinforced the interest and
capacity of the Cerro de Pasco Corporation's workers to create industrial
unions. Leaders who sought to unite their fellow workers, create unions, and
negotiate improved working conditions with the company responded not only
to their fellow miners but also to urban political and labor groups based
outside the mine camps. Because the company played a key role in the
Peruvian economy, urban-based political groups sought to incorporate the
mine unions into rival national and regional labor organizations. Organizers
sent to the camps or miners whom the organizers had won over often gained
election to positions of union leadership. To the extent that these leaders
became focused on controlling the unions, in order to shore up political
alliances, or influence national politics, they tended to lose touch with the
day-to-day economic and social goals of the rank-and-file mineworkers, particularly those still tied to rural life. Miners frequently expressed suspicion that
union leaders tended to become corrupted or to feel themselves superior to
the workers after they went to Lima to negotiate contracts with the company,
the government, and political and labor groups.

Throughout the company's history, the miners militantly and sometimes
violently pursued their demands against the company. Their militancy was
somewhat independent of proletarianization or politicization: Both temporary and long-term workers and both union and nonunion members engaged
in confrontational tactics. Nevertheless, organizers frequently identified the
miners' militancy as a reflection of a proletarian consciousness. Political organizers who usually came from urban backgrounds generally failed to appreciate the extent to which rural ties and nonmining economic aspirations motivated the miners' strike actions. The divergence between the miners and
politicized leaders appeared not only with regard to the nationalization of the
mines during the 1969–71 strike wave but in earlier periods of action as well.

During the Cerro de Pasco Corporation's first three decades of operation,
groups of temporary peasant miners in individual camps periodically joined
together to make demands on the company for higher wage payments, a
reduction of prices in the company store, free carbide for their lamps, and a
shorter workday—in brief, demands that began to assert their control over
their labor, working, and living conditions. Occasionally the protests became

violent. Miners attacked managers, destroyed machinery, derailed trains, and dynamited a company store—returning to work only after the arrival of government troops. The workers' formed mutual aid societies and political groups that were temporary and usually informal, dissolving after the immediate issue was addressed, successfully or not, or when the workers completed their work contracts and returned to their villages.[23]

The Communist Party undertook the first major attempt at formally unionizing the miners in 1930, when the depression had raised fears of layoffs among workers. Delegates from Lima mobilized workers from most of the camps into forming unions within a few weeks. The new unions were united by a congress that formed the Federation of Mine Workers of Peru. Communist organizers believed that workers' unity and their struggles for union recognition, job security, and higher wages would transform the miners' "proletarian instinct" into class consciousness, leading the workers to initiate a revolution. Although the temporary peasant miners took militant actions to protect their employment, they were not a proletariat. When government troops arrested the leaders and killed twenty-seven protesting workers in Mal Paso, a majority of the workers abandoned the mines for their rural villages. The union movement collapsed.[24] Although labor organizers had originally been inspired by Peruvian socialist José Carlos Mariátegui, they ignored his observation that "the Indians in the mines in good part continue[d] to be peasants."[25] Their mistake would be repeated again later.

In 1944, however, workers in the La Oroya smelter took more initiative. A group of section delegates, who had been planning secretly, called an assembly of workers and formed a union. When the company refused to recognize the union, the workers sent a commission to President Prado, who granted them recognition in the hope of winning the miners' support for his successor in the upcoming presidential elections. By 1947, workers in all the mining camps, the railroads, and construction had formed unions. Additional unions were added with the opening of new mines and plants, reaching a total of fifteen separate unions within the Cerro de Pasco by 1968.[26]

The American Popular Revolutionary Alliance, better known by its acronym APRA (Alianza Popular Revolucionaria Americana), was the first national political party to establish a position of leadership in the unions. APRA members helped organize the smelter union at La Oroya, provided legal assistance in the formation of other unions, united the unions into the Federation of Mining and Metallurgical Workers, and affiliated the federation with the Workers' Central of Peru based in Lima. The Cerro de Pasco unions undertook their first strike in 1947, which lasted for twenty-one days. Local merchants who were *apristas* (sympathizers of APRA) supported the miners by providing credit and food. Partly because mineworkers had supported the election of President Bustamante, the minister of labor imposed a settlement that doubled the miners' wages. Over the next decade and a half, APRA's ambitions to win national political influence led it to moderate its union tactics. APRA tried not only to avoid confrontations with the company and the government but also to keep the union leadership from falling into the hands of more militant leaders. *Aprista*-led unions made relatively conciliatory demands—even in 1958, when the company laid off twenty-five hundred workers as a result of the economic recession. Despite more militant actions by workers unhappy with the APRA's timidity, the *apristas* managed to maintain control of the Cerro de Pasco unions.[27]

The political potential of the miners' ties to rural villages became evident in the early 1960s when radical leaders began to take over the unions at the same moment that growing rural poverty led peasants to invade local hacienda lands. The Cerro de Pasco Corporation owned the largest hacienda in central Peru. As a result of noxious fumes from the La Oroya smelter spreading across the countryside since 1920, the company over the years had purchased 270,000 hectares (1 hectare equals 2.47 acres) in lieu of paying indemnities to local landowners.[28] The company and approximately seventy other estate owners possessed 90 percent of the land in the provinces of Junín and Pasco. The other 650,000 rural residents held only 10 percent of the land.[29] Between 1959 and 1963, however, land-hungry peasants carried out at least 103 land invasions in the region. The Cerro de Pasco Corporation lost 35,000 hectares to peasant seizures.[30] *Cholos* who had once worked in the mines and obtained political experience in the unions took leadership roles in these land invasions.[31] The mine unions also offered support to the peasants. When government troops killed eight peasants in 1962, the Cerro de Pasco miners and railroad workers, some of whom were members of local villages and had taken part in the invasions, declared a strike. Peasants and miners barricaded La Oroya's streets until government troops regained control. Two months later, the workers at Morococha, Yauricocha, and Mahr Tunel went on strike. They too demanded both higher wages and the withdrawal of troops used against the peasants.

In this increasingly militant atmosphere during the 1960s, the miners replaced most of the moderate APRA union officials with radical leaders belonging to Trotskyite groups that also supported the peasants. They rejected as insufficient a government offer to increase wages and, in 1962, began another strike. In La Oroya, government troops prevented marching workers from crossing a bridge. The company's main warehouse was burned down in the ensuing melee, causing millions of dollars of damage. Government troops arrested and imprisoned many of the miners, and moderate *apristas* resumed control over the unions until the military revolution.[32]

"Class Struggle"?

In the late 1960s, left-wing political groups regained their leading role in the mine unions. Despite strong sectarian differences, the leftists shared the goal of organizing the miners into acting as a class to revolutionize Peruvian society as a whole. Depending on each group's ideological orientation, they vied with one another to enlist the miners through militant actions to support or challenge the legitimacy of the revolution that had been declared in Lima by the new military junta that took power in 1968 through a bloodless coup d'état. Moscow-oriented communists in the General Confederation of Peruvian Workers (Confederación General de Trabajadores Peruanos, or CGTP) attempted to use the miners' militancy to provide "critical support" for the military reforms. Other Marxist-Leninist, Maoist, and Trotskyite groups competed for the miners' allegiance by revealing what they saw as the military government's illicit alliance with "imperialist" mining ventures in Peru, including the Cerro de Pasco Corporation. These radical leftists set the nationalization of the mines as one of their primary goals. Thus began the political mobilization that produced a thirty-month strike wave that crested in 1971.

In 1969, union insurgents linked to the Moscow communists led the workers in La Oroya and Cobriza on a strike for higher wages. The new leaders organized thirty-five hundred miners to make a "march of sacrifice" to Lima. A women's committee led the march down the mountain road and organized an *olla común*, or common pot, to feed the marchers. Although halted by government troops, the march won a wage increment from the government. Seeking to use this success to build a national organization, the communist leaders for the first time united the separate unions of each of the company's camps into the Federation of Mining and Metallurgical Workers of the Cerro de Pasco Corporation. In turn, the Cerro de Pasco unions affiliated with the communists' newly formed national federation of miners.

The following year, competing leftist groups attempted to use similar organizing tactics to challenge the communist leadership. When the federated company union failed to negotiate a new collective contract, radical leaders called for another strike and another *marcha de sacrificio* to pressure the company. But, once in Lima, the communist leaders skillfully turned the march into a rally to support the military junta, and General Velasco's government granted most of the unions' demands. However, other leftists convinced workers in Cobriza, Morococha, and Cerro de Pasco to continue striking, and they succeeded in obtaining the largest pay increase ever, including an extra cost-of-living bonus for the Cobriza workers.[33] Early in 1971, in an attempt to contain the growing influence of the radical leftists, the government recognized the communists' General Confederation of Peruvian Workers as the official mediator of union disputes. On the basis of their success with wage increases the previous year, however, the radical leftists managed to take over control of the Cerro de Pasco federation, and, in opposing the military government, the Cerro de Pasco unions bolted from the communists' national mining federation.

The issue of support for the military government sharpened a few months later with the military government's announcement of a law requiring the creation of a Comunidad Minera in every mining company. General Velasco's government intended this Mining Community to eliminate class conflict by giving miners a vested interest in the profitable operation of mining companies. The Comunidad Minera was designed to create co-ownership. It would award the miners 6 percent of the company's annual net income, to be reinvested in the company until the workers' share equaled half the company's total capital. The communists supported the new law, whereas the rival radical leaders of the federation of Cerro de Pasco unions denounced the plan.[34]

In September 1971, executives of the Cerro de Pasco Corporation declined to negotiate a new wage agreement. They claimed to have been operating at a loss because of previous wage increases and because of lost mineral sales owing to strikes. The company petitioned the government to postpone any wage increase for two years. However, radical union leaders demanded a 100 percent wage raise, a six-hour working day, and retirement with full benefits after fifteen years. Under pressure, the government offered the unions a small raise, but this was rejected by both the company and the unions. The union federation called a strike and introduced the additional demand for nationalizing the mining industry, which included the Cerro de Pasco Corporation and other large foreign-owned mines. The demand for nationalizing the mines had not been discussed or voted on in the general assemblies of the miners. Rather, the leftist leaders announced that, henceforward, nationalization had become a principal demand of labor.

In conversations with miners from many camps before and during the strike, this author found that many workers agreed with the idea of nationalization in principle, but most opposed it as a practical measure. They felt that having the government run the mines would only make working conditions more difficult. If the North Americans remained as owners, the miners said, then the government would resolve each strike with a compromise guaranteeing them at least a minimal raise. As owner, however, the government would probably regard future strikes as political attacks and would be less likely to grant wage increases. Furthermore, the miners found that North American engineers treated them more fairly than did Peruvian engineers and that the North Americans were better prepared to operate the mines. Government administrators, they predicted, would be nepotistic in hiring and would steal from the company.

The leftist leaders recognized the miners' lack of enthusiasm for nationalization but decided to push forward anyway, intending that the 1971 strike would raise the miners' political consciousness. The leftists speculated that the military's recent approval of wage increases and the proposed Comunidad Minera had confused the workers about the government's true dependence on and allegiance to foreign capitalists. A position paper, which was circulated within the Revolutionary Vanguard before the strike, outlined the argument. "The mining proletariat of the central region, although it constitutes one of the most advanced sectors of the Peruvian working class, has not yet attained a clear class consciousness," the paper said. "Nevertheless, the contradictions of their living conditions have generated the presence of a strong class instinct capable of being transformed into consciousness through the intensification of our own party work. And in this sense, the next fight to introduce and incorporate the call for nationalization of the large mining companies constitutes an important step in this process."[35] Again, as in the 1930s, the leftists misunderstood the nonproletarian motives of most miners' militancy. Although the workers' economic aspirations led them to pursue wage increases militantly and although they did not oppose the nationalization of the mines, they certainly were not prepared to defend the demand for nationalization when faced with government repression.

In the meantime, while the Ministry of Labor was sponsoring contract negotiations between the unions and the company in Lima, the strike at the mines became violent.[36] In Cobriza, perhaps the most militant of the company's seven striking mining camps, some miners interpreted the company's movement of heavy equipment as preparation to bring in strikebreakers. Approximately sixty union members, wives, and children marched up the mountain to Parco, the exclusive compound where the administrators lived. They were met by members of the Civil Guard, company staff, and the mine's superintendent, who emerged from his home with a pistol in his hand. Tempers flared. The guards released tear gas and fired rifles into the air. A boy was shot through the leg by a stray bullet, and the union's secretary-general hit the superintendent in the head with a ball and chain. The miners seized the superintendent and two staff members and took them back to the union hall as hostages. Although they soon released the superintendent for medical treat-

Peruvian miners' poster calling for nationalization of American mines, 1971.
(Courtesy of Josh DeWind)

ment, the union leaders vowed not to free the other hostages until their strike demands were met.

Miners in other camps also took militant action. In Cerro de Pasco, the company's oldest and largest mine, workers trying to take over company offices also clashed with Civil Guards. Contingents of miners from most camps converged at the company's smelter and refinery in La Oroya to begin a *marcha de sacrificio* to Lima. The military government responded by suspending constitutional civil rights in the three provinces of central Peru within which the Cerro de Pasco Corporation operated. North American–trained antiguerrilla army troops were flown into Cobriza. In breaking into the union hall and freeing the hostages, the soldiers shot and killed five workers, including the union's secretary-general. In the succeeding days, the government arrested and imprisoned leftists and union leaders at all the mining camps. More than 120 workers were rounded up in Cobriza. One by one, as miners returned to work, the unions were forced to call off the strikes. Just as the leftist parties had done little to prepare the miners for the demand of nationalization, they had also not prepared public support. Although some urban unions and university-based groups in Lima began a campaign to support the imprisoned and fired miners, particularly after the strike, broad popular support was not forthcoming. The Andean strike wave broke up against a seawall of repression.

Conclusion

Why did the military government, which boasted of its reformist tendencies, send troops to crush the strike in the Cerro de Pasco? The generals had planned to base Peru's industrial development on the mining industry. Although miners constituted less than 5 percent of the nation's labor force, mineral exports provided the government with more than half of its export earnings. The military's plan projected that new foreign investments in unworked mineral deposits would make Peru one of the largest producers of copper in the world, providing the foreign exchange necessary to pay for Peru's industrialization. Labor conflicts and leftist demands to nationalize the large American-owned mining companies threatened the junta's development schemes. Besides diminishing mineral production at a time that foreign exchange reserves were drastically declining, labor strife was also scaring off new investments.

The military government would not permit the unions to enhance workers' control through nationalization, but it was willing to increase state controls over the mining industry through repossession of subsoil rights, mineral production, and marketing. In 1971, the junta decreed that large mining companies must bring unworked mineral deposits into production or lose them. The Cerro de Pasco Corporation scrambled to form a financial consortium to finance the opening of deposits at Tundra, Antamina, Chalcobamba, Ferrobamba, and Toromocho. But the consortium fell apart, and rights to exploit the deposits reverted to the government.[37] Based on negotiations concluded in 1969, however, the Southern Peru Copper Corporation, of which Cerro de Pasco was a major stockholder, managed to retain its claims in Cuajone by arranging to invest $670 in opening the mine. Production began there in 1976. By 1979, copper produced in Cuajone accounted for more than 50 percent of Peru's sales.[38] The government also took a direct role in mineral production and marketing with the creation of Minero-Perú in 1970. This state enterprise eventually took over and developed the Tundra and Cerro Verde deposits and constructed copper and zinc refineries in Ilo and Cajamarquilla respectively. Minero-Perú marketed all of Peru's mineral exports, except copper from Cuajone.

The expectations of leftists notwithstanding, neither the military junta nor the Cerro de Pasco Corporation had ruled out nationalization of the company's mining operations. The company despaired over what seemed to be long-term labor unrest, rising wages, and declines in productivity and metal prices. In December 1971, less than three months after the strike repression, the Cerro de Pasco Corporation itself proposed that the Peruvian government nationalize the company's mining operations. Contentious negotiations proceeded for two years, and nationalization took place on 1 January 1974. The Peruvian government paid $28.5 million, only 16 percent of the company's declared "fair market value."[39] Production and profits increased substantially under Centromín, as the nationalized mining operations are now named. Between 1974 and 1980, profits as a percentage of sales increased to an average of 15.6 percent, up from 5 percent during the last five years under ownership by the Cerro de Pasco Corporation.[40]

Once it had nationalized the Cerro de Pasco mines, the military government lost its interest in worker co-ownership and participation in management through its Mining Community. Rather than give the miners shares in Centromín, the government issued bonds from a state development corporation. In 1978, after union leaders used comanagement to press workers' grievances with administrators and to obtain company information to justify wage increases, the government forbade the union leaders' participation.

Nationalization and state intervention into the mining industry did not provide a firm base for the government's industrialization plan. Between 1970 and 1985, Peru's mining exports increased by 50 percent. Yet the industry's average annual rate of growth was declining. The government incurred heavy foreign debts initiating development projects. It exaggerated the estimates of ore values and underestimated costs. World copper prices fluctuated widely, and the government failed to complete the development projects that it had initiated.[41] Faced with unmanageable debt payments, high inflation, and growing monetary imbalances, the military turned the government back to civilians in 1980. The generals had not succeeded in building Peru's industrialization on the firm foundation of the mining industry.

The military junta's efforts to reduce unrest among the miners of the Cerro de Pasco Corporation had also failed to address the basic economic and social issues that motivated their strikes.[42] The government's attempts to improve the miners' living conditions, not by raising wages but by initiating the construction of new apartment blocks to replace the small, unsanitary, and inhospitable living quarters that decades earlier the Cerro de Pasco Corporation had built.[43] Improved living quarters seem to have attracted some miners to move their families to the camps and enroll their children in the company schools. But these measures did not address the workers' basic consumption needs. If anything, like the company's social work programs of the 1960s, these changes cut miners off from agricultural support; increased their need for furniture, school uniforms, school supplies, and food at the mines; and contributed to their demands for higher wages and workers' control.

During the 1970s, after the nationalization of the Cerro de Pasco Corporation, the miners of Centromín resumed their frequently militant pursuit of economic interests while continuing to avoid a working-class identity despite the rise of such organizing in other mines and industrial sectors. As many miners had predicted, government ownership of the mines placed the unions' activities in a politicized context. But the participation of Centromín unions in national politics remained uneven, particularly in comparison to unions in mines where the workforce was more fully proletarianized, such as the Toquepala mine of the Southern Peru Copper Corporation.[44] The Toquepala miners took a leading role in creating organizational structures through which miners throughout Peru collaborated with one another and with other workers on the basis of their working-class membership. The first step, in 1973, was to take control of the National Federation of Mining and Metallurgical Workers of Peru away from progovernment leadership in order to coordinate economic demands and strikes. The National Federation assumed a leading role in coordinating nationwide, class-based opposition to the military government's increasingly conservative economic and labor policies. This opposition included an effective national work stoppage in 1977—"the country's most important mobilization of the working class to date," according to one historian[45]—and inserted the nations' mine unions, as class organizations, into national political as well as economic affairs.

The involvement of the Centromín unions in class-based, national protests was hesitant and inconsistent. In 1977, the Centromín unions were virtually the only miners' group in Peru not to observe the national strike. But they were still willing to take militant actions to protest dangerous working conditions in their own mines, including a work stoppage when a mine elevator cable broke and killed six workers in mid-1979. They also launched a thirty-two-day *marcha de sacrificio* to Lima to protest severe economic policies imposed by new conservative leadership of the military government. In 1980, an elected civilian regime replaced the military junta, the undermining of which workers' opposition deserves credit.

The hesitance of the Centromín miners to collaborate in class-identified organizations and national political activities may well reflect the continuing incomplete proletarianization of the miners. Most recently, the miners of the central Andes have resisted the overtures of the Maoist guerrilla group Sendero Luminoso (the Shining Path).[46] Apparently, the ties to commercial agriculture and their petite bourgeois aspirations this author noticed in 1970 persist in leading miners away from class-based movements calling for the overthrow of the capitalist economy. The history of the central Peruvian miners' militance demonstrates an independence from narrow proletarian ideologies and class organizations and reflects socioeconomic interests and goals that were more complex than has been anticipated by urban revolutionaries and intellectuals. To these miners, workers' control has always signified the workers' freedom to pursue careers other than working for an industrial wage.

Notes

The author would like to thank Julian Laite for his comments on an earlier draft of this chapter. The field research for this chapter was supported with grants from the Doherty Charitable Foundation at Princeton University and the Department of Anthropology of Columbia University.

1. That the miners would militantly demand government approval for higher wages and, through nationalization of the mines, greater control over the workplace was thus seen as a natural outcome of their employment as industrial workers, an interpretation of the strikes that has been since offered by some social scientists. See especially Alberto Flores Galindo, *Los mineros de la Cerro de Pasco, 1900–1930* (Lima, 1974); Dirk Kruijt and Menno Vellinga, *Labor Relations and Multinational Corporations: The Cerro de Pasco Corporation in Peru (1902–1974)* (Assen, The Netherlands, 1979).

See also Josh DeWind, "A History of the Political Economy of Mining in Peru," 1970, in author's possession, 1–5.

2. *Andean Air Mail and Peruvian Times* (Lima), 11 December 1970, 22–23.

3. Josh DeWind, *Peasants Become Miners: The Evolution of Industrial Mining Systems in Peru, 1902–1974* (New York, 1987), chaps. 1, 2.

4. Ibid., chap. 4.

5. Hildebrando Castro Pozo, *Nuestra comunidad indígena* (Lima, 1924), 97–98.

6. Ibid., 117–24; Alberto Noriega, "El enganche en la minería del Perú," *Boletín de Minas, Industrias, y Construcciones* (Lima, 1911), ser. 2, 3 (nos. 4–6), 43–46; Flores Galindo, *Los mineros de la Cerro de Pasco*, 34–50.

7. Noriega, "El enganche," 42; Dora Mayer de Zulén, *The Conduct of the Cerro de Pasco Corporation* (Lima, 1913), 7.

8. Moisés Poblete Troncoso, *Condiciones de vida y de trabajo de la población indígena del Perú* (Geneva, Switzerland, 1938), 144–45.

9. Comité Interamericano de Desarrollo Agrícola, *Tenencia de la tierra y desarrollo socio-económico del sector agrícola: Perú* (Washington, D.C., 1966), 66–67; Thomas R. Ford, *Man and Land in Peru* (Gainesville, Fla., 1955), 248.

10. Florencia E. Mallon, *The Defense of Community in Peru's Central Highlands: Peasant Struggle and Capitalist Transition, 1860–1940* (Princeton, 1983), chaps. 7–9; Marvin Harris, *Patterns of Race in the Americas* (New York, 1964), 25–36.

11. Edward Alsworth Ross, *South of Panama* (New York, 1921), 153.

12. Heraclio Bonilla, *El minero de los andes* (Lima, 1974), 42–45.

13. Castro Pozo, *Nuestra comunidad indígena*, 120 n.

14. Bonilla, *El minero de los andes*, 53.

15. Like the Cerro de Pasco Corporation earlier in the century, smaller and technologically less advanced mines in Huancavelica during the mid-1960s employed *indígenas* (a more respectful term for *indios*) who maintained ties with traditional peasant communities. While *indígenas* were assigned unskilled jobs, skilled jobs were given to *cholos*. See Henri Favre, "Algunos problemas referentes a la industria minera de Huancavelica," *Cuadernos de Antropología* (Lima), vol. 3, no. 8 (1965): 20.

16. Cerro de Pasco Corporation, Administration Department, *Annual Report* (Lima, 1969), n.p.

17. Ibid., n.p.

18. Cerro de Pasco Corporation, interview with representative of Industrial Relations Department, Cerro de Pasco mine, September 1970.

19. Ibid.

20. Richard N. Adams observed that temporary mine labor in the peasant village of Muquiyauyo provided some of the owners of small plots of land with enough supplemental income to continue traditional subsistence agriculture. Mine labor led others into nonagricultural trades. Richard N. Adams, *Community in the Andes: Problems in Progress in Muquiyauyo* (Seattle, 1959), 93–98.

21. Cerro de Pasco Corporation, *Annual Report*, n.p.

22. Ibid., n.p.

23. Mayer de Zulén, *Conduct of the Cerro de Pasco Corporation*, 41–42; Flores Galinda, *Los mineros de la Cerro de Pasco*, 68; *Engineering and Mining Journal* 103 (1917): 1002. The only evidence of formal labor organizing comes from *El Minero Illustrado*, a newspaper published in the city of Cerro de Pasco, which reported in 1918 that small worker associations and political groups such as the 16 Amigos and the Sociedad Obreros Billinghurst met to support a presidential candidate "representative of the working class." These groups then federated as the Sindicato de Oficios Varios, which described itself as part of the Movimiento Sindicalista Obrera. An assembly attended by three hundred workers elected officers. This *sindicato* apparently represented workers' interests to the company but seems to have quickly vanished without leaving any legacy. See especially Julian Laite, *Industrial Development and Migrant Labor* (Manchester, England, 1981), 76.

24. Ricardo Martínez de la Torre, *Apuntes para una interpretación marxista de historia social del Perú* (Lima, 1949), vol. 4; DeWind, *Peasants Become Miners*, 322–41.

25. As quoted in Denis Sulmont, *El movimiento obrero en el Perú, 1900–1956* (Lima, 1975), 53.

26. Laite, *Industrial Development*, 79–82.

27. Ibid.

28. B. T. Colley, "A History of the Cerro de Pasco Corporation," internal memorandum of the Cerro de Pasco Corporation (1958), Lima, mimeograph.

29. Gerrit Huizer, "Land Invasion as a Non-Violent Strategy of Peasant Rebellion," *Journal of Peace Research* 3 (1966): 124.

30. Julio Cotler and Felipe Portocarrero, "Peru: Peasant Organizations," in *Latin American Peasant Movements*, ed. Henry A. Landsberger (Ithaca, N.Y., 1969), 211.

31. Georgio Alberti, *The Breakdown of Provincial Urban Power Structure and the Rise of Peasant Movements* (Madison, Wis., 1973), 323–27; Howard Handleman, *Struggle in the Andes* (Austin, Tex., 1975), 95, 112; Eric Hobsbawm, "Peasant Land Occupations," in *Past and Present* 62 (1974): 142–47.

32. Laite, *Industrial Development*, 82; Genaro Ledesma Izquieta, *Complot* (Lima, 1964).

33. DeWind, *Peasants Become Miners*, 374–79; Laite, *Industrial Development*, 84–85.

34. Laite, *Industrial Development*, 83.

35. Vanguardia Revolucionaria, "La Célula Primero de Mayo," untitled manuscript (1971), in author's possession.

36. Accounts of the following events are found in DeWind, *Peasants Become Miners*, 383–85; Laite, *Industrial Development*, 85–86; Kruijt and Vellinga, *Labor Relations and Multinational Corporations*, 1–3, 167–80.

37. David G. Becker, *The New Bourgeoisie and the Limits of Dependency: Mining, Class, and Power in "Revolutionary" Peru* (Princeton, 1983), 146–48.

38. Ibid., 124.

39. Ibid., 148–55.

40. Ibid., 156.

41. Elizabeth Dore, *The Peruvian Mining Industry: Growth, Stagnation, and Crisis* (Boulder, Colo., 1988), 55, 177, 179, 184–85, 251.

42. Ibid., 308.

43. Ibid., 296 n.

44. Ibid., 291–97; Elizabeth Bauch, *We Shall Not Lose the Bread of Our Children: Strikes at a U.S. Copper Company in Southern Peru* (New York, 1988).

45. Sulmont, *El movimiento obrero*, 52.

46. Deborah Poole and Gerardo Renique, *Peru: Time of Fear* (London, 1992), 82–83.

CHAPTER TEN

DEFENDING THE NATION'S INTEREST

Chilean Miners and the Copper Nationalization

JOANNA SWANGER

U ntil now, most historical accounts maintain that the 1971 nationalization of the Chilean copper industry came about because the political platform of socialist president Salvador Allende had mandated it.[1] These accounts largely ignore the role that the copper miners played in achieving nationalization. This chapter first delineates the actions taken by the miners of the Gran Minería—through their votes and strikes—to promote the nationalization of the industry in which they worked. The Gran Minería was the name for the large U.S.-owned copper companies: the Braden Copper Company (El Teniente mine), a subsidiary of the Kennecott Corporation; and the Chile Exploration Company (Chuquicamata mine) and the Andes Copper Mining Company (Potrerillos/El Salvador mine), subsidiaries of the Anaconda Corporation. These two corporations had controlled 85 to 90 percent of Chile's copper output from 1920 to 1971.[2]

Second, and more important, this chapter proposes to analyze why the miners sought nationalization. An examination of this central issue provides insight into the conflict between the miners and their employers and between labor and the state in Chile. It also brings to light the fact that nationalization held separate meanings for the Popular Unity government of Allende and for the miners. The government considered it as a means of ensuring Chile's economic sovereignty. It took for granted that the miners supported nationalization because the Popular Unity coalition viewed the miners as a "radical" sector of the Chilean working class—that is, "radical" as opposed to "conservative" in the sense that the miners would sacrifice their own personal interests to those of the nation.

However, once the copper industry was nationalized, the workers demonstrated their independence from the socialist government by striking the El Teniente mine from April to June 1973. Ironically, this most "radical" sector of the Chilean proletariat engaged in a strike that mobilized popular protest against a government that was supposed to have represented the workers. It could well be claimed that the miners were redefining concepts such as "radical" and "national interests" on their own terms. Perhaps the workers were more radical than the socialist coalition that governed. After all, they considered nationalization as a form of workers' control—not merely the replacement of arrogant foreign employers by unresponsive state directors. Obviously, the miners were not radical in the sense that the government claimed. They saw nationalization as a way to guarantee their own political and economic sovereignty. Public ownership of the means of production promised the miners both wage stability and administrative control of their own workplace. To achieve their goals, Chilean miners were prepared to challenge the state just as they had for so long pressed the foreign owners.

The Miners as a Labor Aristocracy

Consensus once held that Chile—along with Costa Rica and Uruguay—had the strongest tradition of stable democracy in all of Latin America. The military did not intervene in domestic politics for the better part of the twentieth century. The Chilean polity also had a long tradition of statism, the use of the state apparatus to allocate resources and control the economy. This statist tradition was Chile's response to the fact that, from the end of the nineteenth century, Chile's integration into the world economy was based almost entirely on the development of the export industries of nitrates and copper, both of which had come under British and United States control respectively.

Chile's democratic institutions and the movement to assert Chile's economic independence both tended to strengthen the labor movement. Labor demonstrated its power through legally recognized union organizations and ties to the stalwart parties of the Left. The Center-Left coalition of the Popular Front government (1938–41) carried on the statist tradition by creating institutions aimed at establishing Chile's economic sovereignty by channeling capital into import-substitution industrialization.[3] The program of the Popular Front emphasized the use of legal means to socialize the economy and attempted to establish a collaborative relationship between labor and the state.

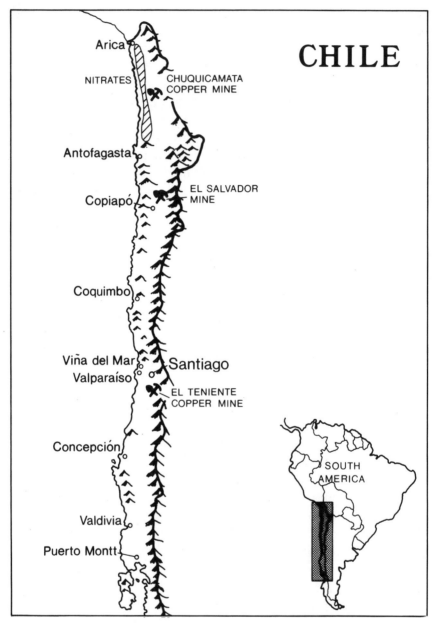

Map 8. *The copper mines of Chile, 1970*

It foreshadowed the coming to power of Allende and the Popular Unity government in 1970.

The relationship between the Gran Minería workers and the rest of the Chilean working class began to deteriorate as the copper unions became stronger in relation to other segments of the working class. The Chilean Workers Confederation (Confederación de Trabajadores de Chile) had played the major role in the labor movement since the 1930s. In 1943, the mineworkers held a strong place within the national labor confederation, their membership accounting for 31.8 percent of total union membership. The confederation defended workers' economic interests. It called for a stable and fair relationship between workers' wages and the cost of living through such means as movable wage scales. The Chilean Workers Confederation also had certain demands that were less strictly economic and more political. For example, it proposed limits on the profits earned by the large companies and urged that labor share in the administration of industry.[4] But this labor organization deteriorated.

In 1953, the National Labor Confederation (Central Unica de Trabajadores, or the CUT) formed from elements of the defunct labor confederation. The development of the CUT marked the beginning of an extensive relationship between the labor movement and the (political) popular movement. By 1963, 51 percent of all Chilean labor unions were affiliated with the new confederation. One of these was the National Copper Workers Confederation (Confederación de Trabajadores del Cobre, or CTC), which arose from a general strike of copper workers in 1951.[5] However, although the copper workers became affiliated with the larger confederation, the copper workers did not, for the most part, play a noticeably active role in the CUT's activities. They did not often cooperate with other kinds of workers. Contemporary observers speculated that the copper miners were much too concerned with their own particular demands.[6]

What were the conditions faced by Gran Minería workers? It is true that they were geographically isolated from the rest of the Chilean proletariat. Both the El Salvador and Chuquicamata mines are located in the Atacama Desert, far north of Santiago. Geographical isolation was less a problem at the El Teniente mine, situated in the mountains just eighty kilometers southeast of Santiago. Nevertheless, at all three locations, the workers and their families lived in communities close to the mines and traveled relatively little. The Gran Minería was largely a capital-intensive operation. In 1966, the Gran Minería employed just 21 percent of the total copper mining workforce, about eighteen thousand workers in all. *Obreros* (blue-collar workers) outnumbered *empleados* (white-collar workers) by two to one. Copper workers recognized three distinct social groups among themselves. At the top of the hierarchy were those people paid in U.S. dollars. These were professional managers, engineers, and technicians, most of whom were U.S. citizens and some of whom were Chilean *empleados*. The Gran Minería did not employ a great number of U.S. citizens, perhaps 1 percent of all employees in 1970. Yet it is certain that all U.S. employees were part of this top social group of copper workers. Next in social prestige were the *empleados* paid in Chilean escudos.

The majority of the copper workers, the *obreros*, formed the group accorded the least prestige. These were the workers who performed the most physically demanding, dirtiest, and dangerous labor. Most of the *obreros* worked as drillers, explosives handlers, or shovelers. Each day they risked fatal accidents from falling rock or electrical shock, and as time passed, each miner ran the risk of partial or complete loss of hearing. Constantly exposed to dust and chemicals in sealed-off underground passages, the *obreros* also ran the risk of contracting the deadly lung disease pneumoconiosis.[7] The miners' working conditions, therefore, always informed their strike demands.

Moreover, the copper miners were generally perceived to be quite radical. Salvador Allende and other officials of the Popular Unity government later shared this assumption. On the other hand, certain other sources have tended to view the copper miners as a kind of "labor aristocracy." Hobsbawm characterizes the labor aristocracy as that segment of privileged workers distinguished from the rest of the proletariat by relatively high wages, better benefits, and increased job security as well as by their perception of themselves as forming a distinct group. The term carries the connotation of conservatism. Labor aristocrats organize with the knowledge that they are defending a privileged position.[8]

Indeed, the copper workers were relatively well off compared with other segments of Chile's working class. Judging from four categories measuring workers' well-being—wages, technological benefits, Christmas bonuses, and social benefits—they were privileged. The wages earned by the Gran Minería workers nearly doubled the wages of the petroleum workers, Chile's second highest paid group of workers. This wage statistic should perhaps be viewed skeptically; it came from the reports of the Braden Copper Company. Nevertheless, the Gran Minería workers enjoyed benefits not shared by most other workers, including paid vacations, better social security benefits, and automatic wage adjustments whenever the cost of living rose significantly.[9]

The fairly good economic position of the copper workers, of course, derived not from the graciousness of the Gran Minería companies but from years of workers' struggle. The miners called the general strike of 1951 for economic reasons. Of all strikes called by the miners from 1956 to 1961, the majority had economic demands (wage increases and wage adjustments) as their basis.[10] Hobsbawm points out that the labor aristocracy, typically militant in defending its own interests, can play the radical role of vanguard for the entire proletariat in that it forms "a strong nucleus of unionism." Yet the copper miners seldom cooperated with the rest of organized labor. Their striking patterns suggest that the Gran Minería workers might have constituted a kind of conservative "labor aristocracy." Copper workers, during this time period, could be said to have remained in Gramsci's "economic-corporate" phase. This is the phase in labor organization in which laborers demonstrate solidarity with others in the same industry but not with the rest of the working class.[11] These analyses are useful as an aperture into the conflicts that were to occur between the copper miners and the Popular Unity in 1973.

Some Marxist observers who obviously supported the Popular Unity during Allende's rule wanted to make the point that the copper workers, despite their relative economic well-being, did not represent a "conservative" labor aristocracy. Barrera wanted to portray them as radicals. He pointed out that the margin of difference in pay for *empleados* and *obreros* working for the Gran Minería diminished steadily between 1955 and 1966, apparently to show the leftist tendencies of both *empleados* and *obreros*. It is true that the Copper Workers Confederation's stipulation that all workers' demands had to be agreed on by both *empleados* and *obreros* tended to pressure the companies for a more even distribution of income.[12] Pro-Allende opinion also emphasized the desire of copper workers themselves for nationalization of the industry and numerous strike repressions the workers had suffered in the recent past. These facts served as evidence to Allende supporters that the miners were fulfilling the role of the proletarian vanguard.[13] The Popular Unity associated nationalization so closely with the achievement of the workers' state that the miners' actions toward that end could not be considered other than "radical."

To Benefit the Country

Nationalization had elements of a "top-down" process as well as meeting the "bottom-up" demands of workers. The concept of anti-imperialism, the desire to rid the nation of the domination of foreign economic interests, held great sway with the middle-class Left and with intellectuals in the Popular Unity. The earliest calls for nationalization found expression under the more general banner of anti-imperialism. The Chilean Left—the socialists and the communists, for the most part—made efforts to couch the workers' strike movement in terms of Chile's anti-imperialist struggle. In this way, every material benefit earned by the striking copper workers became a small victory in the struggle against foreign domination.[14] But how did workers respond to anti-imperialism? The copper workers themselves, though patriotic, did not necessarily make the connection between the concrete fact of a strike and the goal of anti-imperialism.

Anti-imperialism and its corollary, "economic nationalism," the belief that a nation's sovereignty rests on the control of its own economy, already had an extensive history in the country. Chileans began to express concern over foreign economic penetration as early as the 1850s.[15] Economic nationalism with regard to copper did not become significant until the twentieth century. By 1930, copper was Chile's most important product at a time when the foreign interests controlled 52 percent of all capital investment in the country. United States capital accounted for 60 percent of all foreign assets.[16] Thus, when the depression hit, causing real wages to fall and unemployment to rise, Chileans reawakened to their country's fragile position within the global market economy. Calls for the nationalization of industry increased, especially in the Gran Minería, owned entirely by U.S. firms. The Chilean Workers Confederation represented one of the voices calling for nationalization. In the midst of World War II, the confederation linked fascism to "regressive capitalism." It proposed the nationalization of the industry. In its actions, the copper workers' organization did not appear to have supported nationalization only "to benefit the country" (an anti-imperialistic, "political" goal). Rather, the confederation sought to "assure the welfare" of the workers (a more strictly economic goal).[17] An examination of the apparent disparity between voting patterns of the copper workers and the goals of their strikes bears out this conclusion.

There is no doubt that the copper workers' votes aimed to achieve nationalization. The miners demonstrated this through their ties with the Left. The Chilean Communist Party had a well-developed, anti-imperialist rhetoric. It spoke of the need to develop the workers' consciousness and of the role of the working class in breaking the domination of foreign imperialism and its ally, the domestic oligarchy. The party pointed specifically to the evils of the U.S. domination of the Chilean copper industry. Although the Communist Party made the connection between nationalization and the welfare of Chile (and hence, of Chilean workers), it did not make the connection as strongly as did the Socialist Party.[18] After he became president, Salvador Allende, a socialist, elaborated on the need for nationalization. His stance did not radically differ from the longtime program of his Socialist Party. Allende spoke of how the Gran Minería companies had blocked Chilean sovereignty: They had fixed Chilean copper at low prices during World War II and the Korean War, which forced the government to raise exchange rates, resulting in inflation for Chile.[19] Nationalization, then, formed a centerpiece of the Socialist Party and, to a much lesser extent, the Communist Party. The Chilean labor movement had historical links with both parties, but it seems that the workers voted for them less for historical loyalty than for their programs supporting nationalization.[20]

In the three Gran Minería union elections spanning from 1959 to 1965, the Socialist and Communist Parties received absolute majorities each time. Seven of the thirteen Copper Workers Confederation leaders elected in 1951 were members of the Socialist Party. Four were Independents, and two were from the Christian Democratic Party. Ten of twenty-one leaders elected in 1955 were from the Socialist Party; the rest came from the Radical Party, the Independent Party, and the Christian Democratic Party. In CTC elections during 1958, 1961, and 1964, Socialist Party candidates received absolute majorities each time. The Communist, Christian-Democratic, Radical, and Independent Parties all won up to two spots each. Results of parliamentary elections show an identical pattern. In the Gran Minería mining community of Chuquicamata, the Socialist Party received the greatest support in 1957. In 1961, however, the Communist Party began to receive significant electoral support in the mining communities, where it had almost none in 1957. In these years, the same pattern held true for the mining community of Sewell, home of the El Teniente mine.[21]

Two points merit notation. First, support for the Socialist Party had its highest concentrations in the mining areas. In fact, Salvador Allende, a coalition candidate and one of the long-standing pillars of the Socialist Party, consistently received higher vote totals from the mining communities of the Gran Minería than from the country as a whole. The mining community of El Teniente gave Allende nearly double the percentage of votes he received countrywide in the presidential elections of 1958, 1964, and 1970.[22] Second, the miners gave considerably less electoral support to the Communist Party than the Socialist Party. Although a number of reasons accounted for this difference, the fact remained that the Communist Party did not advocate copper nationalization as clearly as did the Socialist Party. The Communist Party's theme of anti-imperialism did not resonate as much with workers as did the Socialist Party's simple and basic call for nationalization. The theme of nationalization played a large role in Allende's near victory in the 1958 election. He lost by just three percentage points.[23] Nationalization did indeed have the miners' support prior to the 1960s. As early as 1953, the CTC wrote: "Chile could, if it wanted to, NATIONALIZE ITS COPPER. This measure would be part of an overall political system."[24]

Some of Allende's supporters had claimed that the miners represented a radical sector of Chile. As evidence, they pointed to their votes for leftist candidates and to their support for nationalization. Many also pointed to the miners' strikes as acts of anti-imperialism. An editorial printed in the newspaper *El Siglo*, a communist and pro-Allende publication, on 3 October 1959, for example, praised the miners' strikes and said: "[The miners] have the conviction that . . . they are defending not only a wage and salary increase that will allow them to provide for their own needs, but also [they are defending] the national interest because their interests are the nation's interests."[25]

The miners' support for nationalization, however, came not solely as an act of anti-imperialism but, more basically, as an act aimed to bring about workers' control of the industry. Their strike patterns prior to the Frei administration show this to be the case. The strike demands from the 1950s and 1960s were not exclusively economic ones. Miners struck in favor of automatic wage adjustments and higher salaries but also in protest of firings and in solidarity with fellow Gran Minería workers.[26] While their votes made them look "radical," their economistic strike demands might have made the miners appear "conservative." However, this "apparent" disparity did not actually exist. The more "radical" goal of workers' control and the more "conservative" goal of ensuring economic security merged in the miners' quest for nationalization. An economic crisis in 1961 and 1962 brought increased opposition to foreign investment in Chile, and people directed much of their hostility specifically at the companies of the Gran Minería. Subsequently, in July 1964, one of the first copper strikes that possibly had more "nationalistic" reasons behind it and that also represented workers' control objectives took place. The miners at El Teniente struck for an increased share in the profits of the Braden Company.[27] The program of Chileanization attempted to deflect these miners' demands.

Breaking the Authority of the State

During the 1960s, Chileans became increasingly disenchanted with the "benefits" of foreign investment. The growing feeling of economic nationalism in 1964 led both presidential candidates, Salvador Allende and Eduardo Frei, to suggest changing the status of the Gran Minería companies. Allende proposed an immediate nationalization, and Frei favored a more gradual process he called Chileanization. Three-quarters of the labor leaders interviewed in 1963 believed that progress for Chile depended on a rapid and complete restructuring of Chile's economy, including nationalization, whereas the remaining quarter favored a gradual restructuring.[28] Labor clearly sided with Allende. But Frei won the 1964 election with the middle-class vote, and the "gradual evolution" of the Gran Minería companies began in October of that year.

The goals of Chileanization received broad support. They included doubling copper production within seven years of the implementation of the program, state participation in the refining and the marketing of copper, and Chile's coparticipation in the administration—and eventual ownership—of the foreign copper companies. The state actually became near half-owner of both of Anaconda's industries. It became more than half-owner of Kennecott's El Teniente mine.[29] The National Mining Company, a government agency involved both in the productive and administrative aspects of the copper industry, supported Chileanization. It argued that, by removing legal barriers to development and offering incentives to the private companies, the program would allow Chile to become the world's largest producer and exporter of copper. Chileanization had obliged the U.S. copper companies to invest 4 percent of their annual profits in Chile for the next twenty years. The newspaper *La Nación* also praised Frei's program, estimating that Chileanization would raise Chile's gross national product the equivalent of $240 million annually, adding 1 percent or more to the annual growth rate. Pointing to Chile's 51 percent equity in El Teniente, *La Nación* concluded that Chileanization reinforced Chile's sovereignty.[30] Actually, by 1970, at the end of Frei's term, Chileanization did not appear to be doing too badly. By that time, the Chilean government owned more than half of each of the three Gran Minería mines and planned for eventual sole ownership of the El Salvador and Chuquicamata mines. Copper production had greatly increased (1967 was a record year), and so had Chile's refining capacity. The final word of praise for Chileanization came from Senator Ignacio Palma. In 1971, he admitted that Chileanization had been flawed but that it had brought the country to a position of economic strength, permitting Chileans to consider full nationalization. Senator Palma claimed that the income Chile received more than doubled the profits taken by the U.S. corporations.[31]

Chileanization also had its detractors, however. The strong points of the law tended to be outweighed by several glaring weaknesses. The incentives offered to the U.S. companies angered the program's opponents. The Frei government had promised that no new taxes would be imposed on the industry. Nor did it increase existing ones. The U.S. companies also retained the right to maintain foreign bank accounts for the deposit of any and all dividends.[32] Furthermore, Chile's gross profits did not reveal the greater burden of costs. The Chilean government incurred interest charges on loans from the U.S. Export-Import Bank and the Braden Copper Company. One cost/benefit analysis for the El Teniente mine showed that Kennecott was benefiting three times more than Chile.[33] Those studies indicating Chileanization's costs for the nation and its benefits for the U.S. companies reinforced the arguments for a true nationalization. Salvador Allende and others reiterated the need for radical change. By the end of Frei's administration, even though the copper industry may have looked healthy, the country as a whole was suffering rising inflation and an unemployment rate of 8 percent.[34] The continuing economic problems also affected the copper workers.

At the beginning of the Frei administration, the Copper Workers Confederation once again had declared favor for a program of nationalization. "The characteristics of our country pose the necessity of struggles to recover our basic resources," the Copper Workers Confederation had declared in 1964, "in order to accelerate our economic development in an independent form."[35] The miners subsequently expressed their dissatisfaction with Chileanization, which they viewed as a cheap substitute for nationalization. In 1965, they wrote an open letter to President Frei: "The politics advocated by the Government for the copper companies mean neither an historical change in copper politics nor much less that [Chile] is going to become the owner of its own copper resources."[36]

The miners, nevertheless, sought to influence the structure of Chileanization, resulting in two huge strikes. The copper workers in 1965 had demanded a greater sharing in the company's profits, worker pensions, and health benefits. These measures were approved by the Senate in early October, only to be rejected by the Christian-Democratic majority in the Chamber of Deputies. The CTC then called a general strike of all the Gran Minería workers. The strike lasted thirty-seven days and cost the country nearly $30 million in lost copper production. The CTC's finalized list of forty-five demands contained mostly demands that may be termed strictly "economic" (e.g., wage increases and Christmas bonuses), as well as several workers' control objectives (e.g., well-defined job descriptions and work schedules, regular evaluations, and the establishment of a scale of seniority). Most important, the strikes made no mention of nationalization.[37] It may be that the miners saw their economic demands not as typically "conservative" or even selfish but rather as "radical," in the sense that the miners were determined not to let the companies reap huge profits at their expense.

The second strike called by the Copper Workers Confederation in March 1966 originated with the El Teniente miners, who were demanding pay raises. Workers at the El Salvador and Chuquicamata mines soon joined the strike. This action so angered the Christian Democratic government that Frei even charged that the miners were no longer striking for better pay but rather to "break the authority of the State and overthrow the Government." The president declared a zone of emergency at the El Salvador mine and sent *carabineros* (federal police) to the scene. In the ensuing conflict, the police killed nine miners and injured thirty-six more. This violence brought the National Labor Confederation into the conflict. It declared a national solidarity strike on 15 March, at which point the labor conflict became more political than economic. The confederation and the newspaper *El Siglo* attributed the labor repression to the government's desire to maintain the long tradition of exploiting the workers.[38] This whole experience undoubtedly politicized the miners. The copper workers moved even closer to the leftist parties and further away from Frei's Christian-Democratic Party. Yet they maintained their own economic and shop floor interests as their driving force.[39]

An examination of relations between the government, the companies, and the workers during the Frei administration reveals an awareness on the part of workers of exploitation and the need for workers' control. In 1963, the general opinion among union leaders held that company/union relations were fairly good, with only 3 percent of those surveyed describing relations as "very bad." As for the Gran Minería companies specifically, the Braden Copper Company portrayed itself as a wonderful employer, "one of the best employers in Chile," in fact. It pointed to such features as high wages, good housing, superb educational and medical facilities, an established record in industrial safety, and "corporate charitable activities." Braden also pointed out that it had helped to found the Chilean Institute for the Rational Administration of Enterprise, an organization promoting "modern management methods and practices" and having the convenient acronym ICARE. Yet, at the time, a majority of union leaders doubted that the companies were interested in the workers' welfare. Union leaders were also aware that economic exploitation was occurring. Fifty-three percent of the leaders opined that wages were too low; 85 percent thought that the companies were financially quite well off. An overwhelming majority of the unionists stated that the companies could afford to pay the workers higher wages with little or no difficulty. The most interesting answers came in response to the question: If the company were to reap huge profits in the next few years, would the workers also benefit? Three out of four labor leaders answered that the workers might receive some slight benefits but not nearly as many as they should receive. Sixteen percent said the workers would benefit in no way whatsoever.[40] These surveys, it should be remembered, came from a variety of industries, including but not limited to copper. However, this notion that foreign companies exploited Chilean workers carried over into the copper industry specifically.

In the Gran Minería, the workers noticed this exploitation in two ways. First, although their wages were higher than in other industries, the productivity of the miners was also proportionally much higher. Second, the Chilean copper workers were aware that they were earning less than half of the wages earned by U.S. employees of the Gran Minería, who received their pay in U.S. dollars rather than Chilean escudos.[41] Nevertheless, this awareness of exploitation did not necessarily translate into the workers' desire to rid Chile of "Yankee imperialists." The workers stuck with their economic goals. In 1967, 920 workers (as opposed to union leaders) of various Chilean industries were polled. Seventy-eight percent said that the long-term goals of the union should be to improve the living conditions of the workers. Only 5 percent expressed interest in having the unions take a political stand on issues. Frei addressed these material demands of the workers when he started to undertake reforms in 1969. His "Habitational Plan" would have helped workers become small homeowners. President Frei had also tapped into another source of worker dissatisfaction. In his 1964 campaign against Allende, he had promised the workers participation in running the industries and in sharing the profits. "The worker will no longer be a machine as in a myopic capitalist regime," a Frei campaign pamphlet read, "nor a functionary of a government which owns all the industries, as happens in a Marxist regime."[42] Through Chileanization, Frei was trying to provide an alternative to nationalization and the economic and political power it promised the workers. Meanwhile, the Copper Workers Confederation reiterated its position on the matter. Its president in 1969 endorsed nationalization instead of Chileanization. "Our position . . . with respect to this issue is decidedly for NATIONALIZATION, in open juxtaposition to 'Chileanization,' " said the leader of the miners union. "Our struggle for nationalization has been ongoing since the birth of the [Copper Workers Confederation] in 1951."[43] The copper miners had an opportunity to carry out their long-term objective in 1970. In that year, Socialist Party candidate Salvador Allende won the three-candidate presidential election with 36.3 percent of the popular vote.

Throughout its three years in power, Allende's Popular Unity referred to to itself as "the government of the people" and "the government of the workers."[44] For Allende, as well as for other Chilean politicians, the prolabor bias of the Popular Unity was tantamount to support of nationalization. Socialist politicians often equated the history of workers' struggle—and that of the Chilean people in general—to a fight for nationalization. "This great national revindication [i.e., nationalization] is . . . the reason for the existence of the popular movement," Allende said. "It is the government made by the people . . . which struggles for complete economic liberty, for the free power of decision over our resources." In the Senate debate preceding the unanimous passage of the law nationalizing the copper industry, senators frequently referred to nationalization coming about as a result of the people's struggle. They also couched their arguments in terms of anti-imperialism and eco-

Chilean workers refining copper at the El Teniente mine, 1964.
(Courtesy of the Library of Congress, Washington, D.C.)

nomic nationalism. Senator Luis Corvalán of the Communist Party spoke of the many generations that had struggled to end the exploitation of the workers and to terminate the power of the oligarchy and the bourgeoisie. For the Socialist Party, legislators praised the martyrs of the El Salvador mine and referred to decades of exploitation by foreigners.[45] The workers' struggle once again was being cast in the mold of anti-imperialism. This does not mean that the workers did not themselves speak of exploitation or that the workers were not wholly supportive of nationalization. It does imply, however, that the politicians of the Popular Unity assumed that their cause was also that of the workers.

For the miners, however, the concept of nationalization meant two important things: an increase in income and worker participation in controlling the copper industry. This second point bears additional discussion. In the debate over nationalization, Senator Altamirano spoke of the need to guarantee the "real, creative, and living" participation of the workers in the copper industry's administration. Many official voices repeated this theme. Luis Figueroa of the National Labor Confederation said that neither the businessmen nor the government but rather the workers themselves would run the mining industry. In fact, the new administrative structure contained a number of workers. The mines were to be run by an administrative council (made up of five democratically elected workers, five government representatives, and one representative of Allende) and a production committee (composed of a supervisor and a worker representative from each mine section). The Popular Unity had been creating this administrative structure in certain public industries as early as April 1971, two and one-half months prior to the nationalization of copper.[46] Luis Figueroa stated, "There is no doubt that the character of the enterprises of the State . . . now fundamentally changes with the incorporation of workers into their administration."[47] A debate over whether nationalization truly did represent a "fundamental change" in terms of the miners' actual power arose later, during the El Teniente strike.

Exploited Now by the Boss State

The miners seemed generally supportive of nationalization and of the Popular Unity government through 1972. Three factors demonstrate evidence of this conclusion: the miners' voting patterns and political participation, the miners' striking patterns, and levels of copper production. As for political participation, the workers at El Teniente began to organize committees of production the very same month that nationalization took effect. This heightened participation in the industry's administration stayed in effect over the next several months. Two important union elections in 1972 indicated strong progovernment sentiment. In June of that year, workers elected roughly 75 percent Popular Unity candidates as leaders of the National Labor Confederation. This election also marked the first time in union history that a labor confederation used secret balloting, so the results probably show true workers' feelings.[48] Second, in July, the Copper Workers Confederation held its Fifth Congress, in whose election for the directorate Popular Unity candidates won eleven of thirteen seats. The Independent and left-wing Popular Socialist Union won the other two seats.[49] The fact that the Christian Democrats may have won seats had they not declined to run candidates should not obscure the backing that miners gave to the Popular Unity.

Strike patterns during this time also show general support for the government and for nationalization, although they may be somewhat difficult to sort out. On the one hand, Allende said in May 1971 that the number of strikes had diminished significantly since he took office. This appears to be true. He also claimed that, in the first half of 1971, *no* strikes at all had occurred in the coal, nitrate, copper, iron, or textile industries, proving that workers supported his revolutionary nationalistic cause. To say that the workers did not strike during this time period, however, was not true. They did.[50] On the other hand, sources opposed to the Popular Unity (Kennecott Copper Company, for example) described an outright "breakdown of labor discipline" once Allende came to power. This too appears to be wishful thinking. True, the workers did strike significantly under the Popular Unity government. But the number of strikes did not increase under Popular Unity compared with previous regimes, and the workers did not intend with their strikes to harm the government (as Kennecott wished to portray). Statistics show that the number of workers who struck in 1971 decreased 55 percent from the number in 1970 under Frei's regime. Strikes in many industries during Allende's first year in office were intended to aid the government in the process of nationalization. For the miners, though, nationalization did not equate merely with nationalism. It also meant increased economic welfare during a time in which inflation was still depressing the workers' real wages. As soon as nationalization had occurred, therefore, the miners struck for wage increases.[51] They did not consider such action as treasonous either to Allende or to the nation.

Production levels of copper also serve as a partial indication of worker support for the government. There occurred in 1971 a 0.3 percent increase in production of refined copper as well as a 3.2 percent increase in primary copper production. Although the production of refined copper dropped off 10 percent for the first semester of 1972, the general trend in primary copper production showed gradual increases each year Allende held office. This trend manifested itself especially in the nationalized Gran Minería, which showed a 4 percent production increase in 1972. The trend continued through March 1973.[52] The miners clearly were committed to making nationalization work. In Chuquicamata, the miners even set up a volunteer work committee so that workers who were so inclined could work one Sunday a month for free.[53] Without doubt, the miners were aware of the importance of copper for Chile and, consequently, of their own importance for the nation. High production increased the workers' bargaining power for economic and political gains.

Nevertheless, the Popular Unity government began to lose support among the miners and among the populace in general. By the beginning of 1973, half of El Teniente's eight unions had Christian Democratic leaders, the former Popular Unity officials having been voted out by the rank and file. At another of the nationalized mines, Chuquicamata, "non-Marxists" won seven of ten spots on the board of directors elected by union members.[54] The decrease in support for the government on the part of the miners testifies to the fact that, although surely concerned with both, the miners gave higher priority to their own economic and political power than to the interests of Chile as defined by the government.[55] This drop-off in support from the miners as well as from other sectors of the Chilean population had its origins in external factors.

According to the monthly financial reports from the Copper Corporation, the Chilean government agency that administered the industry, the U.S. copper strike of 1971 had had a bigger impact on the world copper market than Chilean nationalization. The Copper Corporation mentions nationalization only as an aside in its July report. In its 1972 report, the corporation remarked that not even the conflict between Kennecott and Chile had affected the stability of copper prices.[56] This conflict, however, did have a major impact on Chile itself. In calculating the amount of indemnification owed to Kennecott for nationalizing El Teniente, the Chilean comptroller general determined the sum to be negative $310 million because of years of Kennecott's illegal and "excessive profits." The U.S. copper company recognized the "right of a sovereign nation" to nationalize private property but objected to Chile's refusal to pay compensation as a "violation of international law."[57] Kennecott proceeded to call for a worldwide embargo on Chilean copper. Charges were pressed against Chile in France, Holland, Sweden, Germany, and Italy.[58] The copper embargo hurt Chile severely, preventing it from taking advantage of the low yet fairly stable copper prices.[59] Meanwhile, two significant changes had transformed Chile's relationship to world copper markets. First, nationalization had increased Chile's economic power. From 1970 through September 1973, Chilean copper sold at the recognized London market price, whereas before, Chilean copper had always sold at well below it. Second, although one should not even hint at strict causality, the election of Allende coincided with several decreases in world copper prices. Another huge drop occurred with Allende's inauguration, and thereafter the price gradually decreased and stabilized at pre-1968 levels.[60]

Beyond changes related to the copper industry, Chile faced other, more general economic problems. Inflation was one of them. Although it had dropped from 16 percent in the first three months of 1970 to 3 percent for the comparable period of 1971, inflation did prove to be a growing problem throughout the rest of Allende's administration. One source claims that the cost of living had risen 195 percent from May 1972 to May 1973. Capital flight, which resulted from the elite's unwillingness to invest in Chile under socialist leadership, together with inflation led to shortages of essential goods. Rationing was instituted. World Bank president Robert McNamara summed up

Chile's economic problems in 1972. He listed rampant inflation, a balance of payments deficit of $370 million, and successive annual losses in net foreign exchange reserves; all of these economic problems combined made it impossible for Chile to receive assistance from any international lending institution.[61] Chile's economic problems serve as an example of the "structural trap" of which Howard Richards writes. That is, nationalization brought the same kind of economic problems to Chile in 1971 as it did to Bolivia in 1952, because "the very concept of the control of the means of production is an oxymoron." When a nation-state attempts to gain control over production, it finds that an attempted solution such as nationalization, because it is only partial, may actually prove detrimental. Control of the production site is of little use as long as finance, processing, and marketing are controlled externally.[62] Chile thus fell victim to the "whims" of the international market at the very moment that the copper miners—indeed, all Chileans—looked to Popular Unity for delivery of nationalization's benefits.

Popular Unity government officials were well aware of the external risks that Chile faced. For this reason, government representatives made efforts among the workers to promote the concept of *el hombre nuevo*, the new man, who would sacrifice for the good of the revolution and would respond to moral over material incentives.[63] To this end, Economics Minister Pedro Vuskovic tried to express the massiveness of what Chile was undertaking. "It is a matter not only of making the necessary structural reforms to modify the functioning conditions of the economy and society but rather of qualitatively transforming the nature of society and the economy," Vuskovic said. "It is the long process of the maturation of the Chilean people, the unity of the working classes of the country." Popular Unity supporters felt sure that the Gran Minería miners had already developed this sense of the *hombre nuevo* and would continue to increase production despite anticipated difficulties. Senator Luengo said that "the working class [would] know how to respond to the requirements of the epoch." Senator Altamirano referred specifically to the miners: "We are sure that the workers of [the Gran Minería], whose patriotism no one can doubt, will complete the [task] . . . with efficiency, abnegation, and the will to overcome."[64]

Indeed, the "patriotism" of the Gran Minería workers appeared strong in the beginning of Popular Unity's term in power. In 1971, for example, just a few months after nationalization, Cuban revolutionary leader Fidel Castro visited Chile. He spoke to miners of the need to maintain and increase their discipline, now that their work was serving the interests of the nation rather than of foreign owners. "And this worker, who knows what work is, who knows what sacrifice is, always responds to the interests of his homeland, always responds to the interests of his people," Castro said, "and he is always in the vanguard when his country needs him, when his class needs him!" The miners met his statements with rounds of applause, further reinforcing the opinion that they indeed represented one of Chile's most radical sectors.[65] Because they strongly favored nationalization, the miners made great efforts at maintaining "discipline" and increasing production.

Yet "socialism" and "nationalization" held different meanings for the workers than for the Popular Unity—especially as time went by and Chile encountered economic difficulties. Economics Minister Vuskovic once had to address a working-class crowd upset about the food shortages. The workers did not respond when Vuskovic spoke of nationalization as a way to end Chile's economic dependence. They did applaud when he said that Chile's previous "distribution mechanism" had been set up for the rich, disregarding the working class, and that the Popular Unity would end the suffering. The concept of *el hombre nuevo* was perhaps not shared throughout the population as a whole, as the government had hoped. A principal concern of the Chilean working classes was material well-being. Miners too protested—in the form of strikes—against economic problems caused by external factors. In January 1973, the Chuquicamata workers protested the forced use of rationing cards.[66] The most critical of the strikes, however, took place at the El Teniente mine from April through June 1973.

The prolonged El Teniente strike caused great damage to Chile and to the Popular Unity government. Chile forfeited nineteen thousand metric tons of copper in lost production. The strike also provoked national political problems. The miners demanded that Congress fire Labor Minister Luis Figueroa, longtime labor leader of the National Labor Confederation, and Mining Minister Sergio Bitar. The Congress did indeed suspend these two, along with the ministers of interior and economy. Allende's cabinet was reshuffled as a result of pressures from the El Teniente strike. Furthermore, the strike led to infighting among the executive, legislative, and judicial branches. The supreme court ordered that the nationalized companies be reprivatized.[67] Perhaps even more traumatic for Popular Unity, however, was the fact that the El Teniente strike served as a point of mobilization for other sectors of the population. Agricultural workers, truck drivers, students, and the middle classes all used the opportunity to express their dissatisfaction with inflation and shortages. The political atmosphere became tense during the months of May and June. On several occasions, the government "of the workers" called out the police to control popular demonstrations, and the military attempted a coup on Allende at the end of June 1973.[68] But why did the copper workers strike a nationalized mine in whose administration they participated?

The strike serves as yet another illustration that the Popular Unity and the miners misunderstood each other in terms of what nationalization meant. Because it considered the miners as radical and supportive of nationalization by virtue of their patriotism, Allende's government was taken aback by the El Teniente strike. The government tried to resolve the conflict by appealing to the miners' sense of *el hombre nuevo*. Shortly after the strike began, on 19 April, President Allende called the El Teniente union leaders to the presidential palace to discuss the strike's implications. He detailed the economic and political difficulties facing the country, including efforts by right-wing opposition groups to destabilize the Popular Unity, the damage caused by other strikes (e.g., the infamous truckers' strike of October 1972, in which truckers, subsidized by the U.S. Central Intelligence Agency, effectively paralyzed Chile for nearly a month), and the international problems caused by the copper embargo by France and Holland. Allende presumably intended the leaders to take this information back to the rank and file and convince the workers to call off the strike. Yet the strike continued and even gained momentum, attracting other sectors to the miners' cause. This led Allende to address the issue of Chile's general economic problems in his annual May speech. He said that rationing food so that no one went hungry was preferable to "rationing salaries," as happened in capitalistic societies. He also called for the people to recognize the need for a period of sacrifice in order to make the transformation to socialism a real one. The government could effect an "easy populism," he said, but this would lead to even more inflation, and the workers themselves would be jeopardized.[69] But the strike and the popular uprisings continued into June. So did the government's appeals to the people. Calling for people to put aside egoistic demands and support the revolutionary process, the government circulated leaflets quoting Lenin, Che Guevara, and Fidel Castro. The strike finally had ended by July, but Chile was still suffering from the damage initiated by the strike. President Allende addressed the National Workers Confederation and again appealed for sacrifice.[70] Although he now recognized the economic nature of the strike, the president and his government during the El Teniente strike had viewed it strictly in political terms.

Many officials of the Popular Unity saw the right-wing opposition as manipulating—even inciting—the El Teniente strike in order to destabilize the government and provoke its downfall. Labor Minister Luis Figueroa announced that the government would consider the miners' demands but warned the political Right to stop trying to manipulate the workers. Sergio Bitar stated that Popular Unity representatives had stormed the union hall of the CTC, "proving afterwards that the large majority of its occupants were not [copper] workers but activists of the Right and ultra-right." The statement is of dubious accuracy.[71] Members of Popular Unity claimed that the press had exaggerated the numbers of striking miners. A "significant number" of miners had kept working, they said, and those miners who were striking were being pressured to do so by opportunistic union leaders.

Initially, it is true that significant differences appear to have existed between the leaders' desire to strike and that of the union rank and file. The same disparities may have existed between the *obreros* and the *empleados*. At the time of the strike, a large number of copper union leaders represented the Christian Democratic Party (an opposition party), having been voted into leadership by the rank and file. The union leader who spearheaded the El Teniente strike, Guillermo Medina, later accepted a position in the regime of General Pinochet. At any rate, the government expressed outrage at the fact that right-wing elements were protesting "in the name of the workers."[72] Right-wing opposition groups did indeed latch on to the miners' strike and use it for their own ends. This fact led the government to discredit the strike—or claim that the workers did not truly desire to strike. One Christian Democratic senator illustrated what he believed to be the attitude of the Popular Unity, citing the words of Lenin: "It is necessary to repeat the lie as many times as necessary, until transforming it into truth."[73] However, the lie was not that the El Teniente strike was infiltrated and manipulated by the right wing. It was rather that the rank-and-file miners were so "radical" that they would not have struck against the socialist government for purely economic demands.

The workers, however, considered economic and political goals to be one and the same, and they used the El Teniente strike to express their dissatisfaction with nationalization's unfulfilled promise of increased labor participation. The clamor for increased workers' control in the administration of mining had been growing throughout 1972 and 1973. One year prior to the El Teniente strike, workers in the nationalized Chuquicamata mine had struck to demand increased worker participation in the running of the industry. "Just as before we shouted, 'Take the copper back from the Yankees!'" stated the Chuquicamata strikers, "now we must shout, 'Take the copper back from the communists and give it to the Chileans!'" The Central Committee of the Socialist Party repeated its call for more political power for the workers just a few days before the El Teniente strike broke out, reminding party members of Lenin's dictum that the fundamental problem of revolution is the problem of power. The Socialist Party even demanded workers' control of the national economy. In the midst of the strike, national labor leader Luis Villena addressed the National Workers Confederation. He called on all workers to support the miners. "For eighteen years I've been exploited by imperialism,"

Villena said. "I don't want to be exploited now by the Boss-State." Following the strike, Roberto Córdova resigned as worker representative on the administrative council of El Teniente. "The same injustices and privileges continue as when the gringos were here," he said.[74] Thus, the workers were expressing the feeling that nationalization had brought about a mere transfer of bosses rather than workers' control. The economic element was always present within the workers' more "political" demands. Marxist union leaders had frequently reminded the miners that the foreign companies had been robbing them of the surplus value they produced.[75] The question of who was getting the surplus value now that the mines were nationalized also was foremost in the miners' minds.

Clearly the miners had suffered inflation eroding their wages, which was, after all, the principal cause of the strike. The government in 1972 had attempted to prevent a decrease in workers' real income. It passed a law providing for a 100 percent automatic adjustment, or increase, of all workers' wages and salaries throughout Chile. Those who worked under collective contracts, as did the copper miners, would have sixty days from the publication of the law to incorporate the wage readjustment into existing labor contracts. However, the copper miners had already, since 1943, enjoyed the benefit of the movable wage scale, which automatically adjusted their wages equal to one-half the raise in the consumer price index. Because the wage scale had already granted the miners a 41 percent wage readjustment before the new 100 percent wage law went into effect, the national copper administration deducted the wage increase by that amount. The workers immediately filed a complaint. On 17 April 1973, the appeals board ruled in favor of the administration and ordered the workers to accept the deduction or forgo the readjustment altogether.[76] Thus began the El Teniente strike.

The strike illustrates both the "economic-corporate" spirit of the copper miners and their simultaneous desire to make nationalization work. The fact that the miners were willing to strike for increased wages when the entire working class and Chile as a whole were suffering such severe economic problems shows that the miners were behaving as a labor aristocracy struggling not to lose their status and job security during a time of inflation. Had their strike demands been met, the copper workers would have received pay 10 percent higher than that of any other salaried workers in the country, which they may have felt they deserved given the dangers of mine work and the importance of copper to the national economy. In its negotiations with the miners, the government stated that the spirit of its wage law was not meant to include "readjustments on top of readjustments" or "double readjustments." The workers answered that the letter of the law was clear enough and that it was not necessary to examine the spirit of the law.[77] Chilean copper miners had had a deeply rooted spirit of struggle. That is to say, they had fought the U.S. companies for dozens of years to improve their wages and living conditions, and they were not prepared to abandon this struggle after the government took over the Gran Minería—especially when Chile was experiencing rampant inflation and the world price of copper had just climbed significantly.[78] However, on 29 June, one faction of the army attempted a coup d'état. The coup was put down because of internal dissension within the armed forces, yet the event raised the stakes considerably. The miners then saw that their strike—and all the solidarity strikes and uprisings linked to it— might result in the loss of the Allende government and the reversal of nationalization as well. Therefore, the miners compromised when the government made its next offer. Workers received all the benefits of the government's earlier proposals (paid vacations, pensions, and a guarantee against firing) plus production bonuses for April, May, and June (the months in which very few of the miners had actually produced). In the end, however, the workers had to give up the "double readjustment" that had caused the strike in the first place.[79] Although economic demands obviously held extreme importance for the miners, they were not willing to risk the undoing of nationalization solely for the sake of such demands. The strike ended in July 1973.

Conclusion

The El Teniente strike demonstrates that nationalization occurred within the context of a misunderstanding between the Popular Unity government and the copper miners. This misunderstanding had two main aspects. First of all, the Popular Unity misread the miners' radicalism and their willingness to sacrifice for the survival of the government "of the workers" as it traveled down the path to socialism. Second, the miners and the Popular Unity disagreed as to the meaning of nationalization. Should the El Teniente strike have surprised the government? Perhaps not, if Allende's ministers had examined more closely the history of the miners and those values the miners held dear. Perhaps they might not have tried to manipulate the wage readjustment to the miners' disadvantage. Instead, the Popular Unity would have looked for other ways in which to economize. The miners had engaged in a long struggle for economic benefits, and they saw nationalization as the culmination of this struggle and the victory of the Popular Unity as the guarantee that their victories would be protected. But they were not willing to lose economic benefits especially when a government "of the workers" was in power.

The strike at El Teniente expressed the miners' dissatisfaction with na-

tionalization not only in terms of its inability to meet their economic demands. They were also dissatisfied with nationalization in general. As the
miners saw it, nationalization, in contrast to Chileanization, was to represent a
fundamental change. It was supposed to have given the workers more economic and political power than they had ever had before. Popular Unity
shared this goal, though secondarily to the restoration of Chile's economic
sovereignty. No such thing as economic sovereignty exists, however, within
the structure of modern-day global capitalism. The Popular Unity was aware
of the "structural trap" presented by nationalization. It knew that control of
the means of production offered no guarantee of economic security as long
as the means of exchange remained beyond Chile's control. Therefore, Allende's government sought ways to make internal structural changes that
would combat the external pressures. Such changes included the comptroller
general's determination that Chile owed no compensation to Kennecott and
the government's manipulation of the wage readjustment.

Moreover, the Popular Unity believed that their long history of resistance
meant that the miners were radical enough to sacrifice willingly for the good
of Chile, as defined by the Popular Unity. The strikers' acceptance of the
government's demands after the attempted coup does indicate that the workers were indeed willing to sacrifice to some extent. However, they sacrificed
not as much to protect the Popular Unity as to protect their own conception
of nationalization. Although the miners had expressed their disappointment
with the way nationalization had turned out, they still believed their participation in the industry's administration represented a better alternative to privatization. They hoped that, if Popular Unity stayed in power, nationalization
could eventually become what it was intended to be: a fundamental change
guaranteeing workers' control.

On 11 September 1973, the armed forces, with encouragement from the
U.S. government, launched a coup d'état against Allende and the Popular
Unity, and there began seventeen years of violent repression under the Pinochet military regime. Thousands of Chileans were tortured, killed, or exiled
for perceived subversion. Pinochet's conservative economic advisers instituted the reprivatization of industries that the Popular Unity government had
nationalized. Although reprivatization formed one part of the plan designed
to encourage renewed foreign investment, the "strategic" copper industry remained nationalized during the first several years of Pinochet's rule. The
other element of the plan consisted of severe repression of labor, restoring the
confidence of potential foreign investors. Pinochet dissolved the National
Labor Confederation, froze wages, banned union elections, and outlawed

strikes of more than sixty days' duration. Ironically, the perception of the miners as being a "radical" sector remained; this time it was the miners—and not the government—who suffered the effects of this perception. Many copper miners (especially union leaders) who had been active in the quest for nationalization were jailed or killed. In 1978, the Pinochet regime reinstituted the legality of union elections, yet labor repression continued. In May 1983, nevertheless, the El Teniente copper miners mounted a strike that again mobilized countrywide opposition to the government in power. It was a heroic effort indeed, especially in the face of retaliation much more severe than being fired from the job. Yet here again the same patterns were repeated. After negotiating with the Pinochet regime, the miners agreed to wage concessions.[80] The elected government of Christian Democrat Patricio Aylwin finally succeeded Pinochet's regime in 1990, and although their clout has declined along with the copper industry, it remains to be seen how the miners will take advantage of the political opening to renew their struggle for workers' control.

Notes

The author would like to thank Professor Paul Drake for reading and commenting on a draft of this chapter.

1. See, for example, George M. Ingram, *Expropriation of U.S. Property in South America: Nationalization of Oil and Copper Companies in Peru, Bolivia, and Chile* (New York, 1974); Markos J. Mamalakis, *The Growth and Structure of the Chilean Economy: From Independence to Allende* (New Haven, 1976); Theodore H. Moran, *Multinational Corporations and the Politics of Dependence: Copper in Chile* (Princeton, 1974).

2. Ingram, *Expropriation of U.S. Property*, 220.

3. Paul W. Drake, *Socialism and Populism in Chile, 1932–1952* (Urbana, Ill., 1978), 214–18.

4. United States Department of Labor, Bureau of Labor Statistics, "Chile: Labor Union Membership, 1943," in *Labor Conditions in Latin America*, Latin American Series, no. 21 (Washington, D.C., 1945), 1–2; Confederación de Trabajadores de Chile (CTCh), *Declaración de principios y estatutos de la Confederación de Trabajadores de Chile* (Santiago, 1943), 4–7.

5. Gonzalo Falabella, *Clase, partido y estado: La CUT en el gobierno de la Unidad Popular* (Lima, 1975), 2, 6; Henry Landsberger, Manuel Barrera, and Abel Toro, *El pensamiento del dirigente sindical chileno: Un informe preliminar* (Santiago, 1963), 17–18.

6. Manuel Barrera, *El conflicto obrero en el enclave cuprífero* (Santiago, 1973), 54; Jorge Barría Serón, *Los sindicatos de la Gran Minería del Cobre* (Santiago, 1970), 138–39. A look at the history of the labor movement within the copper industry shows that

the miners had a long history of unrest, starting at El Teniente in 1911. As the century progressed, the copper unions gained in strength and struck for economic petitions such as job security and high wage increases, which they usually received. One early clue suggesting the miners' desire for nationalization consists of the fact that they sought modification of the Código del Trabajo in order to increase the workers' share in profits to more than the listed 6 percent. See Barría, *Los sindicatos de la Gran Minería*, 4–5, 8–9, and Ellen M. Bussey (for the U.S. Department of Labor, Bureau of Labor Statistics), *Foreign Labor Information: Labor in Chile* (Washington, D.C., 1956), 13. Barría attributes the copper miners' isolation from the rest of labor to the fact that the miners were concerned more with their own demands than with those of labor as a whole as well as to the miners' geographical isolation.

7. Barrera, *El conflicto obrero*, 19, 21–22, 28–29, 34. This chapter's author has found no records indicating that women were employed in the Gran Minería. The safe assumption is that the vast majority of workers were men.

8. E. J. Hobsbawm, *Labouring Men: Studies in the History of Labour* (New York, 1964), 273, 277, 286–87.

9. Barrera, *El conflicto obrero*, 85–87, 93–95.

10. Barría, *Los sindicatos de la Gran Minería*, 15, 134, 137; CODELCO (Corporación Del Cobre), *Sección relaciones industriales, 1955–1966*, as cited in Crisóstomo Pizarro, *La huelga obrera en Chile, 1890–1970* (Santiago, 1971), 177.

11. Antonio Gramsci, *Selections from the Prison Notebooks* (New York, 1971), 181; Hobsbawm, *Labouring Men*, 323.

12. Barrera, *El conflicto obrero*, 89; CODELCO, *Estatuto de los trabajadores del cobre* (Santiago, 1970), 8, art. 22.

13. Barrera, *El conflicto obrero*, 74-78, 108.

14. Ibid., 10–11.

15. In that decade, Chilean Augustín Edwards established a monopoly over copper by storing up Chilean copper reserves and hence forcing up the U.S. and British copper prices; for this, he became a national hero. Ingram, *Expropriation of U.S. Property*, 213.

16. Ibid., 213, 218, 226.

17. Mamalakis, *Growth and Structure*, 89–93; CTCh, *Declaración de principios*, 3–4.

18. Gladys Marín, Hugo Fuentes, Mario Juica, Sergio Arriagada, and Pedro Henríquez, *Documentos del XIII Congreso del Partido Comunista de Chile 1965: La juventud chilena junto a la clase obrera por la revolución* (Santiago, 1965), 20, 38–40; Partido Comunista de Chile, *La clase obrera centro de la unidad y motor de los cambios revolucionarios: Documentos del XIII Congreso Nacional del Partido Comunista de Chile* (Santiago, 1965), 20–21, 33, 38.

19. Salvador Allende Gossens, "Mensaje del Ejecutivo, con el que inicia un proyecto de Reforma Constitucional que modifica el Artículo No. 10 de la Constitución Política del Estado," in Eduardo Novoa Monreal, ed., *La nacionalización chilena del cobre: Comentarios y documentos* (Santiago, 1972), 406–7.

20. The historical links are demonstrated in that, in the early twentieth century, labor hero Luis Emilio Recabarren formed the Partido Obrero Socialista, which gave rise to the Federación Obrera de Chile and eventually became the Partido Comunista. Falabella, *Clase, partido y estado*, 3. The statement in the text can only be inferred from the few references to the writings of the CTC listed in Barrera, *El conflicto obrero*, 32, 36, 68.

21. Barrera, *El conflicto obrero*, 62–63; Barría, *Los sindicatos de la Gran Minería*, 98; Manuel Barrera, *El sindicato industrial como instrumento de lucha de la clase obrera chilena* (Santiago, 1971), 155–56.

22. Barrera, *El conflicto obrero*, 67.

23. Ingram, *Expropriation of U.S. Property*, 250.

24. Cited in Barrera, *El conflicto obrero*, 68.

25. Cited in ibid., 96.

26. Pizarro, *La huelga obrera*, 177; Barría, *Los sindicatos de la Gran Minería*, 15, 134, 137.

27. Ingram, *Expropriation of U.S. Property*, 251–52; Barrera, *El conflicto obrero*, 55.

28. Ingram, *Expropriation of U.S. Property*, 252–53; Landsberger, Barrera, and Toro, *El pensamiento del dirigente sindical*, 25.

29. The state of Chile became owner of 51 percent equity in the El Teniente enterprise. As the Kennecott Corporation stated, "In 1967, Kennecott *proposed* that Chile acquire a controlling interest in this profitable venture" (emphasis mine). Kennecott Copper Corporation, *Expropriation of the El Teniente Copper Mine by the Chilean Government* (New York, 1971), 3; Embassy of Chile, *News From Chile*, 31 December 1964; Ingram, *Expropriation of U.S. Property*, 253.

30. Félix Guerrero Páviz, ed., *ENAMI: Memoria y balance, 1969* (Santiago, 1969), 3, 22–23; *News From Chile*, 28 October 1967.

31. Ingram, *Expropriation of U.S. Property*, 269; *News From Chile*, 13 January 1968; El Senado de la República de Chile, "Sesión 25a, en martes 19 de enero de 1971," in *Diario de sesiones del Senado* (Santiago, 1971), 1385–86, 1388.

32. Opponents of Chileanization said the law did not significantly differ from the Nuevo Trato law. The Nuevo Trato law, passed in 1955, attempted to increase Gran Minería production by promising an inverse relation between the amount of production and the tax rate. The law met great criticism because the supposed increased revenue for Chile from increased production was more than canceled out by the loss in tax income. Ingram, *Expropriation of U.S. Property*, 245–47, 256; Barría, *Los sindicatos de la Gran Minería*, 17; Ministerio de Minería, "Decreto No. 1.771, de 23 de diciembre de 1966, sobre franquicias y liberaciones," in Novoa, *La nacionalización chilena*, 384–85, 388.

33. Study by Keith Griffin, cited in Ingram, *Expropriation of U.S. Property*, 262–63; Kennecott Copper Corporation, *Expropriation of the El Teniente Copper Mine*, 3.

34. Allende, "Mensaje del Ejecutivo," 408; El Senado de la República de Chile, "Congreso Pleno, en domingo 11 de julio de 1971," in *Diario de sesiones del Senado* (Santiago, 1971), 18–19; Ingram, *Expropriation of U.S. Property*, 270–71.

35. Cited in Barrera, *El conflicto obrero*, 68.

36. From "Carta abierta [de CTC] al Presidente de la República," *Cobre*, 14 January 1965, as cited in Barría, *Los sindicatos de la Gran Minería*, 24.

37. *El Mercurio*, 24 October 1965, 23; Barrera, *El conflicto obrero*, 56–58, 73–74.

38. Pizarro, *La huelga obrera*, 178–82; Barrera, *El conflicto obrero*, 71, 74–77, 79, 81.

39. Frei's government had in fact committed itself to maintaining a "docile, disciplined labor force" for the foreign companies and, to this end, had enacted legislation to freeze wage increases. Frei quoted in Ingram, *Expropriation of U.S. Property*, 270.

40. Survey information from Landsberger, Barrera, and Toro, *El pensamiento del dirigente sindical*, 7–10, 13; Braden Copper Company, *A Tradition of Service: Community Activities of Braden Copper Company, Chilean Subsidiary of Kennecott Copper Corporation* (New York, [ca. 1965]), 3–5, 9–10, 14–15.

41. Ingram, *Expropriation of U.S. Property*, 240–41; Barrera, *El conflicto obrero*, 95; Marcelo J. Cavarozzi and James F. Petras, "Chile," in *Latin America: The Struggle with Dependency and Beyond* (New York, 1974), 505.

42. Barrera, *El sindicato industrial*, 35; Guerrero, *ENAMI*, 35; *Nuevos Horizontes* (pamphlet for Frei campaign) (Santiago, [ca. 1964]), 2–7.

43. Quoted in Barrera, *El conflicto obrero*, 68–69.

44. See, for example, Pedro Vuskovic, *Exposición del Ministro de Economía, Pedro Vuskovic, ante las mujeres de Santiago, el 29 de julio de 1971, en el Estadio Chile* (Santiago, 1971), 2; El Senado de la República de Chile, "Sesión 25a," 1378.

45. Salvador Allende, "Primer Mensaje del Presidente Salvador Allende ante el Congreso Pleno, 21 mayo 1971," in *Las grandes alamedas: Documentos del Presidente Salvador Allende*, ed. Fundación de Amigos del Centro Gaitán (Bogotá, 1983), 212–13; Allende, "Mensaje del ejecutivo," 404; El Senado de la República de Chile, "Congreso Pleno," 10, 14–17.

46. El Senado de la República de Chile, "Congreso Pleno," 19; Luis Figueroa, "La participación en el Gobierno de la Unidad Popular," in *La vía chilena al socialismo* (Mexico City, 1973), 200; Pedro Vuskovic, "Los rumbos de la economía chilena," *Desarrollo Indoamericano* 5 (1971): 17–18; Salvador Allende, "Segundo Mensaje del Presidente Salvador Allende ante el Congreso Pleno, 21 mayo 1972," in *Las grandes alamedas*, 269.

47. Figueroa, "La participación en el Gobierno," 204. See also Salvador Allende, "Mensaje del Ejecutivo," 418; El Senado de la República de Chile, "Sesión 58a, en martes 20 de abril de 1971," and "Sesión 71a, en miercoles 12 de mayo de 1971," in *Diario de sesiones del Senado* (Santiago, 1971), 3017–54, 3629–44.

48. Sergio Bitar and Crisóstomo Pizarro, *La caída de Allende y la huelga de El Teniente* (Santiago, 1986), 53; Embassy of Chile, *Chile: Summary of Recent Events* (Washington, D.C.), 15 June 1972, 1.

49. Embassy of Chile, *Chile: Summary of Recent Events*, 3 August 1972, 2.

50. For example, the strike at the Yarur textile mill occurred on 28 April 1971. See Peter Winn, *Weavers of Revolution* (Oxford, 1986), 139; Allende, "Primer Mensaje," 223.

51. Kennecott Copper Corporation, *Expropriation of the El Teniente Copper Mine*, 4; Embassy of Chile, *Chile: Summary of Recent Events*, 15 June 1972, 3; Bitar and Pizarro, *La caída de Allende*, 11, 33; El Mercurio, ed., *Breve historia de la Unidad Popular: Documento de "El Mercurio"* (Santiago, 1974), 71; Ingram, *Expropriation of U.S. Property*, 295.

52. CODELCO, *Informe de mercado*, 3 vols. (Santiago, 1971–73), 1:6, 8, 11, 2:13; Allende, "Segundo Mensaje," 247; Salvador Allende, "Tercer Mensaje del Presidente Salvador Allende ante el Congreso Pleno, 21 mayo 1973," in *Las grandes alamedas*, 313; *Chile: Summary of Recent Events* 251 (15 February 1973): 3; Bitar and Pizarro, *La caída de Allende*, 33.

53. Francisco Zapata, *Los mineros de Chuquicamata: ¿Productores o proletarios?* (Mexico City, 1975), 57–58.

54. Ingram, *Expropriation of U.S. Property*, 297–98.

55. Another key instance in the miners' struggle for—and disillusion with—workers' control was the "Strike of Titichoca," which occurred at Chuquicamata in February 1972. The strike was named for a worker who was fired because he had left work early. This conflict demonstrates the tension between the unions and the administrative councils because the strike began when the administrative council defended management in firing the worker. The strike lasted three days and was resolved when Titichoca was rehired. Zapata, *Los mineros de Chuquicamata*, 55–56.

56. CODELCO, *Informe de mercado* 1, no. 7 (July 1971): 3, 5; CODELCO, *Informe de mercado* 2, no. 10 (October 1972): 2.

57. Kennecott Copper Corporation, *Expropriation of the El Teniente Copper Mine*, 2; Kennecott Copper Corporation, *Confiscation of El Teniente, the World's Largest Underground Copper Mine: Kennecott Continues Its Pursuit of Remedies outside of Chile* (New York, 1973), 89.

58. Accounts of the results of these court proceedings are quite interesting. If we look at accounts of the German court ruling, for example, CODELCO and Kennecott agree on the date of the ruling, and that is all. CODELCO stated that the German court ruled in favor of Chile, lifted the embargo, and made Kennecott pay court costs; Kennecott claimed that the German court ruled in its favor because the nationalization violated international law. The Chilean account is supported in other sources. CODELCO, *Informe de mercado* 3, no. 1 (January 1973): 6; Kennecott Copper Corporation, *Confiscation*, i–iv, 69; *Chile: Summary of Recent Events*, 15 February 1973, 3.

59. CODELCO, *Informe de mercado* 2, no. 7 (July 1972): 7–8; no. 8 (August 1972): 9; no. 11 (November 1972): 6.

60. The price in April 1970 (pre-Allende) was 79.2 cents per pound; a year later (prenationalization), it had fallen to 57.2, and by December of that year (postnationalization), the price had dropped to 47.1 cents per pound. In 1973, the world copper price increased and reached especially high levels during the El Teniente strike, when Chile was not able to take advantage of the high price. Then the price dropped during the month of the coup in Chile but made a miraculous recovery the following month.

See CODELCO, *Informe de mercado* 1, no. 12 (December 1971): 17; vol. 2, no. 12 (December 1972): 14; vol. 3, no. 10 (October 1973): 22.

61. Vuskovic, "Los rumbos," 17; El Mercurio, *Breve historia*, 337; "Statement by the Honorable John M. Hennessy, Assistant Secretary of the Treasury for International Affairs before the Subcommittee on Multinational Corporations of the Senate Foreign Relations Committee, March 28, 1973," cited in Kennecott, *Confiscation*, 95. For a good summary of the interplay between the Chilean nationalization and externally driven economic problems, see Paul E. Sigmund, *Multinationals in Latin America: The Politics of Nationalization* (Madison, Wis., 1980), 158–78.

62. Howard Richards, "Six Reflections on *The Political Unconscious*" (letter 59), in *Letters from Quebec* (Toronto, 1992), 23.

63. The concept of *el hombre nuevo* is attributed to Che Guevara.

64. Vuskovic, "Los rumbos," 19; El Senado, "Congreso Pleno," 21, 41.

65. Fidel Castro, "Speech Given by Major Fidel Castro Ruz, Prime Minister of the Revolutionary Government and First Secretary of the Central Committee of the Communist Party of Cuba, before the Miners of Chuquicamata, Chile, on November 14, 1971, Year of Productivity," in *The Speeches of Fidel Castro* (Montreal, 1972), 1:124–25.

66. Vuskovic, "Exposición del Ministro,"27–28; El Mercurio, *Breve historia*, 282.

67. Which rulings these were is not specified. CODELCO, *Informe de mercado* 3, no. 7 (July 1973): 7; El Mercurio, *Breve historia*, 362, 372; Bitar and Pizarro, *La caída de Allende*, 39.

68. El Mercurio, *Breve historia*, 355–62. A brief disclaimer on my sources for this section: I am drawing chiefly on the works of two parties who very much had personal stakes in the matter. One is Sergio Bitar, who was fired from his position as minister of mining. The other is the newspaper *El Mercurio*. *El Mercurio* is known to be an extremely conservative newspaper, one that was consistently hostile to the Popular Unity. The newspaper received $1.5 million in CIA funds during the Popular Unity's stay in power. U.S. Senate, *Hearings before the Select Committee to Study Governmental Operations with Respect to Intelligence Activities of the United States Senate*, 94th Cong., 1st sess., 4–5 December 1975, 176. The Allende government, in fact, sued the newspaper in the summer of 1973 for publishing "an anti-government advertisement which openly called for disobedience." Embassy of Chile, *Chile: A Summary of Recent Events*, 10 July 1973. Furthermore, the same newspaper, which rallied to the cause of the El Teniente miners in 1973, had urged the El Teniente miners not to strike in 1966, saying that their strike only benefited the Soviet Union and would surely bring about the downfall of the " 'Great West.' " Cited in Barrera, *El conflicto obrero*, 72.

69. Bitar and Pizarro, *La caída de Allende*, 20; Allende, "Tercer mensaje," 325–26.

70. Salvador Allende, "Discurso pronunciado por el Presidente de la República, compañero Salvador Allende, en el Plenario de Federaciones de la CUT, 25 julio 1973," in *Las grandes alamedas*, 163–64; El Mercurio, *Breve historia*, 362.

71. Luis Figueroa, "La oposición no puede seguir jugando con los trabajadores," *Las noticias de ultima hora*, 16 April 1973, 14; Bitar and Pizarro, *La caída de Allende*, 27–28 (the accuracy of Bitar's statement is doubtful because it is not footnoted); El Mercurio,

Breve historia, 359; Jaime Ruíz-Tagle, "Huelga en 'El Teniente,'" *El Trimestre Eco-nómico,* no. 40 (October–December 1973): 940–41; reprinted from *Mensaje* 219 (June 1973).

72. *Chile: A Summary of Recent Events,* 10 July 1973, 2; Bitar and Pizarro, *La caída de Allende,* 26–27, 41–42; Vuskovic, *Exposición del ministro,* 8–9. Additional research has indicated that in no other copper strike during the Popular Unity were the social conflicts among the copper workers so sharply present as they were in the El Teniente strike. Contrary to the view presented in *El Mercurio,* it appears that by the end of the first week of May, the entire dynamic of the strike had shifted. More than 60 percent of the original strikers (and the vast majority of these were *obreros*) had returned to work. After this date, the El Teniente strike had become the protest of the *empleados.* See *El Siglo,* 5–6 May, 8–9 May, 12 May, 17 May 1973. It is important to note as well that, as was the case with the October 1972 truckers' strike, the CIA may have been directly or indirectly funding the El Teniente strike. Zapata, *Los mineros de Chuquicamata,* 70; U.S. Senate, *Hearings before the Select Committee,* 30–32.

73. Quoted in El Mercurio, *Breve historia,* 335.

74. El Mercurio, *Breve historia,* 183, 333–34, 398; Comité Central, Partido So-cialista, "Control y dirección de la clase obrera sobre la economía," *Las noticias de ultima hora,* 9 April 1973, 6.

75. Ruíz-Tagle, "Huelga," 940.

76. Bitar and Pizarro, *La caída de Allende,* 16, 19; Ruíz-Tagle, "Huelga," 937–38.

77. Ruíz-Tagle, "Huelga," 938–39.

78. Ibid., 939. Indeed, the copper price had jumped 16¢ in two months at the outbreak of the El Teniente strike.

79. Bitar and Pizarro, *La caída de Allende,* 43; CODELCO, *Informe de mercado* 3, no. 7 (July 1973): 7.

80. Phil O'Brien and Jackie Roddick, *Chile: The Pinochet Decade* (London, 1983), 4–7, 80–81, 104–5; Pamela Constable and Arturo Valenzuela, *A Nation of Enemies: Chile under Pinochet* (New York, 1991), 242–43.

WORKERS' CONTROL IN LATIN AMERICA

JONATHAN C. BROWN

By now, it has become clear that the role of the workers in making history in Latin America cannot be diminished even though their voices are not heard as clearly as those of the politicians and the elite. Workers were, in fact, full participants in the great events that defined their nations during the half century following the Great Depression.

These chapters leave little doubt that laborers participated actively in the restructuring of the economies and societies of their countries. Michael Braga shows that the sugar mill workers, in spite of—or, perhaps, because of—their poverty and hunger, helped set Cuba's reform agenda. Their dramatic seizures of the mills made it impossible for owners and politicians to ignore their demands. The railway workers performed much the same function in Guatemala. They directed their union activities toward defeat of unpopular rulers and support of reformist politicians. Marc McLeod posits that the program of the Guatemalan revolution had originated among the masses themselves. In Bolivia, the miners also had been the driving force behind the revolution of 1952. Andrew Boeger makes clear that the mineworkers had sacrificed and struggled successfully to have their concerns recognized at the national level. In Peru too, as Josh DeWind demonstrates, workers at the foreign-owned copper company contributed to national affairs. DeWind's miners, however, pursued goals often at odds with those of the reformist government and especially contrary to the objectives of their radical labor leaders. That workers had the capacity to make themselves a political force is also evident in the case of Brazil. Joel Wolfe shows that women textile workers would not be deterred even from provoking the activism of their male-dominated unions. Nor had

Brazilian workers been shy about forcing national political leaders like Getúlio Vargas to respond to their concerns.

These chapters also suggest that, from here on out, scholars and students
ought to be wary of analyzing reform movements as if they were creatures of
their middle-class or elite leaders. Most major social and economic reforms
have contained working-class components. In Mexico, workers contributed
mightily to the oil nationalization, for which the government ever since has
claimed sole credit. The same might be said for Argentine railway workers. No
longer can the railway nationalization be attributed merely to the popular
leader, Juan Perón. As María Celina Tuozzo demonstrates, the workers had
been struggling for decades against British owners considerably out of touch
with the technological and managerial requirements of the age. Nor have
workers opposed industrial modernization. They do not resist improvements
to the productivity of industries in which they work. According to Andrea
Spears, Mexican railway workers only opposed being made scapegoats for the
unwillingness of managers to reform themselves as well. Laborers merely
refuse to bear the sole burden of industrial progress while others reap the
benefits.

For all their support of nationalist causes and all their struggles against
foreign exploitation, the workers in Latin America certainly have not allowed
themselves to become the tools of manipulative domestic politicians. Juan
Perón rose to power because he championed what workers for so long had
been advocating, namely social justice. Nonetheless, as Michael Snodgrass
demonstrates, the caudillo's working-class supporters never abandoned their
efforts to define Peronism according to their own criteria. That workers with
independent agendas clashed with their leaders has become a common theme
in this book. The "peaceful road to socialism" in Chile displayed much the
same internal dynamism. The copper miners did not give up their own goals
just because they finally had a government that claimed to represent their
interests. Joanna Swanger shows that even Salvador Allende had to contend
with working-class participation for which his socialist political philosophy
had not quite prepared him. In all these cases, the conclusion is obvious. Latin
American workers have not permitted themselves to be manipulated. If anything, the working class has imposed its demands and agenda on the politicians.[1] How else can one account for the power of the numerous revolutionary,
reformist, and populist movements of twentieth-century Latin America?

Why did these workers impose themselves on historical events? In each
case, they were motivated by their experience in the workplace and in their
communities. Workers' control arises from the shop floor because laborers and

their families respond rigorously to the concrete situations of their lives. They did not merely submit to the new demands of twentieth-century industry but actively attempted to reshape those conditions. Workers fought the racism of their foreign owners and the contempt of middle managers. They struggled to create healthy communities and to provide educational opportunities for their progeny. They intervened to preserve or reassert control over their own lives in the shops and in the mines. It is mistaken, however, to believe that workers will always be unified. Case after case has demonstrated that workers too engage in ethnic and gender discrimination and fight each other tenaciously for jobs. But sometimes, their struggles among themselves and against the employers held important consequences for the nation and for the process of industrialization. As E. P. Thompson says, no worker "ever had surplus value taken out of his hide without finding some way of fighting back," thus forcing the economy to develop in unexpected ways.[2] In Latin America, the "fighting back" also forced political life to take new directions. Finally, these vignettes amply illustrate that, although workers suffered setbacks from middle-class reaction and military repression, their struggles for workers' control continue into the future.

Nowadays, the cynic may say that the labor movements ultimately depicted in this volume have failed, because Latin America currently is reprivatizing major industries and laying off redundant employees by the tens of thousands. If our book proves nothing else, it does show that the working people of Latin America cannot be written off. Their activities often are not apparent, as we explain, because the media is dominated by the elites. Following the long Latin American depression of the 1980s, labor is once again being dismissed as a factor in national life. Yet we know from our research that the working people were not intimidated by the massacres, deportations, arrests, and tortures. They always reemerged afterward to participate in—even instigate—important national events. We also know that the workers were instrumental in resisting and defying the military governments of Brazil, Chile, and Argentina in the 1970s and early 1980s.[3] They helped bring about the transition to democracy, even though the bourgeois media minimizes the evidence of their prominent roles. They were not the subjects of our book, but someday these working people too will have their stories told by another generation of historians.

The notion of "failure" presents several other problems too. Perhaps one might say that working people may have made a mistake during this long middle period in placing too much faith in the state, especially now that it has become painfully clear that the state has failed to live up to its end of the bargain. Our chapters deal with various episodes in the development of populism in Latin America. In this process, the workers and the state moved their separate struggles forward in concert. But the "failure," if that is what one calls the recent neoliberal trend, is the work of the political leadership and not labor's rank and file. In the middle years, corrupt political elites had so badly mismanaged the economies that labor had helped them to consolidate under state control that privatization, the resale of economic assets to private interests, remains their only salvation. (None of the authors of this volume suggests that privatization is the only solution, but governing elites are now advocating just that.) But the perceived need for extensive economic restructuring is not labor's doing. Can labor be blamed for the bank failures in Venezuela? The breakdown of public services in Lima? The monetary devaluation of Mexico? The venality of Brazilian politicians? Nonetheless, in being laid off and having their incomes reduced, workers are made to pay for the folly of those same politicians who are now restructuring and privatizing the economies. These episodes indicate not labor's failure but the failure of the state.

The contribution of workers to the histories of their nations is not linear but cyclical. Twentieth-century resistance of workers has led neither to socialist nirvana nor to permanent defeat. At this moment of apparent retreat, they are simply realigning themselves within the new global economic system, assessing the new environment. Admittedly, their initial assessments have not been favorable. "Up to now, we have not seen that the privatizations have brought anything good to the nation," labor leaders in Córdoba, Argentina, said recently. "We only see unemployment, poverty, and that the nation remains without any recourse while the external debt grows and grows."[4] Workers do not give up. Gradually, they will work out ways to fight for their needs, maybe by developing new strategies. Indeed, Latin America may be poised on the cusp of another round of working-class assertiveness as in the 1930s, previous to which labor had also been written off. As we note in the introduction, "the struggle for workers' control never ends. It is constantly being negotiated everywhere, at all times, and at some level."

What makes these conclusions about workers' control possible? It is the imaginative effort that these and other scholars have expended in discovering the voices of the urban and industrial workers. The introduction to this volume refers to the near monopoly of historical resources by literate Latin Americans and foreigners. But by no means is it impossible to uncover the agency of laborers in the histories of their countries. The researcher can hear the muted voices of workers in the correspondence of employers. Who can read the dispatches of U.S. managers and U.S. diplomats without learning of the artful resistance of Cuban sugar workers? Of Mexican petroleum and railway workers? Of Peruvian and Bolivian miners? The researcher need only discount the obvious prejudices of managers to understand the underlying conflicts between foreign capital and native-born workers in Argentina and Chile.

By the same token, the researcher must also deflect the biases of national sources. For example, political and union leaders who often claim to represent labor may not, in fact, reflect the exact sentiments of the workers. (Government and union officials, after all, have different perspectives—usually those of the middle class.) Yet, the researcher may presume, the workers do find expression, at least indirectly, in official correspondence and in the pronouncements of popular politicians. Tuozzo and Brown find fascinating details about labor's effect on employers in the diplomatic documents of the British Foreign Office and the State Department. The researcher will also learn much from the literature of labor leaders. Tuozzo, McLeod, and Swanger utilize union documents to explore the attitudes and opinions of workers. The chapters by Snodgrass and Swanger indicate that newspapers reveal surprising details about labor conflicts. One may also find much information about workers in government documents and company records. These sources reveal that the workers have been just as willing to resist the shortsighted dictates of domestic capitalists and government officials as of foreign owners, as Braga, Spears, and Boeger clearly demonstrate in this volume.

But the best sources of information, of course, come from the workers themselves. Nothing can substitute for Wolfe's interviews with retired textile workers, for Boeger's conversations with miners at Chojlla, and for DeWind's personal observations of Peruvian miners during the Cerro de Pasco strikes. None of these sources are foolproof, however. Historians would be wise to utilize as many different resources as possible. Moreover, the scholar has to use them with sympathy—with respect—for the workers. Anything less would result in the denigration of their contributions to history. On the issues of culture and gender, the chapter by Joel Wolfe deals with gender; those by DeWind and Boeger treat both gender and culture, particularly the residual influence of indigenous culture from which many mineworkers originated.[5] But our primary contributions—showing how workplace experiences influence behavior and indicating how labor can impact a nation's history—remain in clear focus in each chapter of this volume.

None of the authors in this volume suggests that only the study of the working class will reveal the authentic causality of modern Latin American history. Quite the contrary. We merely desired to isolate one group, the industrial workers, to test our hypotheses concerning workers' control. Our investigations of these few episodes of the activism of the urban working class reveal to us how futile monocausal explanations really are. Consequently, despite their influence, the urban and industrial workers cannot be credited—nor disparaged—for all the twists and turns of modern Latin American history. Nor do we conclude that industrial workers compose the most influential group among the popular classes impinging on the histories of their nations. The peasants and rural proletarians deserve a share of the credit. Even though their voices have been recorded in fewer numbers even than those of urban workers, the peasants ought not be underestimated in their contributions to the histories of their nations. Their role has been particularly relevant to the four social revolutions occurring in Latin America during this century: the Mexican of 1910, the Bolivian of 1952, the Cuban of 1959, and the Nicaraguan of 1979.[6] Many of the industrial workers who figure in this volume, after all, had had intimate experiences with rural life. They had relatives in the hinterlands or themselves had grown up in the countryside. To the new industrial workplace they brought strategies of resistance developed by their peasant forebears. Workers' control, therefore, has complex antecedents. Did first-generation industrial workers return to influence the struggles of their country cousins? Until rural workers receive proper attention from scholars, no one can safely accept facile explanations about Latin America. Indeed, its history contains more puzzles than can be imagined.

Nor do we claim that workers' control is the only paradigm with which to explain the behavior of those who work for a wage. Indeed, human behavior is so complex that gender, ideology, race, ethnicity, economic structure, popular culture, class antagonisms, and state formation must not be discarded as useful tools for discovering the many facets of the working class. One thing is certain. The closer scholars get to the lives and experiences of workers and peasants, the more they can make sense of the complexity of history. Perhaps this is the enduring contribution of the concept of workers' control.

Notes

1. See particularly Ruth Berins Collier and David Collier, *Shaping the Political Arena: Critical Junctures, the Labor Movement, and Regime Dynamics* (Princeton, 1991).

2. E. P. Thompson, "The Poverty of Theory or an Orrery of Errors," in *The Poverty of Theory and Other Essays* (London, 1978), 154.

3. Liza Cox, "Repression and Rank-and-File Pressure during the Argentine Process of National Reorganization" (master's thesis, University of Texas at Austin, 1995); Isabel Ribeiro de Olívera, *Travalho e política: As origenes do Partido dos Trabalhadores* (Petrópolis, Brazil, 1988); Margaret Keck, *The Workers' Party and Democratization in Brazil* (New Haven, 1992).

4. As quoted in *La Jornada* (Mexico City), 7 July 1995.

5. This book is not written to contribute to the discussion on gender and culture per se. The reader instead is referred to several recent contributions: *Rituals of Rule, Rituals of Resistance: Public Celebrations and Popular Culture in Mexico*, ed. William H. Beezley, Cheryl English Martin, and William E. French (Wilmington, Del., 1994); *Everyday Forms of State Formation: Revolution and the Negotiation of Rule in Modern Mexico*, ed. Gilbert M. Joseph (Durham, N.C., 1994); Steve J. Stern, *The Secret History of Gender: Women, Men, and Power in Late Colonial Mexico* (Chapel Hill, 1995).

6. Fortunately, historians are engaged in just such work. Some seminal works for twentieth-century Latin America include Florencia E. Mallon, *The Defense of Community in Peru's Central Highlands* (Princeton, 1986); Barbara Weinstein, *The Amazon Rubber Boom, 1850–1920* (Stanford, 1983); Catherine LeGrand, *The Expansion of the Colombian Frontier, 1830–1936* (Albuquerque, 1986); Peter S. Linder, "Agriculture and Rural Society in Pre-Petroleum Venezuela: The Sur del Lago Zuliano, 1880–1920" (Ph.D. diss., University of Texas at Austin, 1992); Brian Loveman, *Struggle in the Countryside: Politics and Rural Labor in Chile, 1919–1973* (Bloomington, Ind., 1976); David McCreery, *Rural Guatemala: 1760–1940* (Stanford, 1994); Jean Meyer, *The Cristero Rebellion: The Mexican People between Church and State, 1926–1929* (Cambridge, England, 1976); *Riot, Rebellion, and Revolution: Rural Social Conflict in Mexico*, ed. Friedrich Katz (Princeton, 1988); William Roseberry, *Coffee and Capitalism in the Venezuelan Andes* (Austin, Tex., 1983); Mario Samper, *Generations of Settlers: Rural Households and Markets on the Costa Rican Frontier, 1850–1935* (Boulder, Colo., 1990); John Tutino, *From Insurrection to Revolution in Mexico: Social Bases of Agrarian Violence, 1750–1940* (Princeton, 1986); Cliff Welch, "Rivalry and Unification: Mobilising Rural Workers in São Paulo on the Eve of the Brazilian *Golpe* of 1964," *Journal of Latin American Studies* 27, pt. 1 (1995): 161–87; John Womack Jr., *Zapata and the Mexican Revolution* (New York, 1968); Douglas K. Yarrington, "Duaca in the Age of Coffee: Land, Society, and Politics in a Venezuela District, 1830–1936" (Ph.D. diss., University of Texas at Austin, 1992). Particularly relevant to this evolving historiography of the peasants is the approach of "subaltern studies." See Florencia E. Mallon, *Peasant and Nation: The Making of Postcolonial Mexico and Peru* (Berkeley, 1995).

SELECTIVE BIBLIOGRAPHY
of Twentieth-Century
Latin American Labor History

General

Andrews, George Reid. "Latin American Workers." *Journal of Social History* 21 (1987): 311–26.

Bergquist, Charles. *Labor in Latin America: Comparative Essays on Chile, Argentina, Venezuela, and Colombia*. Stanford, 1986.

Chaney, Elsa M., and Mary García Castro, eds. *Muchachas No More: Household Workers in Latin America and the Caribbean*. Philadelphia, 1989.

Collier, Ruth Berins. "Popular Sector Incorporation and Political Supremacy: Regime Evolution in Brazil and Mexico." In *Brazil and Mexico: Patterns in Late Development*, edited by Silvia Ann Hewlitt and Richard S. Weinert. Philadelphia, 1982.

Collier, Ruth Berins, and David Collier. *Shaping the Political Arena: Critical Junctures, the Labor Movement, and Regime Dynamics*. Princeton, 1991.

Conniff, Michael L., ed. *Latin American Populism in Comparative Perspective*. Albuquerque, 1982.

Da Costa, Emilia Viotti. "Experience versus Structure: New Tendencies in the History of Labor and the Working Class in Latin America." *International Labor and Working-Class History* 36 (Fall 1989): 3–24.

Evans, Judith. "Results and Prospects: Some Observations on Latin American Labor Studies." *International Labor and Working Class History* 16 (1979): 29–39.

González Casanova, Pablo, ed. *Historia del movimiento obrero en América Latina*. 4 vols. Mexico City, 1984–85.

Hall, Michael M., and Hobart A. Spalding Jr. "The Urban Working Class and Early Latin American Labour Movements, 1880–1930." In *Cambridge History of Latin America*, edited by Leslie Bethell. Vol. 4. Cambridge, England, 1986.

Kofas, Jon V. *The Struggle for Legitimacy: Latin American Labor and the United States, 1930–1960*. Tempe, Ariz., 1994.

McCreery, David J., Todd A. Diacon, and Cliff Welch, eds. *Latin American Labor: History and Problems*. Birmingham, 1994.

Maram, Sheldon L., and Gerald M. Greenfield, eds. *Latin American Labor Organizations*. Westport, Conn., 1987.

Mörner, Magnus. *Adventurers and Proletarians: The Story of Migrants in Latin America*. Pittsburgh, 1985.

Roseberry, William, Lowell Gudmudson, and Mario Samper Kutschbach, eds. *Coffee, Society, and Power in Latin America*. Baltimore, 1995.

Roxborough, Ian. "Issues in Labor Historiography." *Latin American Research Review* 21 (1986): 178–88.

Sofer, Eugene F. "Recent Trends in Latin American Labor Historiography." *Latin American Research Review* 15 (1980): 167–76.

Spalding, Hobart A., Jr. *Organized Labor in Latin America: Historical Case Studies of Workers in Dependent Societies*. New York, 1977.

Torre, Juan Carlos, and Elizabeth Jelín. "Los nuevos trabajadores en América Latina: Una reflexión sobre la tesis de la aristocracia obrera." *Desarrollo económico* 22, no. 85 (1982): 3–23.

Andean Region (Bolivia, Peru, Ecuador, Colombia, Venezuela)

Archila Neira, Mauricio. *Cultura e identidad obrera: Colombia, 1910–1945*. Bogotá, 1991.

Babb, Florence E. *Between Field and Cooking Pot: The Political Economy of Market Women in Peru*. Austin, 1989.

Barcelli S., Augustín. *Medio siglo de luchas sindicales revolucionarias en Bolivia, 1905–1955*. La Paz, 1956.

Barrios de Changara, Domitila, with Moema Viezzer. *"Let Me Speak!": Testimony of Domitila, a Woman of the Bolivian Mines*. Translated by Victoria Ortiz. London, 1978.

Bauch, Elizabeth. "We Shall Not Lose the Bread of Our Children: Strikes at a U.S. Copper Company in Southern Peru." Ph.D. diss., Columbia University, 1988.

Blanchard, Peter. *The Origins of the Peruvian Labor Movement, 1883–1991*. Albuquerque, 1976.

Bonilla, Heraclio. *El minero de los andes: Una aproximación a su estudio*. Lima, 1974.

Braun, Herbert. *The Assassination of Gaitán: Public Life and Urban Violence in Colombia*. Madison, Wis., 1985.

Brown, Jonathan C., and Peter S. Linder. "Trabajadores en petróleo extranjero: México y Venezuela, 1920–1948." *Las inversiones extranjeras en América Latina, 1850–1930: Nuevos debates y problemas en historia económica*. Edited by Carlos Marichal. Mexico City, 1995.

Caicedo, Edgar. *Historia de las luchas sindicales en Colombia*. Bogotá, 1982.

Collins, Jane L. *Unseasonal Migration: The Effects of Rural Labor Scarcity in Peru*. Princeton, 1989.

Contreras, Manuel E. "Mano de obra en la minería estañífera de principios de siglo, 1900–1925." *Historia y Cultura* 8 (1985): 97–134.

Davis, Charles L. *Political Control and Working Class Mobilization: Venezuela and Mexico*. Lexington, Ky., 1981.

Delgado-Parrado, Guillermo. "Articulations of Group Identity and Class Formation among the Bolivian Tin Miners." Ph.D. diss., University of Texas at Austin, 1987.

DeWind, Josh. "From Peasants to Miners: Background to Strikes in the Mines of Peru." *Science and Society* 39 (1975): 44–72.

——. *Peasants Become Miners: The Evolution of Industrial Mining Systems in Peru, 1902–1974*. New York, 1987.

Dunkerley, James. *Rebellion in the Veins: Political Struggle in Bolivia*. London, 1984.

Ellner, Steve. *Los partidos políticos y su disputa por el control del movimiento sindical en Venezuela, 1936–1948*. Caracas, 1980.

——. "Welfare, Oil Workers, and the Labor Movement in Venezuela." In *Welfare, Equity, and Development in Latin America*, edited by Christopher Abel and Colin Lewis. London, 1989.

Flores Galindo, Alberto. *Los mineros de la Cerro de Pasco, 1900–1930*. Lima, 1974.

Godio, Julio. *El movimiento obrero venezolano, 1850–1980*. 3 vols. Caracas, 1980–84.

Greaves, Thomas, and Xavier Albó. "An Anatomy of Dependency: A Bolivian Tin Miners' Strike." In *Political Participation in Latin America*, edited by Mitchell A. Seligson and John A. Booth. Vol. 2. New York, 1979.

Greenfield, Gerald, ed. *Organized Labor in Venezuela*. Westport, Conn., 1990.

Jiménez, Michael F. "Citizens of the Kingdom: Towards a Social History of Radical Christianity in Latin America." *International Labor and Working Class History* 35 (1988): 3–21.

Keremitsis, Dawn. "Women Workers in Transition: The Sexual Divison of the Labor Force in Mexico and Colombia." *Americas* 4 (1984): 491–504.

Kruijt, Dirk, and Menno Vellinga. *Labor Relations and Multinational Corporations: The Cerro de Pasco Corporation in Peru (1902–1974)*. Assen, The Netherlands, 1979.

Laite, Julian. *Industrial Development and Migrant Labor in Latin America*. Austin, 1981.

——. "Miners and National Politics in Peru, 1900–1974." *Journal of Latin American Studies* 12 (1980): 317–40.

Langer, Erick D. "Labor Strikes and Reciprocity on Chuquisaca Haciendas." *Hispanic American Historical Review* 65 (1985): 255–78.

LeGrand, Catherine. "Colombian Transformations: Peasants and Wage-Labourers in the Santa Marta Banana Zone." *Journal of Peasant Studies* 11 (1984): 178–200.

Linder, Peter S. "Coerced Labor in Venezuela, 1880–1936." *Historian* 57 (1994): 43–58.

Lora, Guillermo. *A History of the Bolivian Labour Movement, 1848–1971*. Edited and abridged by Laurence Whitehead and translated by Christine Whitehead. Cambridge, England, 1977.

Martin, Gail. "The Bolivian Mineworkers Federation (FSTMB), 1952–1965: Labour, Politics, and Economic Development." Ph.D. diss., Portsmouth Polytechnic University, England, 1984.

Mata, Celestino. *Historia sindical de Venezuela, 1813–1985*. Caracas,1985.

Medhurst, Kenneth N. *The Church and Labour in Colombia*. Manchester, England, 1984.

Middleton, Alan. "Division and Cohesion in the Working Class: Artisans and Wage Labourers in Ecuador." *Journal of Latin American Studies* 14 (May 1982): 171–94.

Moncayo, Víctor, and Fernando Rojas. *Luchas obreras y política laboral en Colombia*. Bogotá, 1978.

Nash, June. "Resistance as Protest: Women in the Struggle of Bolivian Tin Mining Communities." In *Women Cross-Culturally: Change and Challenge*, edited by Ruby Rohrlich-Leavitt. The Hague, 1975.

———. *We Eat the Mines and the Mines Eat Us: Dependency and Exploitation in Bolivian Tin Mines*. New York, 1979.

O'Connor, Alan. "The Miner's Radio Stations in Bolivia: A Culture of Resistance." *Journal of Communication* 40 (1990): 102–10.

Parker, David S. "Peruvian Politics and the Eight-Hour Day: Rethinking the 1919 General Strike." *Canadian Journal of History* 30 (1995): 417–38.

Parker, Dick. "Sources on Working-Class History in Venezuela, 1850–1964." *International Labor and Working Class History* 27 (1985): 83–99.

Pineo, Ronn F. "Reinterpreting Labor Militancy: The Collapse of the Cacao Economy and the General Strike of Guayaquil, Ecuador, 1922." *Hispanic American Historical Review* 68 (1988): 707–36.

Platt, Tristan. "Conciencia andina y conciencia proletaria: *Ohuyaruna* y *ayllu* en el norte de Potosí." *HISLA* 2 (1983): 47–73.

Rodríguez Ostria, Gustavo. *El socavón y el sindicato: Ensayos históricos sobre los trabajadores mineros, siglos xix–xx*. La Paz, 1991.

Sowell, David. *The Early Colombian Labor Movement: Artisans and Politics in Bogotá, 1832–1919*. Philadelphia, 1992.

Sulmont, Denis. *Historia del movimiento minero metalúrgico*. Lima, 1980.

———. *El movimiento obrero en el Perú, 1900–1956*. Lima, 1975.

Tennassee, Paul Nehru. *El papel de los obreros petroleros en Venezuela durante el período 1918–1948*. Caracas, 1980.

Urrutia Montoya, Miguel. *The Development of the Colombian Labor Movement*. New Haven, 1969.

Volk, Steven S. "Class, Union, Party: The Development of a Revolutionary Union Movement in Bolivia (1905–1952)." *Science and Society* 39 (1975): 26–43.

Whitehead, Laurence. "Miners as Voters: The Electoral Process in Bolivia's Mining Camps." *Journal of Latin American Studies* 13 (1981): 313–46.

———. "Sobre el radicalismo de los trabajadores mineros de Bolivia." *Revista mexicana de sociología* 42 (1980): 465–96.

Brazil

Andrews, George Reid. "Black and White Workers: São Paulo, Brazil, 1888–1928." *Hispanic American Historical Review* 68 (1988): 491–524.

———. *Blacks and Whites in São Paulo, Brazil, 1888–1988*. Madison, Wis., 1991.

Benevides, Maria Victoria. *O PTB e o trabalhismo: Partido e sindicato em São Paulo*. São Paulo, 1989.

Castro e Gomes, Angela Maria. *A invenção do trabalhismo*. Rio de Janeiro, 1988.

Conniff, Michael L. *Urban Politics in Brazil: The Rise of Populism, 1925–1945*. Pittsburgh, 1981.

———. "Voluntary Associations in Rio de Janeiro, 1870–1945: A New Approach to Urban Social Dynamics." *Journal of Interamerican Studies* 17 (1975): 64–81.

Da Costa, Emilia Viotti. "Brazilian Workers Rediscovered." *International Labor and Working-Class History* 22 (1982): 217–32.

Diacon, Todd A. *Millenarian Vision, Capitalist Reality: Brazil's Contestado Rebellion, 1912–1916.* Durham, N.C., 1991.

Fausto, Boris. *Trabalho urbano e conflito social.* São Paulo, 1976.

French, John D. *The Brazilian Workers' ABC: Class Conflict and Alliances in Modern São Paulo.* Chapel Hill, 1991.

——. "Workers and the Rise of Adhemarista Populism in São Paulo, 1945–1947." *Hispanic American Historical Review* 68 (1988): 1–43.

Grossi, Yonne de Souza. *Mina de Morro Velho: A extração do homen: Uma história de experiência operária.* Rio de Janeiro, 1981.

Hahner, June. *Poverty and Politics: The Urban Poor in Brazil, 1870–1920.* Albuquerque, 1986.

Harding, Timothy. "The Political History of Organized Labor Movement in Brazil." Ph.D. diss., Stanford University, 1973.

Humphrey, John. *Capitalist Control and Workers' Struggle in the Brazilian Auto Industry.* Princeton, 1983.

Leite Lopes, José Sérgio. *A tecelagem dos conflitos de classe na cidade das Chaminés.* São Paulo, 1988.

Levine, Robert M. *Urban Workers under the Brazilian Republic.* Glasgow, Scotland, 1981.

Loyola, Maria Andréa. *Os sindicatos e o PTB: Estudo de um caso em Minas Gerais.* Petrópolis, Brazil, 1980.

Malloy, James M. *The Politics of Social Security in Brazil.* Pittsburgh, 1979.

Maranhão, Ricardo. *Sindicato e democratização: Brasil, 1945–1950.* São Paulo, 1979.

Mericle, Kenneth S. "Conflict Resolution in the Brazilian Industrial Relations System." Ph.D. diss., University of Wisconsin–Madison, 1974.

Moisés, José Alvaro. *Greve de massa e crise política: Estudo da greve dos 300 mil em São Paulo, 1953–1954.* São Paulo, 1978.

Paoli, Maria Célia. "Working-Class São Paulo and Its Representations, 1900–1940." *Latin American Perspectives* 14 (1987): 204–25.

Ribeiro de Olivera, Isabel. *Trabalho e política: As origenes do Partido dos Trabalhadores.* Petrópolis, Brazil, 1988.

Skidmore, Thomas E. "Workers and Soldiers: Urban Labor Movements and Elite Responses in Twentieth-Century Latin America." In *Elites, Masses, and Modernization in Latin America, 1850–1930,* edited by Virginia Bernhard. Austin, Tex., 1979.

Vianna, Luiz Werneck. *Liberalismo e sindicato no Brasil.* 2d ed. Rio de Janeiro, 1978.

Weffort, Francisco C. *O populismo na política brasileira.* Rio de Janeiro, 1980.

Weinstein, Barbara. *The Amazon Rubber Boom, 1850–1920.* Stanford, 1983.

——. "The Industrialists, the State, and the Issue of Worker Training and Social Services in Brazil, 1930–1950." *Hispanic American Historical Review* 70 (1990): 397–404.

Welch, Cliff. *Lutas camponesas no interior paulista: Memorias de irineu Luis de Moraes.* Rio de Janeiro, 1992.

——. "Rivalry and Unification: Mobilizing Rural Workers in São Paulo on the Eve of the Brazilian *Golpe* of 1964." *Journal of Latin American Studies* 27 (1995): 161–88.

Wolfe, Joel. "Anarchist Ideology, Worker Practice: The 1917 General Strike and the Formation of São Paulo's Working Class." *Hispanic American Historical Review* 71 (1991): 809–46.

——. "'Father of the Poor' or 'Mother of the Rich'?: Getúlio Vargas, Industrial Workers, and Constructions of Class, Gender, and Populism in São Paulo, 1930–1954." *Radical History Review* 58 (1994): 80–111.

——. *Working Women, Working Men: São Paulo and the Rise of Brazil's Industrial Working Class, 1900–1955.* Durham, N.C., 1993.

Central America and the Caribbean

Aguilar, Luis E. *Cuba 1933: Prologue to Revolution.* Ithaca, N.Y., 1972.

Bishop, Edwin. "The Guatemalan Labor Movement, 1944–1959." Ph.D. diss., University of Wisconsin, 1959.

Bourgois, Philippe I. *Ethnicity at Work: Divided Labor on a Central American Banana Plantation.* Baltimore, 1989.

Bush, Archer C. "Organized Labor in Guatemala, 1944–1949: A Case Study of an Adolescent Labor Movement in an Underdeveloped Country." Latin American Seminar Reports no. 2, Colgate University, 1950.

Carr, Barry. "Mill Occupations and Soviets: The Mobilisation of Sugar Workers in Cuba, 1917–1933." *Journal of Latin American Studies* 28 (1996): 129–58.

Chomsky, Aviva. *"A Perfect Slavery": West Indian Workers and the United Fruit Company in Costa Rica, 1870–1950.* Baton Rouge, 1996.

Conniff, Michael L. *Black Labor on a White Canal: Panama, 1904–1981.* Pittsburgh, 1985.

Córdova, Efrén. *Castro and the Cuban Labor Movement: Statecraft and Society in a Revolutionary Period (1959–1961).* Lanham, Md., 1987.

——. *El trabajador cubano en el estado de obreros y campesinos.* Miami, 1990.

Galvin, Miles E. *The Organized Labor Movement in Puerto Rico.* London, 1979.

García, Angel, and Piotr Mironchuk. *Los soviets obreros y campesinos en Cuba.* Havana, 1987.

Ghai, Dharam P., Cristóbal Kay, and Peter Peek. *Labour and Development in Rural Cuba.* New York, 1988.

Gleijeses, Piero. *Shattered Hope: The Guatemalan Revolution and the United States, 1944–1954.* Princeton, 1991.

Goldston, James A. *Shattered Hope: Guatemalan Workers and the Promise of Democracy.* Boulder, Colo., 1989.

Gould, Jeffrey C. *To Lead as Equals: Rural Protest and Political Consciousness in Chinandega, Nicaragua, 1912–1979.* Chapel Hill, 1990.

Groban, Fabio. "The Cuban Working Class Movement from 1925 to 1933." *Science and Society* 39 (1975): 73–103.

Instituto del Movimiento Comunista y de la Revolución Socialista de Cuba. *Historia del movimiento obrero cubano, 1865–1958.* 2 vols. Havana, 1985.

Knight, Franklin. "Jamaican Migrants and the Sugar Industry, 1900–1934." In *Between Slavery and Free Labor: The Spanish-Speaking Caribbean in the Nineteenth Century,* edited by Manuel Moreno Fraginals, Frank Moya Pons, and Stanley L. Engerman. Baltimore, 1985.

LaWare, David C. "From Christian Populism to Social Democracy: Workers, Populists, and the State in Costa Rica, 1940–1956." Ph.D. diss., University of Texas at Austin, 1996.

Levenson-Estrada, Deborah. *Trade Unionists against Terror: Guatemala City, 1954–1985.* Chapel Hill, 1994.

Lewis, Lancelot S. *The West Indian in Panama, 1850–1914.* Washington, D.C., 1980.

Lewis, Oscar, Ruth M. Lewis, and Susan M. Rigden. *Living the Revolution: An Oral History of Contemporary Cuba.* 2 vols. Urbana, Ill., 1977–78.

López Larrave, Mario. *Breve historia del movimiento sindical guatemalteco.* Guatemala, 1979.

MacCameron, Robert. *Bananas, Labor, and Politics in Honduras, 1954–1963.* Syracuse, N.Y., 1983.

McCreery, David. *Rural Guatemala, 1760–1940.* Stanford, 1994.

——. "This Life of Misery and Shame: Female Prostitution in Guatemala City, 1880–1920." *Journal of Latin American Studies* 18 (1986): 333–53.

Medina, Medófilo. *Artesanos y obreros costaricenses, 1880–1914.* San José, 1985.

Mejía, Medardo. *El movimiento obrero en la Revolución de Octubre.* Guatemala, 1949.

Mintz, Sidney W. *Worker in the Cane: A Puerto Rican Life History.* New York, 1974.

Obando Sánchez, Antonio. *Memorias: La historia del movimiento obrero en Guatemala en este siglo.* Guatemala, 1978.

Pérez, Louis A. "Aspects of Hegemony: Labor, State, and Capital in Plattist Cuba." *Cuban Studies* 16 (1986): 44–70.

Quintero-Rivera, A. G. "Socialists and Cigarmakers: Artisans' Proletarianization in the Making of the Puerto Rican Working Class." *Latin American Perspectives* 10 (1983): 19–38.

Rivero Múñoz, José. *El movimiento laboral cubano durante el período 1906–1911.* Havana, 1962.

——. *El movimiento obrero durante la primera intervención.* Havana, 1961.

Schneider, Ronald M. *Communism in Guatemala, 1944–1954.* 2d ed. New York, 1979.

Sims, Harold. "Cuban Labor and the Cold War." In *Latin America from the Second World War to the Cold War,* edited by Leslie Bethell and Ian Roxborough. Cambridge, England, 1991.

Smith, Carol A., ed. *Guatemalan Indians and the State, 1540 to 1988.* Austin, Tex., 1990.

Soto, Lionel. *La revolución del 33.* Havana, 1977.

Stubbs, Jean. *Tobacco on the Periphery: A Case Study in Cuban Labour History, 1860–1958.* Cambridge, England, 1985.

Zeitlin, Maurice. *Revolutionary Politics and the Cuban Working Class.* Princeton, 1967.

Mexico

Adleson G., S. Lief. "Historia social de los obreros industriales de Tampico, 1906–1919." Doctoral thesis, El Colegio de México, 1982.

Anderson, Rodney. "Mexican Workers and the Politics of Revolution, 1906–1911." *Hispanic American Historical Review* 54 (1974): 94–113.

——. *Outcasts in Their Own Land: Mexican Industrial Workers, 1906–1911.* DeKalb, Ill., 1976.

Barbosa Cano, Fabio. *La CROM, de Luis N. Morones a Antonio J. Hernández*. Puebla, Mexico, 1980.

Basurto, Jorge. *Del avilacamachismo al alemanismo (1940–1952): La clase obrera en la historia de México*. Mexico City, 1984.

——. *En el régimen de Echeverría: La clase obrera en la historia de México*. Mexico City, 1984.

——. *El proletariado industrial en México (1850–1930)*. Mexico City, 1975.

Bortz, Jeffrey L. "The Genesis of the Mexican Labor Relations System: Federal Labor Policy and the Textile Industry, 1925–1940." *Americas* 52 (1995): 43–70.

——. *Industrial Wages in Mexico City, 1939–1975*. New York, 1986.

Brown, Jonathan C. "Foreign and Native-Born Workers in Porfirian Mexico." *American Historical Review* 98 (1993): 787–818.

——. "Foreign Oil Companies, Oil Workers, and the Mexican Revolutionary State." In *Multinational Enterprise in Historical Perspective*, edited by A. Teichova, M. Lévy-Leboyer, and H. Nussbaum. Cambridge, England, 1986.

——. *Oil and Revolution in Mexico*. Berkeley, 1993.

——. "Los trabajadores y el capital foráneo en la industria petrolera mexicana." *Secuencia: Revista de historia y ciencias sociales* 34 (1996): 93–128.

Brown, Jonathan C., and Alan Knight, eds. *The Mexican Petroleum Industry in the Twentieth Century*. Austin, Tex., 1992.

Carr, Barry. *Marxism and Communism in Twentieth-Century Mexico*. Lincoln, Nebr., 1992.

——. *El movimiento obrero y la política en México, 1910–1929*. Mexico City, 1981.

Collier, Ruth Berins. *The Contradictory Alliance: State-Labor Relations and Regime Change in Mexico*. Berkeley, 1992.

Durand Ponte, Víctor M. *La ruptura de la nación: Historia del movimiento obrero mexicano desde 1938 hasta 1952*. Mexico City, 1986.

French, William E. *A Peaceful and Working People: Manners, Morals, and Class Formation in Northern Mexico*. Albuquerque, 1996.

——. "*Progreso Forzado*: Workers and the Inculcation of the Capitalist Work Ethic in the Parral Mining District." In *Rituals of Rule, Rituals of Resistance: Public Celebrations and Popular Culture in Mexico*, edited by William H. Beezley, Cheryl English Martin, and William E. French. Wilmington, Del., 1994.

——. "Prostitutes and Guardian Angels: Women, Work, and the Family in Porfirian Chihuahua." *Hispanic American Historical Review* 72 (1992): 529–53.

Frost, Elsa Cecilia, Michael C. Meyer, and Josefina Zoraida Vásquez, eds. *El trabajo y los trabajadores en la historia de México*. Mexico City, 1979.

Gómez Tagle, Silvia. *Insurgencia y democracia en los sindicatos electricistas*. Mexico City, 1980.

Hart, John M. *Anarchism and the Mexican Working Class, 1860–1931*. Austin, Tex., 1987.

Illades, Carlos. *Hacia la Republica del Trabajo: La organización artesanal en la ciudad de México, 1853–1876*. Mexico City, 1996.

Joseph, Gilbert M., and Daniel Nugent, eds. *Everyday Forms of State Formation: Revolution and the Negotiation of Rule in Modern Mexico*. Durham, N.C., 1994.

Knight, Alan. "The Working Class and the Mexican Revolution, c. 1900–1920." *Journal of Latin American Studies* 16 (1984): 51–97.

La Botz, Dan. *The Crisis of Mexican Labor*. New York, 1988.

Lear, John R. "Workers, Vecinos, and Citizens: The Revolution in Mexico City, 1909–1917." Ph.D. diss., University of California at Berkeley, 1993.

Middlebrook, Kevin. *Unions, Workers, and the State in Mexico*. La Jolla, Calif., 1989.

Morgan, Tony. "Proletarians, Politicos, and Patriarchs: The Use and Abuse of Cultural Customs in the Early Industrialization of Mexico City, 1880–1910." In *Rituals of Rule, Rituals of Resistance: Public Celebrations and Popular Culture in Mexico*, edited by William H. Beezley, Cheryl English Martin, and William E. French. Wilmington, Del., 1994.

Novelo, Victoria, and Augusto Urteaga. *La industria en los magueyales: Trabajo y sindicatos en Ciudad Sahagún*. Mexico City, 1979.

Ortega, Max. *Estado y movimiento ferrocarrilero, 1958–1959*. Mexico City, 1988.

Parlee, Lorena M. "The Impact of United States Railroad Unions on Organized Labor and Government Policy in Mexico (1880–1911)." *Hispanic American Historical Review* 64 (1984): 443–75.

Pérez Toledo, Sonia. *Los hijos del trabajo: Los artesanos de la ciudad de México, 1780–1853*. Mexico City, 1996.

Reyna, José Luis, and Raúl Trejo Delarbre. *De Adolfo Ruíz Cortines a Adolfo López Mateo (1952–1964): La clase obrera en la historia de México*. Mexico City, 1981.

Rodea, Marcelo. *Historia del movimiento obrero ferrocarrilero en México, 1890–1943*. Mexico City, 1944.

Roxborough, Ian. *Unions and Politics in Mexico: The Case of the Automobile Industry*. Cambridge, England, 1984.

Ruiz, Ramón Eduardo. *Labor and the Ambivalent Revolutionaries: Mexico, 1911–1923*. Baltimore, 1976.

Salazar, Rosendo, and José G. Escobedo. *Las pugnas de la gleba, 1907–1922*. Mexico City, 1923.

Southern Cone Region (Uruguay, Argentina, Paraguay, Chile)

Adelman, Jeremy, ed. *Essays in Argentine Labour History, 1870–1930*. Houndsmills, England, 1992.

———. "Reflections on Argentine Labour and the Rise of Peron." *Bulletin of Latin American Research* 11, no. 3 (1992): 243–59.

———. "State and Labour in Argentina: The Port Workers of Buenos Aires, 1910–1921." *Journal of Latin American Studies* 25 (1993): 73–102.

Alexander, Robert J. *Labor Relations in Argentina, Brazil, and Chile*. New York, 1962.

Angell, Alan. *Politics and the Labour Movement in Chile*. London, 1972.

Baily, Samuel. "The Italians and the Development of Organized Labor in Argentina, Brazil, and the United States, 1880–1916." *Journal of Social History* 3 (1969): 123–34.

———. *Labor, Nationalism, and Politics in Argentina*. Buenos Aires, 1967.

Barrera, Manuel. *El conflicto obrero en el enclave cuprífero*. Santiago, 1973.

——. *El sindicato industrial como instrumento de lucha de la clase obrera chilena*. Santiago, 1971.

——. *Worker Participation in Company Management in Chile: A Historical Experience*. Geneva, 1981.

Barría Serón, Jorge. *Historia de la CUT*. Santiago, 1971.

——. *Los sindicatos de la Gran Minería del Cobre*. Santiago, 1970.

——. *Trayectoria y estructura del movimiento sindical chileno, 1946–1962*. Santiago, 1963.

Bitar, Sergio, and Crisóstomo Pizarro. *La caída de Allende y la huelga de El Teniente*. Santiago, 1986.

Brennan, James. *The Labor Wars of Córdoba, 1955–1976: Ideology, Work, and Labor Politics in an Argentine Industrial City*. Cambridge, Mass., 1994.

Del Campo, Hugo. *Sindicalismo y peronismo: Los comienzos de un vínculo perturable*. Buenos Aires, 1983.

Delich, Francisco José. *Crisis y protesta social: Córdoba, mayo de 1969*. Buenos Aires, 1970.

DeShazo, Peter. *Urban Workers and Labor Unions in Chile, 1902–1907*. Madison, Wis., 1983.

Di Tella, Guido. *Argentina under Perón, 1973–1976: The Nation's Experience with a Labour-Based Government*. New York, 1990.

Di Tella, Torcuato S. "Working-Class Organizations and Politics in Argentina." *Latin America Research Review* 16 (1981): 47–51.

Doyon, Louisa M. "Conflictos obreros durante el régimen peronista (1946–1955)." *Desarrollo Económico* 17, no. 67 (1977): 437–73.

——. "El crecimiento sindical bajo el peronismo." *Desarrollo Económico* 15, no. 57 (1975): 151–61.

——. "La organización del movimiento sindical peronista, 1946–1958." *Desarrollo Económico* 24, no. 94 (1984): 203–34.

Drake, Paul W. *Socialism and Populism in Chile, 1932–1952*. Champaign, Ill., 1978.

Espinoza, John G., and Andrew S. Zimbalist. *Economic Democracy: Workers' Participation in Chilean Industry*. New York, 1978.

Germani, Gino. "El surgimiento de Peronismo: El rol de los obreros y los migrantes internos." *Desarrollo Económico* 13, no. 51 (1973): 435–88.

Godio, Julio. *El movimiento nacional y la cuestión nacional, Argentina: Inmigrantes asalariados y lucha de clases, 1880–1910*. Buenos Aires, 1972.

——. *El movimiento obrero argentino (1943–1955)*. Buenos Aires, 1990.

Goldberg, Heidi. "Railroad Unionization in Argentina, 1912–1929." Ph.D. diss., Yale University, 1979.

Goodwin, Paul B., Jr. *Los ferrocarriles británicos y la Unión Cívica Radical, 1916–1930*. Buenos Aires, 1974.

Gordillo, Mónica. *El movimiento obrero ferroviario desde del interior del país*. Buenos Aires, 1988.

James, Daniel. "October 17th and 18th: Mass Protest, Peronism, and the Argentine Working Class." *Journal of Social History* 21 (1988): 441–61.

——. "Rationalisation and Working Class Response: The Context and Limits of Factory Floor Activity in Argentina." *Journal of Latin American Studies* 13 (1981): 375–402.

———. *Resistance and Integration: Peronism and the Argentine Working Class, 1946–1976*. Cambridge, England, 1988.

Horowitz, Joel. "Argentina's Failed General Strike of 1921: A Critical Moment in the Radicals' Relations with Unions." *Hispanic American Historical Review* 75 (1995): 57–79.

———. *Argentine Unions, the State, and the Rise of Peron*. Berkeley, 1990.

———. "Ideologías sindicales y políticas estatales en la Argentina, 1930–1943." *Desarrollo Económico* 25, no. 98 (1984): 275–96.

———. "The Impact of Pre-1943 Labor Union Traditions on Peronism." *Journal of Latin American Studies* 15 (1983): 101–16.

———. "Occupational Community and the Creation of a Self-Styled Elite: Railway Workers in Argentina." *Americas* 42 (1985): 55–81.

Jelín, Elizabeth. "Labor Conflicts under the Second Peronist Regime: Argentina, 1973–1976." *Development and Change* 10 (1979): 233–58.

Korzeniewicz, Roberto P. "The Labor Politics of Radicalism: The Santa Fe Crisis of 1928." *Hispanic American Historical Review* 73 (1993): 1–32.

———. "Labor Unrest in Argentina, 1887–1907." *Latin American Research Review* 24 (1989): 71–98.

———. "Labor Unrest in Argentina, 1930–1943," *Latin American Research Review* 28 (1993): 7–40.

———. "The Labour Movement and the State in Argentina, 1887–1907." *Bulletin of Latin American Research* 8 (1989): 25–45.

Landsberger, Henry, Manuel Barrera, and Abel Toro. *El pensamiento del dirigente sindical chileno: Un informe preliminar*. Santiago, 1963.

Landsberger, Henry, and Tim McDaniel. "Hypermobilization in Chile, 1970–1973." *World Politics* 28 (1976): 502–41.

Lobato, Mirta Zaída. *El "Taylorismo" en la gran industria exportadora argentina, 1907–1945*. Buenos Aires, 1988.

Matsushita, Hiroshi. *Movimiento obrero argentino: Sus proyecciones en los orígenes del peronismo*. Buenos Aires, 1983.

Moran, Theodore. *Multinational Corporations and the Politics of Dependence: Copper in Chile*. Princeton, 1974.

Munck, Ronaldo. "Cycles of Class Struggle and the Making of the Working Class in Argentina, 1890–1920." *Journal of Latin American Studies* 19 (1987): 19–39.

Munck, Ronaldo, Ricardo Falcón, and Bernardo Galitelli. *Argentina from Anarchism to Peronism: Workers, Unions, and Politics, 1855–1985*. London, 1987.

Murmís, Miguel, and Juan Carlos Portantiero, eds. *Estudios sobre los orígenes del peronismo*. 2 vols. Buenos Aires, 1971.

Navarro, Marysa. "Hidden, Silent, and Anonymous: Woman Workers in the Argentine Trade Union Movement." In *The World of Women's Trade Unionism*, edited by N. C. Soldon. Westport, Conn., 1985.

Petras, James F. "Chile: Nationalization, Socioeconomic Change, and Popular Participation." In *Latin America: From Dependence to Revolution*, edited by James F. Petras. New York, 1973.

———. *Politics and Social Forces in Chilean Development*. Berkeley, 1970.

Pinto Vallejos, Julio. *Expansión minera y desarrollo industrial: Un caso de crecimiento asociado (Chile, 1850–1914).* Santiago, Chile, 1990.

Pizarro, Crisóstomo. *La huelga obrera en Chile, 1890–1970.* Santiago, 1971.

Raga, Adriana. "Workers, Neighbours, and Citizens: A Study of an Argentine Industrial Town, 1930–1945." Ph.D. diss., Yale University, 1988.

Rock, David. *Argentina in the Twentieth Century.* Pittsburgh, 1975.

———. "Lucha civil en la Argentina: Semana trágica en enero de 1919." *Desarrollo Ecónomico* 22, no. 44 (1971): 165–215.

———. *Politics in Argentina, 1890–1930: The Rise and Fall of Radicalism.* London, 1975.

Salvatore, Ricardo. "Labor Control and Discrimination: The *Contratista* System in Mendoza, Argentina, 1880–1920." *Agricultural History* 60 (1986): 52–80.

Stickell, Arthur L. "Migration and Mining: Labor in Northern Chile in the Nitrate Era, 1880–1930." Ph.D. diss., Indiana University, 1979.

Tamarin, David. *The Argentine Labor Movement, 1930–1945: A Study in the Origins of Peronism.* Albuquerque, 1985.

Thompson, Ruth. "The Limitation of Ideology in the Early Argentine Labour Movement: Anarchism in the Trade Unions, 1890–1920." *Journal of Latin American Studies* 16 (1984): 81–99.

Torre, Juan Carlos, ed. *La formación del sindicalismo peronista.* Buenos Aires, 1988.

———. *La vieja guardia sindical y Perón: Sobre los orígenes del peronismo.* Buenos Aires, 1990.

Whiteford, Scott. *Workers from the North: Plantations, Bolivian Labor, and the City in Northwest Argentina.* Austin, Tex., 1981.

Winn, Peter. *Weavers of Revolution: The Yarur Workers and Chile's Road to Socialism.* New York, 1986.

Zapata, Francisco. *Los mineros de Chuquicamata: ¿Productores o proletarios?* Mexico City, 1975.

Zeitlin, Maurice, and James F. Petras. *El radicalismo político de la clase trabajadora chilena.* Buenos Aires, 1969.

NOTES ON THE CONTRIBUTORS

Andrew Boeger is assistant professor of history at North Carolina A&T State University in Greensboro. He obtained his doctorate at the University of Texas at Austin, completing a dissertation on the miners of Chojlla, Bolivia. Before entering graduate school, Boeger spent four years as a labor and community organizer in the Midwest. As a graduate student, he was active with the Texas State Employees Union/Communications Workers of America Local 6186.

Michael Marconi Braga is a prizewinning journalist who currently writes for the *Gulf Coast Business Journal* in Sarasota, Florida. He covers banking, finance, insurance, and international trade and labor relations. Graduating from the University of Texas at Austin with a master's degree in economics, Braga wrote his thesis on the Cuban sugar industry and its workers from 1920 to 1934. His bachelor's degree is from Duke University. Braga has also worked for the *Buenos Aires Herald* and *Cuba News*, a publication of the *Miami Herald*.

Jonathan C. Brown teaches Latin American history at the University of Texas at Austin. He has published articles and books on Mexico and Argentina and specializes in economic and labor history. At the moment, he is completing a book on the social history of colonial Latin America.

Josh DeWind is currently director of the International Migration Program of the Social Science Research Council. He is on leave from the Department of Anthropology at Hunter College, City University of New York, where he directs programs on Latin American and Caribbean studies and human rights. DeWind received his Ph.D. in anthropology from Columbia University in 1977. His research and writing has covered various aspects of economic development in Latin America and the Caribbean and of international migration to the United States.

Marc Christian McLeod is a Ph.D. candidate in the Department of History at the University of Texas at Austin. He is currently working on a dissertation that compares the histories of Haitian and British West Indian immigrants to Cuba in the early twentieth century. His master's thesis examines the history of railway workers in Guatemala from 1912 to 1954. He is a graduate of the School of Foreign Service at Georgetown University.

Michael Snodgrass was born to a family of poor sharecroppers and graduated with a bachelor's degree from the University of Iowa. In 1993, he completed his master's thesis at the University of Texas at Austin on Argentine workers during Perón's first presidency. Snodgrass is currently writing a doctoral thesis on working-class formation, industrial relations, and unionism in Monterrey, Mexico, prior to World War II.

Andrea Spears, who is a candidate for the Ph.D. degree in history at the University of Texas at Austin, is writing her dissertation on Mexican railway workers in the 1940s. She obtained her master's degree in international studies from Florida State University at Tallahassee, learning her first Mexican labor history with Rodney Anderson. As a graduate student, she has also completed research on the militancy of Argentine railway workers during the first presidency of Juan Perón.

Joanna Swanger is writing a doctoral dissertation on rural and urban workers in Las Villas, Cuba, between the 1933 and 1959 revolutions. Swanger received her B.A. in peace and global studies from Earlham College in 1990 and her M.A. from the University of Texas at Austin in 1993. Her master's thesis deals with Chile's copper industry under Allende.

María Celina Tuozzo is a doctoral candidate who is doing field research in La Serena, Chile, for a dissertation on gender and community. Before entering the history program at the University of Texas at Austin, she was a student of sociology working with Torcuato Di Tella in Argentina. Tuozzo has written a master's thesis on the workers of the St. John d'el Rey Mining Company in Brazil.

Joel Wolfe, who obtained his doctorate at the University of Wisconsin at Madison, teaches as associate professor of history at Rice University. He has written a book and numerous articles on the social and political struggles of workers in São Paulo throughout the twentieth century. At present, he is engaged in research on the Brazilian auto industry with special reference to the influence of the automobile on Brazilian culture and lifestyles.

INDEX